Understanding Music

Past and Present

N. Alan Clark, PhD | Thomas Heflin, PhD | Jeffrey Kluball, PhD | Elizabeth Kramer, PhD

D1225962

UNG
UNIVERSITY of NORTH GEORGIA
UNIVERSITY PRESS
Dahlonega, GA

ISBN: 978-1-940771-33-5

Produced by:
University System of Georgia

Published by:
University of North Georgia Press
Dahlonega, Georgia

Cover Design and Layout Design:
Corey Parson

For more information, please visit http://ung.edu/university-press
Or email ungpress@ung.edu

Table of Contents

1

Music Fundamentals

N. Alan Clark, Thomas Heflin, Elizabeth Kramer

1.1 OBJECTIVES

1. Recognize a wide variety of sounds, comparing and contrasting them using musical elements of pitch, volume, articulation, and timbre.
2. Aurally identify important performing forces (use of the voice and instruments) of Western music.
3. Define basic elements of melody, harmony, rhythm, and texture and build a vocabulary for discussing them.
4. Identify basic principles and types of musical form.
5. Listen to music and describe its musical elements and form.
6. Compare and contrast categories of art music, folk music, and pop music.
7. Identify ways in which humans have used music for social and expressive purposes.

1.2 KEY TERMS AND INDIVIDUALS

- Accidentals
- Acoustics
- Acoustical Engineer
- Acoustician
- Amplitude
- Beat
- Brass
- Chord
- Chord Progression
- Chromatic
- Composition
- Conjunct
- Consonant
- Cycles per Second (cps)
- Disjunct
- Dissonant
- Dynamics
- Equalization
- Form
- Frequency

- Fundamental Pitch
- Guido of Arezzo
- Improvisation
- Instrumentation
- Interval
- Harmony
- Hertz (Hz)
- Homophonic
- Key
- Keyboard
- Measure
- Melody
- Meter
- Monophonic
- Motive
- Music
- Noise
- Octave
- Overtones
- Partials
- Percussion
- Performing Forces
- Phrase
- Pitch
- Polyphony
- Polyrhythm
- Range
- Register
- Rhythm
- Scale
- Sequence
- Seventh Chord
- Sine Wave
- Sound
- Sound Waves
- Step
- Strings
- Syncopation
- Synthesizers
- Tempo
- Texture
- Timbre
- Time Signature
- Tonic
- Triad
- Twelve-Bar Blues
- Vocal
- Woodwinds

1.3 WHAT IS MUSIC?

Music moves through time; it is not static. In order to appreciate music we must remember what sounds happened, and anticipate what sounds might come next. Most of us would agree that not all sounds are music! Examples of sounds not typically thought of as music include noises such as alarm sirens, dogs barking, coughing, the rumble of heating and cooling systems, and the like. But, why? One might say that these noises lack many of the qualities that we typically associate with music.

We can define **music** as the intentional organization of sounds in time by and for human beings. Though not the only way to define music, this definition uses several concepts important to understandings of music around the world. "Sounds in time" is the most essential aspect of the definition. Music is distinguished from many of the other arts by its temporal quality; its sounds unfold over and through time, rather than being glimpsed in a moment, so to speak. They are also perceptions of the ear rather than the eye and thus difficult to ignore; as one can do by closing his or her eyes to avoid seeing something. It is more difficult for us to close our ears. Sound moves through time in waves. A sound wave is generated when an object vibrates within some medium like air or water. When the wave is received by our ears it triggers an effect known as sound, as can be seen in the following diagram:

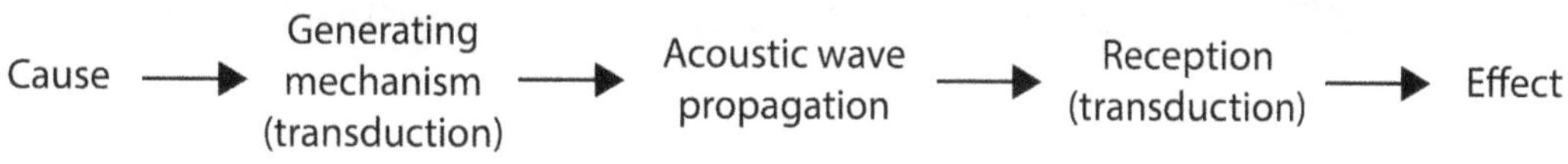

Figure 1.1 | Movement of a sound wave
Author | Corey Parson
Source | Original Work
License | CC BY-SA 4.0

As humans, we also tend to be interested in music that has a plan, in other words, music that has intentional organization. Most of us would not associate coughing or sneezing or unintentionally resting our hand on a keyboard as the creation of music. Although we may never know exactly what any songwriter or composer meant by a song, most people think that the sounds of music must show at least a degree of intentional foresight.

A final aspect of the definition is its focus on humanity. Bird calls may sound like music to us; generally the barking of dogs and hum of a heating unit do not. In each of these cases, though, the sounds are produced by animals or inanimate objects, rather than by human beings; therefore the focus of this text will only be on sounds produced by humans.

1.3.1 Acoustics

Acoustics is essentially "the science of sound." It investigates how sound is produced and behaves, elements that are essential for the correct design of music rehearsal spaces and performance venues. Acoustics is also essential for the design and manufacture of musical instruments. The word itself derives from the Greek word *acoustikos* which means "of hearing." People who work in the field of acoustics generally fall into one of two groups: **Acousticians,** those who study the theory and science of acoustics, and **acoustical engineers,** those who work in the area of acoustic technology. This technology ranges from the design of rooms, such as classrooms, theatres, arenas, and stadiums, to devices such as microphones, speakers, and sound generating synthesizers, to the design of musical instruments like strings, keyboards, woodwinds, brass, and percussion.

1.3.2 Sound and Sound Waves

As early as the sixth century BCE (500 years before the birth of Christ), Pythagoras reasoned that strings of different lengths could create harmonious (pleasant) sounds (or tones) when played together if their lengths were related by certain ratios. Concurrent sounds in ratios of two to three, three to four, four to five, etc.

are said to be harmonious. Those not related by harmonious ratios are generally referred to as **noise**. About 200 years after Pythagoras, Aristotle (384-322 BCE) described how sound moves through the air—like the ripples that occur when we drop a pebble in a pool of water—in what we now call waves. **Sound** is basically the mechanical movement of an audible pressure wave through a solid, liquid, or gas. In physiology and psychology, sound is further defined as the recognition of the vibration caused by that movement. **Sound waves** are the rapid movements back and forth of a vibrating medium—the gas, water, or solid—that has been made to vibrate.

1.3.3 Properties of Sound: Pitch

Another element that we tend to look for in music is what we call "definite pitch." A definite **pitch** is a tone that is composed of an organized sound wave. A note of definite pitch is one in which the listener can easily discern the pitch. For instance, notes produced by a trumpet or piano are of definite pitch. An indefinite pitch is one that consists of a less organized wave and tends to be perceived by the listener as **noise**. Examples are notes produced by percussion instruments such as a snare drum.

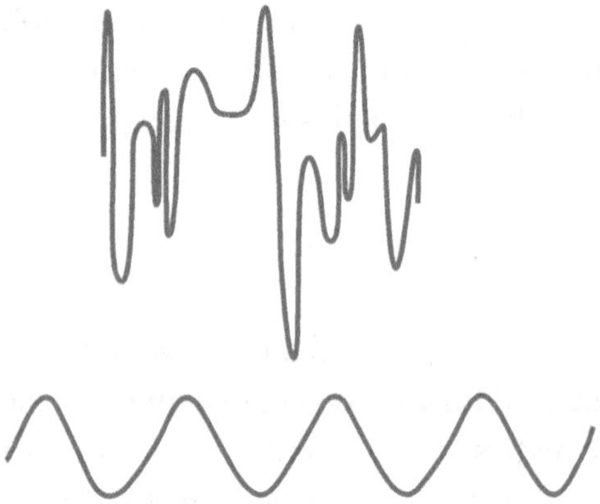

Figure 1.2 | Two sound waves, the first an indefinite pitch and the second a definite pitch.
Author | Corey Parson
Source | Original Work
License | CC BY-SA 4.0

Numerous types of music have a combination of definite pitches, such as those produced by keyboard and wind instruments, and indefinite pitches, such as those produced by percussion instruments. That said, most tunes, are composed of definite pitches, and, as we will see, melody is a key aspect of what most people hear as music.

The sound waves of definite pitches may come in many frequencies.

Frequency refers to the repetitions of a wave pattern over time and is normally measured in **Hertz** or **cycles per second (cps)**. Humans normally detect types of sound called musical tones when the vibrations range from about twenty vibrations per second (anything slower sounds like a bunch of clicks) to about 20,000 vibrations per second (anything faster is too high for humans to hear.) Watch the first five minutes of this excellent explanation of

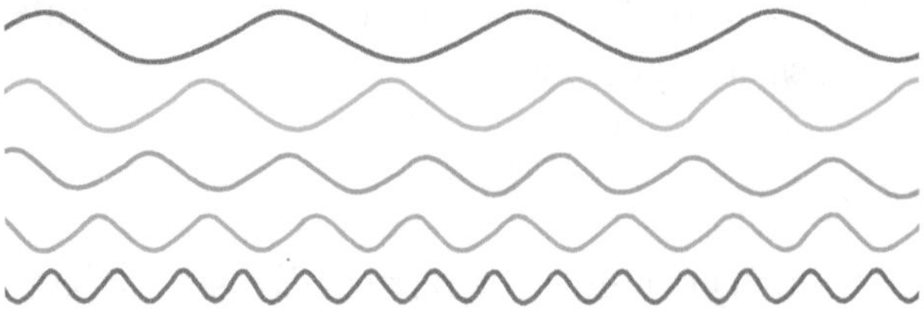

Figure 1.3 | Sine waves of varying frequencies
Author | Corey Parson
Source | Original Work
License | CC BY-SA 4.0

how different types of sounds result from the combination of the **partials** above the basic tone. In actuality, all sounds result from different variations of this process, as it naturally occurs in our environment.

Ex. 1.1: The Audio Kitchen; Sawtooth and Square Waves (2012)

http://www.youtube.com/watch?v=A1gwC8YoyMU

In the Western world, musicians generally refer to definite pitches by the "musical alphabet." The musical alphabet consists of the letters A-G, repeated over and over again (...ABCDEFGABCDEFGABCDEFG...), as can be seen from this illustration of the notes on a keyboard. These notes correspond to a particular frequency of the sound wave. A pitch with a sound wave that vibrates 440 times each second, for example, is what most musicians would hear as an A above middle C. (Middle C simply refers to the note C that is located in the middle of the piano keyboard.) As you can see, each white key on the keyboard is assigned a particular note, each of which is named after the letters A through G. Halfway between these notes are black keys, which sound the sharp and flat notes used in Western music. This pattern is repeated up and down the entire keyboard.

SIDEBAR: How Waves Behave

Reflection – sound waves reflect off of hard surfaces

Absorption – sound waves are absorbed by porous surfaces

Amplitude – refers to how high a wave appears on an oscilloscope; i.e., how much energy it has and therefore how loud it is

Frequency – refers to how many times a wave vibrates each second. This vibrating speed is measured using cycles per second (cps) or the more modern Hertz (Hz)

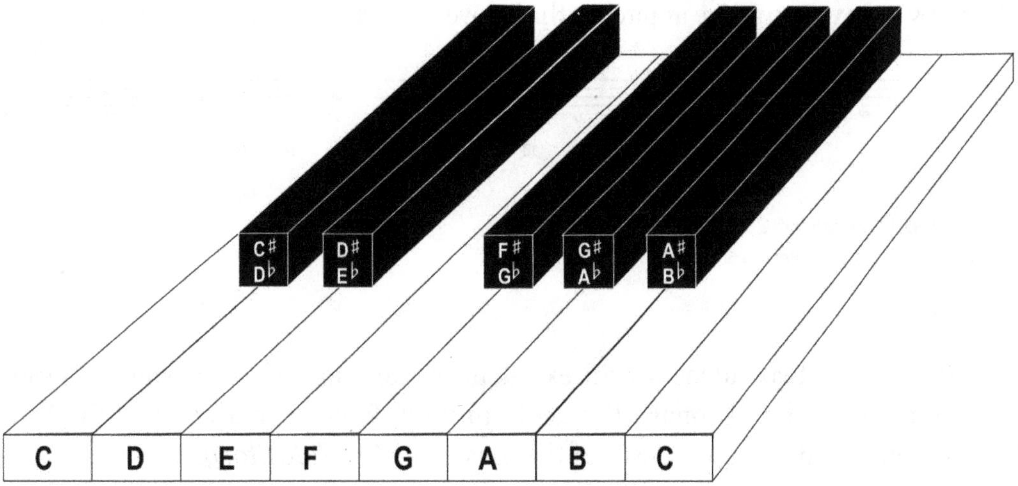

Figure 1.4 | The keyboard and the musical alphabet.
Author | Corey Parson
Source | Original Work
License | CC BY-SA 4.0

When a sound wave is generated, it often generates other waves or ripple effects, depending on the medium through which it travels. When a string of a certain length is set into motion, for example, its waves may also set other strings of varying lengths into motion.

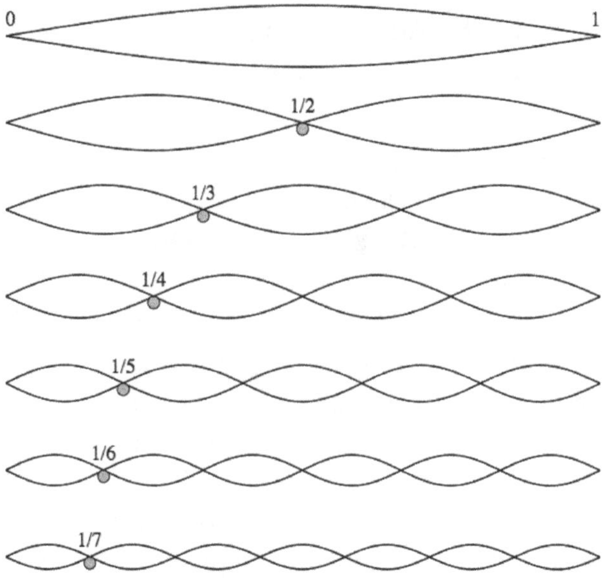

Figure 1.5 | Overtones of a vibrating string
Author | User "Qef"
Source | Wikimedia Commons
License | Public Domain

The vibration with the lowest frequency is called the **fundamental pitch.** The additional definite pitches that are produced are called **overtones**, because they are heard above or "over" the fundamental pitch (tone). Our musical alphabet consists of seven letters repeated over and over again in correspondence with these overtones. Please see Figure 1.6 for the partials for the fundamental pitch C:

To return to the musical alphabet: the first partial of the overtone series is the loudest and clearest overtone heard "over" the fundamental pitch. In fact, the sound wave of the first overtone partial is vibrating exactly twice as fast as its fundamental tone. Because of this, the two tones sound similar, even though the first overtone partial is clearly higher in pitch than the fundamental pitch. If you follow the overtone series, from one partial to the next, eventually you will see that all the other pitches on the keyboard might be generated from the fundamental pitch and then displaced by **octaves** to arrive at pitches that move by **step** (refer to Figure 1.6).

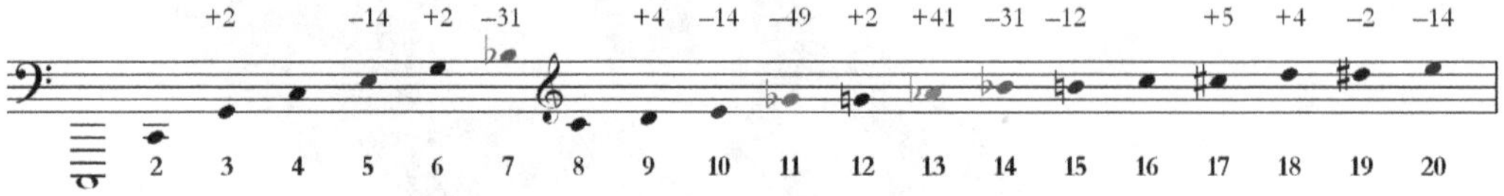

Figure 1.6 | Partials of C
Author | User "MusicMaker5376"
Source | Wikimedia Commons
License | CC BY-SA 3.0

Watch these two videos for an excellent explanation of the harmonic series from none other than Leonard Bernstein himself, famous conductor of the New York Philharmonic and composer of the music of *West Side Story*.

Ex. 1.2: The Harmonic Series

https://www.youtube.com/watch?v=8n3qMB6AD_o
https://www.youtube.com/watch?v=iDTj6tBnHlA

The distance between any two of these notes is called an **interval**. On the piano, the distance between two of the longer, white key pitches is that of a step. The longer, white key pitches that are not adjacent are called leaps. The interval between C and D is that of a second, C and E that of a third, the interval between C and F that of a fourth, the interval between C and G that of a fifth, the interval of C to A is a sixth, the interval of C to B is a seventh, and the special relationship between C and C is called an octave.

1.3.4 Other Properties of Sound: Dynamics, Articulation, and Timbre

The volume of a sound is its **dynamic**; it corresponds with the **amplitude** of the sound wave. The articulation of a sound refers to how it begins and ends, for example, abruptly, smoothly, gradually, etc. The **timbre** of a sound is what we mean when we talk about tone color or tone quality. Because sound is somewhat abstract, we tend to describe it with adjectives typically used for tactile objects, such as "gravelly" or "smooth," or adjectives for visual descriptions, such as "bright" or "metallic." It is particularly affected by the ambience of the performing space, that is, by how much echo occurs and where the sound comes from. Timbre is also shaped by the **equalization (EQ)**, or balance, of the fundamental pitch and its overtones.

The video below is a great example of two singers whose voices have vastly different timbres. How would you describe Louis Armstrong's voice? Perhaps you would call it "rough or "gravelly." How would you describe Ella Fitzgerald's voice? Perhaps it could be called "smooth" or "silky."

Ex. 1.3: Louis Armstrong and Ella Fitzgerald

https://www.youtube.com/watch?v=J20EmPP5dTM

1.4 MUSIC NOTATION

The development of music notation was absolutely critical to the rise of music that used more than just one melody. Everything that has developed in Western music after 1040 CE—from music of many independent voices (polyphonic), to solo voices with keyboard or group accompaniments, to the popular music we enjoy today—grew from this development. Though modern scholars have found examples of written musical symbols as far back as 900 CE, the staff notation system developed by **Guido of Arezzo** and others who followed him allowed for the accurate preservation and distribution of music. Music notation also greatly contributed to the growth, development, and evolution of the many musical styles over the past one thousand years.

Because of his contributions to the development of music notation, Guido of Arezzo is arguably the most important figure in the development of written music in the Western world. He developed a system of lines and spaces that enabled musicians to notate the specific notes in a melody. The development of music notation made it possible for composers to notate their music accurately, allowing others to perform the music exactly the way each composer intended. This ability allowed polyphonic (many voiced) music to evolve rapidly after 1040 CE. The video linked below is an excellent resource that explains Guido's contributions in more detail.

Ex. 1.4: Guido of Arezzo

http://www.youtube.com/watch?v=LxkstaYPztM

The popularity of staff notation after Guido paved the way for the development of a method to notate rhythm. The system of rhythmic notation we use today in Western music has evolved over many years and is explained in the following link.

Ex. 1.5: Rhythmic Notation by Andrew Poushka (2003)

http://www.studybass.com/lessons/reading-music/rhythmic-notation

The following prepared college marching band arrangement is adapted from DJ Khaled's popular tune "All I Do is Win," which shows an example of how staff notation is used today.

Figure 1.7 | "All I Do Is Win"
Author | N. Alan Clark
Source | Original Work
License | CC BY-SA 4.0

1.5 PERFORMING FORCES FOR MUSIC

Music consists of the intentional organization of sounds by and for human beings. In the broadest classification, these sounds are produced by people in three ways: (1) through the human voice, the instrument with which most of us are born, (2) by using musical instruments, or (3) by using electronic and digital equipment to generate purely electronic sounds.

1.5.1 The Human Voice as a Performing Force

The human voice is the most intimate of all the music instruments in that it is the one that most of us are innately equipped. We breathe in, and, as we exhale, air rushes over the vocal chords causing them to vibrate. Depending on the length of the vocal chords, they will tend to vibrate more slowly or more quickly, creating pitches of lower or higher frequencies. The muscles in the larynx contract, causing the vocal chords to close, and air pressure forces them open. This closing and opening can happen hundreds of times a second. To reach a higher pitch vocal chords vibrate more rapidly.

Changing the shape of your vocal cavity allows for different timbres and vowel sounds. Changing the position of the mouth and lips allows for further variety in sound and for the production of consonants. Because men tend to have thicker and longer vocal chords, they tend to have lower voices than women, whose vocal chords tend to be shorter and slimmer.

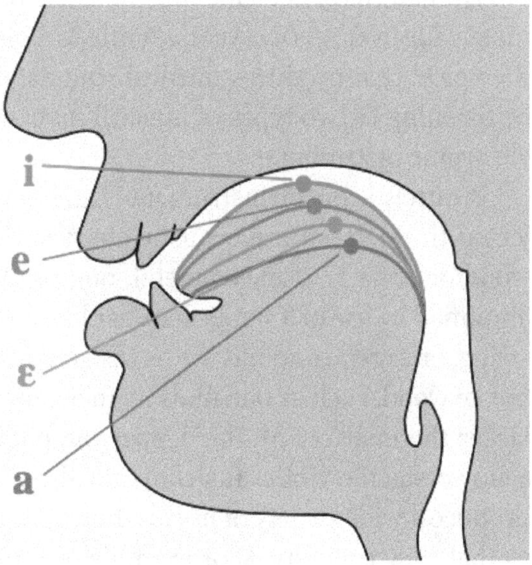

Figure 1.8 | Position of the larynx for various vowel sounds.
Author | User "Badseed"
Source | Wikimedia Commons
License | CC BY-SA 4.0

The natural speaking voice exhibits some variation in pitch. One's voice often rises at the end of a question. When you have a cold and the vocal chords are swollen, you often speak in lower pitches than normal. Singing generally differs from speaking in that it uses a wider **range** of definite pitches that often occur in a regular meter (discussed later). By range, we mean the number of pitches, expressed as an intervallic distance. A trained opera singer might have a range of three to four octaves, whereas the average person has a range of a little over an octave.

Additionally, as we speak we generally focus on consonants, which articulate the beginnings and ends of syllables and help make our meaning plain. In singing, performers often focus on the vowels, as vowels tend to carry better than consonants. Also, the meaning of the words is sometimes deemed less significant than the melodies themselves.

In Western music, voice ranges are typically split into four categories:

1. Bass: lowest male voices; sing in a low **register**, below middle C (middle C being the C approximately in the middle of the range of the piano)
2. Tenor: highest male voices; sing in a register around and below middle C
3. Alto: lowest female voices; sing in a register around and above middle C
4. Soprano: highest female voices; sing almost exclusively above middle C

Western classical music tends to use all four of these ranges, whereas melodic register and range in jazz, rock, and pop tends to be somewhat more limited. As you listen to jazz, rock, and pop, pay attention to ranges and registers used as well as any trends. Are most female jazz vocalists altos or sopranos? Do most doo-wop groups sing in higher or lower registers? Different musical voices exhibit different musical timbres as well, as you heard earlier with Louis Armstrong and Ella Fitzgerald.

1.5.2 Musical Instruments as Performing Forces

Humans have been making music with bone, stone, wood, textiles, pottery, and metals for over 35,000 years. A musical instrument is any mechanism, other than the voice, that produces musical sounds. As we study jazz, rock, and pop we will be listening to two types of musical instruments, purely acoustic instruments and electronic instruments.

A purely acoustic instrument is an instrument whose sound is created and projected through natural acoustic characteristics of its media. Thus, when one hits wood or bone or stone or metal, one sends vibrations through it which might be amplified by use of a small chamber like a sound box or a gourd. When one plucks a string, one creates sound waves that might be amplified through a piece of wood or box of wood, such as one finds in an acoustic guitar or violin. As with the voice, the larger the instrument, the deeper the pitches it plays—consider for example, the cello versus the violin. Instruments also differ in their ranges, some being able to produce a wide variety of notes while others are much more restricted in the pitches that they can play. (For example, the piano has a range of over seven octaves, while the saxophone normally plays only two and a half).

The timbre of a sound coming from a musical instrument is affected by the materials used and the way in which the sound is produced. Based on these two characteristics, we categorize acoustic instruments into five groups: strings, woodwinds, brass, percussion, and keyboard.

1. **Strings:** instruments whose sound is produced by setting strings in motion. These strings can be set in motion by plucking the strings with your finger, or a pick (a piece of plastic). They can also be set in motion by bowing. In bowing, the musician draws a bow across the string, creating friction and resulting in a sustained note. Most bows consist of horse hair held together on each end by a piece of wood. String examples: violins; violas; violoncellos; string bass (also known as double bass or stand-up bass); classical, acoustic, and bass guitars; harps. For more information and listening examples of the

Figure 1.9 | Horsehair Bow
Author | User "Feitscherg"
Source | Wikimedia Commons
License | CC BY-SA 3.0

different orchestral string instruments, go to http://www.philharmonia.co.uk/explore/instruments. Click on the individual instruments for an introduction and demonstration of the instrument.

2. **Woodwinds:** instruments traditionally made of wood whose sound is generated by forcing air through a tube, thus creating a vibrating air column. This can be done in one of several ways. The air can travel directly through an opening in the instrument, as in a flute. The air can pass through an opening between a reed and a wooden or metal mouthpiece as in a saxophone or clarinet, or between two reeds as in a bassoon or oboe. Although many woodwind instruments are in fact made of wood, there are exceptions. Instruments such as the saxophone and the modern flute are made of metal while some clarinets are made of plastic. These instruments are still considered woodwinds because the flute was traditionally made of wood and the saxophone and clarinet still use a wooden reed to produce the tone. Woodwind examples: flute, clarinet, oboe, bassoon. For more information and listening examples of the different orchestral woodwind instruments, go to http://www.philharmonia.co.uk/explore/instruments. Click on the individual instruments for an introduction and demonstration of the instrument.
3. **Brass:** instruments traditionally made of brass or another metal (and thus often producing a "bright" or "brassy" tone) whose sound is generated by "buzzing" (vibrating the lips together) into a mouthpiece attached to a coiled tube. This "buzzing" sets the air within the tube vibrating. The pitches are normally amplified by a flared bell at the end of the tube. Brass examples: trumpet, bugle, cornet, trombone, (French) horn, tuba, and euphonium. For more information and listening examples of the different orchestral brass instruments, go to http://www.philharmonia.co.uk/explore/instruments. Click on the individual instruments for an introduction and demonstration of the instrument.
4. **Percussion:** instruments that are typically hit or struck by the hand, with sticks, or with hammers, or that are shaken or rubbed. Some percussion instruments (such as the vibraphone) play definite pitches, but many play indefinite pitches. The standard drum set used in many jazz and rock ensembles, for example, consists of mostly indefinite-pitch instruments. Percussion examples: drum set, agogo bells (double bells), glockenspiel, xylophone, vibraphone, bass drum, snare or side drum, maracas, claves, cymbals, gong, triangle, tambourine. For more information and listening examples of the different orchestral percussion instruments, go to http://www.philharmonia.co.uk/explore/instruments. Click on the individual instruments for an introduction and demonstration of the instrument.
5. **Keyboards:** instruments that produce sound by pressing, or striking keys on a keyboard. The keys set air moving by the hammering of a

string (in the case of the piano) or by the opening and closing of a pipe through which air is pushed (as in the case of the vibraphone, organ, and accordion). All of these instruments have the capacity of playing more than one musical line at the same time. Keyboard examples: piano, organ, vibraphone, and accordion. For more information and listening examples of the different orchestral keyboard instruments, go to http://www.philharmonia.co.uk/explore/instruments. The keyboard link is found within the percussion instruments.

1.5.3 Non-acoustic instruments

Electric sounds and instruments: instruments can be electric in several ways. In some cases, an acoustic instrument, such as the guitar, violin, or piano may be played near a microphone that feeds into an amplifier. In this case, the instrument is not electric. In other cases, amplifiers are embedded in or placed onto the body of an acoustic instrument. In still other cases, acoustic instruments are altered to facilitate the amplification of their music. Thus, solid body violins, guitars, and basses may stand in for their hollow-bodied cousins.

Another category of electronic instruments are those that produce sound through purely electronic or digital means. Synthesizers and the modern electric keyboard, as well as beat boxes, are examples of electronic instruments that use wave generators or digital signals to produce tones.

SIDEBAR: Moog - Inventor of the Synthesizer

https://www.youtube.com/watch?v=y5HRa9nEVVU

Figure 1.10 | Early Minimoog by R. A. Moog Inc. (ca. 1970)
Author | User "glacial23"
Source | Wikimedia Commons
License | CC BY-SA 2.0

Synthesizers are electronic instruments (often in keyboard form) that create sounds using basic wave forms in different combinations. The first commercially available compact synthesizers marketed for musical performance were designed and built by Dr. Robert Moog in the mid-1960s.

A staple of twenty-first century music, synthesizers are widely used in popular music and movie music. Their sounds are everywhere in our society. Synthesizers are computers that combine tones of different frequencies. These combinations of frequencies result in complex sounds that do not exist in nature. Listen to the recording below of Bjork, which incorporates a live band with a variety of strange and interesting synthesized sounds.

Ex. 1.6: Björk – Voltaic Paris HD

https://www.youtube.com/watch?v=HeKAVX2s6hM

Solid-state electronics have enabled the synthesizer to shrink in size from its early days in the 1970s. Compare the number of electronic components in the photo of Keith Emerson's "rig" with the much smaller keyboard synthesizers used by Chick Corea linked below.

Ex. 1.7: Emerson, Lake, and Palmer – "Tarkus" 1971

https://www.youtube.com/watch?v=TpvOVNfu4VQ

Ex. 1.8: Chick Corea, Live at North Sea Jazz 2003

https://www.youtube.com/watch?v=SL34LYIWQ6M

Synthesizers can also be used to imitate the complex sounds of real instruments, making it possible for a composer to create music and have it played without having to hire a real orchestra. The video below features music created using sample-based synthesis, a method that incorporates recorded audio "samples" to approximate the sound of an orchestra through a computer.

Ex. 1.9: Vienna Symphonic Library

https://www.youtube.com/watch?v=Cwbgp26g-QQ

Many photographs of all different types of instruments may be found using Google images.

1.6 NEW RECORDING TECHNOLOGIES

Today, the ability to make high quality recordings is within the reach of anyone with a laptop and a microphone. But only a few years ago, recordings were an expensive endeavor available only to those with the financial backing of a record label. Musicians of the twenty-first century have access not only to recording technologies, but also to new and cutting-edge tools that are fundamentally changing how music is created, enjoyed, and disseminated. The synthesizer discussed above can be a recording technology, but there are others such as Auto-Tune.

1.6.1 Auto-Tune and Looping

Auto-Tune is a technique originally invented to correct for intonation mistakes in vocal performances. However, the technique quickly evolved into a new form of expression, allowing singers to add expressive flourishes to their singing. Even-

Figure 1.11 | Boss RC-50 Loop Station
Author | User "Massygo"
Source | Wikimedia Commons
License | CC BY 2.0

tually, the technique was used to turn regular speech into music, making it possible to create music out of everyday sounds. Listen to the clip below of the musical group, the Gregory Brothers, who regularly use Auto-Tune to create songs from viral Internet videos and news clips.

Ex. 1.10: Obama Mixtape: 1999 - Songify the News Special Edition

https://www.youtube.com/watch?v=eq1FIvUHtt0

Looping is another technique that musicians now use to create music on the spot. The technique involves recording audio samples which are then repeated or "looped" over and over again to a single beat. The performer then adds new loops over the old ones to create complex musical backdrops. The clip below features a street musician named Dub FX, who uses only his voice, a loop pedal, and some audio effects to replicate the effect of a full band.

Ex. 1.11: Dub FX

https://www.youtube.com/watch?v=lvyDy15vW6U

1.7 MELODY

The melody of a song is often its most distinctive characteristic. The ancient Greeks believed that melody spoke directly to the emotions. **Melody** is the part of the song that we hum or whistle, the tune that might get stuck in our heads. A more scientific definition of melody might go as follows: melody is the coherent succession of definite pitches in time. Any given melody has range, register, motion, shape, and phrases. Often, the melody also has rhythmic organization.

The first of these characteristics, range, is one that we've already encountered as we talked about pitch. The range of a melody is the distance between its lowest and highest notes. We talk about melodies having narrow or wide ranges. Register is also a concept we discussed in relation to pitch. Melodies can be played at a variety of registers: low, medium, high.

As melodies progress, they move through their given succession of pitches. Each pitch is a certain distance from the previous one and the next. Melodies that are meant to be sung tend to move by small intervals, especially by intervals of seconds or steps. A tune that moves predominantly by step is a stepwise melody. Other melodies have many larger intervals that we might describe as "skips" or "leaps." When these leaps are particularly wide and with rapid changes in direction (that is, the melody ascends and then descends and then ascends and so forth), we say that the melody is **disjunct**. Conversely, a melody that moves mostly by step, in a smoother manner—perhaps gradually ascending and then gradually descending—might be called **conjunct**.

Shape is a visual metaphor that we apply to melodies. Think of a tune that you know and like: it might be a pop tune, it might be from a musical, or it might be a song you recall from childhood. Does it correspond with any of the shapes in Figure 1.12?

In other words, do the pitches of the melody primarily ascend; shape A? Descend; shape B? Oscillate, much like a wave; shape C? Ascend, arch up, and then descend; shape D? These are shapes that we might hear unfolding over time. As we think back to a melody that we know, we can replay it in our mind and visualize the path that it traces.

Sing the childhood tune "Row, Row, Row Your Boat" to yourself. Which shape from Figure 1.12 do you think it is most like? "D" is the best answer. Now look at the musical notation for "Row, Row, Row Your Boat."

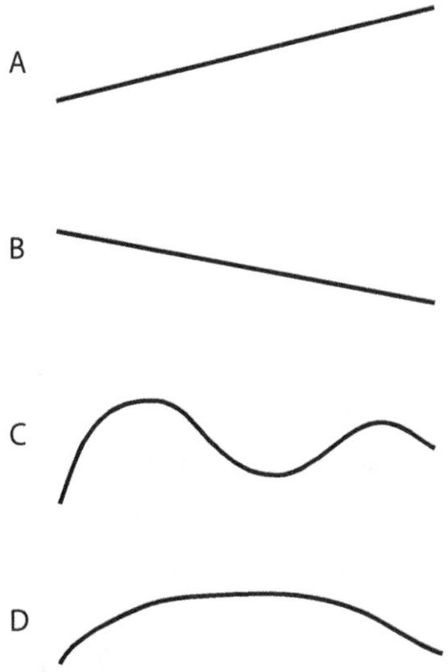

Figure 1.12 | Melodic Shapes
Author | Corey Parson
Source | Original Work
License | CC BY-SA 4.0

Figure 1.13 | "Row, Row, Row Your Boat"
Author | Arranged by N. Alan Clark
Source | Traditional Melody
License | CC BY-SA 4.0

Even if you can't read music, hopefully you can see how the note heads trace an arch-like shape, similar to the shape labeled "D" in Figure 1.12. Most melodies have smaller sub-sections called **phrases**. These phrases function somewhat like phrases in a sentence. They are complete thoughts, although generally lacking a sense of conclusion. In the song "Row, Row, Row Your Boat," the music corresponding with the words "Row, row, row your boat," might be heard as the first phrase and "gently down the stream," as the second phrase. "Merrily, merrily, merrily, merrily," comprises a third phrase, and "life is but a dream," a fourth, and final, phrase.

Melodies are also composed of **motives**. A motive is the smallest musical unit, generally a single rhythm of two or three pitches. In "Row, Row, Row Your Boat," the music set to "merrily" might be heard as a motive. Motives repeat, often in sequence. A **sequence** is a repetition of a motive or phrase at a different pitch level. Thus, in "Row, Row, Row Your Boat," the first time you hear "merrily" is when it is at the top of the melody's range. The next time, it is a bit lower in pitch, the next time a bit lower still, and the final time you hear the word, it is sung to the lowest pitch of the melody. Another song that you might know that has sequences is "My Country, 'Tis of Thee."

Ex. 1.12: Mormon Tabernacle Choir "My Country, 'Tis of Thee" (2014)

https://www.youtube.com/watch?v=eWJIooA7fLM

1.8 HARMONY

Most simply put, **harmony** is the way a melody is accompanied. It refers to the vertical aspect of music and is concerned with the different music sounds that occur in the same moment. Western music culture has developed a complex system to govern the simultaneous sounding of pitches. Some of its most complex harmonies appear in jazz, while other forms of popular music tend to have fewer and simpler harmonies.

We call the simultaneous sounding of three or more pitches a **chord**. Like intervals, chords can be consonant or dissonant. **Consonant** intervals and chords tend to sound sweet and pleasing to our ears. They also convey a sense of stability in the music. **Dissonant** intervals and chords tend to sound harsher to our ears, and often convey a sense of tension or instability. In general, dissonant intervals and chords tend to resolve to consonant intervals and chords. Seconds, sevenths, and tri-tones sound dissonant and resolve to consonance. Some of the most consonant intervals are unisons, octaves, thirds, sixths, fourths, and fifths. From the perspective of physics, consonant intervals and chords are simpler than dissonant intervals and chords. However, the fact that most individuals in the Western world hear consonance as sweet and dissonance as harsh probably has as much to do with our musical socialization as with the physical properties of sound.

A listening example of consonance may be found at the following links:

http://real.darton.edu/faculty/kluball/MUSC1100/Question 11.mp3
http://real.darton.edu/faculty/kluball/MUSC1100/Question 23.mp3

An example of dissonance may be found at the following links:

http://real.darton.edu/faculty/kluball/MUSC1100/Question 9.mp3
http://real.darton.edu/faculty/kluball/MUSC1100/Question 10.mp3

The **triad** is a chord that has three pitches. On top of its root pitch is stacked another pitch at the interval of a third higher than the root. On top of that second pitch, another pitch is added, another third above. If you add a fourth pitch that is a third above the previous pitch, you arrive at a **seventh chord**. (You may be wondering why we call chords with three notes "triads" and notes with four chords "seventh chords." Why not "fourth chords?" The reason has to do with the fact that the extra note is the "seventh" note in the scale from which the chord is derived. (We will get to scales shortly.) Seventh chords are dissonant chords. They are so common in jazz, however, that they do not always sound like they need to resolve to consonant chords, as one might expect. One also finds chords with other additional tones in jazz: for example, ninth chords, eleventh chords, and thirteenth chords. These chords are related by stacking additional thirds on top of the chord.

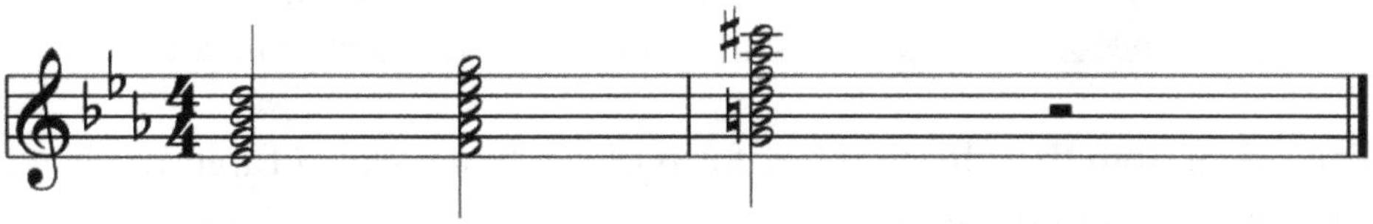

Figure 1.14 | Seventh, ninth, and eleventh chords in musical notation
Author | Corey Parson
Source | Original Work
License | CC BY-SA 4.0

Key (sometimes called "tonality") is closely related to both melody and harmony. The key of a song or composition refers to the pitches that it uses. A key is a collection of pitches, much like you might have with a collection of stamps, bottles, etc. The most important pitch of a key is its **tonic,** that is, the note from which the other pitches are derived. For example, a composition in C major has C as its tonic; a composition in A minor has A as its tonic; a blues in the key of G has G as its tonic. A key is governed by its **scale.** A scale is a series of pitches, ordered by the interval between its notes. There are a variety of types of scales. Every major scale, whether it is D major or C major or G-sharp major, has pitches related by the same intervals in the same order. Likewise, the pitches of every minor scale comprise the same intervals in the same order. The same could be said for a variety of other scales that are found in jazz, rock, and popular music, including the blues scale and the pentatonic scale.

C-major scale			C	D	E	F	G	A	B	C
A-minor scale	A	B	C	D	E	F	G	A		
Blues scale on A	A		C	D	E		G	A		
					(E-flat)					

Table 1.1: C major scale, A minor scale, Blues scale on A

Major and minor scales are most often found in Western music today. The difference of sound in the major scale as opposed to the minor scale is in the perception of the sound. Major sounds relatively bright and happy. "Happy Birthday" and "Joy to the World" (the Christmas Carol) are based on the major mode.

Examples of Major scales excerpts may be heard at the following links:
http://real.darton.edu/faculty/kluball/MUSC1100/Question 14.mp3
http://real.darton.edu/faculty/kluball/MUSC1100/Question 3.mp3

Minor sounds relatively more subdued, sad, or melancholy. The Christmas Carol "We Three Kings" is in the minor mode.

Examples of Minor mode excerpts may be heard at the following links:
http://real.darton.edu/faculty/kluball/MUSC1100/Question 24.mp3
http://real.darton.edu/faculty/kluball/MUSC1100/Question 16.mp3

You might note that the simplest form of the blues scale (Table 1.1) is a type of pentatonic or five-note scale. This reflects the origins of the blues in folk music; much of the folk music around the world uses pentatonic scales. You might also note that the blues scale on A, has a note suspended below it, an E-flat (a pitch that is a half-step higher than D and a half-step lower than E). Otherwise, it is devoid of its blue notes. Blue notes are pitches that are sometimes added to blues scales and blues pieces. The most important blues note in the key of A is E-flat. In a sense, blues notes are examples of accidentals. **Accidentals** are notes that are not normally found in a given key. For example, F-sharp and B-flat are accidentals in the key of C. Accidentals are sometimes called **chromatic** pitches: the word chromatic comes from the ancient Greek word meaning color, and accidentals and chromatic pitches add color and excitement to a composition.

Chords can be built on every pitch of a scale. See Table 1.2 for the triads of C major.

C	**D**	**E**	**F**	**G**	**A**	**B**
E	**F**	**g**	**A**	**B**	**c**	**D**
G	**A**	**b**	**C**	**D**	**e**	**F**
I	**ii**	**iii**	**IV**	**V**	**vi**	**vii°**

Table 1.2: Chords of C Major

One can build seventh chords on these same pitches, by simply adding pitches. In the key of C major, the C major triad is considered the tonic triad (I), because it is built on the tonic of the key. Every other chord in C major tends to resolve to the tonic chord. The two next important chords are the F chord, which we call the IV chord or subdominant, and the G chord, which we call the V chord or dominant. Popular music also uses the VI chord a lot. The chords of a key tend to progress in an orderly fashion. Certain chords tend to resolve to other chords. The dominant or V chord, normally resolves directly to the tonic or I chord. We call a series of chords a **chord progression**.

One of the most important chord progressions for jazz and rock is the blues progression.

In the blues, the tonic chord (I) moves to the subdominant chord (IV) and then back to the tonic chord (I) before moving to the dominant chord (V) and finally back to the tonic (I). This often happens in the space of twelve bars or measures and thus this progression is sometimes called the **twelve-bar blues**. In the key of D, it would look like the following:

Root of the chord	D	G	D	A	G
Chord Symbol	I	(IV)	I	V	(IV)
Number of bars	4	2	2	2	2

Table 1.3: Twelve-bar blues in the key of D

As you can see, sometimes the dominant chord (V) briefly shifts back to the subdominant chord (IV) before finally resolving to the tonic chord.

Chord progressions play a major role in structuring jazz, rock, and popular music, cueing the listener to beginnings, middles, and ends of phrases and the song as a whole. Chord progressions in particular, and harmony in general, may be the most challenging aspects of music for the beginner. Hearing chords and chord progressions requires that one recognize several music phenomena at the same time. Chords may change rapidly, and a listener has to be ready to move on to the next chord as the music progresses.

The best way to learn to hear harmonies is to start with simple examples and ask general questions. Listen to "Light My Fire" (1967) by the Doors, using the link below. See if you can hear the general difference between the verses, which use mostly minor chords, and the chorus, which uses mostly major chords. If you continue to listen, you will eventually be able to hear both.

Ex. 1.13: The Doors, "Light my Fire" (1967)

https://www.youtube.com/watch?v=deB_u-to-IE

1.9 RHYTHM

When you think of the word rhythm, the first thing that might pop into your head is a drum beat. But rhythm goes much deeper than that. Earlier, we defined music as intentional organization of sounds. **Rhythm** is the way the music is organized in respect to time. It works in tandem with melody and harmony to create a feeling of order. The most fundamental aspect of rhythm is the **beat**, which is the basic unit of time in music. It is the ***consistent*** pulse of the music, just like your heartbeat creates a steady, underlying pulse within your body. The beat is what you tap your feet to when you listen to music. Imagine the beat as a series of equidistant dots passing through time as in the Figure 1.15.

Figure 1.15 | The Beat
Author | Thomas Heflin
Source | Original Work
License | CC BY-SA 4.0

It should be noted that the beat does not measure exact time like the second hand on a clock. It is instead a fluid unit that changes depending on the music being played. The speed at which the beat is played is called the **tempo**. At quick tempos, the beats pass by quickly, as represented by Figure 1.16 below showing our beats pressed against each other in time.

Figure 1.16 | Fast Tempos
Author | Thomas Heflin
Source | Original Work
License | CC BY-SA 4.0

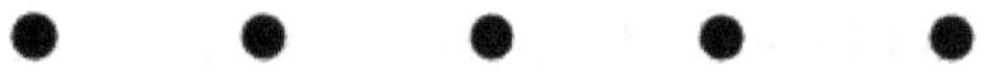

Figure 1.17 | Slow Tempos
Author | Thomas Heflin
Source | Original Work
License | CC BY-SA 4.0

At slow tempos, the beats pass by slowly, as seen in Figure 1.17 showing our beats with plenty of space between them.

Composers often indicate tempo markings by writing musical terms such as "allegro" which indicates that the piece should be played at a quick, or brisk, tempo. In other cases, composers will write the tempo markings in beats per minute (BPM), when they want more precise tempos. Either way, the tempo is one of the major factors in establishing the character of a piece. Slow tempos are used in everything from sweeping love songs to the dirges associated with sadness or death. Take for example, Chopin's famous funeral march:

Ex. 1.14: Chopin "Piano Sonata Op.35 No.2"

https://www.youtube.com/watch?v=Hgw_RD_1_5I

Fast tempos can help to evoke anything from bouncy happiness to frenzied madness. One memorable example of a fast tempo occurs in "Flight of the Bumblebee," an orchestral interlude written by Nikolai Rimsky-Korsakov for his opera *The Tale of Tsar Saltan*, which evokes the busy buzzing of a bee.

Ex. 1.15: Nikolai Rimsky-Korsakov "Flight of the Bumblebee"

https://www.youtube.com/watch?v=aYAJopwEYv8

Beats are the underlying pulse behind music, while **meter** refers to the way in which those beats are grouped together in a piece. Each individual grouping is called a **measure** or a **bar** (referring to the bar lines that divide measures in written music notation). Most music is written in either duple meter (groupings of two), triple meter (groupings of three), or quadruple meter (groupings of four). These meters are conveyed by stressing or "accenting" the first beat of each grouping. In the figure below, you can see examples of triple and quadruple meter. The first beat of each bar is larger than the rest to indicate this accent. These larger beats are often referred to as strong beats, while the smaller beats between them. are referred to as weak beats.

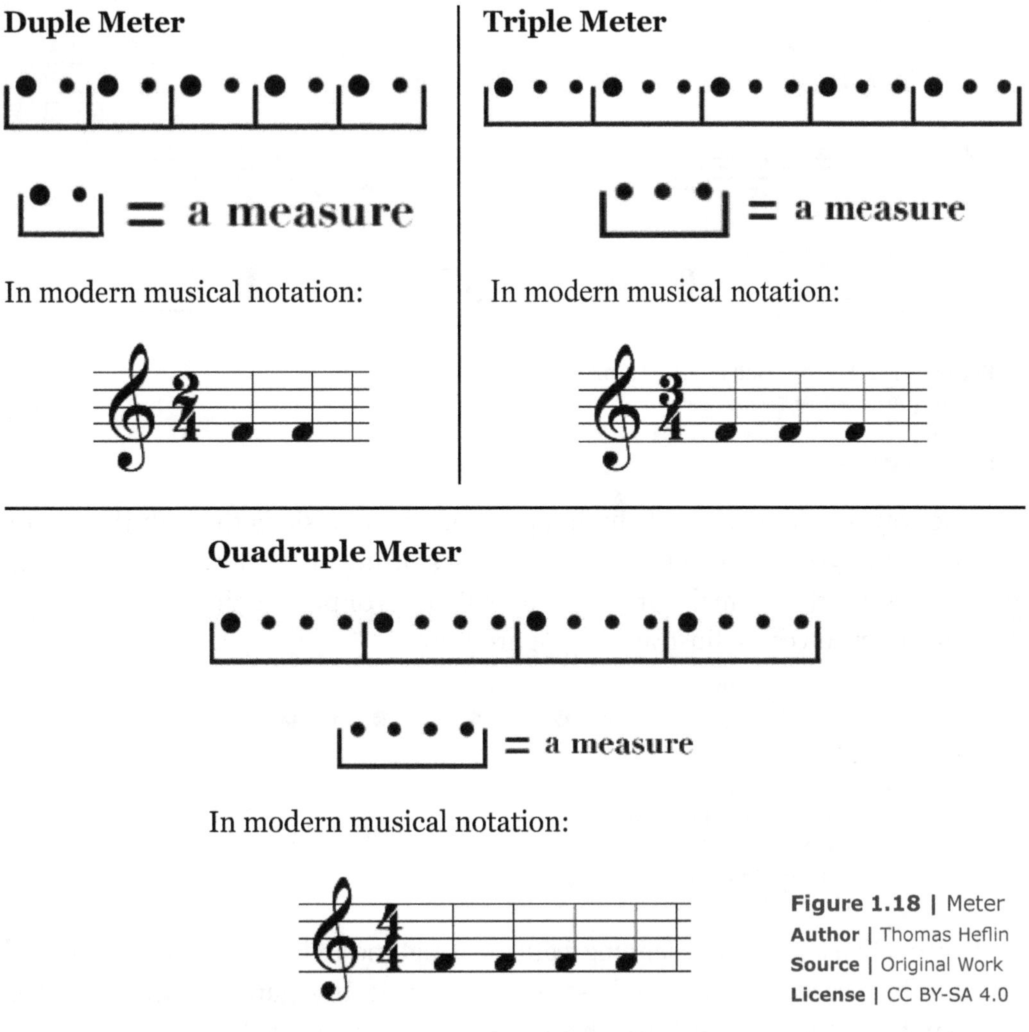

Figure 1.18 | Meter
Author | Thomas Heflin
Source | Original Work
License | CC BY-SA 4.0

To illustrate how vital rhythm is to a piece of music, let's investigate the simple melody "Mary Had a Little Lamb." Below, the melody and chords are conveyed through standard musical notation. The meter is indicated by the two numbers four over four. (This is known to music readers as the **time signature**.) This particular time signature is also known as "common time" due to the fact that it is so widely used. The top number indicates the meter, or how many beats there are per measure. The bottom number indicates which type of note in modern musical notation will represent that beat (in this case, it is the quarter note). The vertical lines are there to indicate each individual measure. As you can see, the melody on the top staff and the chords on the bottom staff line up correctly in time due to the fact that they are grouped into measures together. In this way, rhythm is the element that binds music together in time.

Figure 1.19 | "Mary Had a Little Lamb"
Author | Arranged by Thomas Heflin
Source | Traditional Melody
License | CC BY-SA 4.0

One way to add a sense of rhythmic variation to music is through the use of syncopation. **Syncopation** refers to the act of shifting of the normal accent, usually by stressing the normally unaccented weak beats or placing the accent between the beats themselves as illustrated in Figure 1.20.

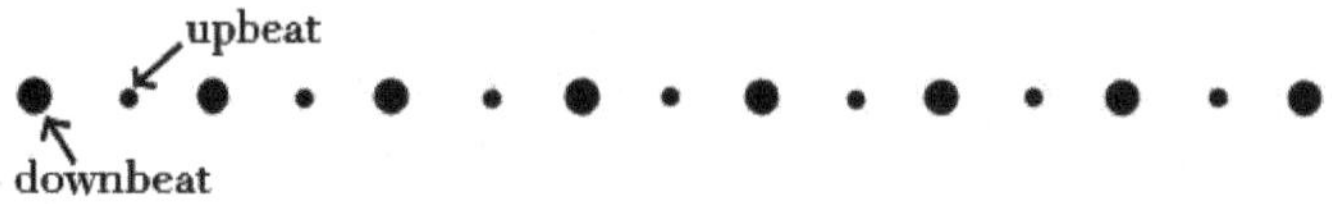

Figure 1.20 | Syncopation
Author | Thomas Heflin
Source | Original Work
License | CC BY-SA 4.0

Syncopation is one of the defining features of ragtime and jazz, and is one aspect of rhythmic bounce associated with those genres of music. In Figure 1.21 below, it is the circled notes on the weak beats which are accented or emphasized.

Figure 1.21 | "The Entertainer" by Scott Joplin
Author | Corey Parson
Source | Original Work
License | CC BY-SA 4.0

In some cases, certain types of music may feature the use of a **polyrhythm**, which simply refers to two or more different rhythms being played at the same time. A common polyrhythm might pit a feeling of four against a feeling of three. Polyrhythms are often associated with the music of Africa. However, they can be found in American and European music of the twentieth century, such as jazz.

Listen to the example below of Duke Ellington playing his signature song, the Billy Strayhorn composition "Take the A Train." You will notice that the beats in the piece are grouped as four beats per measure. Pay special attention to what happens at 1:32 in the video. The horns begin to imply groupings of three beats (or triple meter) on top of the existing four beat groupings (or quadruple meter). These concurrent groupings create a sense of rhythmic tension that leads the band into the next section of the piece at 1:38 in the video.

Ex. 1.16: Duke Ellington "Take the A Train"

https://www.youtube.com/watch?v=hRGFqSkNjHk

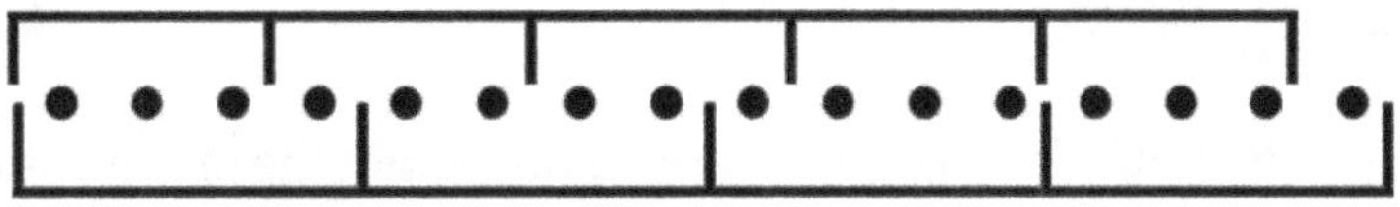

Figure 1.22 | Polyrhythm
Author | Thomas Heflin
Source | Original Work
License | CC BY-SA 4.0

1.10 TEXTURE

Texture refers to the ways in which musical lines of a musical piece interact. We use a variety of general adjectives to describe musical texture, words such as transparent, dense, thin, thick, heavy, and light. We also use three specific musical terms to describe texture: monophony, homophony, and polyphony. Of these three terms, homophony and polyphony are most important for jazz, rock, and popular music.

Monophonic music is music that has one melodic line. This one melodic line may be sung by one person or 100 people. The important thing is that they are all singing the same melody, either in unison or in octaves. Monophony is rare in jazz, rock, and popular music. An example would be a folk melody that is sung by one person or a group of people without any accompaniment from instruments. Gregorian chant is another excellent example of monophonic music.

Ex. 1.17: Gregorian Chant

https://www.youtube.com/watch?v=3ElL8hdQD_4

Homophonic music is music that has one melodic line that is accompanied by chords. A lot of rock and popular music has a homophonic texture. Anytime the tune is the most important aspect of a song, it is likely to be in homophonic texture. Elvis Presley's "Hound Dog" (1956), The Carter Family's version of "Can the Circle be Unbroken" (1935), and Billy Joel's "Piano Man" (1973), are relatively good examples of homophony.

Polyphony simultaneously features two or more relatively independent and important melodic lines. Dixieland jazz and bebop are often polyphonic, as is the music of jam bands such as the Allman Bros. "Anthropology" (ca. 1946) for example, a jazz tune recorded by Dizzy Gillespie, Charlie Parker, and others reflects the busy polyphony typical in bebop. Some jazz played by larger ensembles, such as big bands, is also polyphonic at points, although in this case, there is generally a strong sense of a main melody. Much of the music that we will study in this text exists somewhere between homophony and polyphony. Some music will have a strong main melody, suggesting homophony, and yet have interesting countermelodies that one would expect in polyphony. Much rap is composed of many layers of sounds, but at times those layers are not very transparent, as one would expect in polyphony.

1.11 PUTTING IT ALL TOGETHER

1.11.1 Form in Music

When we talk about musical **form**, we are talking about the organization of musical elements—melody, harmony, rhythm, texture, timbre—in time. Because music is a temporal art, memory plays an important role in how we experience musical form. Memory allows us to hear repetition, contrast, and variation in music. And it is these elements that provide structure, coherence, and shape to musical compositions.

A composer or songwriter brings myriad experiences of music, accumulated over a lifetime, to the act of writing music. He or she has learned how to write music by listening to, playing, and studying music. He or she has picked up, consciously and/or unconsciously, a number of ways of structuring music. The composer may intentionally write music modeled after another group's music: this happens all of the time in the world of popular music where the aim is to produce music that will be disseminated to as many people as possible. In other situations, a composer might use musical forms of an admired predecessor as an act of homage or simply because that is "how it's always been done." We find this happening a great deal in the world of folk music, where a living tradition is of great importance. The music of the "classical" period (1775-1825) is rich with musical forms as heard in the works of masters such as Joseph Haydn and Wolfgang Amadeus Mozart. In fact, form plays a vital role in most Western art music (discussed later in the chapter) all the way into the twenty-first century. We will discuss these forms, such as the rondo and sonata-allegro, in later chapters, but for the purpose of this introduction, we will focus on those that might be more familiar to the modern listener.

1.11.2 The Twelve-Bar Blues

Many compositions that on the surface sound very different use similar musical forms. A large number of jazz compositions, for example, follow either the twelve-bar blues or an AABA form. The twelve-bar blues features a chord progression of I-IV-I-V-IV-I. Generally the lyrics follow an AAB pattern, that is, a line of text (A) is stated once, repeated (A), and then followed by a response statement (B). The melodic idea used for the statement (B) is generally slightly different from that used for the opening a phrases (A). This entire verse is sung over the I-IV-I-V-IV-I progression. The next verse is sung over the same pattern, generally to the same melodic lines, although the singer may vary the notes in various places occasionally.

Listen to Elvis Presley's version of "Hound Dog" (1956) using the link below, and follow the chart below to hear the blues progression.

Ex. 1.18: Elvis Presley "Hound Dog" (1956)

https://www.youtube.com/watch?v=-eHJ12Vhpyc

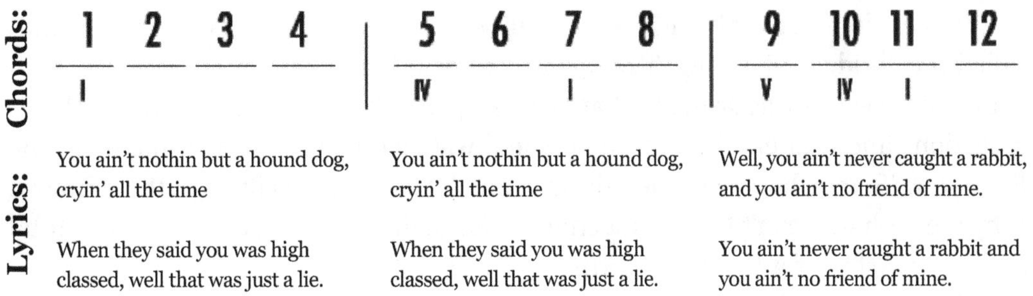

Figure 1.23 | Format Breakdown of Elvis's "Hound Dog"
Author | Thomas Heflin
Source | Original Work
License | CC BY-SA 4.0

This blues format is one example of what we might call musical form. It should be mentioned that the term "blues" is used somewhat loosely and is sometimes used to describe a tune with a "bluesy" sound, even though it may not follow the twelve-bar blues form. The blues is vitally important to American music because it influenced not only later jazz but also rhythm and blues and rock and roll.

1.11.3 AABA Form

Another important form to jazz and popular music is AABA form. Sometimes this is also called thirty-two-bar form; in this case, the form has thirty-two measures or bars, much like a twelve-bar blues has twelve measures or bars. This form was used widely in songs written for Tin Pan Alley, Vaudeville, and musicals from the 1910s through the 1950s. Many so-called jazz standards spring from that repertoire. Interestingly, these popular songs generally had an opening verse and then a chorus. The chorus was a section of thirty-two-bar form, and often the part that audiences remembered. Thus, the chorus was what jazz artists took as the basis of their improvisations.

"(Somewhere) Over the Rainbow," as sung by Judy Garland in 1939 (accompanied by Victor Young and his Orchestra), is a well-known tune that is in thirty-two-bar form.

Ex. 1.19: Judy Garland "(Somewhere) Over the Rainbow" (1939)

https://www.youtube.com/watch?v=PSZxmZmBfnU

After an introduction of four bars, Garland enters with the opening line of the text, sung to melody A. "Somewhere over the rainbow way up high, there's a land that I heard of once in a lullaby." This opening line and melody lasts for eight bars. The next line of the text is sung to the same melody (still eight bars long) as the first line of text. "Somewhere over the rainbow skies are blue, and the dreams that you dare to dream really do come true." The third part of the text is contrasting in character. Where the first two lines began with the word "somewhere," the third line begins with "someday." Where the first two lines spoke of a faraway place, the third line focuses on what will happen to the singer. "Someday I'll wish upon a star, and wake up where the clouds are far, behind me. Where troubles melt like lemon drops, away above the chimney tops, that's where you'll find me." It is sung to a contrasting melody B and is eight bars long. This B section is also sometimes called the "bridge" of a song. The opening a melody returns for a final time, with words that begin by addressing that faraway place dreamed about in the first two A sections and that end in a more personal way, similar to the sentiments in the B section. "Somewhere over the rainbow, bluebirds fly. Birds fly over the rainbow. Why then, oh why can't I?" This section is also eight bars long, adding up to a total of thirty-two bars for the AABA form.

Although we've heard the entire thirty-two-bar form, the song is not over. The arranger added a conclusion to the form that consists of one statement of the A section, played by the orchestra (note the prominent clarinet solo); another re-statement of the A section, this time with the words from the final statement of the A section the first time; and four bars from the B section or bridge: "If happy little bluebirds...Oh why can't I." This is a good example of one way in which musicians have taken a standard form and varied it slightly to provide interest. Now listen to the entire recording one more time, seeing if you can keep up with the form.

1.11.4 Verse and Chorus Forms

Most popular music features a mix of verses and choruses. A chorus is normally a set of lyrics that recur to the same music within a given song. A chorus is sometimes called a refrain. A verse is a set of lyrics that are generally, although not always, just heard once over the course of a song.

In a simple verse-chorus form, the same music is used for the chorus and for each verse. "Can the Circle Be Unbroken" (1935) by The Carter Family is a good example of a simple verse-chorus form. Many childhood songs and holiday songs also use a simple verse-chorus song.

Ex. 1.20: The Carter Family "Can the Circle Be Unbroken" (1935)

https://www.youtube.com/watch?v=qjHjm5sRqSA

In a simple verse form, there are no choruses. Instead, there is a series of verses, each sung to the same music. Hank Williams's "I'm So Lonesome I Could Cry" (1949) is one example of a simple verse form. After Williams sings two verses, each sixteen bars long, there is an instrumental verse, played by guitar. Williams sings a third verse followed by another instrumental verse, this time also played by guitar. Williams then ends the song with a final verse.

Ex. 1.21: Hank Williams: I'm So Lonesome I Could Cry (1949)

https://www.youtube.com/watch?v=oyTOZCfp8OY

A contrasting verse-chorus form features different music for its chorus than for the statement of its verse(s). "Light my Fire" by the Doors is a good example of a contrasting verse-chorus form. In this case, each of the two verses are repeated one time, meaning that the overall form looks something like: intro, verse 1, chorus, verse 2, chorus, verse 2, chorus, verse 1, chorus. You can listen to "Light my Fire" by clicking on the link below.

Ex. 1.22: The Doors, "Light my Fire" (1967)

https://www.youtube.com/watch?v=deB_u-to-IE

Naturally, there are many other forms that music might take. As you listen to the music you like, pay attention to its form. You might be surprised by what you hear!

1.11.5 Composition and Improvisation

Music from every culture is made up of some combination of the musical elements. Those elements may be combined using one of two major processes; composition and improvisation.

Composition

Composition is the process whereby a musician notates musical ideas using a system of symbols or using some other form of recording. We call musicians who use this process "composers." When composers preserve their musical ideas using notation or some form of recording, they intend for their music to be reproduced the same way every time.

Listen to the recording of Mozart's music linked below. Every element of the music was carefully notated by Mozart so that each time the piece is performed, it can be performed exactly the same way.

Ex. 1.23: Mozart "Piano Sonata K.457 in C minor" (1989)

https://www.youtube.com/watch?v=JrUH5VAetEg

Improvisation

Improvisation is a different process. It is the process whereby musicians create music spontaneously using the elements of music. Improvisation still requires the musician to follow a set of rules. Often the set of rules has to do with the scale to be used, the rhythm to be used, or other musical requirements using the musical elements.

Listen to the example of Louis Armstrong below. Armstrong is performing a style of early New Orleans jazz in which the entire group improvises to varying degrees over a set musical form and melody. The piece starts out with a statement of the original melody by the trumpet, with Armstrong varying the rhythm of the original written melody as well as adding melodic embellishments. At the same time, the trombone improvises supporting notes that outline the harmony of the song and the clarinet improvises a completely new melody designed to complement the main melody of the trumpet. The rhythm section of piano, bass, and drums are improvising their accompaniment underneath the horn players, but are doing so within the strict chord progression of the song. The overall effect is one in which you hear the individual expressions of each player, but can still clearly recognize the song over which they are improvising. This is followed by Armstrong interpreting the melody. Next we hear individual solos improvised on the clarinet, the trombone, and the trumpet. The piece ends when Armstrong sings the melody one last time.

Ex. 1.24: Louis Armstrong, "When the Saints Go Marching In" (1961)

https://www.youtube.com/watch?v=5WADCJ4_KmU

Composition and Improvisation Combined

In much of the popular music we hear today, like jazz and rock, both improvisation and composition are combined. Listen to the example linked below of Miles Davis playing "All Blues." The trumpet and two saxophones play an arrangement of a composed melody, then each player improvises using the scale from which the melody is derived. This combined structure is one of the central features of the jazz style and is also often used in many popular music compositions.

Ex. 1.25: Miles Davis "All Blues" (1949)

https://www.youtube.com/watch?v=uRBgy43gCoQ

1.11.6 Music and Categories

Categorizing anything can be difficult, as items often do not completely fit in the boxes we might design for them. Still, categorizing is a human exercise by which we attempt to see the big picture and compare and contrast the phenomenon we encounter, so that we can make larger generalizations. By categorizing music we can attempt to better understand ways in which music has functioned in the past and continues to function today. Three categories which are often used in talking about music are (1) art music, (2) folk music, and (3) popular music. These categories can be seen in the Venn diagram below:

Image 1.24 | Venn Diagram of the Three Categories of Music
Author | Elizabeth Kramer
Source | Original Work
License | CC BY-SA 4.0

Much of the music that we consider in this book falls into the sphere of art music in some way or form. It is also sometimes referred to as classical music and has a written musical tradition. Composers of art music typically hope that their creative products will be played for many years. Art music is music that is normally learned through specialized training over a period of many years. It is often described as music that stands the test of time. For example, today, if you go to a symphony orchestra concert you will likely hear music composed over a hundred years ago.

Folk music is another form of music that has withstood the test of time, but in a different way. Folk music derives from a particular culture and is music that one might be expected to learn from a family at a young age. Although one can study folk music, the idea is that it is accessible to all; it generally is not written down in musical notation until it becomes an object of scholarship. Lullabies, dance music, work songs, and some worship music are often considered folk music as they are integrated with daily life.

Popular music is marked by its dissemination to large groups of people. As such, it is like folk music. But popular music is generally not expected to be passed down from one generation to the next as happens with folk music. Instead, as its name implies, it tends to appeal to the masses at one moment in time. To use twentieth-century terminology, it often hits the charts in one month and then is supplanted by something new in the next month. Although one might find examples of popular music across history, popular music has been especially significant since the rise of mass media and recording technologies in the twentieth century. Today, music can be put online and instantly go viral around the world. Some significant twentieth-century popular music is discussed in chapter eight.

1.12 CHAPTER SUMMARY

In this chapter, we learned a basic definition of music as well as definitions of the basic elements of music. We also explored some basic facts about acoustics, including the nature of sound. We learned how tones comprised of organized sound waves sound to us like definite pitches, while disorganized sound waves are perceived as noise. We briefly touched on the harmonic series and how it influenced the nature of music, including properties of sound such as timbre.

Next, we explored how the development of musical notation made it possible to organize sounds into a wide variety of configurations. There are an infinite number of possible **performing forces**, but the most common would have to be the human voice followed by a wide variety of instruments including strings, woodwinds, brass, percussion, keyboards, and electric instruments.

Next we discussed the four main components of music: melody, harmony, rhythm and texture. Melody is defined primarily by its shape, and can be broken up into smaller components called motives. Harmony, which is the vertical aspect of music, can be described in its most basic terms as dissonant or consonant. Harmony is often built in thirds through the use of three-note chords called triads or four-note chords called seventh chords. Whole sequences of chords are known as chord progressions. Compositions are harmonically grounded through the use of key centers, tonic notes, and scales.

Rhythm is the way the music is organized in respect to time. The fundamental unit of time is the beat, which is further broken into groupings called measures. These groupings are determined by the meter of the piece, which is often either duple, triple, or quadruple. The speed at which these beats go by is known as the tempo. Other rhythmic devices such as syncopation and polyrhythm can add further variety to the music. On a larger scale, music is put together in terms of its form. We discussed three common song forms, the blues, AABA and the Verse and Chorus.

Texture refers to the ways in which musical lines of a musical piece interact. Common textures include monophonic texture (one melodic line), homophonic texture (accompanied by chords), and polyphonic texture (simultaneous melodies). We also saw that composition and improvisation are the two major processes used to combine the musical elements we discussed. They may be used independently or they may be combined within a composition. These topics are key concepts to remember while reading the upcoming chapters where they are further expanded upon.

1.13 GLOSSARY

Accidentals – notes that are not normally found in a given key

Acoustics – the study of how sound behaves in physical spaces

Acoustical Engineer – a person who works in the area of acoustic technology

Acoustician – a person who studies the theory and science of acoustics

Amplitude – refers to how high the wave form appears to vibrate above zero when seen on an oscilloscope; louder sounds create higher oscilloscope amplitude readings

Bar – see *measure*

Beat – the basic unit of time in music

Brass – instruments traditionally made of brass or another metal (and thus often producing a "bright" or "brassy" tone) whose sound is generated by blowing into a mouthpiece that is attached to a coiled tube

Chord – the simultaneous sounding of three or more pitches; like intervals, chords can be consonant or dissonant

Chord Progression – a series of chords

Chromatic – musical pitches which move up or down by successive half-steps

Composition – the process whereby a musician notates musical ideas using a system of symbols or using some other form of recording

Conjunct – a melody that moves mostly by step, in a smooth manner

Consonant – (adjective) term used to describe intervals and chords that tend to sound sweet and pleasing to our ears; consonance (noun), as opposed to dissonance, is stable and needs no resolution.

Cycles per Second (cps) – a definition of frequency of vibration; replaced by Hertz in 1960

Disjunct – a melody with wide leaps and rapid changes in direction

Dissonant – (adjective) intervals and chords that tend to sound harsh to our ears; dissonance (noun) is often used to create tension and instability, and the interplay between dissonance and consonance provides a sense of harmonic and melodic motion in music

Dynamic – the variation in the volume of musical sound (the amplitude of the sound waves)

Equalization (EQ) – the process of raising or lowering different frequencies of sound, either in a recording, or within a tone (overtones)

Form – the structure of the phrases and sections within a musical composition (Does it repeat?)

Frequency – how quickly or slowly a medium (solid, liquid, gas) vibrates and produces a sound

Fundamental Pitch – the lowest pitch in the harmonic series

Guido of Arezzo – a medieval music theorist who developed a system of lines and spaces that enabled musicians to notate the specific notes in a melody

Improvisation – the process whereby musicians create music spontaneously using the elements of music as building blocks

Instrumentation – the instruments comprising a musical group (including the human voice)

Interval – the distance in pitch between any two notes

Harmony – any simultaneous combination of tones and the rules governing those combinations (the way a melody is accompanied is also another way to define harmony)

Hertz (Hz) – the unit of frequency defined as one cycle per second and named after Heinrich Hertz (1957-1894) in 1960

Homophonic – musical texture comprised of one melodic line accompanied by chords

Key – the set of pitches on which a composition is based

Keyboard – instruments that are characterized by keyboards, such as the piano, organ, vibraphone, and accordion

Measure – a unit of time that contains a specific number of beats defined by the meter/ time signature

Melody – a succession of single tones in musical compositions

Meter – the way in which the beats are grouped together in a piece

Monophonic – musical texture comprised of one melodic line; a melodic line may be sung by one person or 100 people

Motive – the smallest musical unit of a melody, generally a single rhythm of two or three pitches

Music – sound and silence organized in time

Noise – a disorganized sound with no observable pitch

Octave – the distance between two musical pitches where the higher pitch vibrates exactly twice as many times per second as the lower

Oscilloscope - an electronic device that displays a visual representation of the different types of sound waves

Overtones (also known as harmonics) – a musical tone heard above a fundamental pitch

Partials – the sounds of different frequency that naturally occur above a fundamental (primary) tone

Percussion – instruments that are typically hit or struck by the hand, with sticks, or with hammers or that are shaken or rubbed by hand

Performing Forces – see instrumentation

Phrase – smaller sub-sections of a melody

Pitch – a tone that is composed of an organized sound wave

Polyphony – musical texture that simultaneously features two or more relatively independent and important melodic lines

Polyrhythm – two or more different rhythms played at the same time

Range – the number of pitches, expressed as an intervallic distance

Register – the low, medium, and high sections of an instrument or vocal range

Rhythm – the way the music is organized in respect to time

Scale – a series of pitches, ordered by the interval between its notes

Sequence – a repetition of a motive or phrase at a different pitch level

Seventh Chord – a chord that has four pitches stacked in intervals of thirds

Sine Wave – the simplest sound wave that occurs in nature. A pure sine wave contains no partials and is perfectly smooth and rounded in appearance on an oscilloscope.

Sound – the mechanical movement of an audible pressure wave through a solid, liquid, or gas

Sound Waves – longitudinal waves (compression and rarefaction waves) that travel through a solid, liquid, or gas

Step – the distance between adjacent notes in a musical scale

Strings – instruments whose sound is produced by setting strings in motion

Syncopation – the act of shifting the normal accent, usually by stressing the normally unaccented weak beats or placing the accent between the beats themselves

Synthesizers – electronic instruments (often in keyboard form) that create sounds using basic wave forms in different combinations

Tempo –the speed at which the beat is played

Texture – the ways in which musical lines of a musical piece interact

Timbre – the tone color or tone quality of a sound

Time signature – the numeric notation at the beginning of a line of music where the top number indicates how many beats are in each measure and the bottom number indicates which type of note will represent that beat

Tonic – the most important pitch of a key; the note from which the other pitches are derived

Triad – a chord that has three pitches stacked in intervals of thirds

Twelve-Bar Blues – a twelve-bar musical form commonly found in American music

Vocal – having to do with the human voice

Woodwinds – instruments traditionally made of wood whose sound is generated by forcing air through a tube, thus creating a vibrating air column

2 Music of the Middle Ages

Elizabeth Kramer

2.1 OBJECTIVES

1. Demonstrate knowledge of historical and cultural contexts of the Middle Ages
2. Recognize musical styles of the Middle Ages
3. Identify important genres and uses of music of the Middle Ages
4. Identify aurally, selected compositions of the Middle Ages and critically evaluate its style
5. Compare and contrast music of the Middle Ages with today's contemporary music

2.2 KEY TERMS AND INDIVIDUALS

- *a cappella*
- Alfonso the Wise
- bubonic plague
- cadence
- cathedrals
- Catholic Church
- chant
- classical Greece and Rome
- clergy
- commoners
- courtly love
- courts
- Crusades
- drone
- gothic
- Guillaume de Machaut
- Hildegard of Bingen
- hymn
- mass
- melisma
- Middle Ages (450-1400 CE)
- nobility
- Perotin
- polyphony
- Pope
- Pythagoras

- refrain
- rhythm according to the text
- Roman Empire (27 BCE – 476 CE)
- song
- strophes
- syllabic
- university
- vernacular literatures
- verse
- Virgin Mary

2.3 INTRODUCTION AND HISTORICAL CONTEXT

2.3.1 Musical Timeline

Events in History	Events in Music
	2nd millennia BCE: First Hebrew Psalms are written
	7th Century BCE: Ancient Greeks and Romans use music for entertainment and religious rites
	6th Century BCE: Pythagoras and his experiments with acoustics
From the 1st Century CE: Spread of Christianity through the Roman Empire	
	4th Century BCE: Plato and Aristotle write about music
4th Century CE: Founding of the monastic movement in Christianity	
	c. 400 CE: St Augustine writes about church music
c. 450 CE: Fall of Rome	
	4th – 9th Century CE: Development/Codification of Christian Chant
	c. 800 CE: First experiments in Western Music
11th Century CE: Rise of Feudalism & the Three Estates	
	11th Century CE: Guido of Arezzo refines of music notation and development of solfège
11th Century: Growth of Marian Culture	
1088 CE: Founding of the University of Bologna	
	12th Century CE: Hildegard of Bingen writes Gregorian chant
c. 1095-1291 CE: The Crusades	
c. 1163-1240s CE: Building of Notre Dame in Paris and the rise of Gothic architecture	
	13th Century CE: Development of Polyphony
	c. 1275 CE: King Alfonso the Wise collects early songs in an exquisitely illuminated manuscript
1346-53: Height of the Bubonic Plague (Black Death)	14th Century CE: Further refinement of musical notation, including notation for rhythm
	1300-1377 CE: Guillaume de Machaut composes songs and church music

2.3.2 Introduction

What do you think of when you hear the term the Middle Ages (450-1450)? For some, the semi-historical figures of Robin Hood and Maid Marian come to mind. Others recall Western Christianity's Crusades to the Holy Land. Still others may have read about the arrival in European lands of the bubonic plague or Black Death, as it was called. For most twenty-first-century individuals, the Middle Ages seem far removed. Although life and music were quite different back then, we hope that you will find that there are cultural threads that extend from that distant time to now.

We normally start studies of Western music with the Middle Ages, but of course, music existed long before then. In fact, the term Middle Ages or medieval period got its name to describe the time in between (or "in the middle of") the ancient age of classical Greece and Rome and the Renaissance of Western Europe, which roughly began in the fifteenth century. Knowledge of music before the Middle Ages is limited, and some of our most ancient sources refer to the Greek mathematician Pythagoras, who died around 500 B.C.E. (See his profile on a third century ancient coin: Figure 2.1.)

Figure 2.1 | Profile of Pythagoras on ancient coin
Author | User "Schaengel89"
Source | Wikimedia Commons
License | Public Domain

Pythagoras might be thought of as a father of the modern study of acoustics due to his experimentation with bars of iron and strings of different lengths. Images of people singing and playing instruments, such as those found on the Greek vases provide evidence that music was used for ancient theater, dance, and worship. The Greek word *musicka* referred to not music but also referred to poetry and the telling of history. Writings of Plato and Aristotle referred to music as a form of ethos (an appeal to ethics). As the Roman Empire expanded across Western Europe, so too did Christianity (see Figure 2.2, a map of Western Europe around 1000). Considering that Biblical texts from ancient Hebrews to those of early Christians, provided numerous records of music used as a form of worship, the Empire used music to help unify its people: the theory was that if people worshipped together in a similar way, then they might also stick together during political struggles.

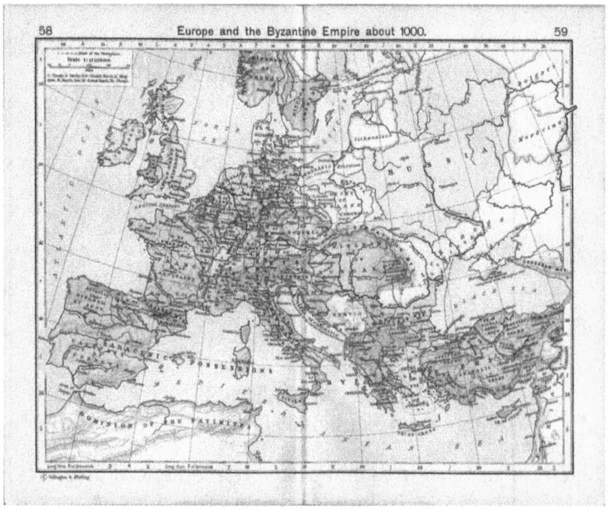

Figure 2.2 | Map of Western Europe
Author | User "Roke"
Source | Wikimedia Commons
License | Public Domain

Later, starting around 800 CE, Western music is recorded in a notation that we can still decipher today. This brief overview of these five hundred years of the Roman Empire will help us better understand the music of the Middle Ages.

2.3.3 Historical Context for Music of the Middle Ages (800-1400)

During the Middle Ages, as during other periods of Western history, sacred and secular worlds were both separate and integrated. However during this time, the Catholic Church was the most widespread and influential institution and leader in all things sacred. The Catholic Church's head, the Pope, maintained political and spiritual power and influence among the noble classes and their geographic territories; the life of a high church official was not completely different from that of a noble counterpart, and many younger sons and daughters of the aristocracy found vocations in the church. Towns large and small had churches, spaces open to all: commoners, clergy, and nobles. The Catholic Church also developed a system of monasteries, where monks studied and prayed, often in solitude, even while making cultural and scientific discoveries that would eventually shape human life more broadly. In civic and secular life, kings, dukes, and lords wielded power over their lands and the commoners living therein. Kings and dukes had courts, gatherings of fellow nobles, where they forged political alliances, threw lavish parties, and celebrated both love and war in song and dance.

Many of the important historical developments of the Middle Ages arose from either in the church or the court. One such important development stemming from the Catholic Church would be the developments of architecture. During this period, architects built increasingly tall and imposing cathedrals for worship through the technological innovations of pointed arches, flying buttresses, and large cut glass windows. This new architectural style was referred to as "gothic," which vastly contrast the Romanesque style, with its rounded arches and smaller windows. Another important development stemming from the courts occurred in the arts. Poets and musicians, attached to the courts, wrote poetry, literature, and music,

Figure 2.3 | Notre-Dame de Paris
Author | User "Zuffe"
Source | Wikimedia Commons
License | CC BY 3.0

Figure 2.4 | The ambulatory of Notre Dame
Author | User "Zmorgan"
Source | Wikimedia Commons
License | Public Domain

less and less in Latin—still the common language of the church—and increasingly in their own vernacular languages (the predecessors of today's French, Italian, Spanish, German, and English). However, one major development of the Middle Ages spanned sacred and secular worlds: universities shot up in locales from Bologna, Italy, and Paris, France, to Oxford, England (the University of Bologna begin the first). At university, a young man could pursue a degree in theology, law, or medicine. Music of a sort was studied as one of the seven liberal arts and sciences, specifically as the science of proportions. (Look for music in this twelfth-century image of the seven liberal arts from the Hortus deliciarum of the Herrad of Landsberg: Figure 2.5.)

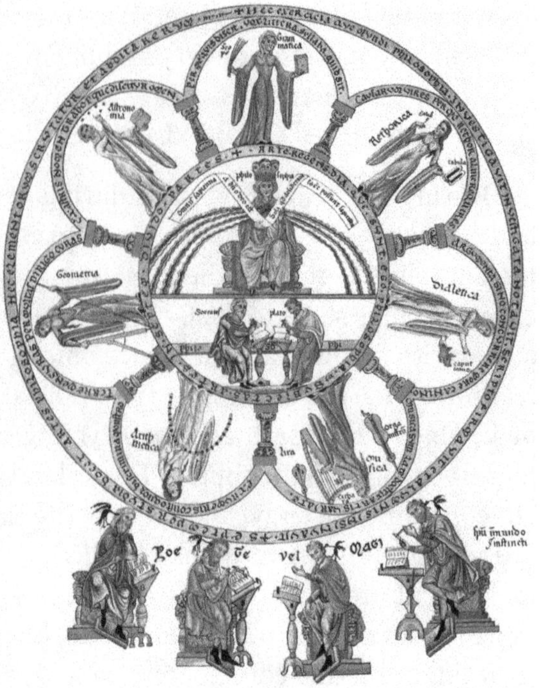

Figure 2.5 | Hortus deliciarum of the Herrad of Landsberg
Author | Herrad von Landsberg
Source | Wikimedia Commons
License | Public Domain

2.4 MUSIC IN THE MIDDLE AGES: AN OVERVIEW

Not surprisingly, given their importance during the Middle Ages, both the Catholic Church and the network of aristocratic courts left a significant mark on music of the time. Much of the music from that era that was written down in notation and still exists comes from Christian worship or court entertainment. Churches and courts employed scribes and artists to write down their music in beautifully illuminated manuscripts such as this one that features Guillaume Machaut's "Dame, avous sans retollir," discussed later. Churchmen such as the monk Guido of Arezzo devised musical systems such as "solfège" still used today.

Figure 2.6 | Group of people dancing depicted in Machaut's manuscript
Author | Guillaume de Machaut
Source | Wikimedia Commons
License | Public Domain

As we study a few compositions from the Middle Ages, we will see the following musical developments at play: (1) the development of musical texture from monophony to polyphony, and (2) the shift from music whose rhythm is hinted at by its words, to music that has what we refer to today as meter. Although we know that instrumental music existed in the Middle Ages, most of the music that has survived is vocal.

2.5 MUSIC FOR MEDIEVAL CHRISTIAN WORSHIP

The earliest music of Catholic Christianity was **chant**, that is, monophonic *a cappella* music, most often sung in worship. As you learned in the first chapter of this book, monophony refers to music with one melodic line that may be performed by one or many individuals at the same time. Largely due to the belief of some Catholics that instruments were too closely associated with secular music, instruments were rarely used in medieval worship; therefore most chant was sung a cappella, or without instruments. As musical notation for rhythm had not yet developed, the exact development of rhythm in chant is uncertain. However, based on church traditions (some of which still exist), we believe that the rhythms of medieval chants were guided by the natural rhythms provided by the words.

Medieval Catholic worship included services throughout the day. The most important of these services was the **Mass**, at which the Eucharist, also known as communion, was celebrated (this celebration includes the consumption of bread and wine representing the flesh and blood of Jesus Christ). Five chants of the mass (the Kyrie, Gloria, Credo, Sanctus, and Agnus Dei) were typically included in every mass, no matter what date in the church calendar. Catholics, as well as some Protestants, still use this Liturgy in worship today.

In the evening, one might attend a Vespers service, at which chants called hymns were sung. Hymns, like most of the rest of the Catholic liturgy, were sung in Latin. **Hymns** most often featured four-line strophes in which the lines were generally the same length and often rhymed. Each strophe of a given hymn was sung to the same music, and for that reason, we say that hymns are in strophic form. Hymns like most chants generally had a range of about an octave, which made them easy to sing.

Throughout the Middle Ages, Mary the mother of Jesus, referred to as the Virgin Mary, was a central figure in Catholic devotion and worship. Under Catholic belief, she is upheld as the perfect woman, having been chosen by God to miraculously give birth to the Christ while still a virgin. She was given the role of intercessor, a mediator for the Christian believer with a petition for God, and as such appeared in many medieval chants.

Figure 2.7 | The Virgin Mary featured in a panel from an altarpiece painted by Cimabue around 1280
Author | Cimabue
Source | Wikimedia Commons
License | Public Domain

Focus Composition:

Ave Generosa by Hildegard of Bingen (Twelfth Century)

Many composers of the Middle Ages will forever remain anonymous. Hildegard of Bingen (1098-1179) from the German Rhineland is a notable exception. At the age of fourteen, Hildegard's family gave her to the Catholic Church where she studied Latin and theology at the local monastery. Known for her religious visions, Hildegard eventually became an influential religious leader, artist, poet, scientist, and musician. She would go on to found three convents and become an abbess, the chief administrator of an abbey.

Figure 2.8 | Depiction of Hildegard of Bingen in the Rupertsberger Codex of her *Liber Scivias*
Author | Hildegard
Source | Wikimedia Commons
License | Public Domain

Writing poetry and music for her fellow nuns to use in worship was one of many of Hildegard's activities, and the hymn "Ave Generosa" is just one of her many compositions. This hymn has multiple strophes in Latin that praise Mary and her role as the bearer of the Son of God. The manuscript contains one melodic line that is sung for each of the strophes, making it a strophic monophonic chant. Although some leaps occur, the melody is conjunct. The range of the melody line, although still approachable for the amateur singer, is a bit wider than other church chant of the Middle Ages. The melody also contains melismas at several places. A **melisma** is the singing of multiple pitches on one syllable of text. Overall, the rhythm of the chant follows the rhythm of the syllables of the text.

Chant is by definition monophonic, but scholars suspect that medieval performers sometimes added musical lines to the texture, probably starting with drones (a pitch or group of pitches that were sustained while most of the ensemble sang together the melodic line). Performances of chant music today often add embellishments such as occasionally having a fiddle or small organ play the drone instead of being vocally incorporated. Performers of the Middle Ages possibly did likewise, even if prevailing practices called for entirely *a cappella* worship.

LISTENING GUIDE
For audio, go to: https://www.youtube.com/watch?v=RJzeD4HHnxs&feature=youtu.be UCLA Early Music Ensemble; Soloist Arreanna Rostosky; Audio & video by Umberto Belfiore; listen through 3:17 for the first four strophes.
Composer: Hildegard of Bingen

Composition: *Ave Generosa*		
Date: 12th century		
Genre: Hymn (a type of chant)		
Form: Strophic		
Nature of Text: multiple, four-line strophes in Latin, praising the Virgin Mary [text and translation found at Norma Gentile, http://www.healingchants.com/contact2.html]		
Performing Forces: small ensemble of vocalists		
What we want you to remember about this composition: • It is chant. • It is *a cappella.* • Its rhythms follow the rhythms of the text. • It is monophonic (although this performance adds a drone).		
Other things to listen for: • Its melodic line is mostly conjunct. • Its melody contains many melismas. • It has a Latin text sung in a strophic form.		
Timing	**Performing Forces, Melody, and Texture**	**Text and Form**
0:00	Solo vocalist enters with first line using a monophonic texture. The melody opens with an upward leap and then moves mostly by step: conjunct	**Strophe 1:** Ave, generosa, "Hail generous one"
0:10	Group joins with line two, some singing a drone pitch. The melody continues mostly conjunctly, with melismas added. Since the drone is improvised, this is still monophony.	**Strophe 1 continues:** Gloriosa et intacta puella... "Noble, glorious, and whole woman..."
0:49	Repetition of the melody to new words sung by all with monophonic texture (the drone continues)	**Strophe 2:** Nam hec superna infusio in te fuit... "The essences of heaven flooded into you..."

1:37	Repetition of the melody to new words sung by all with monophonic texture (the drone continues)	**Strophe 3**: O pulsherrima et dulcissima... "O lovely and tender one..."
2:34	Repetition of the melody to new words sung by all with monophonic texture (the drone continues)	**Strophe 4**: Venter enim tuus gaudium havuit... "Your womb held joy..."

2.5.1 The Emergence of Polyphonic Music for the Medieval Church

Initial embellishments such as the addition of a musical drone to a monophonic chant were probably improvised during the Middle Ages. With the advent of musical notation that could indicate polyphony, composers began writing polyphonic compositions for worship, initially intended for select parts of the Liturgy to be sung by the most trained and accomplished of the priests or monks leading the mass. Originally, these polyphonic compositions featured two musical lines at the same time; eventually, third and fourth lines were added. Polyphonic liturgical music, originally called organum, emerged in Paris around the late twelfth and thirteenth centuries. In this case, growing musical complexity seems to parallel growing architectural complexity.

Composers wrote polyphony so that the **cadences**, or ends of musical phrases and sections, resolved to simultaneously sounding perfect intervals. Perfect intervals are the intervals of fourths, fifths, and octaves. Such intervals are called perfect because they are the first intervals derived from the overtone series (see chapter one). As hollow and even disturbing as perfect intervals can sound to our modern ears, the Middle Ages used them in church partly because they believed that what was perfect was more appropriate for the worship of God than the imperfect.

Figure 2.9 | Depiction of Guillaume de Machaut
Author | Anonymous
Source | Wikimedia Commons
License | Public Domain

In Paris, composers also developed an early type of rhythmic notation, which was important considering that individual singers would now be singing different musical lines that needed to stay in sync. By the end of the fourteenth century, this rhythmic notation began looking a little bit like the rhythmic notation recognizable today. Beginning a music composition, a symbol fell indicating something like our modern meter symbols (see chapter one). This symbol told the performer whether the composition was in two or in three and laid out the note value that provided the basic beat. Initially almost all metered church music used triple time, because the number three was associated with perfection and theological concepts such as the trinity.

Elsewhere in what is now France, Guillaume de Machaut (c. 1300-13) emerged as the most important poet and composer of his century. He is the first composer about which we have much biographical information, due in part to the fact that Machaut himself, near the end of his life, collected his poetry into volumes of manuscripts, which include a miniature image of the composer (see Figure 2.9 of Machaut at work from a fourteenth century manuscript). We know that he traveled widely as a cleric and secretary for John, the King of Bohemia. Around 1340, he moved to Reims (now in France), where he served as a church official at the cathedral. There he had more time to write poetry and music, which he seems to have continued doing for some time.

Focus Composition:

Agnus Dei from the *Nostre Dame Mass* (c. 1364 CE) by Guillaume de Machaut

We think that Machaut wrote his *Mass of Nostre Dame* around 1364. This composition is famous because it was one of the first compositions to set all five movements of the mass ordinary as a complete whole: these movements are the pieces of the Catholic liturgy comprising every Mass, no matter what time of the year. Movement in music refers to a musical section that sounds complete but that is part of a larger musical composition. Musical connections between each movement of this Mass cycle—the Kyrie, Gloria, Credo, Sanctus, and Agnus Dei—suggest that Machaut intended them to be performed together, rather than being traded in and out of a Mass, based on the preferences of the priest leading the service. Agnus Dei was composed after the Machaut's brother death in 1372, this Mass was likely performed every week in a side chapel of the Reims Cathedral. Medieval Catholics commonly paid for Masses to be performed in honor of their deceased loved ones.

As you listen to the Agnus Dei movement from the *Nostre Dame Mass*, try imagining that you are sitting in that side chapel of the cathedral at Reims, a cathedral that looks not unlike the Cathedral of Notre in Paris. Its slow tempo might remind us that this was music that memorialized Machaut's dead brother, and its triple meter allegorized perfection. Remember that although its perfect intervals may sound disturbing to our ears, for those in the Middle Ages they symbolized that which was most appropriate and musically innovative.

LISTENING GUIDE

For audio, go to:
https://www.youtube.com/watch?v=mvIEA2dBKGA
Oxford Camerata directed by Jeremy Summerly

Composer: Guillaume de Machaut

Composition: Agnus Dei from the *Nostre Dame Mass*

Date: c. 1364 CE

Genre: Movement from the Ordinary of the Mass

Form: A – B – A

Nature of Text: Latin words from the Mass Ordinary: Agnus Dei, qui tollis peccata mundi, Miserere nobis" (Lamb of God, who takes away the sin, have mercy on us)

Performing Forces: small ensemble of vocalists

What we want you to remember about this composition:

- It is part of the Latin mass.
- It uses four-part polyphony.
- It has a slow tempo.

Other things to listen for:

- Its melodies lines have a lot of melismas
- It is in triple meter, symbolizing perfection
- It uses simultaneous intervals of fourths, fifths, and octaves, also symbolizing perfection.
- Its overall form is A-B-A.

Timing	**Performing Forces, Melody, and Texture**	**Text & Form**
0:00	Small ensemble of men singing in four-part polyphony; a mostly conjunct melody with a lot of melismas in triple meter at a slow tempo. The section ends with a cadence on open, hollow-sounding harmonies such as octaves and fifths.	**A:** Agnus Dei, qui tollis peccata mundi, Miserere nobis

1:11	This section begins with faster notes sung by the alto voice. Note that it ends with a cadence to hollowing-sounding intervals of the fifth and octave, just like the first section had.	**B:** Agnus Dei, qui tollis peccata mundi, Miserere nobis
2:27	Same music as at the beginning.	**A:** Agnus Dei, qui tollis peccata mundi, Miserere nobis

2.6 MUSIC IN MEDIEVAL COURTS

Like the Catholic Church, medieval kings, dukes, lords and other members of the nobility had resources to sponsor musicians to provide them with music for worship and entertainment. Individuals roughly comparable to today's singer-songwriters served courts throughout Europe. Like most singer-songwriters, love was a favored topic. These poet-composers also sang of devotion to the Virgin Mary and of the current events of the day.

Many songs that merge these two focus points appear in a late thirteenth-century manuscript called the *Cantigas de Santa Maria* (Songs for the Virgin Mary), a collection sponsored by **King Alfonso the Wise** who ruled the northwestern corner of the Iberian peninsula. *Cantigas de Santa Maria* also includes many illustrations of individuals playing instruments. The musician on the left in Figure 2.10 is playing a rebec and the one to the right a lute. Elsewhere in the manuscript these drummers and fifers appear (see Figure 2.11). These depictions suggest to us that, outside of worship services, much vocal music was accompanied by instru-

Figure 2.10 | Rebec and Lute Players depicted in *Cantigas de Santa Maria*
Author | Unknown
Source | Wikimedia Commons
License | Public Domain

Figure 2.11 | Drummers and fifers depicted in *Cantigas de Santa Maria*
Author | Unknown
Source | Wikimedia Commons
License | Public Domain

ments. We believe such songs as these were also sung by groups and used as dance music, especially as early forms of rhythmic notation indicate simple and catchy patterns that were danceable. Other manuscripts also show individuals dancing to the songs of composers such as Machaut.

Focus Composition:

Song of Mary, No. 181: "The Virgin will aid those who most love her"

"The Virgin will aid those who most love her," is one of over four hundred songs praising the Virgin Mary in the *Cantigas de Santa Maria* described above. "The Virgin will aid those who most love her" praises Mary for her help during the crusades in defeating a Moroccan king in the city of Marrakesh. It uses a verse and refrain structure similar to those discussed in chapter one. Its two-lined chorus (here called a **refrain**) is sung at the beginning of each of the eight four-lined strophes that serve as verses. The two-line melody for the refrain is repeated for the first two lines of the verse; a new melody then is used for the last two lines of the verse. In the recent recording done by Jordi Savall and his ensemble, a relatively large group of men and women sing the refrains, and soloists and smaller groups of singers perform the verses. The ensemble also includes a hand drum that articulates the repeating rhythmic motives, a medieval fiddle, and a lute, as well as medieval flutes and shawms, near the end of the excerpt below. These parts are not notated in the manuscript, but it is likely that similar instruments would have been used to accompany this monophonic song in the middle ages.

LISTENING GUIDE For audio, go to: https://www.youtube.com/watch?v=770O53MCpQo&feature=youtu.be Performed by Jordi Savall and Ensemble; listen from 0:13 through 3:29.
Composer: Anonymous
Composition: Song of Mary, No. 181: "The Virgin will aid those who most love her" (Pero que seja a gente d'outra lei [e]descreuda)
Date: c. 1275
Genre: Song
Form: Refrain [A] & verses [ab] = A-ab
Nature of Text: Refrain and strophes in an earlier form of Portuguese, praising the Virgin Mary
Performing Forces: small ensemble of vocalists, men and women singing together and separately

What we want you to remember about this composition:

- It is music for entertainment, even though it has a sacred subject.
- It is monophonic.
- Its narrow-ranged melody and repetitive rhythms make it easy for non-professionals to sing.

Other things to listen for:

- In this recording, the monophonic melody is sung by men and women and is played by a medieval fiddle and lute; a drum plays the beat; near the end of the excerpt, you can also hear flutes and shawms.
- Its musical form is A-ab, meaning that the refrain is always sung to the same music.

Timing	Performing Forces, Melody, and Texture	Text and Form
0:00	Fiddles and lute playing melody for refrain; Drum playing rhythmic motive; monophonic texture throughout; Mostly conjunct melody with a narrow range; Repeated motive shifts back and forth between twos and threes	**A:** Intro
0:12	Sung by men and women	**A:** Refrain
0:23	One woman starts and then others join, singing monophonically the same the same melodic phrase as the refrain	**a:** First two lines of the first verse
0:37	Several women singing with a monophonic texture a different melodic phrase	**b:** Second two lines of the first verse,
0:48	Men and women; same melody as in the Refrain above	**A:** Refrain
1:00	One man, joined by other men; same melody as in the first half of the verse above	**a:** First two lines of the second verse
1:14	Several men; same melody as in the second half of the verse above	**b:** Second two lines of the second verse
1:26	Men and women; same melody as in the Refrain above	**A:** Refrain

1:37	Women; same melody as the other verses; men join them for the b phrase of the melodic theme.	**ab:** Verse three
2:03	Men and women	**A:** Refrain
2:13	Men start and women sing the b-phrase of the melodic theme.	**ab:** Verse four
2:40	Men and women	**A:** Refrain
2:52	Played by flutes, medieval fiddle, lutes, drums, zither	**a:** First two lines of the fifth verse
3:05	Played by same instruments as above	**b:** Second two lines of the second verse
3:17	Played by the above instruments plus shawms.	**A:** Refrain

Medieval poet composers also wrote a lot of music about more secular love, a topic that continues to be popular for songs to the present day. Medieval musicians and composers, as well as much of European nobility in the Middle Ages, were particularly invested in what we call courtly love. Courtly love is love for a beloved, without any concern for whether or not the love will be returned. The speakers within these poems recounted the virtues of their beloved, acknowledging the impossibility of ever consummating their love and pledging to continue loving their beloved to the end of their days.

Guillaume de Machaut, who wrote the famous *Mass of Nostre Dame* discussed above, also wrote many love songs, some polyphonic and others monophonic. In his "Lady, to you without reserve I give my heart, thought and desire," a lover admires his virtuous beloved and pledges undying love, even while suspecting that they will remain ever apart. Like "The Virgin will aid," its sung words are in the original French. Also like "The Virgin will aid," it consists of a refrain that alternates with verses. Here the refrain and three verses are in a fixed medieval poetic and musical form that can be notated as Abba-Abba-Abba-Abba. Machaut's song, written over fifty years after "The Virgin will aid," shows medieval rhythms becoming increasingly complex. The notes are grouped into groups of three, but the accentuation patterns often change. We suspect that this song was also used as dance music, given the illustration of a group dancing in a circle appearing above its musical notation in Machaut's manuscript. As we noted earlier, songs like this were most likely sung with accompaniment, even though this accompaniment wasn't notated; the recording excerpt in the link below uses tambourine to keep the beat.

LISTENING GUIDE

For audio, go to:
https://www.youtube.com/watch?v=7VM99EwcXNU
Studio der Frühen Musik

Composer: Guillaume de Machaut

Composition: "Lady, to you without reserve I give my heart, thought and desire" (Dame, à vous sans retollir")

Date: Fourteenth century

Genre: song

Form: Refrain [A] & Verses [bba]

Nature of Text: French poem about courtly love with a refrain alternating with three verses.

Performing Forces: soloist alternating with small ensemble of vocalists

What we really want you to remember about this composition:

- It is a French song about courtly love.
- It is monophonic, here with tambourine articulating the beats
- Its form consists of an alternation of a refrain and verses

Other things to listen for:

- Its melodic line is mostly conjunct, the range is a little over an octave, and it contains several short melismas.
- Its specific form is Abba, which repeats three times

Timing	Performing Forces, Melody, and Texture	Text and Form
0:00	Small group of women singing in monophonic text with tambourine; Mostly conjunct melody with a narrow range; Notes fall in rhythmic groups of three, but the accent patterns change often	**A**: Refrain
0:14	Female soloist still in monophonic texture without tambourine; the b phrase is mostly conjunct, starts high and descends, repeats, then returns to the a phrase as heard in the refrain	**bba**: Verse
0:40	Same music as in the A phrase above with the words of the refrain	**A**: Refrain

0:53	Female soloist as heard above to new words	**bba**: Verse
1:18	As heard in the Refrain above, words and music	**A**: Refrain
1:31	As heard above verses, with new words	**bba**: Verse
1:57	As heard in the Refrain above, words and music	**A**: Refrain

2.7 CHAPTER SUMMARY

In this chapter, we have studied music that dates back almost 1500 years from today. In some ways, it differs greatly from our music today, though some continuous threads exist. Individuals in the Middle Ages used music for worship and entertainment, just as occurs today. They wrote sacred music for worship and also used sacred ideas in entertainment music. Music for entertainment included songs about love, religion, and current events as well as music that might be danced to. Though the style and form of their music is quite different from ours in many ways, some aspects of musical style have not changed. Conjunct music with a relatively narrow range is still a typical choice in folk and pop music, owing to the fact that it is easy for even the amateur to sing. Songs in strophic form and songs with a refrain and contrasting verses also still appear in today's pop music. As we continue on to study music of the Renaissance, keep in mind these categories of music that remain to the present day.

2.8 GLOSSARY

A cappella – vocal music without instrumental accompaniment

Cadence – the ending of a musical phrase providing a sense of closure, often through the use of one chord that resolves to another

Chant – text set to a melody written in monophonic texture with un-notated rhythms typically used in religious worship

Courtly Love – love for a beloved, without any concern for whether or not the love will be returned, called "courtly" because it was praised by those participating in medieval courts

Drone – a sustained pitch or pitches often found in music of the middle ages or earlier and in folk music

Hymn – religious song most generally having multiple strophes of the same number and length of lines and using strophic form

Mass – Catholic celebration of the Eucharist consisting of liturgical texts set to music by composers starting in the middle ages

Melisma – multiple pitches sung to one syllable of text

Polyphony – musical texture that simultaneously features two or more relatively independent and important melodic lines

Refrain – a repeating musical section, generally also with repeated text; sometimes called a "chorus"

Rhythm According to the Text – rhythm that follows the rhythm of the text and is not notated

Song – a composition sung by voice(s)

Strophe – section of a poem or lyric text generally of a set number of lines and line length; a text may have multiple strophes

Strophic – musical form in which all verses or strophes of a song are sung to the same music

Syllabic – music in which each syllable of a text is set to one musical note

Verse and Refrain Form – a musical form (sometimes referred to as verse and chorus) in which one section of music is sung to all the verses and a different section of music is sung to the repeating refrain or chorus

3 Music of the Renaissance

Jeff Kluball

3.1 OBJECTIVES

1. Demonstrate knowledge of historical and cultural contexts of the Renaissance
2. Recognize musical styles of the Renaissance
3. Identify important genres and uses of music of the Renaissance
4. Identify selected music of the Renaissance aurally and critically evaluate its style and uses
5. Compare and contrast music of the Renaissance with their own contemporary music

3.2 KEY TERMS AND INDIVIDUALS

- Anthem
- Chanson
- Chapel Master
- Consort
- Counter-Reformation
- Galliard
- Giovanni Pieruigi da Palestrina
- Jig
- Josquin des Prez
- Madrigal
- Martin Luther
- Motet
- Pavanne
- Reformation
- Renaissance
- Thomas Weelkes
- William Byrd
- William Kemp
- Word painting

3.3 INTRODUCTION AND HISTORICAL CONTEXT

3.3.1 What is the Renaissance?

The term **Renaissance** literally means "rebirth." As a historical and artistic era in Western Europe, the Renaissance spanned from the late 1400s to the early 1600s. The Renaissance was a time of waning political power in the church, somewhat as a result of the Protestant Reformation. Also during this period, the feudal system slowly gave way to developing nation-states with centralized power in the courts. This period was one of intense creativity and exploration. It included such luminaries as Leonardo da Vinci, Christopher Columbus, Ferdinand Magellan, Nicolaus Copernicus, and William Shakespeare. The previous medieval period was suppressive, firmly established, and pious. The Renaissance however, provided the thinkers and scholars of the day with a revival of Classical (Greek and Roman) wisdom and learning after a time of papal restraint. This "rebirth" laid the foundation for much of today's modern society, where humans and nature rather than religion become the standard for art, science, and philosophy.

The School of Athens (1505), Figure 3.1, by Raphael demonstrates the strong admiration, influence, and interest in previous Greek and Roman culture. The painting depicts the Greek philosophers Aristotle and Plato (center), with Plato depicted in the likeness of Leonardo da Vinci.

Figure 3.1 | The School of Athens
Author | Raphael
Source | Wikimedia Commons
License | Public Domain

3.3.2 Renaissance Timeline

Events in History	Events in Music and the Arts
1440: Gutenberg's printing press	
1453: Fall of Constantinople	
1456: Gutenberg Bible	
	c. 1475: Josquin Desprez, *Ave Maria*
1492: Columbus reaches America	c. 1482: Bottecelli, *La Primavera*
	c. 1503: Leonardo da Vinci, *Mona Lisa*
	1504 Michelangelo, *David*
1517: Martin Luther nails The Ninety-Five Theses on Wittenberg Church Door	c. 1505: Raphael, *School of Athens, Madonna del Granduca*
1545-1563: Council of Trent	
1558-1603: Elizabeth I, Queen of England	
	1563: Giovanni Pierluigi da Patestrina, *Pope Marcellus Mass*
1588: Spanish Armada defeated	c. 1570: Titian, *Venus and the Lute Player*
	1597: Shakespeare, *Romeo and Juliet*
	1601: Thomas Weelkes, *As Vesta Was Descending*

Occurrences at the end of the Middle Ages accelerated a series of intellectual, social, artistic, and political changes and transformation that resulted in the Renaissance.

By the 1500s, Catholic liturgical music had become extremely complex and ornate. Composers such as Josquin des Prez and Palestrina were composing layered Masses that utilized musical textures such as polyphony and imitative counterpoint (more on these techniques later). The mass is a sacred choral composition historically composed as worship liturgy.

The complexity of the music in the Catholic Mass garnered criticism from **Martin Luther**, a Roman Catholic priest and the eventual father of the Protestant Reformation, who complained that the meaning of the words of the mass, formal worship liturgy, were lost in the beautiful polyphony of the music. Also, Catholic Masses were always performed in Latin, a language seldom used outside the church. Early Protestant hymns stripped away contrapuntal textures, utilized regular beat patterns, and set biblical texts in German. Martin Luther himself penned a few hymns, many of which the great classic composer Johann Sebastian Bach would revisit about 125 years later.

3.3.3 Renaissance Humanism

The Humanism movement is one which expressed the spirit of the Renaissance era that took root in Italy after eastern European scholars fled from Constantinople to the region bringing with them books, manuscripts, and the traditions of Greek scholarship. Humanism is a major paradigm shift from the ways of thought during the medieval era where a life of penance in a feudal system was considered the accepted standard of life. As a part of this ideological change there was a major intellectual shift from the dominance of scholars/clerics of the medieval period (who developed and controlled the scholastic institutions) to the secular men of letters. Men of letters were scholars of the liberal arts who turned to the classics and philosophy to understand the meaning of life.

Humanism has several distinct attributes as it focuses on human nature, its diverse spectrum, and all its accomplishments. Humanism syncretizes all the truths found in different philosophical and theological schools. It emphasizes and focuses on the dignity of man, and studies mankind's struggles over nature.

Medieval vs. Renaissance

Figure 3.2 | (above) Rendition of David Fighting Goliath found on a Medieval Cast plate; 613-630
Author | Unknown
Source | Met Museum
License | OASC

Figure 3.3 | (right) Michelangelo's rendition of David preparing to fight Goliath, stone in hand and sling over his shoulder; 1501-1504
Photographer | Jörg Bittner Unna
Source | Wikimedia Commons
License | CC BY 3.0

3.3.4 Rebirth of ancient civilizations

Predecessors to the Renaissance and the Humanist movement include Dante and Petrarch. In 1452, after the fall of Constantinople, there was considerable boost in the Humanist movement. Humanism was accelerated by the invention of the printing press, which permitted mass reproduction of the classical text—once only found in hand-written manuscripts—the availability of literature improved immensely. Thus, literacy among the common people increased dramatically. The scholastic and intellectual stimulation of the general public facilitated by Humanism initiated a power and knowledge shift from the land-owning upper class and the church to the individual. This shift facilitated and contributed to the beginning of the Reformation. As mentioned above, Martin Luther was a leading religious reformer who challenged the authority of the central Catholic Church and its role in governance, education, and religious practices. Like most other European groups of the era, the Humanists at the time, were divided in their support of the reformation and counter-reformation movements.

3.3.5 Symmetry and Perspective in Art

Figure 3.4 | Cimabue's Madonna; 1280
Author | Cimabue
Source | Wikimedia Commons
License | Public Domain

Figure 3.5 | Giotto's Madonna; 1310
Author | Giotto
Source | Wikimedia Commons
License | Public Domain

Figure 3.6 | Raphael's Madonna; 1504
Author | Raphael
Source | Wikimedia Commons
License | Public Domain

The shift away from the power and authority of the church between the Medieval period and the Renaissance period is not only evident in music but is also found in the visual arts. Artists and authors of the Renaissance became interested in classical mythology and literature. Artists created sculptures of the entire human body, demonstrating a direct lineage from ancient Greek culture to the Renaissance. In the Middle Ages, such depictions of the nude body were thought to be objects of shame or in need of cover. Artists of the Middle Ages were more focused on religious symbolism than the lifelike representation created in the Renaissance era. Medieval artists perceived the canvas as a flat medium/surface on which subjects are shown very two dimensionally. Painters of the Renaissance were more interested in portraying real life imagery in three dimensions on their canvas. See the evolution of the Virgin Mary from the Medeival period to the Renaissance period in Figures 3.4, 3.5, and 3.6 above. You can see the shift from the religious symbolism to the realistic depiction of the human body features.

Raphael and Leonardo da Vinci focused on portraying realism, utilizing linear perspective and creating illusions of space in their works. A geometric system was effectively used to create space and the illusion of depth. This shift from the religious symbolism to the real portrayal of the human is representative of the decline of the church in the arts as well as music. Music outside of the church, secular music, increased in importance.

3.3.6 The Protestant Reformation

Figure 3.7 | Wittenburg Church
Author | User "Fewskulchor"
Source | Wikimedia Commons
License | CC BY-SA 3.0

In the Middle Ages, people were thought to be parts of a greater whole: members of a family, trade guild, nation, and church. At the beginning of the Renaissance, a shift in thought led people to think of themselves as individuals, sparked by Martin Luther's dissent against several areas and practices within the Catholic Church. On October 31, 1517, Luther challenged the Catholic Church by posting The Ninety-Five Theses on the doors of the Castle Church in Wittenberg, Germany. The post stated Luther's various beliefs and interpretations of Biblical doctrine which challenged the many practices of the Catholic Church in the early 1500s. Luther felt that educated/literate believers should be able to read the scriptures and become individual church entities themselves. With the invention of the Gutenberg Press, copies of the scriptures and hymns became available to the masses which helped spread the Reformation. The empowerment of the common worshiper or middle class continued to fuel the loss of authority of the church and upper class.

3.3.7 Gutenberg Press

Few inventions have had the significance to modernization as the Gutenberg Press. Up until the invention of the press, the earliest forms of the books with edge bounding, similar to the type we have today, called codex books were hand produced by monks. This process was quite slow, costly, and laborious, often taking months to produce smaller volumes and years to produce a copy of the Bible and hymn books of worship.

Gutenberg's invention of a much more efficient printing method made it possible to distribute a large amount of printed information at a much accelerated and labor efficient pace. The printing press enabled the printing of hymn books for the middle class and further expanded the involvement of the middle class in their worship service-a key component in the reformation. Gutenberg's press served as a major engine for the distribution of knowledge and contributed to the Renaissance, Scientific Revolution, and Protestant reformation.

3.3.8 Columbus's Voyage

Columbus's discovery of the New World in 1492 also contributed to the spirit and spread of the Humanist movement. The discovering of new land and the potential for colonization of new territory added to the sense of infallibility and ego of the human race. The human spirit of all social classes was invigorated. The invigoration of the middle class influenced the arts and the public's hunger for art and music for the vast middle class population.

3.4 MUSIC OF THE RENAISSANCE

Characteristics of the Renaissance Music include: steady beat, balanced phrases (the same length), polyphony (often imitative), increasing interest in text-music relationships, Petrucci and the printing of music, and a growing merchant class singing/playing music at home. **Word painting** was utilized by Renaissance composers to represent poetic images musically. For example, an ascending melodic line would portray the text "ascension to heaven." Or a series of rapid notes would represent running.

Art music in the Renaissance served three basic purposes: (1) worship in both the Catholic and burgeoning Protestant Churches, (2) music for the entertainment and edification of the courts and courtly life, and (3) dance music. Playing musical instruments became a form of leisure and a significant, valued pastime for every educated person. Guests at social functions were expected to contribute to the evening's festivities through instrumental performance. Much of the secular music in the Renaissance was centered on courtly life. Vocal music ranged from **chansons** (or songs) about love and courtly intrigue to madrigals about nymphs, fairies, and, well, you name it. Both chansons and madrigals were often set for one or more voices with plucked-string accompaniment, such as by the lute, a gourd-shaped instrument with frets, raised strip on the fingerboard, somewhat similar to the modern guitar.

A **madrigal** is a musical piece for several solo voices set to a short poem. They originated in Italy around 1520. Most madrigals were about love. Madrigals were published by the thousands and learned and performed by cultured aristocrats. Similar to the motet, a madrigal combines both homophonic and polyphonic textures. Unlike the motet, the madrigal is secular and utilizes unusual harmonies and word painting more often. Many of the refrains of these madrigals utilized the text "Fa La" to fill the gaps in the melody or to possibly cover risqué or illicit connotations. Sometimes madrigals are referred to as Renaissance Fa La songs.

A volume of translated Italian madrigals were published in London during the year of 1588, the year of the defeat of the Spanish Armada. This sudden public interest facilitated a surge of English madrigal writing as well as a spurt of other secular music writing and publication. This music boom lasted for thirty years and was as much a golden age of music as British literature was with Shakespeare and Queen Elizabeth I. The rebirth in both literature and music originated in Italy and migrated to England; the English madrigal became more humorous and lighter in England as compared to Italy.

Renaissance music was mostly polyphonic in texture. Comprehending a wide range of emotions, Renaissance music nevertheless portrayed all emotions in a balanced and moderate fashion. Extreme use of and contrasts in dynamics, rhythm, and tone color do not occur. The rhythms in Renaissance music tend to have a smooth, soft flow instead of a sharp, well-defined pulse of accents.

Composers enjoyed imitating sounds of nature and sound effects in their compositions. The Renaissance period became known as the golden age of *a cappella* choral music because choral music did not require an instrumental accompaniment.

Instrumental music in the Renaissance remained largely relegated to social purposes such as dancing, but a few notable virtuosos of the time, including the English lutenist and singer John Dowland, composed and performed music for Queen Elizabeth I, among others.

Dowland was a lutenist in 1598 in the court of Christian IV and later in 1612 in the court of King James I. He is known for composing one of the best songs of the Renaissance period, *Flow, my Teares*. This imitative piece demonstrates the melancholy humor of the time period. Dowland's *Flow, My Teares* may be heard at https://www.youtube.com/watch?v=jkRrzAo9Wl4. For more information on Dowland, and lyrics to *Flow My Tears*, go to http://genius.com/John-dowland-flow-my-tears-annotated.

The instruments utilized during the Renaissance era were quite diverse. Local availability of raw materials for the manufacture of the instrument often determined its assembly and accessibility to the public. A renaissance consort is a group of renaissance instrumentalists playing together. A whole consort is an ensemble performing with instruments from the same family. A broken consort is an ensemble comprised of instruments from more than one family.

Instruments from the Medieval and Renaissance may be found at: http://www.music.iastate.edu/antiqua/instrumt.html.

3.4.1 Style Overview

Medieval Music

- Mainly monophony
- Majority of the music's rhythm comes from the text
- Use of perfect intervals such as fourths, fifths, and octaves for cadences
- Most music comes from the courts or church
- Music instruction predominantly restricted to the church and patron's courts

Renaissance Music

- Mainly polyphony (much is imitative polyphony/overlapped repetition–please see music score below)
- Majority of the music's rhythms is indicated by musical notation
- Growing use of thirds and triads
- Music – text relationships increasingly important with the use of word painting
- Invention of music publishing
- Growing merchant class increasingly acquires musical skills

3.5 WORSHIP MUSIC

During the Renaissance from 1442 to 1483, church choir membership increased dramatically in size. The incorporation of entire male ensembles and choirs singing in parts during the Renaissance is one major difference from the Middle Ages' polyphonic church music, which was usually sung by soloists. As the Renaissance progressed, the church remained an important supporter of music although, musical activity gradually shifted to secular support. Royalty and the wealthy of the courts seeking after and competing for the finest composers replaced what was originally church supported. The motet and the mass are the two main forms of sacred choral music of the Renaissance.

3.5.1 Motet

The **motet**, a sacred Latin text polyphonic choral work, is not taken from the ordinary of the mass. A contemporary of Leonardo da Vinci and Christopher Columbus, **Josquin des Prez** was a master of Renaissance choral music. Originally from the region that is today's Belgium, Josquin spent much of his time serving in chapels throughout Italy and partly in Rome for the papal choir. Later, he worked for Louis XII of France and held several church music directorships in his native land. During his career, he published masses, motets, and secular vocal pieces, and was highly respected by his contemporaries.

Josquin's "Ava Maria ...Virgo Serena"("Hail, Mary ... Serene Virgin") ca. 1485 is an outstanding Renaissance choral work. A four part (Soprano, Alto, Tenor, Bass) Latin prayer, the piece weaves one, two, three and four voices at different times in polyphonic texture.

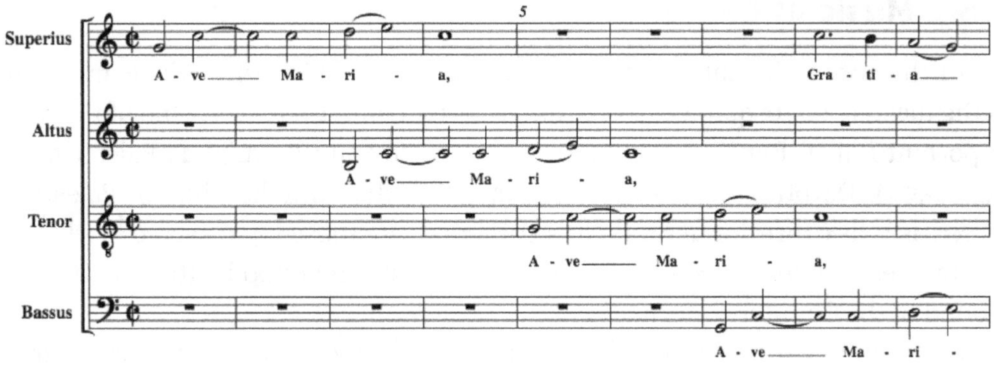

Figure 3.8 | Opening Line of Ave Maria
Author | Josquin Des Prez
Source | Wikimedia Commons
License | Public Domain

LISTENING GUIDE

For audio go to:

https://www.youtube.com/watch?v=LUAgAF4Khmg

To view a full text score of Josquin des Prez "Ave Maria...Virgo Serena" while listening, go to:

http://www.cengage.com/music/book_content/049557273X_wright-Simms/assets/more/scores/JosquinAveMaria.pdf

Composer: Josquin des Prez

Composition: Ava Maria...Virgo Serena

Date: c. 1485, possibly Josquin's earliest dated work

Genre: motet

Form: through composed in sections

Translation:
Available at the following link:

http://unam-ecclesiam.blogspot.com/2007/10/another-beautiful-ave-maria-by-josquin.html

Performing Forces: four-part choir

What we want you to remember about this composition: The piece is revolutionary in how it presented the imitative weaving of melodic lines in polyphony. Each voice imitates or echoes the high voice (soprano).

Other things to listen for: After the initial introduction to Mary, each verse serves as a tribute to the major events of Mary's life—her conception, the nativity, annunciation, purification, and assumption. See above translation and listening guide.

3.5.2 Music of Catholicism—Renaissance mass

In the sixteenth century, Italian composers excelled with works comparable to the mastery of Josquin des Prez and his other contemporaries. One of the most important Italian Renaissance composers was Giovanni Pieruigi da Palestrina (c. 1525-1594). Devoting his career to the music of the Catholic Church, Palestrina served as music director at St. Peter's Cathedral, composed 450 sacred works and 104 masses. His influence in music history is best understood with a brief background of the Counter-Reformation.

Protestant reformists like Martin Luther and others, sought to correct malpractices and abuses within the structure of the Catholic Church. The Reformation began with Martin Luther and spread to two more main branches: The Calvinist and The Church of England. The protestant reformists challenged many practices that benefitted only the church itself and did not appear to serve the lay members (parishioners). A movement occurred within the church to counter the protestant reformation and preserve the original Catholic Church. The preservation movement or "Counter-Reformation" against the protestant reform led to the development of the Jesuit order (1540) and the later assembling of the Council of Trent (1545-1563) which considered issues of the church's authority and organizational structure. The Council of Trent also demanded simplicity in music in order that the words might be heard clearly.

The Council of Trent discussed and studied the many issues facing the Catholic Church, including the church's music. The papal leadership felt that the music had gotten so embellished and artistic that it had lost its purity and original meaning. It was neither easily sung nor was its words (still in Latin) understood. Many accused the types of music in the church as being theatrical and more entertaining rather than a way of worship (something that is still debated in many churches today). The Council of Trent felt melodies were secular, too ornamental, and even took dance music as their origin. The advanced weaving of polyphonic lines could not be understood, thereby detracting from their original intent of worship with sacred text. The Council of Trent wanted a paradigm shift of religious sacred music back toward monophonic Gregorian chant. The Council of Trent finally decreed that church music should be composed to inspire religious contemplation and not just give empty pleasure to the ear of the worshipper.

Renaissance composer Palestrina heeded the recommendations from The Council of Trent and composed one of the period's most famous works, "Missa Papae Marcelli" (Pope Marcellus Mass). Palestrina's restraint and serenity reflect the recommendations of The Council of Trent. The text, though quite polyphonic, is easily understood. The movement of the voices does not distract from the sacred meaning of the text. Through history, Palestrina's works have been the standard for their calmness and quality.

LISTENING GUIDE

For audio go to: https://www.youtube.com/watch?v=oeLIgzAe5sI&feature=youtu.be&list=PLlu9u9ap3Q8ySADTqkhuoNyX_NeL44yrQ

Composer: Giovanni Pieruigi da Palestrina (1525-1594)

Composition: "Missa Papae Marcelli" (Pope Marcellus Mass)- 1. Kyrie

Date: c. 1562

Genre: Choral, Kyrie of Mass

Form: through-composed (without repetition in the form of verses, stanzas, or strophes) in sections

Nature of Text:

Latin Text	English Translation
Kyrie eleison,	Lord have mercy,
Christe eleison,	Christ have mercy,
Kyrie eleison,	Lord have mercy,

Performing Forces: Unknown vocal ensemble

What we want you to remember about this composition: Listen to the polyphony and how the voices move predominantly stepwise after a leap upward. After initial voice begins the piece, the other voices enter imitating the initial melody and then continue to weave the voices as more enter. Palestrina's mass would come to represent proper counterpoint/polyphony and become the standard for years to come.

Other things to listen for: even though the voices overlap in polyphony, the text is easily understood. The masses were written as to bring out the text and make it simple to understand. The significance of the text is brought out and easily understood.

Listening Guide: Follow the musical score as you listen to the selection.

Figure 3.9 | Musical score of "Kyrie" opening
Author | User "Joonasl"
Source | Wikimedia Commons
License | GNU

3.5.3 Music of the Protestant Reformation

As a result of the Reformation, congregations began singing strophic hymns in German with stepwise melodies during their worship services. This practice enabled full participation of worshipers. Full participation of the congregations' members further empowered the individual church participant, thus contributing to the Renaissance's Humanist movement. Early Protestant hymns stripped away contrapuntal textures, utilized regular beat patterns, and set biblical texts in German.

Instead of a worship service being led with a limited number of clerics at the front of the church, Luther wanted the congregation to actively and fully participate, including in the singing of the service. Since these hymns were in German, members of the parish could sing and understand them. Luther, himself a composer, composed many hymns and chorales to be sung by the congregation during worship, many of which Johann Sebastian Bach would make the melodic themes of his Chorale Preludes 125 years after the original hymns were written. These hymns are strophic (repeated verses as in poetry) with repeated melodies for the different verses. Many of these chorales utilize syncopated rhythms to clarify the text and its flow (rhythms). Luther's hymn "A Mighty Fortress" is a good example of this practice. The chorales/hymns were usually in four parts and moved with homophonic texture (all parts changing notes in the same rhythm). The melodies of these four-part hymn/chorales used as the basis for many chorale preludes performed on organs prior to and after worship services are still used today.

An example of one such Chorale Prelude based on Luther's him can be found at:
https://www.youtube.com/watch?v=hVNoCIcqRYs

LISTENING GUIDE
For audio go to: https://www.youtube.com/watch?v=G42xwWoUS-o; This recording is in English and performed by the Mormon Tabernacle Choir.
Composer: Martin Luther
Composition: "A Mighty Fortress Is Our God" (also known as the "Battle Hymn of the Reformation")
Date: 1529
Genre: Four-Part homophonic church anthem. This piece was written to be sung by the lay church membership instead of just by the church leaders a was practiced prior to the Reformation.
Form: Four part Chorale, Strophic
Nature of Text (topic, lyrics, translations): Originally in German so it could be sung by all church attendees.

Performing Forces: Congregation-This recording is the Mormon Tabernacle Choir
Things to listen for: Stepwise melody, Syncopated rhythms centered around text
Translation: Translated from original German to English by Frederic H. Hedge in 1853. A mighty fortress is our God, a bulwark never failing; Our helper He, amid the flood of mortal ills prevailing: For still our ancient foe doth seek to work us woe; His craft and power are great, and, armed with cruel hate, On earth is not his equal. Did we in our own strength confide, our striving would be losing; Were not the right Man on our side, the Man of God's own choosing: Dost ask who that may be? Christ Jesus, it is He; Lord Sabaoth, His Name, from age to age the same, And He must win the battle. And though this world, with devils filled, should threaten to undo us, We will not fear, for God hath willed His truth to triumph through us: The Prince of Darkness grim, we tremble not for him; His rage we can endure, for lo, his doom is sure, One little word shall fell him. That word above all earthly powers, no thanks to them, abideth; The Spirit and the gifts are ours through Him Who with us sideth: Let goods and kindred go, this mortal life also; The body they may kill: God's truth abideth still, His kingdom is forever.

You can view a PBS Luther documentary at:
https://www.youtube.com/watch?v=PyVrPIp4QsA
For another movie on Martin Luther, go to:
https://www.youtube.com/watch?v=jmcKlPyRxSM

3.5.4 Anthem

Composer **William Byrd** (1543 – 1623) became very distinguished from many of his contemporary composers because of his utilization of many different compositional tools that he used in his music. His works represent several musical personalities instead of one single style. As his career progressed, Byrd become more interested and involved in Catholicism. The influence of Catholicism through the use of biblical text and religious styles increasingly permeated his music. The mandates established and requirements imposed by the Council of Trent placed a serious stumbling block in the path of the development of church music compositional techniques after the reformation. Several denominations had to adapt to the mandates required by the Council of Trent. The music in the Catholic Church experienced relatively little change as the result of the reformation. This lack of change was the result composers such as Byrd who remained loyal to the religion and their refusal to change their "traditional catholic" style of composing.

Figure 3.10 | William Byrd
Author | Vandergucht
Source | Wikimedia Commons
License | Public Domain

In Byrd's Anglican Anthem, "Sing Joyfully Unto God," the opening phrase of the text is set with a single voice on each part. This technique is very similar to the Catholic Church settings of Chant incipits. This full anthem by Byrd is much more polyphonic in nature than that of verse anthems. It also borrows heavily from both madrigal and motet styles, though modified for the liturgy. "Sing Joyfully Unto God" is one of the most thoroughly motet-like of the many Byrd anthems. Within the anthem there is a new point of imitation for each new phrase of text. Byrd extensively uses the text depictions to creatively illustrate the music's meaning. Below is an example of how Byrd's "Sing Joyfully, Unto God" emphasizes the trumpet call of the text. All voices are singing together to depict the fullness of a trumpet fanfare, thickening the texture to illustrate the musical concept. This section begins with homophony, but polyphony is employed throughout the work. Byrd uses this technique primarily for a structural contrast device.

Figure 3.11 | Homophony as text depiction in Byrd's *Sing Joyfully Unto God*
Author | Edward Tambling
Source | ChoralWiki
License | CPDL

The use of imitation as a structural tool is maintained primarily within full anthems. Byrd also uses a technique called pairing of voices, which was highly popular within the Renaissance period.[1]

1 Mitchell, Shelley. "William Byrd: Covert Catholic Values with Anglican Anthems Comparison of Style to Catholic Gradualia." MA thesis. Indiana State University, 2008. Web. 15 December 2015.

LISTENING GUIDE
For audio, go to: https://www.youtube.com/watch?v=4mPkPnN-T9o University of Wisconsin Eau Claire Concert Choir
Composer: William Byrd
Composition: *Sing Joyfully Unto God*
Date: circa 1580-1590
Genre: Choral (Anthem)
Form: Through-composed
Nature of Text: SSAATB Sing joyfully to God our strength; sing loud unto the God of Jacob! Take the song, bring forth the timbrel, the pleasant harp, and the viol. Blow the trumpet in the New Moon, even in the time appointed, and at our feast day. For this is a statute for Israel, and a law of the God of Jacob.
Performing Forces: six-part choir
What we want you to remember about this composition: This is a very much a motet-like sounding church anthem. It sounds very much like a mass but the text does not come from any of the five sections of the mass. The work incorporated many of the polyphony techniques used in the mass. Listen how the six voices interweave. Significant points: One of the most popular pieces from the time period. The Psalm 81 text is set in English. Scored in SSAATB (two sopranos, two alsos, one tenor, and one bass). • imitative polyphony • a capella in English • some word painting

3.6 SECULAR MUSIC-ENTERTAINMENT MUSIC OF THE RENAISSANCE

Royalty sought the finest of the composers to employ for entertainment. A single court, or royal family, may employ as many as ten to sixty musicians, singers, and instrumentalists. In Italy, talented women vocalists began to serve as soloists in the courts. Secular pieces for the entertainment of nobility and sacred pieces for the chapel were composed by the court music directors. Musicians were often transported from one castle to another to entertain the court's patron, travelling in their patron's entourage.

The Renaissance town musicians performed for civic functions, weddings, socials, and religious ceremonies/services. Due to market, that is, the supply and demand of the expanding Renaissance society, musicians experience higher status and pay unlike ever before. The Flanders, Low Countries of the Netherlands, Belgium, and northern France became a source of musicians who filled many important music positions in Italy. As in the previous era, vocal music maintained its important status over instrumental music.

Germany, England, and Spain also experienced an energetic musical expansion. Secular vocal music became increasingly popular during the Renaissance. In Europe, music was set to poems from several languages, including English, French, Dutch, German, and Spanish. The invention of the printing press led to the publication of thousands of collections of songs that were never before available. One instrument or small groups of instruments were used to accompany solo voices or groups of solo voices.

3.6.1 Thomas Weelkes

Thomas Weelkes, a church organist and composer, became one of the finest English madrigal composers. Thomas Weelkes' "As Vesta Was Descending" serves as a good example of word painting with the melodic line following the meaning of the text in performance.

LISTENING GUIDE For audio, go to: https://www.youtube.com/watch?v=95DJ70qTWK8
Composer: Thomas Weelkes
Composition: "As Vesta Was From Latmos Hill Descending"
Date: 1601
Genre: Madrigal
Form: Through-composed
Performing Forces: Choral ensemble

One thing to remember about this composition:
This composition is a great example of "word painting" where the text and melodic line work together. When the text refers to descending down a hill, the melody descends also.

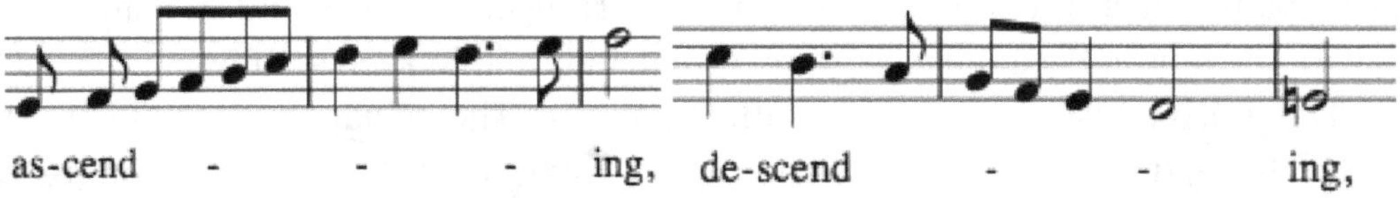

Figure 3.12 | Examples of "word painting" in Weelkes's "As Vest Was From Latmos Hill Descending"
Author | Diana Thompson
Source | ChoralWiki
License | CPDL

Timing	Performing Forces, Melody, and Texture	Text and Form
0:00	Descending melodic/scales on "descending"	As Vesta was from Latmos hill descending,
0:14	Ascending melodic/scales on "ascending"	she spied a maiden queen the same ascending,
0:31	Melody gently undulates, neither ascending nor descending.	attended on by all the shepherds swain,
0:45	Rapid imitative descending figures on running down	to whom Diana's darlings came running down amain.
1:05	Two voices, three voices, and then all voices	First two by two, then three by three together,
1:12	solo voice or unison	leaving their goddess all alone, hasted thither,
1:24	All voices in delicate polyphony	and mingling with the shepherds of her train with mirthful tunes her presence entertain.
1:40	All voices unite to introduce the final proclamation	Then sang the shepherds and nymphs of Diana,
1:52	Brief, joyful phrase imitated among voices is repeated over and over	Long live fair Oriana!

3.6.2 Renaissance Dance Music

With the rebirth of the Renaissance, came a resurgence of the popularity of dance. This resurgence led to instrumental dance music becoming the most widespread genre for instrumental music. Detailed instruction books for dance also included step orders and sequences that followed the music accompaniment. The first dances started, similar to today's square dances, soon evolved into more elaborate and unique forms of expression. Examples of three types of Renaissance dances include the pavanne, galliard, and jig.

The **pavanne** is a more solemn stately dance in a duple meter (in twos). Its participants dance and move around with prearranged stopping and starting places with the music. Pavannes are more formal and used in such settings.

The **galliard** is usually paired with a pavanne. The galliard is in triple meter (in threes) and provides an alternative to the rhythms of the pavanne. The **jig** is a folk dance or its tune in an animated meter. It was originally developed in the 1500s in England. The instrumental jig was a popular dance number. Jigs were regularly performed in Elizabethan theatres after the main play. **William Kemp** actor, song and dance performer, and a comedian, is immortalized for having created comic roles in Shakespeare. He accompanied his jig performances with pipe and tabor and snare drum. Kemp's jig started a unique phrasing/cadence system that carried well past the Renaissance period.

LISTENING GUIDE
For audio, go to: https://www.youtube.com/watch?v=YWO2UWOrV2o
Composer: Composer unknown but was performed by William Kemp. The piece became known as Kemp's Jig
Composition: "Kemp's Jig"
Date: late 1500s
Genre: Jig (Dance Piece instrumental)
Form: abb (repeated in this recording) Most dances of the period had a rhythmic and harmony pause or repose (cadence) every four or eight measures to mark a musical or dancing phrase.
Performing Forces: Lute solo instrumental piece
What we want you to remember about this composition: A jig is a light folk dance. It is a dance piece of music that can stand alone when played as an instrumental player. This new shift in instrumental music from strictly accompaniment to stand alone music performances begins a major advance for instrumental music. Will Kemp was a dancer and actor. He won a bet that he could dance from London to Norwich (80 miles). "Kemps Jig" was written to celebrate the event.
One thing to remember about this composition: This piece of dance music is evolving from just a predictable dance accompaniment to a central piece of instrumental music. Such alterations of dance music for the sake of the music itself are referred to as the stylization of dance music that has carried on through the centuries.

To view an informative Renaissance Music Timeline, go to:
http://musiced.about.com/od/famousmusicians1/a/trenaissance.htm

3.7 CHAPTER SUMMARY

The Renaissance period was truly a time of great discovery in science, music, society, and the visual arts. The reemergence and renewed interests of Greek and Roman history/culture is still current in today's modern society. Performing music outside of the church in courts and the public really began to thrive in the Renaissance and continues today in the music industry. Many of the master works, both sacred and secular, from the Renaissance are still appreciated and continue to be the standard for today's music industry. Songs of love, similar to Renaissance chansons, are still composed and performed today. The beauty of Renaissance music, as well as the other arts, is reintroduced and appreciated in modern-day theater performances and visually in museums. The results of the Protestant Reformation are still felt today, and the struggles between contemporary and traditional church worship continues very much as it did during the Renaissance. As we continue our reading and study of music through the Baroque period, try to recall the changes and trends of the Medieval and Renaissance eras and how they thread their way through history to today. Music and the Arts do not just occur; they evolve and also remain the same.

3.8 GLOSSARY

Anthem – a musical composition of celebration, usually used as a symbol for a distinct group, particularly the national anthems of countries. Originally, and in music theory and religious contexts, it also refers more particularly to short sacred choral work and still more particularly to a specific form of Anglican

Church Music – Sacred music written for performance in church, or any musical setting of ecclesiastical liturgy, or music set to words expressing propositions of a sacred nature, such as a hymn. Church Music Director is a position responsible the musical aspects of the church's activities.

Chanson – is in general any lyric-driven French song, usually polyphonic and secular. A singer specializing in chansons is known as a "chanteur" (male) or "chanteuse" (female); a collection of chansons, especially from the late Middle Ages and Renaissance, is also known as a chansonnier.

Chapel Master – Director of music, secular and sacred, for the courts' official functions and entertainment.

Consort – A renaissance consort is a group of renaissance instrumentalists playing together. A whole consort is an ensemble performing with instruments from the same family. A broken consort is an ensemble comprised of instruments from more than one family.

Counter-Reformation – The preservation movement or "Counter-Reformation" against the protestant reform led to the development of the Jesuit order (1540) and the later assembling of the Council of Trent (1545-1563) which considered issues of the church's authority and organizational structure.

Dance Music [WM1] – is music composed specifically to facilitate or accompany dancing

Frets – is a raised strip on the neck of a stringed instrument. Frets usually extend across the full width of the neck and divide the string into half steps for most western musical instruments. Most guitars have frets.

Galliard – was a form of Renaissance dance and music popular all over Europe in the 16th century.

Jig – is the accompanying dance tune for an energetic fold dance usually in a compound meter.

Madrigal – a musical piece for several solo voices set to a short poem. They originated in Italy around 1520. Most madrigals were about love.

Motet – is a highly varied sacred choral musical composition. The motet was one of the pre-eminent polyphonic forms of Renaissance music.

Pavanne – is a slow processional dance common in Europe during the 16th century Renaissance.

Reformation – was a succession and division from the practices of the Roman Catholic Church initiated by Martin Luther. Led to the development of Protestant churches.

Word painting – was utilized by Renaissance composers to represent poetic images musically. For example, an ascending melodic line would portray the text "ascension to heaven." Or a series of rapid notes would represent running.

4 Music of the Baroque Period

Jeff Kluball and Elizabeth Kramer

4.1 OBJECTIVES

1. Demonstrate knowledge of historical and cultural contexts of the Baroque Period
2. Recognize musical performing forces (voices, instruments, and ensembles), styles, composers, and genres of the Baroque
3. Explain ways in which music and extra-musical influences interact in music of the Baroque Period
4. Aurally identify selected music of the Baroque, making critical judgments about its style and use

4.2 KEY TERMS AND INDIVIDUALS

- absolute monarchs
- antiphonal
- Antonio Stradavarius
- Antonio Vivaldi
- aria
- basso continuo
- Bernini
- cantata
- Cervantes
- chorale
- Claudio Monteverdi
- concerto
- cori spezzati
- Descartes
- Florentine Camerata
- fugue
- Galileo Galilei
- George Frideric Handel
- Giovanni Gabrieli
- homophony
- J. S. Bach
- libretto
- Louis XIV
- melisma
- motor rhythm
- movement

- Newton
- opera
- oratorio
- *Passions of the Soul*
- Polychoral
- polyphony
- program music
- recitative
- ritornello form
- sectional form
- Shakespeare
- solo
- sonata
- stylized dance
- subject
- suite
- terraced dynamics
- Thirty Years War
- through-composed
- tutti

4.3 INTRODUCTION AND HISTORICAL CONTEXT

This brief introduction to the Baroque period is intended to provide a short summary of the music and context in the Baroque Era, which lasted from about 1600-1750. This period includes several composers that we now hear on so-called "classical" music stations. You are probably familiar with such names as Bach, Handel, and Pachelbel, whose Canon is used in many modern weddings. You have almost certainly heard snippets of these composers on TV shows, commercials, or movies. In this section, we will add some context and history to these and many other personalities from the Baroque Era.

It's appropriate that we hear Handel and his contemporaries in commercials today considering the Baroque era was essentially the first age in which music became a commercial commodity. Opera in the seventeenth century was the entertainment equivalent of movies today. The biggest opera stars in 1720 were followed around by paparazzi and gossiped about just as are, say, Brad Pitt and Angelina Jolie. You'll encounter more on that when you get to the opera portion of this learning chapter.

The term "Baroque" has an interesting and disputed past. Baroque ultimately is thought to have derived from the Italian word ***barocco***. Philosophers during the Middle Ages used this term to describe an obstacle or veerings from schematic logic. Later the term came to denote or bring attention to any contorted idea, obscure thought, or anything different, out of the ordinary, or strange. Another possible origin is from the Portuguese term ***barrocco***, in Spanish ***barrueco***. Jewelers use this term even today to describe irregular or imperfectly shaped pearls: a baroque pearl. The baroque period is a time of extremes resulting from events stemming back to the renaissance. The conflict between the reformation and counter-reformation, and the influence of Greek/Roman culture as opposed to medieval roots are present throughout the Baroque era.

In art circles, the term baroque came to be used to describe the bizarre, irregular, grotesque, or anything that departs from the regular or expected. This definition was adhered to until 1888 when Heinrich Woolfflin coined the word as

a stylistic title or designation. The baroque title was then used to describe the style of the era. The term "rococo" is sometimes used to describe art from the end of the Baroque period, from the mid to late eighteenth century. The rococo took the extremes of baroque architecture and design to new heights with ornate design work and gold gilding (see figure of a rococo church). Historical events and advances in science influenced music and the other arts tremendously. It is not possible to isolate the trends of music during this period without briefly looking into what was happening at the time in society.

4.3.1 Science

Sir Isaac Newton and his studies made a great impact on Enlightenment ideology. In addition to creating calculus, a discipline of mathematics still practiced today, he studied and published works on universal gravity and the three laws of motion. His studies supported heliocentrism, the model of the solar system's planets and their orbits with the sun. Heliocentrism invalidated several religious and traditional beliefs.

Johannes Kepler (b. 1571-1630), a German astronomer, similarly re-evaluated the Copernican theory that the planets move in a circular motion in their orbits around the sun. In utilizing Brahe's records, Kepler concluded that the planets move in ellipses in their orbits around the sun. He was the first to propose elliptical orbits in the solar system

William Harvey conducted extensive anatomical research concerning the circulatory system. He studied the veins and arteries of the human arm and also concluded that the blood vessel system is an overall circle returning back to the heart while passing through the lungs.

4.3.2 Philosophy

Descartes (1595-1650) was a famous philosopher, mathematician, and scientist from France. He is arguably considered to be one of the pioneer modern philosophers to make an effort to defeat skepticism. His opinions on the relationship of the body and mind as well as certainty and knowledge have been very influential. He laid the foundation for an analysis and classification of human emotions at a time when more and more writers were noting the powers of music to evoke emotional responses in their listeners

John Locke (1632-1704) is regarded as the founder of the Enlightenment movement in philosophy. Locke is believed to have originated the school of thought known as British Empiricism, laid the philosophical foundation for the modern idea of limited liberal government. Locke believed each person has "natural rights," that government has obligations to its citizens, that government has very limited rights over its citizens and, in certain circumstances, it can be overthrown by its citizens.

4.3.3 Art

Gian Lorenzo Bernini (1598-1680) was a famous Italian sculptor of the Baroque era. He is credited with establishing the Baroque sculpture style. He was also a well-known architect and worked most of his career in Rome. Although he enjoyed the patronage of the cardinals and popes, he challenged artistic traditions. His art reflects a certain sense of drama, action, and sometimes playfulness. Compare for instance his sculpture of David (1623-1624) with the David sculpture (1501-1504) of Renaissance artist Michelangelo. (Figures 4.1 and 4.2)

Figure 4.1 | Michelangelo's David
Author | Jörg Bittner Unna
Source | Wikimedia Commons
License | CC BY 3.0

Where Michelangelo's David appears calmly lost in contemplation, Bernini's David is in the act of flinging his slingshot, jaw set and muscles tensed. We see similar psychological intensity and drama in music of the Baroque period.

Elaborate formal Baroque gardens indicating man's control over nature were used to demonstrate the owner's power and prestige. France was a major contributor to the development of these highly ornamental gardens. These gardens became associated with autocratic government. The designs of these elaborate gardens were from "Cartesian" geometry (science and mathematics) while drawing the landscape into the composition. Look at the Leonard Knyff oil rendering of the Hampton Court Baroque garden.

Figure 4.2 | Bernini's David
Author | Galleria Borghese Official Site
Source | Wikimedia Commons
License | CC BY-SA 4.0

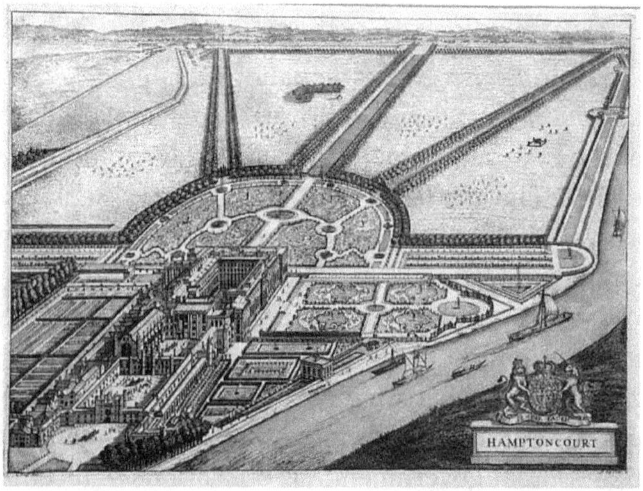

Figure 4.3 | Hampton Court Gardens
Author | Leonard Knyff
Source | Wikimedia Commons
License | Public Domain

4.3.4 Literature

Literature during the Baroque period often took a dramatic turn. William Shakespeare (1564-1616), playwright and poet, wrote the play *Hamlet* and many other great classics still enjoyed by millions of readers and audiences today. Music composers have long used Shakespeare's writing for text in their compositions; for example, his *Hamlet* was used as the basis for an opera. Shakespeare's writings depict an enormous range of human life, including jealousy, love, hate, drama, humor, peace, intrigue, war, as well as all social classes—matter that provides great cultural entertainment.

Jean Racine (1639-1699) wrote tragedies in the neoclassic (anti-Baroque) and Jansenism literary movements. Many works of the classical era utilized rather twisted complicated plots with simple psychology. Racine's neoclassic writing did just the opposite, incorporating simple and easy to understand plots with challenging uses of psychology. Racine is often grouped with Corneille, known for developing the classic tragedy form. Racine's dramas portray his characters as human with internal trials and conflicting emotions. His notable works include *Andromaque, Phèdre*, and *Athalie.*

Miguel de Cervantes (1547-1616) was a Spanish playwright, poet, and novelists. *Don Quixote* is his most famous work and is often considered the first modern novel from Europe. It was published in 1605 and portrays the traditions of Sevilla, Spain. Legend has it that the early portions of *Don Quixote* were written while the author was in jail for stealing.

Other Baroque-era authors include John Milton (1608-1674), author of the epic *Paradise Lost;* John Dryden (1631-1700), dramatist and poet who wrote several semi-operatic works incorporating music by contemporary composer Henry Purcell; Jonathan Swift (1667-1745) an Anglo-Irish essayist and proto-novelist, poet, and cleric who authored *Gulliver's Travels;*, and Henry Fielding (b. 1707-1754) a proto-novelist and dramatist who authored *Tom Jones.*

We will find a similar emphasis on drama as we study Baroque music, especially in the emergence of genres such as opera and oratorio.

4.3.5 Politics

In **politics**, three changes that started in the Renaissance became defining forces in the Baroque period. First, nation-states (like France and England) developed into major world powers, ruled by absolutist monarchs. These absolute monarchs were kings and queens whose authority, it was believed, was divinely bestowed upon them. They amassed great power and wealth, which they often displayed through their patronage of music and the other arts. With the rise of this system of absolutism, the state increasingly challenged the power base of the Church. In the case of Germany, these nation-states were smaller and often unstable. Second, Protestantism spread throughout northern Europe. Places such as England, where Georg Frideric Handel spent most of his adult life, and central Germany, where Johann Sebastian Bach spent all of his life, were Protestant strongholds. J. S. Bach wrote a great deal of music for the Lutheran Church. Third, the middle class continued to grow in social and economic power with the emergence of printing and textile industries and open trade routes with the New World (largely propelled by the thriving slave trade of the time).

4.3.6 Exploration and Colonialism

The 1600s saw the first era of the Colonization of America. France and England were the most active in the colonization of America. The quest for power in Europe, wealth/economics and religious reasons energized the colonial progression. Hudson explores the later-named Hudson River (1609); landing of Pilgrims at Plymouth (1620); Manhattan bought from Native Americans (1626); Boston founded (1630); Harvard University founded (1636).

4.3.7 Musical Timeline

Events in History	Events in Music
	1597: Giovanni Gabrieli writes his *Sacrae Symphoniae*
	1607: Monteverdi performs *Orfeo* in Mantua, Italy
1618-1648: Thirty Years War	
1623: Galileo Galileo publishes *The Assayer*	
1642-1651: English Civil War	
1643-1715: Reign of Louis XIV in France	
1649: Descartes publishes *Passions of the Soul*	
	1678: Vivaldi born in Venice, Italy
1687: Isaac Newton publishes his *Principia*	1685: Handel and Bach born in Germany
	1741: Handel *Messiah* performed in Dublin, Ireland
1740-1846: Reign of Frederick the Great of Prussia	
	1750: J. S. Bach dies

4.4 MUSIC IN THE BAROQUE PERIOD

4.4.1 Music Comparison Overview

Renaissance Music	Baroque Music
• Much music with rhythms indicated by musical notation • Mostly polyphony (much is imitative polyphony) • Growing use of thirds and triads • Music – text relationships increasingly important with word painting • Invention of music publishing • Growing merchant class increasingly acquires musical skills	• Meter more important than before • Use of polyphony continues • Rise of homophony. Rise of instrumental music, including the violin family • New genres such as opera, oratorio, concerto, cantata, and fugue • Emergence of program music • First notation of dynamics and use of terraced dynamics • Continued present of music at church and court • Continued increase of music among merchant classes

4.4.2 General Trends of Baroque Music

The characteristics highlighted in the chart above give Baroque music its unique sound and appear in the music of Monteverdi, Pachelbel, Bach, and others. To elaborate:

1. Definite and regular rhythms in the form of meter and "motor rhythm" (the constant subdivision of the beat) appear in most music. Bar lines become more prominent.
2. The use of polyphony continues with more elaborate techniques of imitative polyphony used in the music of Handel and Bach.
3. Homophonic (melody plus accompaniment) textures emerge including the use of basso continuo (a continuous bass line over which chords were built used to accompany a melodic line)
4. Homophonic textures lead to increased use of major and minor keys and chord progressions (see chapter one)
5. The accompaniment of melodic lines in homophonic textures are provided by the continuo section: a sort of improvised "rhythm section" that features lutes, viola da gambas, cellos, and harpsichords. Continuo sections provide the basso continuo (continuous bass line) and are used in Baroque opera, concerti, and chamber music

6. Instrumental music featuring the violin family—such as suites, sonatas, and concertos emerge and grow prominent.
7. These compositions are longer, often with multiple movements that use defined forms having multiple sections, such as ritornello form and binary form.
8. Composers start to notate dynamics and often write abrupt changes between loud and softs, what are called terraced dynamics.

4.4.3 Genres of the Baroque Period

Much great music was composed during the Baroque period, and many of the most famous composers of the day were extremely prolific. To approach this music, we'll break the historical era into the early period (the first seventy-five years or so) and the late period (from roughly 1675 to 1750). Both periods contain vocal music and instrumental music.

The main genres of the early Baroque vocal music are: madrigal, motet, and opera. The main genres of early Baroque instrumental music include the canzona (also known as the sonata) and suite. The main genres of the late Baroque instrumental music are the concerto, fugue, and suite. The main genres of late Baroque vocal music are: Italian opera seria, oratorio, and the church cantata (which was rooted in the Lutheran chorale, already discussed in chapter three). Many of these genres will be discussed later in the chapter.

Solo music of the Baroque era was composed for all the different types of instruments but with a major emphasis on violin and keyboard. The common term for a solo instrumental work is sonata. Please note that the non-keyboard solo instrument is usually accompanied by a keyboard, such as the organ, harpsichord or clavichord.

Small ensembles are basically named in regard to the number of performers in each (trio = three performers, etc.). The most common and popular small ensemble during the Baroque period was the trio sonata. These trios feature two melody instruments (usually violins) accompanied by basso continuo (considered the third single member of the trio).

The large ensembles genre can be divided into two subcategories, orchestral and vocal. The concerto was the leading form of large ensemble orchestral music. Concerto featured two voices, that of the orchestra and that of either a solo instrument or small ensemble. Throughout the piece, the two voices would play together and independently, through conversation, imitation, and in contrast with one another. A concerto that pairs the orchestra with a small ensemble is called a **concerto grosso** and a concert that pairs the orchestra with a solo instrument is called a **solo concerto**.

The two large vocal/choral genres for the Baroque period were **sacred works** and **opera**. Two forms of the sacred choral works include the **oratorio** and the **mass**. The oratorio is an opera without all the acting. Oratorios tell a story using a cast of characters who speak parts and may include **recitative** (speak singing) and **arias** (sung solos). The production is performed to the audience without the performers interacting. The **Mass** served as the core of the Catholic religious service and commemorates the Last Supper. **Opera** synthesizes theatrical performance and music. Opera cast members act and interact with each other. Types of vocal selections utilized in an opera include recitative and aria. Smaller ensembles (duets, trios etc.) and choruses are used in opera productions.

Oratorio	Opera Seria	Cantata
• Similar to opera except: No costumes or staging • A lot of choral numbers • Typically on biblical topics • Some examples of Handels biblical oratorios: *Saul, Solomon*, and *Judas Maccabeus* • Some examples of Handel's non-biblical oratorios: *Hercules, Acis and Galatea*, and *The Triumph of Time and Truth* • Vocal soloist perform in front instruments utilized for accompaniment	• Serious opera • Historical or Mythological plots • Lavish costumes • Spectacular sets • Showcased famous solo singers • All sung; no narration • Acted and performed on stage • Examples of Baroque opera: *L'Orfeo, L'Arianna, The Fairy Queen* (based on Shakespeare's *Midsummer Night's Dream*), and *Ottone in Villa*	• A work for voices and instruments • Either sacred and resembling a short oratorio or secular as a lyrical drama set to music. • Sacred cantata often involves church choirs and are not acted out • Can utilize narration • Example is Bach's famous Reformation *Cantata* BWV 80: *Ein feste Burg ist unser Got* (A Mighty Fortress is Our God)

4.5 BIRTH OF OPERA

The beginning of the Baroque Period is in many ways synonymous with the birth of opera. Music drama had existed since the Middle Ages (and perhaps even earlier), but around 1600, noblemen increasingly sponsored experiments that combined singing, instrumental music, and drama in new ways. As we have seen in Chapter Three, Renaissance Humanism led to new interest in ancient Greece and Rome. Scholars as well as educated noblemen read descriptions of the emotional power of ancient dramas, such as those by Sophocles, which began and ended with choruses. One particularly active group of scholars and aristocrats interested in the ancient world was the Florentine Camerata, so called because they met in the rooms (or camerata) of a nobleman in Florence, Italy. This group, which included Vicenzo Galilei, father of Galileo Galilei, speculated that the reason for ancient drama's being so moving was its having been entirely sung to a sort of declamatory style that was midway between speech and song. Although today we believe that actually only the choruses of ancient drama were sung, these circa 1600 beliefs led to collaborations with musicians and the development of opera.

Less than impressed by the emotional impact of the rule-driven polyphonic church music of the Renaissance, members of the Florentine Camerata argued that a simple melody supported by sparse accompaniment would be more moving. They identified a style that they called recitative, in which a single individual would sing a melody line that follows the inflections and rhythms of speech (see figure one with an excerpt of basso continuo). This individual would be accompanied by just one or two instruments: a keyboard instrument, such as a harpsichord or small organ, or a plucked string instrument, such as the lute. The accompaniment was called the **basso continuo**.

Basso continuo is a continuous bass line over which the harpsichord, organ, or lute added chords based on numbers or figures that appeared under the melody that functioned as the bass line, would become a defining feature of Baroque music. This system of indicating chords by numbers was called figured bass, and allowed the instrumentalist more freedom in forming the chords than had every note of the chord been notated. The flexible nature of basso continuo also underlined its supporting nature. The singer of the recitative was given license to speed up and slow down as the words and emotions of the text might direct, with the instrumental accompaniment following along. This method created a homophonic texture, which consists of one melody line with accompaniment, as you might recall from chapter one.

Composers of early opera combined recitatives with other musical numbers such as choruses, dances, arias, instrumental interludes, and the overture. The choruses in opera were not unlike the late Renaissance madrigals that we studied in chapter three. Operatic dance numbers used the most popular dances of the day, such as pavanes and galliards. Instrumental interludes tended to be sectional, that is, having different sections that sometimes repeated, as we find in other instrumental music of the time. Operas began with an instrumental piece called the Overture.

Like recitatives, arias were homophonic compositions featuring a solo singer over accompaniment. Arias, however, were less improvisatory. The melodies sung in arias almost always conformed to a musical meter, such as duple or triple, and unfolded in phrases of similar lengths. As the century progressed, these melodies became increasingly difficult or virtuosic. If the purpose of the recitative was to convey emotions through a simple melodic line, then the purpose of the aria was increasingly to impress the audience with the skills of the singer.

Opera was initially commissioned by Italian noblemen, often for important occasions such as marriages or births, and performed in the halls of their castles and pal-

aces. By the mid to late seventeenth century, opera had spread not only to the courts of France, Germany, and England, but also to the general public, with performances in public opera houses first in Italy and later elsewhere on the continent and in the British Isles. By the eighteenth century, opera would become almost as ubiquitous as movies are for us today. Most Baroque operas featured topics from the ancient world or mythology, in which humans struggled with fate and in which the heroic actions of nobles and mythological heroes were supplemented by the righteous judgments of the gods. Perhaps because of the cosmic reaches of its narratives, opera came to be called opera seria, or serious opera. Librettos, or the words of the opera, were to be of the highest literary quality and designed to be set to music. Italian remained the most common language of opera, and Italian opera was popular in England and Germany; the French were the first to perform operas in their native tongue.

Focus Composition:

"Tu se morta" ("You are dead") from Monteverdi's *Orfeo* (1607)

One of the very first operas was written by an Italian composer named Claudio Monteverdi (1567-1643). (See Figure 4.4.) For many years, Monteverdi worked for the Duke of Mantua in central Italy. There, he wrote *Orfeo* (1607), an opera based on the mythological character of Orpheus from Ovid's *Metamorphoses*. In many ways, Orpheus was an ideal character for early opera (and indeed many early opera composers set his story): he was a musician who could charm with the playing of his harp not only forest animals but also figures from the underworld, from the river keeper Charon to the god of the underworld Pluto. Orpheus's story is a tragedy. He and Eurydice have fallen in love and will be married. To celebrate, Eurydice and her female friends head to the countryside where she is bitten by a snake and dies. Grieving but determined, Orpheus travels to the underworld to bring her back to the land of the living. Pluto grants his permission on one condition: Orpheus shall lead Eurydice out of the underworld without looking back. He is not able to do this (different versions give various causes), and the two are separated for all eternity.

Figure 4.4 | Claudio Monteverdi
Author | Bernardo Strozzi
Source | Wikimedia Commons
License | Public Domain

One of the most famous recitatives of Monteverdi's opera is sung by Orpheus after he has just learned of the death of his beloved Eurydice. The words of his recitative move from expressing astonishment that his beloved Eurydice is dead to expressing his determination to retrieve her from the underworld. He uses poetic images, referring to the stars and the great abyss, before, in the end, bidding farewell to the earth, the sky, and the sun, in preparation for his journey.

As recitative, Orpheus's musical line is flexible in its rhythms. Orpheus sings to the accompaniment of the basso continuo, here just a small organ and a long-necked Baroque lute called the theorbo, which follows his melodic line, pausing where he pauses and moving on where he does. Most of the chords played by the basso continuo are minor chords, emphasizing Orpheus's sadness. There are also incidents of word painting, the depiction of specific images from the text by the music.

Whether you end up liking "Tu se morta" or not, we hope that you can hear it as dramatic, as attempting to convey as vividly as possible Orpheus's deep sorrow. Not all the music of *Orfeo* is slow and sad like "Tu se morta." In this recitative, the new Baroque emphasis on music as expressive of emotions, especially tragic emotions such as sorrow on the death of a loved one, is very clear.

LISTENING GUIDE For audio, go to: https://www.youtube.com/watch?v=8ll_u87oPG8&feature=youtu.be Features Jordi Savall and Le Concert des Nations, La Capella Reial de Catalunya, Furio Zanasi singing the role of Orfeo
Composer: Claudio Monteverdi
Composition: "Tu Se Morta" ("You are dead") from *Orfeo*
Date: 1607
Genre: recitative followed by a short chorus
Form: through-composed
Nature of Text: Lyrics in Italian *Tu se' morta, se morta, mia vita* *ed io respiro, tu se' da me partita,* *se' da me partita per mai piu,* *mai piu' non tornare, ed io rimango-* *no, no, che se i versi alcuna cosa ponno,* *n'andra sicuro a' piu profondi abissi,* *e, intenerito il cor del re de l'ombre,* *meco trarotti a riverder le stelle,* *o se cia negherammi empio destino,* *rimarro teco in compagnia di morta.* *Addio terra, addio cielo, e sole, addio* [Translation can be found at http://faculty.deanza.edu/mitchell/music1/stories/storyReader$40]
Performing Forces: solo vocalist and basso continuo (here organ and theorbo), followed by chorus accompanied by a small orchestra

What we want you to remember about this composition:

- It is one of the first operas.
- It is homophonic, accompanied by basso continuo
- It uses word painting to emphasize Orfeo's sorrow

Other things to listen for:

- Its melodic line is mostly conjunct and the range is about an octave in range.
- Most of its chords are minor and there are some dissonances
- Its notated rhythms follow the rhythms of the text and are sung flexibly within a basic duple meter
- It is sung in Italian like much Baroque opera

Timing	Performing Forces, Melody, and Texture	Text and Form
0:00	Solo vocalist and basso continuo in homophonic texture; Singer registers sadness and surprise through pauses and repetition of words such as "never to return"	"Tu se morta, se morta mia vita, e io respiro" And I breathe, you have left me./ *"se' da me partita per mai piu,"*You have left me forevermore,/ *"mai piu' non tornare,"* Never to return,
0:52	"No, No" (declaration to rescue Eurydice) intensified by being sung to high notes; melody descends to its lowest pitch on the word "abyss"	*"ed io rimango-"* and I remain- / *"no, no, che se i versi alcuna cosa ponno,"* No, no, if my verses have any power,/ *"n'andra sicuro a' piu profondi abissi,"* I will go confidently to the deepest abysses,
1:11	Descending pitches accompanied by dissonant chords when referring to the king of the shadows; Melody ascends to high pitch for the word "stars"	*"e, intenerito il cor del re de l'ombre,"* And, having melted the heart of the king of shadows,/ *"meco trarotti a riverder le stelle,"* Will bring you back to me to see the stars again,
1:30	Melody descends for the word "death"	*"o se cia negherammi empio destino,"* Or, if pitiless fate denies me this,/ *"rimarro teco in compagnia di morta."* I will remain with you in the company of death.

1:53	"Earth," "sky," and "sun" are set on ever higher pitches suggesting their experienced position from a human perspective	*"Addio terra, addio cielo, e sole, addio*;" Farewell earth, farewell sky, and sun, farewell.
2:28	Chorus & small orchestra responds; Mostly homophonic texture, with some polyphony; Dissonance on the word "cruel."	Oh cruel destiny, oh despicable stars, oh inexorable skies

4.6 NEW MUSIC FOR INSTRUMENTS

The Baroque period saw an explosion in music written for instruments. Had you lived in the Middle Ages or Renaissance, you would have likely heard instrumental music but much of it would have been either dance music or vocal music played by instruments. Around 1600, composers started writing more music specifically for musical instruments that might be played at a variety of occasions. One of the first composers to write for brass instruments was Giovanni Gabrieli (1554-1612). His compositions were played by ensembles having trumpets and sackbuts (the trombones of their day) as well as violins and an instrument called the cornet (which was something like a recorder with a brass mouth piece). The early brass instruments, such as the trumpet and sackbut, as well as the early French horn, did not have any valves and were extremely difficult to play. Extreme mastery of the air column and embouchure (musculature around the mouth used to buzz the lips) were required to control the pitch of the instruments. Good Baroque trumpeters were highly sought after and in short supply. Often they were considered the aristocrats in the orchestra. Even in the wartime skirmishes of the Baroque era, trumpeters were treated as officers and given officer status when they became prisoners of war. Composers such as Bach, Vivaldi, Handel, and others selectively and carefully chose their desired instrumentation in order to achieve the exact tone colors, blend, and effects for each piece.

Giovanni Gabrieli was an innovative composer of the late Renaissance Venetian School. His masterful compositional technique carried over and established technique utilized during the Baroque era. Giovanni succeeded Andrea Gabrieli, his uncle, at Venice's St. Marks Basilica as the organist following his uncle's death in 1586. Giovanni held the position until his death in 1612. Giovanni's works represent the peak of musical achievement for Venetian music.

Gabrieli continued and perfected the masterful traditional compositional technique known as **cori spezzati** (literally, "split choirs"). This technique was developed in the sixteenth century at St. Mark's where composers would contrast different instrumentalists and groups of singers utilizing the effects of space in the performance venue, that is, the church. Different sub-ensembles would be placed in different areas of the sanctuary. One sub-ensemble would play the "call" and another would give the "response." This musical back and forth is called antiphonal performance and creates a stereophonic sound between the two ensembles. Indeed, this placement of performers and the specific writing of the parts created the first type of stereo sound and three-dimensional listening experiences for parishioners in the congregation. Many of Gabrieli's works were written for double choirs and double brass ensembles to perform simultaneously. See the interior image of St. Mark's Basilica with its chamber on the left and right that are used for opposing brass ensembles (Figure 4.5).

Figure 4.5 | Interior of St. Mark's Basilica
Author | User "Morn"
Source | Wikimedia Commons
License | CC BY-SA 3.0

An example of one such piece with an eight-part setting is Gabrieli's ***Jubilate***. The interior of the Basilica had multiple coves and lofts where musicians could be placed for performing Gabrieli's stereophonic works. In later years, Giovanni became known as a famous music teacher. His most recognized student was Heinrich Schütz of Germany.

Focus Composition:

Gabrieli, "Sonata pian'e forte" from *Sacrae Symphoniae* (1597)

Another famous composition by Gabrieli in eight parts, consisting of two four-part groups, is the *Sonata pian'e forte* which is included in the *Sacrea Symphoniae* composed in 1597. This collection includes several instrumental **canzoni** for six- to eight-part ensembles. These, in addition to several **Toccatas** and **Ricercars,** have provided a great deal of interesting repertoire for brass players. Many of the original works by Gabrieli were written for sackbuts (early versions of the modern trombone) and cornetti (cupped shape mouth pieces on a curved wooden instrument) but have since been transcribed for various brass ensembles.

Let's listen to and study the *Sonata pian'e forte* from Gabrieli's *Sacrea Symphoniae*. This collection is pioneering in musical scoring in that Gabrieli wrote specific louds and softs (volume) into the individual parts for the performers to observe. Through the use of its two keyboards played simultaneously, the pian'eforte could achieve two relative dynamic (volume) levels, soft and loud. The introduction of writing in dynamics (volume p-soft to f-loud) into music by composers is a major step toward notating expression into the music score. Gabrieli also incorporated imitative polyphony and the use of **polychoral** techniques.

LISTENING GUIDE

For audio, go to:
https://www.youtube.com/watch?v=Jx2xgbBkjbg
As performed on instruments from the Renaissance/Baroque transition era, directed by Bernard Fabre-Garrus at the Festival des Cathedrales in Picardie (timings below correspond to this version).

Composer: Giovanni Gabrieli

Composition: *Sonata pian e forte for 8 parts, C. 176* from *Sacrea Symphoniae*

Date: 1597

Genre: Sonata

Form: through-composed in sections

Nature of Text: Antiphonal instrumental work in eight parts

Performing Forces: Two "choirs" **(**Double instrumental quartet—8 parts) of traditional instruments—sackbuts (early trombones) and wooden cornets

What we want you to remember about this composition:

- Antiphonal call and response;
- the use of musical **dynamics** (louds and softs written in the individual parts);
- and contrapuntal imitation

Other things to listen for:

- listen to the noted balance so the melody is heard throughout and how the instruments sound very "vocal" as from earlier time periods (the Renaissance)
- The piece's texture is the division of the forces into two alternating groups in polychoral style.

Timing	Performing Forces, Melody, and Texture
0:00	Choir 1 introduces the first theme in a piano dynamic in a slow tempo and duple meter. Like many early sonatas and canzonas, the composition starts with a repeated-note motive. The notes and harmonies come from the Dorian mode, a predecessor to the minor scale. The composition starts in the key of G.
0:29	As the first choir cadences, the second choir begins, playing a new theme still at a piano dynamic and slow tempo. Later in the theme the repeated note motive (first heard in the first theme of the composition) returns.
0:52	Choirs 1 and 2 play together in a *tutti* section at a forte dynamic. The new theme features faster notes than the first two themes and the parts are more (The key moves to the Mixolydian mode, a predecessor to the major scale, and the key moves to C.)

1:02	Central antiphonal section. Choir 1 opens with a short phrase using a piano dynamics and answered by choir 2 with a different short phrase, also with a piano dynamics. This call and response continues. Some times, the phrases last for only two measures; other times they are as long as four measures. After each passage of antiphonal exchanges, there is music of three to four measures in length where the whole ensemble joins together, usually with different melodic material (e.g. 40-43). The tonal or key center shifts during this section. There is a new theme that uses dotted rhythms that starts in measure 60 (approximately 2:07 in the recording).
2:34	Repetition of the melody to new words sung by all with monophonic texture (the drone continues)

To hear other Giovanni Gabrieli musical compositions, go to:
https://www.google.com/webhp?sourceid=chrome-instant&ion=1&espv=2&ie=UTF-8#q=giovanni+gabrieli+canzon+duodecimi+toni&stick=H4sIAAAAAAAAAONgFuLQz9U3yC4ySlHiArEMLdPLy7K1B-H1LizOTHYtKMotLQvKD8_PSAbASq34rAAAA

4.6.1 Rise of the Orchestra and the Concerto

The Baroque period also saw the birth of the orchestra, which was initially used to accompany court spectacle and opera. In addition to providing accompaniment to the singers, the orchestra provided instrumental only selections during such events. These selections came to include the overture at the beginning, the interludes between scenes and during scenery changes, and accompaniments for dance sequences. Other predecessors of the orchestra included the string bands employed by absolute monarchs in France and England and the town collegium musicum of some German municipalities. By the end of the Baroque period, composers were writing compositions that might be played by orchestras in concerts, such as concertos and orchestral suites.

The makeup of the Baroque orchestra varied in number and quality much more than the orchestra has varied since the nineteenth century; in general, it was a smaller ensemble than the later orchestra. At its core was the violin family, with woodwind instruments such as the flute, recorder, and oboe, and brass instruments, such as the trumpet or horn, and the timpani for percussion filling out the texture. The Baroque orchestra was almost always accompanied by harpsichord, which together with the one or more of the cellos or a bassonist, provided a basso continuo.

The new instruments of the violin family provided the backbone for the Baroque orchestra (see Figures 4.6, 4.7, 4.8, and 4.9). The violin family—the violin, viola, cello (long form violoncello), and bass violin—were not the first bowed string instruments in Western classical music. The Middle Ages had its fiddle (see Figure 4.10), and the Renaissance had the viola da gamba (see Figure 4.11). Bowed strings attained a new prominence in the seventeenth century with the widespread and increased manufacturing of violins, violas, cellos, and basses. Some of these instru-

Figure 4.6 | (far left) Violin
Author | User "Just Plain Bill"
Source | Wikimedia Commons
License | Public Domain

Figure 4.7 | (second from left) Viola
Author | User "Just Plain Bill"
Source | Wikimedia Commons
License | Public Domain

Figure 4.8 | (second from right) Cello
Author | Georg Feitscher
Source | Wikimedia Commons
License | CC BY-SA 3.0

Figure 4.9 | (far right) Double Bass
Author | User "AndrewKepert"
Source | Wikimedia Commons
License | CC BY-SA 3.0

ments, such as those made by Antonio Stradavari (1644-1737), are still sought after today as some of the finest specimens of instruments ever made. With the popularity of the violin family, instruments of the viola da gamba family fell to the sidelines. Composers started writing compositions specifically for the members of the violin family, often arranged with two groups of violins, one group of violas, and a group of cellos and double basses, who sometimes played the same bass line as played by the harpsichord.

One of the first important forms of this instrumental music was the concerto. The word concerto comes from the Latin and Italian root *concertare*, which has connotations of both competition and cooperation. The musical concerto might be thought to reflect both meanings. A concerto is a composition for an instrumental soloist or soloists and orchestra; in a sense, it brings together these two forces in concert; in another sense, these two forces compete for the attention of the audience. Concertos are most often in three movements that follow a tempo pattern of fast – slow – fast. Most first movements of concertos are in what has come to be called **ritornello form**. As its name suggests, a ritornello is a returning or refrain, played by the full orchestral ensemble. In a concerto, the ritornello alternates with the solo sections that are played by the soloist or soloists.

Figure 4.10 | Vielle player
Author | Unknown
Source | Wikimedia Commons
License | Public Domain

One of the most important composers of the Baroque concerto was the Italian Antonio Vivaldi (1678-

1741). His father taught him to play at a young age and he probably began lessons in music composition as a young teen.

Figure 4.11 | Regola Rubertina Titelbild
Author | Silvestro Ganassi
Source | Wikimedia Commons
License | Public Domain

Vivaldi began studying for the priesthood at age fifteen and, once ordained at age twenty-five, received the nickname of "The Red Priest" because of his hair color. He worked in a variety of locations around Europe, including at a prominent Venetian orphanage called the Opsedale della Pietà. There he taught music to girls, some of whom were illegitimate daughters of prominent noblemen and church officials from Venice. This orphanage became famous for the quality of music performed by its inhabitants. Northern Europeans, who would travel to Italy during the winter months on what they called "The Italian Tour"—to avoid the cold and rainy weather of cities such as Paris, Berlin, and London—wrote home about the fine performances put on by these orphans in Sunday afternoon concerts.

These girls performed concertos such as Vivaldi's well known *Four Seasons.* The *Four Seasons* refers to a set of four concertos, each of which is named after one of the seasons. As such, it is an example of program music, a type of music that would become more prominent in the Baroque period. **Program music** is instrumental music that represents something extra musical, such as the words of a poem or narrative or the sense of a painting or idea. A composer might ask orchestral instruments to imitate the sounds of natural phenomenon, such as a babbling brook or the cries of birds. Most program music carries a descriptive title that suggests what an audience member might listen for. In the case of the *Four Seasons*, Vivaldi connected each concerto to an Italian sonnet, that is, to a poem that was descriptive of the season to which the concerto referred. Thus in the case of Spring, the first concerto of the series, you can listen for the "festive song" of birds, "murmuring streams," "breezes," and "lightning and thunder."

Figure 4.12 | Portrait of Antonio Vivaldi
Author | Anonimo Bolognese
Source | Wikimedia Commons
License | Public Domain

Each of the concertos in the *Four Seasons* has three movements, organized in a fast – slow – fast succession. We'll listen to the first fast movement of Spring. Its "Allegro" subtitle is an Italian tempo marking that indicates music that is fast. As a first movement, it is in ritornello form. The movement opens with the ritornello, in which the orchestra presents the opening theme. This theme consists of motives, small groupings of notes and rhythms that are often repeated in sequence. This ritornello might be thought to reflect the opening line from the sonnet. After the ritornello, the soloist plays with the accompaniment of only a few instruments, that is, the basso continuo. The soloist's music uses some of the same motives found in the ritornello but plays them in a more virtuosic way, showing off one might say.

As you listen, try to hear the alternation of the ritornellos and solo sections. Listen also for the motor rhythm, the constant subdivision of the steady beat, and the melodic themes that unfold through melodic sequences. Do you hear birds, a brook, and a thunderstorm? Do you think you would have associated these musical moments with springtime, if, instead of being called the Spring Concerto, the piece was simply called Concerto No. 1?

LISTENING GUIDE For audio, go to: https://www.youtube.com/watch?v=zWopEIymWK8&feature=youtu.be&list=PLoD30A7BBDC001432 Giuliano Carmignola (solo violin); Giorgio Fava (violin I); Gino Mangiocavallo (violin II); Enrico Parizzi (viola); Walter Vestidello (violoncello); Alberto Rasi (violone); Giancarlo Rado (archlute); Andrea Marcon (harpsichord); I Sonatori de la Gioiosa Marca / Giuliano Carmignola (conductor)
Composer: Antonio Vivaldi
Composition: The first movement of Spring from *The Four Seasons*
Date: 1720s
Genre: solo concerto and program music
Form: ritornello form
Nature of Text: the concerto is accompanied by an Italian sonnet about springtime. The first five line are associated with the first movement: Springtime is upon us. The birds celebrate her return with festive song, and murmuring streams are softly caressed by the breezes. Thunderstorms, those heralds of Spring, roar, casting their dark mantle over heaven, Then they die away to silence, and the birds take up their charming songs once more.
Performing Forces: solo violinist and string orchestra
What we want you to remember about this composition: • It is the first movement of a solo concerto that uses ritornello form • This is program music • It uses terraced dynamics • It uses a fast allegro tempo

Other things to listen for: • The orchestral ritornellos alternate with the sections for solo violin • Virtuoso solo violin lines • Motor rhythm • Melodic themes composed of motives that spin out in sequences		
Timing	**Performing Forces, Melody, and Texture**	**Text and Form**
0:00	Orchestra plays the Ritornello. Repetitive motives played by all the violins; cellos subdivide the beat, provided the motor rhythm; Dynamics terraced from loud to soft to loud to soft, every three measures; In E major	"Coming of spring"
0:36	Solo Section featuring the solo violin, joined by two other violins. Solo violin imitates the birds with repeated notes that are ornamented by trills and then repeated in shorter note values	"Birds celebrate" with "festive song."
1:08	Ritornello starts with opening phrase. Opening phrase returns and then a softer new phrase with oscillating notes to depict the murmuring brook; Forte for the return of the opening phrase; then forte repeated low notes foreshadowing the appearance of lightening.	"Murmuring streams" "caressed by the breezes";
1:49	Solo section. Solo violinist playing rapid notes in groups of three to represent lightning; answered by low repeated note in other strings representing thunder	"Thunderstorms...roar"
2:07	Orchestra plays the ritornello. Opening theme (just three measures)	

2:15	Solo section: Solo violin + 2 violins; cello sustains a drone pitch. More high-pitched, ornamented and repeated notes to represent	More chirping birds
2:33	Orchestra. Return of a motivic fragment from the opening phrase now more legato and repeated in a sequence.	
2:45	Solo violin + basso continuo. More fast, repeated and oscillating notes	Final reference to birds and streams
2:58	Orchestra: ritornello. Forte for the first melodic phrase of the ritornello; last phrase ends piano	

4.7 MUSIC OF GEORGE FRIDERIC HANDEL (1685-1759)

George Frideric Handel was one of the superstars of the late Baroque period He was born the same year as one of our other Baroque superstars, Johann Sebastian Bach, not more than 150 miles away in Halle, Germany. His father was an attorney and wanted his son to follow in his footsteps, but Handel decided that he wanted to be a musician instead. With the help of a local nobleman, he persuaded his father to agree. After learning the basics of composition, Handel journeyed to Italy to learn to write opera. Italy, after all, was the home of opera, and opera was the most popular musical entertainment of the day. After writing a few operas, he took a job in London, England, where Italian opera was very much the rage, eventually establishing his own opera company and producing scores of Italian operas, which were initially very well received by the English public. After a decade or so, however, Italian opera in England imploded. Several opera companies there each competed for the public's business. The divas who sang the main roles and whom the public bought their tickets to see demanded high salaries. In 1728, a librettist name John Gay and a composer named Johann Pepusch premiered a new sort of opera in London called ballad opera. It was sung entirely in English and its music was based on folk tunes known by most inhabitants of the British Isles. For the English public, the majority of whom had been attending Italian opera without understanding the language in which it was sung, English language opera was a big hit. Both Handel's opera company

Figure 4.13 | Georg Friedrich Händel
Author | Philip Mercier
Source | Wikimedia Commons
License | Public Domain

and his competitors fought for financial stability, and Handel had to find other ways to make a profit. He hit on the idea of writing English oratorio.

Oratorio is sacred opera that is not staged. Like operas, they are relatively long works, often spanning over two hours when performed in entirety. Like opera, oratorios are entirely sung to orchestral accompaniment. They feature recitatives, arias, and choruses, just like opera. Most oratorios also tell the story of an important character from the Christian Bible. But oratorios are not acted out. Historically-speaking, this is the reason that they exist. During the Baroque period at sacred times in the Christian church year such as Lent, stage entertainment was prohibited. The idea was that during Lent, individuals should be looking inward and preparing themselves for the death and resurrection of Christ, and attending plays and operas would distract from that. Nevertheless, individuals still wanted entertainment, hence, oratorios. These oratorios would be performed as concerts not in the church but because they were not acted out, they were perceived as not having a "detrimental" effect on the spiritual lives of those in the audience. The first oratorios were performed in Italy; then they spread elsewhere on the continent and to England.

Handel realized how powerful ballad opera, sung in English, had been for the general population and started writing oratorios but in the English language. He used the same music styles as he had in his operas, only including more choruses. In no time at all, his oratorios were being lauded as some of the most popular performances in London.

His most famous oratorio is entitled ***Messiah*** and was first performed in 1741. About the life of Christ, it was written for a benefit concert to be held in Dublin, Ireland. Atypically, his librettist, took the words for the oratorio straight from the King James Version of the Bible instead of putting the story into his own words. Once in Ireland, Handel assembled solo singers as well as a chorus of musical amateurs to sing the many choruses he wrote for the oratorio. There it was popular, if not controversial. One of the soloists was a woman who was a famous actress. Some critics remarked that it was inappropriate for a woman who normally performed on the stage to be singing words from sacred scripture. Others objected to sacred scripture being sung in a concert instead of in church. Perhaps influenced by these opinions, ***Messiah*** was performed only a few times during the 1740s. Since the end of the eighteenth century, however, it has been performed more than almost any other composition of classical music. While these issues may not seem controversial to us today, they remind us that people still disagree about how sacred texts should be used and about what sort music should be used to set them.

We've included three numbers from Handel's ***Messiah*** as part of our discussion of this focus composition. We'll first listen to a recitative entitled "Comfort Ye" that is directly followed by an aria entitled "Every Valley." These two numbers are the second and third numbers in the oratorio. Then we'll listen to the Hallelujah Chorus, the most famous number from the composition that falls at the end of the second of the three parts of the oratorio.

LISTENING GUIDE

For audio, go to:
https://www.youtube.com/watch?v=GDEi38TxBME&feature=youtu.be
Tenor Anthony Rolfe Johnson with The Monteverdi Choir and the English Baroque Soloists and John Eliot Gardiner, Conductor

Composer: George Frideric Handel

Composition: "Comfort Ye" and "Every Valley" from *Messiah*

Date: 1741

Genre: accompanied recitative and aria from an oratorio

Form: accompanied recitative—through composed; aria—binary form AA'

Nature of Text: English language libretto quoting the Bible

Performing Forces: solo tenor and orchestra

What we want you to remember about this composition:

- As an oratorio, it uses the same styles and forms as operas but is not staged
- The aria is very virtuoso with its melismas, and alternates between orchestral ritornellos and solo sections

Other things to listen for:

- The accompanied recitative uses more instruments than standard basso continuo-accompanied recitative, but the vocal line retains the flexibility of recitative
- Motor rhythm in the aria
- In a major key
- In the aria, the second solo section is more ornamented than the first, as was often the custom.

Accompanied Recitative: "Comfort Ye"

Timing	Performing Forces, Melody, and Texture	Text and Form
0:00		Reduced orchestra playing *piano* repeated notes
0:13	Mostly stepwise, conjunct sung melody; Homophonic texture	Vocalist & light orchestral accompaniment: "Comfort Ye my people"

0:27	Orchestra and vocalist alternate phrases until the recitative ends	Vocalist and light orchestral accompaniment: Comfort ye my people says your God; speak ye comforter of Jerusalem; and cry upon....that her inquity is pardoned. A voice of him that cry-eth in the wilderness. Prepare ye the way for the Lord. Make straight in the desert a highway for our God
Aria: "Every Valley"		
Timing	**Performing Forces, Melody, and Texture**	**Text and Form**
2:22	Repeated motives; starts loud, ends with an echo	Orchestra plays ritornello
2:39	Soloist presents melodic phrase first heard in the ritornello and the orchestra echoes this phrase	Tenor and orchestra: Every valley shall be exalted
2:52	Long melisma on the word exalt-ed...repeats High note on mountain and low note on "low"	Tenor and orchestra: Shall be exalted And every mountain and hill made low
3:17	Repeated oscillation between two notes to represent crookedness; then one note is sustained on the word straight.	Tenor and orchestra: The crooked straight
3:23	Repeated oscillation between two notes to represent roughness; then one note is sustained on the word plain.	Tenor and orchestra: And the rough places plain
3:38	Melismatic descending sequence on the word "Plain"	Continued
3:53	Goes back to the beginning, but with even more ornamentation from the melismas	Tenor and Orchestra: "Every valley shall be exalted" (Repetition of text and music)
5:10	Repeats the music of the ritornello one final time	Orchestra: ritornello

LISTENING GUIDE		
For audio, go to: https://www.youtube.com/watch?v=ptBZwDYKA14&feature=youtu.be Performed by English Baroque Soloists and Monteverdi Choir, Conducted by John Eliot Gardiner		
Composer: George Frideric Handel		
Composition: "Hallelujah" from *Messiah*		
Date: 1741		
Genre: chorus from an oratorio		
Form: sectional; sections delineated by texture changes		
Nature of Text: English language libretto quoting the Bible		
Performing Forces: solo tenor and orchestra		
What we want you to remember about this composition: • It is for four-part chorus and orchestra • It uses a sectional form where sections are delineated by changes in texture		
Other things to listen for: • In a major key, using mostly major chords • Key motives repeat over and over, often in sequence		
Timing	**Performing Forces, Melody, and Texture**	**Text and Form**
0:00	Orchestra: Introduces main musical motive in a major key with a homophonic texture where parts of the orchestra play the melody and other voices provide the accompaniment	
0:09	Chorus + orchestra: Here the choir and the orchestra provide the melody and accompaniment of the homophonic texture	Hallejulah
0:26	Chorus + orchestra: Dramatic shift to monophonic with the voices and orchestra performing the same melodic line at the same time.	For the Lord God omnipotent reigneth

0:34	Chorus + orchestra: Homophonic texture, as before.	Hallelujah
0:38	Chorus + orchestra: Monophonic texture, as before.	For the Lord God omnipotent reigneth
0:45	Chorus + orchestra: Homophonic texture, as before.	Hallelujah
0:49	Chorus + orchestra: Texture shifts to non-imitative polyphonic with the initial entrance of the sopranos, then the tenors, then the altos.	For the Lord God omnipotent reigneth
1:17	Chorus + orchestra: Homophonic texture, as before.	The Kingdom of this world is begun
1:36	Chorus + orchestra: Imitative polyphony starts in basses, then is passed to tenors, then to the altos, and then to the sopranos.	And he shall reign for ever and ever
1:57	Chorus + orchestra: Monophonic texture, as before.	King of Kings
2:01	Chorus + orchestra: Homophonic texture, as before.	Forever, and ever hallelujah hallelujah
2:05	Chorus + orchestra: Each entrance is sequenced higher; the women sing the monophonic repeated melody motive Monophony alternating with homophony	And Lord of Lords...Repeated alternation of the monophonic king of kings and lord of lords with homophonic for ever and ever
2:36	Chorus + orchestra: Homophonic texture	King of kings and lord of lords
2:40	Chorus + orchestra: Polyphonic texture (with some imitation)	And he shall reign for ever and ever
2:52	Chorus + orchestra: The alternation of monophonic and homophonic textures.	King of kings and lord of lords alternating with "for ever and ever"
3:01	Chorus + orchestra: Mostly homophonic	And he shall reign...Hallelujah

Focus Composition:

Movements from Handel's Water Music Suite

Although Handel is perhaps best known today for his operas and oratorios, he also wrote a lot instrumental music, from concertos like Vivaldi wrote to a kind of music called the suite. Suites were compositions having many contrasting movements. The idea was to provide diverse music in one composition that might be interesting for playing and listening. They could be written for solo instruments such as the harpsichord or for orchestral forces, in which case we call them orchestral suites. They often began with movements called overtures and modeled after the overtures played before operas. Then they typically consisted of **stylized dance** movements. By stylized dance, we mean a piece of music that sounds like a dance but that was not designed for dancing. In other words, a stylized dance uses the distinct characteristics of a dance and would be recognized as sounding like that dance but might be too long or too complicated to be danced to.

Figure 4.14 | An illustration from Kellom Thomlinson's Art of Dancing, London, 1735
Author | Kellom Tomlinson
Source | Wikimedia Commons
License | Public Domain

Dancing was very popular in the Baroque period, as it had been in the Middle Ages and Renaissance. We have several dancing textbooks from the Baroque period that mapped out the choreography for each dance. Some of the most popular dances included the saraband, gigue, minuet, and bourée. The saraband was a slow dance in triple meter, whereas the gigue (or jig) was a very fast dance with triple subdivisions of the beats. The minuet was also in triple time but danced at a much more stately tempo. The bourrée, on the other hand, was danced at a much faster tempo, and always in duple meter.

When King George I asked Handel to compose music for an evening's diversion, the suite was the genre to which Handel turned. This composition was for an event that started at 8pm on Wednesday the seventeenth of July, 1717. King George I and his noble guests would launch a barge ride up the Thames River to Chelsea. After disembarking and spending some time on shore, they re-boarded at 11pm and returned via the river to Whitehall Palace, from whence they came. A contemporary newspaper remarked that the king and his guests occupied one barge while another held about fifty musicians and reported that the king liked the music so much that he asked it to be repeated three times.

Many of the movements that were played for the occasion were written down and eventually published as three suites of music, each in a different key. You have two stylized dance movements from one of these suites here, a bourée and a minuet. We do not know with any certainty in what order these movements were played or even exactly who played them on that evening in 1717, but when the music was published in the late eighteenth century, it was set for two trumpets, two horns, two oboes, first violins, second violins, violas, and a basso continuo, which included a bassoon, cello(s), and harpsichord.

The bourée, as noted above, is fast and in duple time. The minuet is in a triple meter and taken at a more moderate tempo. They use repeated strains or sections of melodies based on repeated motives. As written in the score, as well as interpreted today in the referenced recording, different sections of the orchestra—the strings, woodwinds, and sometimes brass instruments—each get a time to shine, providing diverse timbres and thus musical interest. Both are good examples of binary form.

Figure 4.15 | Westminster Bridge from the North on Lord Mayor's Day
Author | Canaletto
Source | Wikimedia Commons
License | Public Domain

LISTENING GUIDE
For audio, go to: https://www.youtube.com/watch?v=58f6NVMSSXA The English Concert, on period instruments. Trevor Pinnock, conductor. [Bourée at 8:26]
Composer: George Frideric Handel
Composition: Bourée from *Water Music*
Date: 1717
Genre: stylized dance movement from a suite
Form: Binary form, AABB, performed here three times; B is twice as long as A
Performing Forces: Baroque orchestra: according to the musical score, 2 trumpets, 2 horns, 2 oboes, 1 bassoons, 1st violins, 2nd violins, violas, cello, and basso continuo (the cellos play the same music as the bassoon)
What we want you to remember about this composition: • It's a stylized dance. • It's in duple time and starts with a pick up (a note that appears before the first beat of the measure). • It has a relatively fast tempo.

Other things to listen for:

- The A section is half the length of the B section; each section is repeated
- The strings and woodwind instruments alternate taking the lead in this performance
- The cello, bassoon, and harpsichord make up the basso continuo

Timing	Performing Forces, Melody, and Texture	Text and Form
45:23	Strings, basso continuo, trumpet Short phrase A of four measures, repeated	A, repeated
45:23	Same instruments play an answer phrase B of eight measures with descending motivic sequences	B
45:41	Repeated	B
45:50	Flute, oboe, bassoon, trumpets, strings Play the same A phrase as above	A
45:57	Same instruments play the B phrase	B
46:05	Repeated	B
46:13	Strings, trumpets, flute, oboe bassoon, and basso continuo play the A phrase.	A, repeated
46:22	Same instruments play the B phrase.	B
46:30	Repeated	B

LISTENING GUIDE
For audio, go to: https://www.youtube.com/watch?v=58f6NVMSSXA The English Concert, on period instruments. Trevor Pinnock, conductor.
Composer: George Frideric Handel
Composition: Minuet from *Water Music*
Date: 1717
Genre: Stylized dance from a suite
Form: AA BB, to be performed three times according to the score

Performing Forces: Baroque orchestral: according to the musical score, 2 trumpets, 2 horns, 2 oboes, 1 bassoons, 1st violins, 2nd violins, violas, cello, and basso continuo (the cellos play the same music as the bassoon)		
What we want you to remember about this composition: • It is a stylized dance • It is in triple meter and at a moderate and stately tempo		
Other things to listen for: • It uses repeated sections or strains, A and B (A is half the length of B) • We don't know exactly which instruments would have played it but probably different families of instruments would have taken different sections to provide contrast		
Timing	**Performing Forces, Melody, and Texture**	**Text and Form**
50:55	Strings, trumpets: triple meter in a major key; Melody starts with repeated notes and is very conjunct; some ornaments on the first beats of some measures	A
51:11	Repeated	A
51:21	Starts with repeated notes in just strings, oboes, and bassoon and ascends and then the trumpets and horns join: melody ascends and descends, mostly by step; trumpet becomes more prominent new phrases with a three-note motive that repeatedly ascends and then descends by step	B
51:44	As with B above	B
52:07	Flute, oboes, bassoons, horns, trumpets, basso continuo including cello play the opening strain	A
52:17	Repeated	A
52:29	First just double reeds, then adding horns	B
52:50	Repeated	B
53:13	Full orchestra	A

53:24	Repeated	A
53:36	First strings and then the full orchestra	B
53:57	First strings and then the full orchestra	B

4.8 MUSIC OF JOHANN SEBASTIAN BACH (1685-1750)

Figure 4.16 | Portrait of Johann Sebastian Bach
Author | Elias Gottlob Haussmann
Source | Wikimedia Commons
License | Public Domain

Johann Sebastian Bach (B. 1685-1750) During the seventeenth century, many families passed their trades down to the next generation so that future generations may continue to succeed in a vocation. This practice also held true for Johann Sebastian Bach. Bach was born into one of the largest musical families in Eisenach of the central Germany region known as Thuringia. He was orphaned at the young age of ten and raised by an older brother in Ohrdruf, Germany. Bach's older brother was a church organist who prepared the young Johann for the family vocation. The Bach family, though great in number, were mostly of the lower musical stature of town's musicians and/or Lutheran Church organist. Only a few of the Bachs had achieved the accomplished stature of court musicians, but the Bach family members were known and respected in the region. Bach also in turn taught four of his sons who later became leading composers for the next generation.

Bach received his first professional position at the age of eighteen in Arnstadt, Germany as a church organist. Bach's first appointment was not a good philosophical match for the young aspiring musician. He felt his musical creativity and growth was being hindered and his innovation and originality unappreciated. The congregation seemed sometimes confused and felt the melody lost in Bach's writings. He met and married his first wife while in Arnstadt, marrying Maria Barbara (possibly his cousin) in 1707. They had seven children together; two of their sons, Wilhelm Friedemann and Carl Phillipp Emmanuel, as noted above, became major composers for the next generation. Bach later was offered and accepted another position in Műhlhausen.

He continued to be offered positions that he accepted and so advanced in his professional position/title up to a court position in Weimer where he served nine years from 1708-1717. This position had a great number of responsibilities. Bach was required to write church music for the ducal church (the church for the duke that hired Bach), to perform as church organist, and to write organ music and sacred choral pieces for choir, in addition to writing sonatas and concertos (instrumental music) for court performance for his duke's events. While at this post, Bach's fame as an organist and the popularity of his organ works grew significantly.

Bach soon wanted to leave for another offered court musician position, and his request to be released was not received well. This difficulty attests to the work relations of court musicians and their employers. Dukes expected and demanded loyalty from their court musician employees. Because musicians were looked upon somewhat as court property, the duke of the court often felt betrayed when a court musician wanted to leave. Upon hearing of Bach's desire to leave and work for another court for the prince of Cöthen, the Duke at Weimer refused to accept Bach's resignation and threw Bach into jail for almost a month for submitting his dismissal request before relenting and letting Bach go to the Cöthen court.

The Prince at Cöthen was very interested in instrumental music. The Prince was a developing amateur musician who did not appreciate the elaborate church music of Bach's past; instead, the Prince desired instrumental court music, so Bach focused on composing instrumental music. In his five year (1717-1723) tenure at Cöthen, Bach produced an abundance of clavier music, six concerti grossi honoring the Margrave of Brandenburg, suites, concertos and sonatas. While at Cöthen (1720), Bach's first wife Maria Barbara died. He later married a young singer, Anna Magdalena and they had thirteen children together. Half of these children did not survive infancy. Two of Bach's sons birthed by Anna, Johann Christoph and Johann Christian, also went on to become two of the next generation's foremost composers.

At the age of thirty-eight, Bach assumed the position as cantor of the St. Thomas Lutheran Church in Leipzig, Germany. Several other candidates were considered for the Leipzig post, including the famous composer Telemann who refused the offer. Some on the town council felt that, since the most qualified candidates did not accept the offer, the less talented applicant would have to be hired. It was in this negative working atmosphere that Leipzig hired its greatest cantor and musician. Bach worked in Leipzig for twenty-seven years (1723-1750).

Leipzig served as a hub of Lutheran church music for Germany. Not only did Bach have to compose and perform, he also had to administer and organize music for all the churches in Leipzig. He was required to teach in choir school in addition to all of his other responsibilities. Bach composed, copied needed parts, directed, rehearsed, and performed a cantata on a near weekly basis. Cantatas are major church choir works that involve soloist, choir, and orchestra. Cantatas have several movements and last for fifteen to thirty minutes. Cantatas are still performed today by church choirs, mostly on special occasions such as Easter, Christmas, and other festive church events.

Bach felt that the rigors of his Leipzig position were too bureaucratic and restrictive due to town and church politics. Neither the town nor the church really ever appreciated Bach. The church and town council refused to pay Bach for all the extra demands/responsibilities of his position and thought basically that they would merely tolerate their irate cantor, even though Bach was the best organist in Germany. Several of Bach's contemporary church musicians felt his music was not according to style and types considered current, a feeling which may have resulted from professional jealousy. One contemporary critic felt Bach was "old Fashioned."

Beyond this professional life, Bach had a personal life centered on his large family. He had seven children by his first wife, one by a cousin, and thirteen by his second wife, Anna Magdalena, who was also a singer. He wrote a little home school music curriculum entitled *The Notebook of Anna Magdalena Bach.* At home, the children were taught the fundamentals of music, music copying, performance skills, and other musical content. Bach's children utilized their learned music copying skills in writing the parts from the required weekly cantatas that Sebastian was required to compose. Bach's deep spirituality is evident and felt in the meticulous attention to detail of Bach's scared works, such as his cantatas. Indeed, the spirituality of Bach's Passions and his Mass are unequalled by other composers.

Bach did not travel much, with the exception of being hired as a consultant with construction contracts to install organs in churches. He would be asked to test the organs and to be part of their inauguration ceremony and festivities. The fee for such a service ranged from a cord of wood or possibly to a barrel of wine. In 1747, Bach went on one of these professional expeditions to the Court of Frederick the Great in Potsdam, an expedition that proved most memorable. Bach's son, Carl Philipp Emanuel, served as the accompanist for the monarch of the court who played the flute. Upon Bach's arrival, the monarch showed Bach a new collection of pianos—pianos were beginning to replace harpsichords in homes of society. With Bach's permission, the king presented him with a theme/melody that Bach based one of his incredible themes for the evening's performance. Upon Bach's return to Leipzig, he further developed the king's theme, adding a trio sonata, and entitled it *The Musical Offering* attesting to his highest respect for the monarch and stating that the King should be revered.

Bach later became blind but continued composing through dictating to his children. He had also already begun to organize his compositions into orderly sets of organ chorale preludes, preludes and fugues for harpsichord, and organ fugues. He started to outline and recapitulate his conclusive thoughts about Baroque music, forms, performance, composition, fugal techniques, and genres. This knowledge and innovation appears in such works as *The Art of Fugue*—a collection of fugues all utilizing the same subject left incomplete due to his death—the thirty-three *Goldberg Variations* for harpsichord, and the *Mass* in B minor.

Bach was an intrinsically motivated composer who composed music for himself and a small group of student and close friends. This type of composition was a break from the previous norms of composers. Even after his death, Bach's music was ignored nor valued by the musical public. It was, however, appreciated and admired by great composers such as Mozart and Beethoven.

Over the course of his lifetime, Bach produced major works, including *The Well-Tempered Clavier* (forty-eight preludes and fugues in all major and minor keys), three sets of harpsichord suites (six movements in each set), the *Goldberg Variations,* many organ fugues and chorale preludes (chorale preludes are organ solos based upon church hymns—several by Luther), the *Brandenburg Concertos,* and composite works such as *A Musical Offering* and *The Art of Fugue,* an excess of 200 secular and sacred cantatas, two Passions from the gospels of St. Matthew and St. John, a *Christmas Oratorio,* a *Mass* in B minor, and several chorale/hymn harmonizations, concertos, and other orchestral suites and sonatas.

Focus Composition:

Bach, *A Mighty Fortress is Our God* Cantata, BWV 80

Bach's *A Mighty Fortress is Our God* cantata, like most of his cantatas, has several movements. It opens with a polyphonic chorus that presents the first verse of the hymn. After several other movements (including recitatives, arias, and duets), the cantata closes with the final verse of the hymn arranged for four parts. For a comparison of cantatas, oratorios and opera, please see the chart earlier in this chapter. For more information on cantatas go to:

http://www.britannica.com/art/cantata-music

Bach composed some of this music when he was still in Weimar (BWV 80A) and then revised and expanded the cantata for performance in Leipzig around 1730 (BWV 80B), with additional re-workings between 1735 and 1740 (BWVA 80).

LISTENING GUIDE
For audio, go to: http://www.baroquecds.com/723Cantata80.mp3 Performed by the Bach Chorus & Orchestra of the Amsterdam Philharmonic Society / A. Vandernoot
Composer: Johann Sebastian Bach
Composition: *Ein feste Burg ist unser Gott* translated to *A Mighty Fortress is Our God* from Bach Cantata 80 (BWV 80)
Date: 1715-1740
Genre: First-movement polyphonic chorus and final movement chorale from a church cantata
Form: sectional, divided by statements of Luther's original melody line in sustained notes in the trumpets, oboes, and cellos.
Nature of Text: For a translation from the original German to Enligsh, go to: http://www.bach-cantatas.com/BWV80.htm
Performing Forces: choir and orchestra (vocal soloists appear elsewhere in the cantata)
What we want you to remember about this composition: • This is representative of Bach's mastery of taking a Martin Luther hymn and arranging it in imitative polyphony for all four voice parts and instrumental parts

Other things to listen for:

- them to the first verse or strophe of the hymn. He weaves these new melody lines into a beautiful polyphonic choral work.
- Most of the time the instruments double (or play the same music as) the four voice parts.
- He also has the trumpets, oboes, and cellos divide up Luther's exact melody into nine phrases. They present the first phrase after the first section of the chorus and then subsequent phrases throughout the chorus. When they play the original melody, they do so in canon: the trumpets and oboes begin and then the cellos enter after about a measure.
- Also listen to see if you can hear the **augmentation** in the work. The original tune is performed in this order of the voices: Tenors, Sopranos, Tenors, Sopranos, Basses, Altos, Tenors, Sopranos, and then the Tenors.

Figure 4.17 | *Ein' feste Burg ist unser Gott* Sheet Music
Author | User "Drboisclair"
Source | Wikimedia Commons
License | Public Domain

Figure 4.18 | Harpsichord
Author | Gérard Janot
Source | Wikimedia Commons
License | CC BY-SA 3.0

Bach was born into a century that saw great advancements in keyboard instruments and keyboard music. The keyboard instruments included harpsichord, clavichord, and organ. The **harpsichord** is a keyboard instrument whose strings are put into motion by pressing a key that facilitates a plucking of a string by quills of feathers (instead of being struck by hammers like the piano). The tone produced on the harpsichord is bright but cannot be sustained without re-striking the key. Dynamics are very limited on the harpsichord. In order for the tone to continue on the harpsichord, keys are replayed, trills are utilized, embellishments are added, and chords are broken into arpeggios. Harpsichords are used a great deal for counterpoint in the middle voices.

During the early Baroque era, the clavichord remained the instrument of choice for the home; indeed, it is said that Bach preferred it to the harpsichord.

It produced its tone by a means of keys attached to metal blades that strike the strings. As we will see in the next chapter, by the end of the 1700s, the piano would replace the harpsichord and clavichord as the instrument of choice for residences.

Figure 4.19 | Clavichord
Author | Gérard Janot
Source | Wikimedia Commons
License | CC BY-SA 3.0

Bach was best known as a virtuoso organist, and he had the opportunity to play on some of the most advanced pipe organs of his day. Sound is produced on the organ with the depression of one or more of the keys which activates a mechanism that opens pipes of a certain length and pitch through which wind from a wind chest rushes. The length and material of the pipe determines the tones produced. Levers called stops provide further options for different timbres. The Baroque pipe organ operated on relatively low air pressure as compared to today's organs, resulting in a relatively thin transparent tone and volume.

Most Baroque organs had at least two keyboards, called manuals (after the Latin word for hand), and a pedal board, played by the two feet. The presence of multiple keyboards and a pedal board made the organ an ideal instrument for polyphony. Each of the keyboards and the pedal board could be assigned different stops and thus could produce different timbres and even dynamic levels, which helped define voices of the polyphonic texture. Bach composed many of his chorale preludes and fugues for the organ.

Figure 4.20 | Pipe Organ
Author | Gérard Janot
Source | Wikimedia Commons
License | Public Domain

Focus Composition:

Bach, "Little" Fugue in G Minor (BWV 578)

The fugue is one of the most spectacular and magnificent achievements of the Baroque period. During this era of fine arts innovation, scientific research, natural laws, and systematic approaches to imitative polyphony were further developed and standardized. Polyphony first emerged in the late Middle Ages. Independent melodic lines overlapped and were woven. In the Renaissance, the polyphony was further developed by a greater weaving of the independent melodic lines. The Baroque composers, under the influence of science, further organized it into a system—more on this later. The term fugue comes from the Latin word *"fuga"* that means running away or to take flight. The fugue is a contrapuntal (polyphonic) piece for a set number of musicians, usually three of four. The musical theme of a fugue is called the **subject**.

You may think of a fugue as a gossip party. The subject (of gossip) is introduced in one corner of the room between to people. Another person in the room then begins repeating the gossip while the original conversation continues. Then another person picks up on the story and begins repeating the now third-hand news and it then continues a fourth time. A new observer walking into the room will hear bits and pieces from four conversations at one time—each repeating the original subject (gossip). This is how a fugue works. Fugues begin with an exposition. This is when the subject is introduced until the original subject has been played or sung in all the voices or parts. Most fugues are in the four standard voices: soprano, alto, tenor, and bass. We will refer to the parts in these voices for both voices and instruments.

At the beginning of the fugue, any of the four voices can begin with the subject. Then another voice starts with the subject at a time dictated in the music while the first voice continues to more material. The imitation is continued through all the voices. The exposition of the fugue is over when all the voices complete the initial subject.

Voice 1	Soprano	Subject-continues in a counter subject
Voice 2	Alto	Subject-continues in a counter subject
Voice 3	Tenor	Subject-continues in a counter subject
Voice 4	Bass	Subject-continues in a counter subject

After the exposition is completed, it may be repeated in a different order of voices or it may continue with less weighted entrances at varying lengths known as episodes. This variation provides a little relaxation or relief from the early regiment systematic polyphony of the exposition. In longer fugues, the episodes are followed by a section in another key with continued overlapping of the subject. This episode and modulation can continue to repeat until they return to the original key.

Fugues are performed as a prelude to traditional worship on the pipe organ and are quite challenging to perform by the organist. Hands, fingers, and feet must all be controlled independently by the single organist and all at the same time. Often in non-fugal music, this type of polyphony is briefly written into a piece of music as an insert, called a fugato or fugato section. When voices overlap in a fugue, it is called **stretto** (similar to strata). When the original voice continues after the second voice jumps in, the first voice is said to be singing the **countersubject**. The development of musical themes or subjects by lengthening or multiplying the durations of the notes or pitches is called **augmentation**. The shortening or dividing the note and pitch durations is called **diminution**. Both augmentation and diminution are utilized in the development of the musical subjects in fugues and in theme development in other genres. The "turning up-side down" of a musical line from an ascending passage to a descending passage is called **inversion.**

Let's listen to one of Bach's most famous fugues. You may immediately recognize the piece from your past. The *Little Fugue in G Minor* is Bach's most famous organ piece.

LISTENING GUIDE
For live performance, go to: https://www.youtube.com/watch?v=PhRa3REdozw To Listen and view the score, go to: https://www.youtube.com/watch?v=z6Kq6ow-AXk
Composer: Johann Sebastian Bach
Composition: *Organ Fugue in G Minor* (BWR 578)
Date: circa 1709
Genre: Organ Fugue
Form: Fugue
Nature of Text: Bach was able to take the earlier vocal polyphony of the renaissance period and apply it to the organ fugue. This is regarded as one of Bach's great achievements.
Performing Forces: Organ
What we want you to remember about this composition: • Listen to how Bach weaves and overlaps the subject throughout the piece.
Other things to listen for: • The subject (tune) is introduced in the highest voices and then is imitated in each lower voice in order: soprano, alto, tenor and then bass in the pedals. After the exposition is completed in the bass pedals, the subject is introduced in the first voice. Upon the entrance of the second layer, the first voice goes into a counter subject. Just before the subject is introduced five more times, it is preceded by a brief episode. In each episode the subject is not played in its entirety. • Even though the fugue is in G minor, the piece ends with a major chord, a practice utilized during the Baroque period. Major chords were thought more conclusive than minor chords.

Timing	Performing Forces, Melody, and Texture
00:00	Subject in soprano voice alone, minor key
00:18	Subject in alto, countersubject in running notes in soprano
00:42	Subject in tenor, countersubject above it; brief episode follows
01:01	Subject in bass (pedals), countersubject in tenor
01:17	Brief episode
01:28	Subject begins in tenor, continues in soprano
01:48	Brief episode, running notes in a downward sequence
01:56	Subject in alto, major key; countersubject in soprano

02:13	Episode in major, upward leaps and running notes
02:25	Subject in bass (pedals), major key, countersubject and long trill above it
02:42	Longer episode
03:00	Subject in soprano, minor key, countersubject below it
03:16	Extended episode
03:47	Subject in bass (pedals), countersubject in soprano; fugue ends with major chord
04:12	End (Source: http://www.austincc.edu/mwoodruf/music/Bach.htm)

4.9 CHAPTER SUMMARY

As we have seen, the Baroque period introduced the rise of musical superstar composers such as G. F. Handel and his contemporary, J. S. Bach, who, although he may have not been the most famous musician of his day, since then has become one of the most appreciated composers of Western classical music. The period between roughly 1600 and 1750 also saw the birth of genres such as opera, oratorio, cantata, concerto, and fugue. In many cases these new genres were propelled by a focus on instrumental music written for the increasingly sophisticated instruments such as harpsichords and organs of the keyboard family. The violin family also flourished and formed the basis for a new ensemble: the orchestra.

Genres such as opera, oratorio, and concerto will continue to be important in the Classical Period, as will keyboard music. Orchestral music will become even more important, with the opera overtures and orchestral suites of the Baroque Period giving way to the symphonies of the Classical period.

4.10 GLOSSARY

Antiphonal – A genre of sacred music featuring multiple choirs, or a choir that has been divided into different groups that can perform call and responses.

Aria – Homophonic compositions featuring a solo singer over orchestral accompaniment. homophonic compositions featuring a solo singer over accompaniment. Arias are very melodic primarily utilized in operas, cantatas, and oratorios.

Basso continuo – continuous realization of harmony throughout a musical piece, usually by a harpsichord and/or cello. The Basso continuo provides a framework/template for harmonic accompaniments.

Cantata – A composite major church choir form from the Baroque period that involves soloist, choir, and orchestra. Cantatas have several movements and last for fifteen to thirty minutes. Cantatas are performed without staging but they utilize narration, arias, recitatives, choruses and smaller vocal ensembles.

Chorale – Originally the result from the German protestant church's reformation, the chorale is the hymn (tune) is a four part homophonic work that is sung by the church congregation. Chorales became the foundation for several cantatas and chorale preludes for organ.

Concerto – A musical composition for a soloist and orchestra.

Concerto Grosso – a musical composition for a small group of soloists and orchestra.

Cori spezzati – A divided choir that is utilized to perform in a polychoral style—able to perform "call and response". Large churches were designed with multiple choir seating sections to perform such works.

Fugue – perfected by J.S. Bach during the baroque period, fugues are a form written in an imitative contrapuntal style in multiple parts. Fugues are based upon their original tune that is called the **subject.** The subject is then imitated and overlapped by the other parts by the called the answer, countersubject, stretto, and episode

Homophony – Music where the melody is supported by a chordal accompaniment the move in the same rhythm. Homophony is generally the opposite of polyphony where the voices imitative and weave with each other.

Libretto – The text or actual words of an opera, musical, cantata or oratorio, written or compiled by a librettist

Melisma – More than one note sung during one syllable of the text. The melismatic style was used extensively in gregorian chant.

Motor rhythm – The constant repeated subdivision of the beat. The motor rhythm provide unity and stability within the musical piece.

Movement – a subsection or independent section/piece of a larger work. (Ex. A symphony is divided into movements.)

Opera – A staged musical drama for voices and orchestra. Operas are fully blocked and performed in costume with sets. Operas utilize arias and recitatives without no narration.

Oratorio – a major work with religious or contemplative character for solo voices, chorus and orchestra. Oratorios do not utilize blocking, costumes, or scenery.

Polychoral (style) – a compositional style where the chorus/choir is divided into two or more groups that can perform with or independently for each other (see antiphonal).

Polyphony – Two or more melodic voices or instruments combine weaving together.

Program music – instrumental Music written to portray an non-musical idea. A descriptive piece.

Recitative – An operatic number using speech-like melodies and rhythms, performing using a flexible tempo, to sparse accompaniment, most often provided by the basso continuo. Recitatives are often performed between arias and have texts that tend to be descriptive and narrating.

Ritornello Form – Repeated unifying sections founds in between the solo sections of a concerto grosso

Sectional form – A piece where distinct sections can be identified due to changes in texture and other musical compositional techniques.

Solo – A musical piece that features on musician either with or without accompaniment. In larger scored piece, the solo is the main part that should be brought out while performing.

Sonata – a musical composition in multiple movements for solo instrument, usually accompanied by the piano.

Stylized dance – piece of music that sounds like a dance but that was not designed for dancing. In other words, a stylized dance uses the distinct characteristics of a dance and would be recognized as sounding like that dance but might be too long or too complicated to be danced to.

Subject – The main melody or tune of a fugue.

Suite – A multi-movement instrumental musical composition of baroque music—usually in dance form.

Terraced dynamics – Used during the Baroque period, this is where the different sections have a piece of music have a set volume unique for that particular section. The next section may be written to be performed at another volume.

Through-composed – Songs or musical selections where new music is composed for each stanza or section with no repetition.

Tutti – Where the entire musical ensemble performs together as a whole as opposed to a soloist.

Word painting – the depiction of specific images from the text by vocal music. If the text refers to quickly running up a hill, the melody will ascend quickly to portray running up a hill musically.

5 Music of the Classical Period

Jeff Kluball and Elizabeth Kramer

5.1 OBJECTIVES

1. Demonstrate knowledge of historical and cultural contexts of the classical period
2. Recognize musical performing forces (voices, instruments, and ensembles), styles, composers, and genres of the classical period
3. Aurally identify selected music of Haydn, Mozart, and Beethoven and explain how it interacts with forms of the day

5.2 KEY TERMS AND INDIVIDUALS

- American War for Independence
- cadenza
- chamber music
- coda
- concerto
- cotton gin
- da capo
- first-movement concerto form/double-exposition form
- French Revolution
- hemiola
- Industrial Revolution
- Jean-Jacques Rousseau
- Joseph Haydn
- Ludwig van Beethoven
- minuet and trio form
- Napoléon Bonaparte
- opera buffa
- pizzicato
- rondo
- scherzo
- sonata
- sonata form (exposition, development, recapitulation)
- steam engine
- string quartet
- Symphony
- ternary form
- The Enlightenment

- theme and variation form
- Thomas Paine
- Voltaire
- Wolfgang Amadeus Mozart

5.3 INTRODUCTION AND HISTORICAL CONTEXT

Of all the musical periods, the Classical period is the shortest, spanning less than a century. Its music is dominated by three composers whose works are still some of the best known of all Western art music: Joseph Haydn (1732-1809), Wolfgang Amadeus Mozart (1756-1791), and Ludwig van Beethoven (1770-1827). Although born in different European regions, all three spent a substantial amount of time in Vienna, Austria, which might be considered the European musical capital of the time.

Music scholars have referred to this time as the Classical period in music for several reasons. For one, the music of Haydn, Mozart, and Beethoven has served as the model for most composers after their time and is still played today; in this way, the music is "classic" in that it has provided an exemplar and has stood the test of time. As we will also see, this music has often been perceived as emulating the balance and portion of ancient Greek and Roman art, the time period to which the word "classical" is affixed within literature and art history, as well as the wider field of history.

Our use of the Classical period to refer to music of roughly 1750 to 1815, however, should not be confused with our broader use of the term "classical music" to refer to art music (music that does not otherwise fall within the spheres of popular music or folk music).

Beginning towards the end of the 16th century, citizens in Europe became skeptical of traditional politics, governance, wealth distribution, and the aristocracy. Philosophers and theorists across Europe began to questioning these norms and issues and began suggesting instead that humanity could benefit from change. Publications and scientific discoveries of these thinkers proving and understanding many of nature's laws spurred the paradigm shift of logic referred to as the Age of Reason, or the Enlightenment.

The seeds for the Enlightenment can be found in England in approximately the 1680s. In that decade, Newton published *Principia Mathematica* and John Locke published his "Essay Concerning Human Understanding." These two works provided the philosophical, mathematical, and scientific foundation for the Enlightenment's great developments. Locke stressed that knowledge is gained through accumulated life experience rather than by acquired outside truth. Newton's mathematics and optical theory showed that humans can observe, study, define, and test the world around them and can also mathematically measure and prove natural occurrences.

Besides Locke and Newton, Enlightenment thinkers included Voltaire, Montesquieu, Jean-Jacque Rousseau, Benjamin Franklin, and Immanuel Kant. Their works especially stressed improving humanity's condition through the use of reason and common sense in order to provide liberty and justice for all. Many Enlightenment thinkers challenged blind and unconditional following of the authority of religious traditions and institutions and emphasized what they saw as "universal human goods and rights." They believed that if humankind would simply act with common sense—found in ideas such as "the golden rule"—then societies might advance with greater universal justice and liberty.

Figure 5.1 | Benjamin Franklin, 1759
Author | Benjamin Wilson
Source | Wikimedia Commons
License | Public Domain

Being able to solve and understand many of the mysteries of the universe in a quantifiable manner using math and reason, was empowering. Much of the educated middle class applied these learned principles to improve society. Enlightenment ideals lead to political revolutions throughout the Western world. Governmental changes such as Britain's embrace of constitutional democratic form of government and later the United States of America's establishment of democratic republic completely changed the outlook of the function of a nation/state. The overall well-being and prosperity of all in society became the mission of governance.

Up until the mid-1700s art, including music, was under the direct control or patronage of the monarchy/aristocracy, the class whose unquestioned rule was founded on divine hereditary right. The arts were their (and the church's) privilege, luxury, and adornment for generations to come. In its infancy, the Enlightenment's power shift toward the middle class was neither perceived nor anticipated by those in power. America's successful revolution against England landed a devastating blow to the doctrine of the divine ruling rights of kings. Shortly afterward, the ensuing French Revolution had an unintentional impact on the arts and is one of the greatest influences on Western classical music.

Artists and architects of the second half of the eighteenth century looked to classical antiquity as its model; their work is referred to as neoclassical. You can see this interest when one compares the Parthenon in Athens to the columns of the White House. While in power, aristocrats and their wealthy peers exalted the Hellenism that protected them from getting too involved in the current issues of life. The aristocrats saw the ancient Roman gods, heroes, and kings as semblances of themselves. They viewed themselves in the same light as super humans entitled to rule, possess great wealth, and be powerful. This detachment shaped their relationship with the arts in architecture and the visual arts. The rising middle class, on the contrary, viewed and interpreted neoclassical arts as representations of Roman and Greek city-states. This view assisted their resolve to rebel against the tyrants and abolish despotism. Here musical terminology diverges from that used by art historians (Neoclassicism in music would have to wait for the 20th century). As we have few musical exemplars from classical antiquity and as the music of Haydn, Mozart, and Beethoven would become the model for nineteenth century music, music historians have referred to this period as a time of Musical Classicism.

The mid and second half of the 18th century saw a revolutionary political and economic shift in Europe. Here the dramatic paramount shift of power from the aristocracy to the middle class began and strengthened. The wealth of the middle class had been expanding due the growing capitalism from the Industrial Revolution. This revolution resulted from a series of momentous inventions of the mid-1700s, including the Watt Steam Engine, James Hargreaves's spinning jenny, Edmund Cartwright's power loom, and Eli Whitney's cotton gin.

The following decades witnessed great scientific achievements and discoveries including: electricity by Benjamin Franklin, medical smallpox vaccination by Edward Jenner, the discovery of oxygen by Joseph Priestly, the advancement of the mechanistic view of the universe by Pierre-Simon Laplace, and the invention of the voltaic pile (battery) by Alessandro Volta Pierre Laplace (b. 1749-1827) a gifted and talented scientist and mathematician, felt that due to scientific explanation for the planets, their motion, and possibly how they began, humans no longer had any need for God. This mindset even further reduces the influence of the church on society and music.

During the enlightenment, the burgeoning middle class became a major market for art superseding the aristocracy as the principal consumer of music and art. This market shift facilitated a great demand for new innovations in the humanities. While the increased literacy of the middle class led to the proliferation of newspapers, periodicals, and novels throughout Western Europe. These sources provide us with reviews of concerts and published music and capture eighteenth century impressions of and responses to music.

5.3.1 The Visual Arts and Architecture

The visual arts developed two major styles in the Enlightenment. Both are representative of the dualism found in the arts during the classical era. As the aristocracy tried to adhere to the Greek and Roman mythological antiquity, artists such as the painter Jacques-Louis David (b.1748-1835), of the French revolution adorned his canvases with themes of Roman and Athenian democracy. David's paintings were admired by Thomas Jefferson, but David's painting ***The Death of Marat*** (1793) received particular praise. Marat, to whom the painting refers, is the murdered Jean-Paul Marat, an influential French revolutionary leader. Marat's previous influence paired with his murder and David's painting instantly transposed him into a political martyr. David's painting thus became a symbol of sacrifice in the name of the republic.[1]

Architecture in the late eighteenth century leaned toward the clean lines of ancient buildings such as the Athenian Parthenon and away from the highly ornate decorative accents of Baroque and Rococo design. One might also argue that the music of Haydn, Mozart, and early Beethoven aspires toward a certain simplicity and calmness stemming from ancient Greek art.

1 "Jacques-Louis David." *Biography.com*. A&E Television Networks, n.d. Web. 18 December 2015.

5.3.2 Music in Late Eighteenth Century

The three most important composers of the Classical period were Joseph Haydn, Wolfgang Amadeus Mozart, and Ludwig van Beethoven. Although they were born in different places, all three composers spent the last years of their lives in Vienna, Austria, a city which might be considered the musical capitol of the Classical period (see map below).

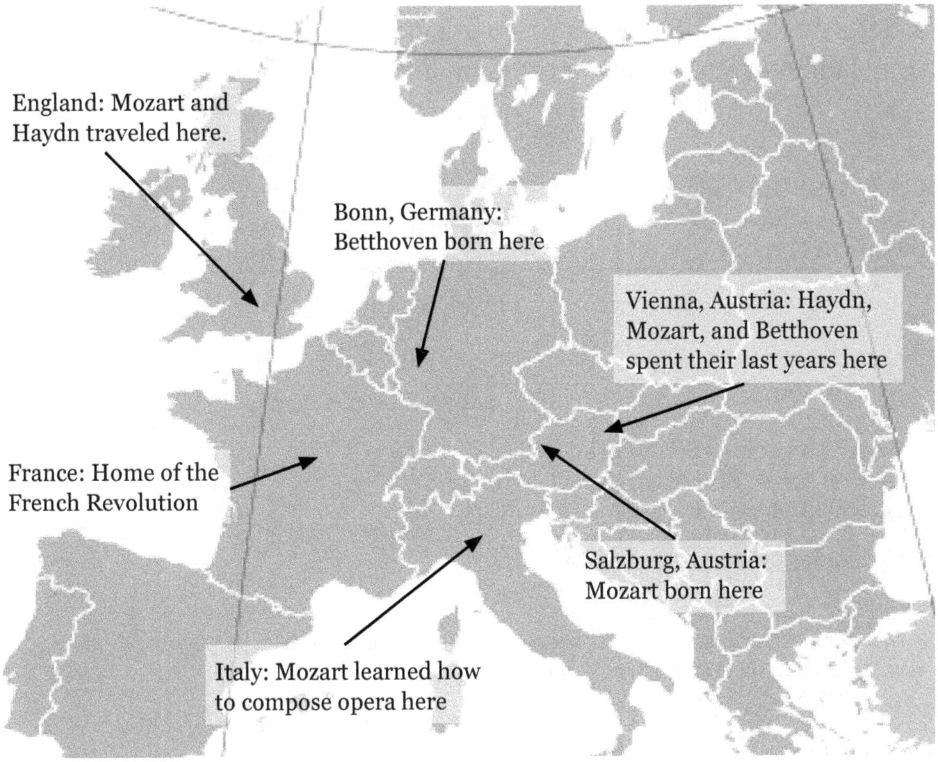
England: Mozart and Haydn traveled here.
Bonn, Germany: Betthoven born here
Vienna, Austria: Haydn, Mozart, and Betthoven spent their last years here
France: Home of the French Revolution
Salzburg, Austria: Mozart born here
Italy: Mozart learned how to compose opera here

Figure 5.3 | Map of Europe
Author | User: "Ssolbergj"
Source | Wikimedia Commons
License | CC BY-SA 3.0

Their music careers illustrate the changing role of the composer during this time. The aristocratic sponsors of the Classical artists—who were still functioning under the patronage system—were more interested in the final product than in the artists' intrinsic motivations for creating art for its own sake. For most of his life, Haydn worked for the aristocracy composing to order and wearing the livery of the Esterházy family, who were his patrons. Though successful working under their patronage, Haydn had more freedom to forge his own career after Prince Nikolaus Esterházy's death and staged concerts for his own commercial benefit in London and Vienna. Beethoven, the son of a court musician, was sent to Vienna to learn to compose. By 1809, he had succeeded in securing a lifetime annuity (a promise from local noblemen for annual support). Beethoven did not have to compose music for them; he simply had to stay in Vienna and compose. In some ways, the role of aristocratic patron and composer was turned on its head. When philosophically compatible with a sponsor, the artist flourished and could express his/her creativity. But in Mozart's case, the patronage system was stifling and counterproductive to his abilities. Mozart was also born and raised by a father who was a court musician, though his father was a court musician for the Archbishop of Salzburg. It was expected that Mozart would also enter the service of the Archbishop; instead, he escaped to Vienna, where he attempted the life of a freelancer. After initial successes, he struggled to earn enough money to make ends meet and died a pauper in 1791. The journey through the Classical period is one between two camps, the old and the new: the old based upon an aristocracy with city states and the new in the rising and more powerful educated middle class. The traditional despotism is dying while the new class system increasingly thrives.

5.3.3 Musical Timeline

Events in History	Events in Music
	1732: Haydn born
	1750: J. S. Bach dies
	1756: Mozart born
1762: French philosopher Rousseau publishes *Émile, or Treatise on Education*, outlining Englightenment educational ideas	
	1770: Beethoven born
1776: Declaration of Independence in the U.S.A.	
1789: Storming of the Bastille and beginning of the French Revolution (Paris, France)	1781: Mozart settles in Vienna
	1791: Mozart dies
	1791-95: Haydn travels to London
	1792: Beethoven moves to Vienna
1793: In the U.S.A., invention of the Cotton Gin, an innovation of the Industrial Revolution	
	1809: Haydn dies
	1827: Beethoven dies

5.4 MUSIC IN THE CLASSICAL PERIOD

5.4.1 Music Comparison Overview

Baroque Music	Classical Music
• Rise of homophony; polyphony still used • Rise of instrumental music, including the violin family • Meter more important than before • New genres such as opera, oratorio, concerto, cantata, and fugue • Emergence of program music • Continued presence of music at church and court • Continued increase of music among merchant classes • Motor rhythm	• Mostly homophony, but with variation • New genres such as the symphony and string quartet • Use of crescendos and decrescendos • Question and answer (aka antecedent consequent) phrases that are shorter than earlier phrases • New emphasis on musical form: for example, sonata form, theme and variations, minuet and trio, rondo, and first-movement concerto form • Greater use of contrasting dynamics, articulations, and tempos

5.4.2 General Trends of Classical Music

Musical Style

The Classical style of music embodies balance, structure, and flexibility of expression, arguably related to the noble simplicity and calm grandeur that the eighteenth century art historian Johann Joachim Winckelmann saw in ancient Greek art. In the music of Haydn, Mozart, and the early Beethoven, we find tuneful melodies using question/answer or antecedent/consequent phrasing; flexible deployment of rhythm and rests; and slower harmonic rhythm (harmonic rhythm is the rate at which the chords or harmonies change). Composers included more expressive marks in their music, such as the crescendo and decrescendo. The homophony of the Classical period featured predominant melody lines accompanied by relatively interesting and independent lines. In the case of a symphony or operatic ensemble, the texture might be described as homophony with multiple accompanying lines or polyphony with a predominant melodic line.

Performing Forces

The Classical period saw new performing forces such as the piano and the string quartet and an expansion of the orchestra. Initially called the fortepiano, then the pianoforte, and now the piano was capable of dynamics from soft to loud; the player needed only to adjust the weight applied when depressing a key. This feature was not available in the Baroque harpsichord. Although the first pianos were developed in the first half of the eighteenth century, most of the technological advancements that led the piano to overtaking all other keyboard instruments in popularity occurred in the late eighteenth century.

Besides the keyboard instruments, the string quartet was the most popular new chamber music ensembles of the Classical period and comprised two violins, a viola, and a cello. In addition to string quartets, composers wrote duets, trios, quintets, and even sextets, septets, and octets. Whether performed in a palace or a more modest middle class home, chamber music, as the name implies, was generally performed in a chamber or smaller room.

In the Classical period, the orchestra expanded into an ensemble that might include as many as thirty to sixty musicians distributed into four sections. The sections include the strings, woodwinds, brass, and percussion. Classical composers explored the individual unique tone colors of the instruments and they did not treat the instrumental sections interchangeably. An orchestral classical piece utilizes a much larger tonal palette and more rapid changes of the ensemble's timbre through a variety of orchestration techniques. Each section in the classical orchestra has a unique musical purpose as penned by the composer. The string section still holds its prominence as the center-piece for the orchestra. Composers continue to predominantly assign the first violins the melody and the accompaniment to the lower strings. The woodwinds are orchestrated to provide diverse tone colors and often assigned melodic solo passages. By the beginning of the nineteenth century, clarinets were added to the flutes and oboes to complete the woodwind section. To add volume and to emphasize louder dynamic, horns and trumpets were used. The horns and trumpets also filled out the harmonies. The brass usually were not assigned the melody or solos. The kettle drum or timpani were used for volume highlights and for rhythmic pulse. Overall, the Classical orchestra matured into a multifaceted tone color ensemble that composers could utilize to produce their most demanding musical thoughts acoustically through an extensive tonal palette. General differences between the Baroque and Classical (1750-1815) orchestras are summarized in the following chart.

Baroque Orchestras	Classical Orchestras
• Strings at the core • Woodwind and brass instruments such as the flutes or oboes and trumpets and horns doubled the themes played by the strings or provided harmonies • Any percussion was provided by timpani • Harpsichord, sometimes accompanied by cello or bassoon, provided the basso continuo • Generally led by the harpsichord player	• Strings at the core • More woodwind instruments—flutes and oboes and (increasingly) clarinets—which were sometimes given their own melodic themes and solo parts • More brass instruments, including, after 1808, trombones. • More percussion instruments, including cymbals, the triangle, and other drums • Phasing out of the basso continuo • Generally led by the concertmaster (the most important first violinist) and increasingly by a conductor

Emergence of New Musical Venues

The Classical period saw performing ensembles such as the orchestra appearing at an increasing number of concerts. These concerts were typically held in theaters or in the large halls of palaces and attended by anyone who could afford the ticket price, which was reasonable for a substantial portion of the growing middle class. For this reason, the birth of the public concert is often traced to the late eighteenth century. At the same time, more music was incorporated into a growing number of middle class households.

The redistribution of wealth and power of this era affected the performing forces and musical venues in two ways. First, although the aristocracy still employed musicians, professional composers were no longer exclusively employed by the wealthy. This meant that not all musicians were bound to a particular person or family as their patron/sponsor. Therefore, public concerts shifted from performances in the homes and halls of the rich to performances for the masses which evolved the symphony into a genre for the public concert, as they were eventually written for larger and larger ensembles. Second, middle class families incorporated more music into their households for personal entertainment. For example, middle class households would have their children take music lesson and participate in chamber music or small musical ensembles. Musicians could now support themselves through teaching lessons, composing and publishing music, and performing in public venues, such as in public concerts. Other opportunities included the public opera house, which was the center for vocal music experimentation during the Classical era. Composers also continued to write music for the church.

Musical Form

As musical compositions of the Classical period incorporated more performing forces and increased in length, a composition's structure became more important. As an element of organization and coherence, form helps give meaning to a musical movement or piece, we have some evidence to suggest that late eighteenth and early nineteenth century audiences heard form in music that was especially composed to play on their expectations.

Sonata Form

The most important innovation in form during the Classical period is what we call **Sonata Form**. This form got its name from being used as the first movement of most piano sonatas of the Classical period. Consisting of three sections—exposition, development, and recapitulation—it was also used for the first movements (and sometimes final movements) of almost all Classical symphonies and string quartets. The **exposition** of a sonata form presents the primary themes and keys of the movement. After the first theme is presented in the home or tonic key, the music modulates to a different key during a sub-section that is called a "transition." Once the new key is established, subsequent themes appear. The exposition generally ends with a rousing confirmation of the new key in a sub-section called the "closing." The exposition then often repeats.

As its name implies, the **development** "develops" the primary themes of the movement. The motives that comprise the musical themes are often broken apart and given to different parts of the orchestra. These motives are often repeated in sequences (refer back to chapter 1 for more about sequences), and these sequences often lead to frequent modulations from one musical key to another that contribute to an overall sense of instability. Near the end of the development, there is sometimes a sub-section called the "retransition" during which the harmonies, textures, and dynamics of the music prepare the listener for the final section of the form, the recapitulation.

Also true to its name, the **recapitulation** brings back the primary themes and home key of the movement. A simultaneous return of the first theme and home key generally marks its beginning. In the recapitulation, the listener hears the same musical themes as in the first presented in the exposition. The main difference between the exposition and the recapitulation is that the recapitulation stays in the home key. After all, the movement is about to end and ending in the home key provides the listener a sense of closure. Recapitulations often end with sub-sections called codas. The **coda**, or "tail," of the movement is a sub-section that re-emphasizes the home key and that generally provides a dramatic conclusion.

Starting in the late eighteenth century, there are reports of listeners recognizing the basic sections of sonata form, and contemporary music theorists outlined them in music composition treatises. Their descriptions are generalizations based on the multitudinous sonata form movements composed by Haydn, Mozart, and Beethoven. Although the sonata form movements of Haydn, Mozart, and Beethoven share many of the characteristics outlined above, each sonata form is slightly different. Perhaps that is what makes their music so interesting: it takes what is expected and does something different. In fact, composers continued to write sonata forms through the nineteenth and twentieth centuries. By the end of the nineteenth century, some of these sonata forms were massive, almost-hour-long movements. You will have the opportunity to hear sonata form in several of our focus compositions from the Classical period.

Other Important Forms in Classical Music

Another form of the Classical period is the **Theme and Variations**. Theme and Variations form consists of the presentation of a theme and then the variations upon it. The theme may be illustrated as A with any number of variations following it: A', A", A"', A"", etc. Each theme is a varied version of the original, keeping enough of the theme to be recognizable, but providing enough variety in style for interest. Variations change melodies (often through ornamentation), harmonies, rhythms, and instrumentation. Theme and variations forms were often found in slow movements of symphonies and string quartets. Some fast movements are also in theme and variations form.

The **Minuet and Trio** form found in many Classical symphonies and string quartets stems from the stylized dances of the Baroque Period (see chapter 4), and then followed by the Minuet A section: A B A for short. To save paper, the return of the A section was generally not written out. Instead, the composer wrote the words **da capo**, meaning to the head, at the end of the B section indicating a return to the A section. As a movement in three parts, Minuet and Trio form is sometimes called a ternary form. As we will see in our discussion of Beethoven's Fifth Symphony, by the beginning of the nineteenth century, the Minuet and Trio was perceived as dated, and composers started writing fast ABA ternary form movements called **scherzos**.

The **rondo** is another popular instrumental form of the late eighteenth and early nineteenth centuries. Rondo consists of the alternation of a refrain "A" with contrasting sections ("B," "C," "D," etc.). Rondos are often the final movements of string quartets, classical symphonies, concerti, and sonata (instrumental solos).

Genres

We normally classify musical compositions into genres by considering their performing forces, function, the presence and quality of any text, and their musical style and form. Changes in any of these factors can lead to changes in genres. The two most important new genres of the Classical period were the symphony and the string quartet; instrumental genres that continued from the Baroque period include the concerto.

Although one might trace its origins to the opera overture, the symphony developed as an orchestral composition for the public concert. By the end of the Classical period, it typically had four movements. The first movement was generally fast in tempo and in sonata form. The final movement was normally fast in tempo and used sonata, rondo, or theme and variations form. The interior movements consisted of a slow and lyrical movement and a moderate-tempo dancelike movement generally using the style of the minuet, a popular eighteenth century dance.

The string quartet became one of the most popular genres of Classical chamber music. Its overall structure and form was exactly like the symphony. However, it was always performed by two violins, one viola, and one cello (thus its name) and commonly used as entertainment in the home, although on occasion string quartets were performed in public concerts. Also popular for personal diversion was the piano sonata, which normally had only three movements (generally lacking the minuet movement found in the string quartet and the symphony).

The most pronounced change in the Classical period vocal music was the growing popularity of **opera buffa**, or comic opera, over the more serious plot and aristocratic characters of Baroque opera seria. Opera buffa portrayed the lives of middle class characters and often mixed tragedy with comedy; as we will see, Mozart would produce some of the most famous opera buffa of all time. (As a side note, Mozart also transformed the opera overture into a preview of the musical themes to follow in the opera proper.) Composers Haydn and Beethoven also continued to write oratorios.

5.5 MUSIC OF JOSEPH HAYDN (1732-1809)

Born in 1732, Joseph Haydn grew up in a small village that was located about a six-hour coach ride east of Vienna (today the two are about an hour apart by car). His family loved to sing together, and perceiving that their son had musical talent, apprenticed six-year-old Joseph Haydn to a relative who was a schoolmaster and choirmaster. As an apprentice, Haydn learned harpsichord and violin and sang in the church. So distinct was Haydn's voice that he was recommended to Vienna's St. Stephen's Cathedral's music director. In 1740 Haydn became of student of St. Stephen's Cathedral. He sang with the St. Stephen's Cathedral boys' choir for almost ten years, until his voice broke (changed). After searching, he found a job as valet to the Italian opera composer Nicola Porpora and most likely started studying music theory and music composition in a systematic way at that time. He composed a comic musical and eventually became a chapel master for a Czech nobleman. When this noble family fell into hard times, they released Haydn. In 1761, he became a Vice-Chapel Master for an even wealthier nobleman, the Hungarian Prince Esterházy. Haydn spent almost thirty years working for their family. He was considered a skilled servant, who soon be-

Figure 5.4 | Joseph Haydn, 1791
Author | Thomas Hardy
Source | Wikimedia Commons
License | Public Domain

came their head Chapel Master and was highly prized, especially by the second and most musical of the Esterházy princes for whom Haydn worked.

The Esterházys kept Haydn very busy: he wrote music, which he played both for and with his patrons, ran the orchestra, and staged operas. In 1779, Haydn's contract was renegotiated, allowing him to write and sell music outside of the Esterházy family. Within a decade, he was the most famous composer in Europe. In 1790, the musical Prince Nikolaus Esterházy died and his son Anton downsized the family's musical activities. This shift allowed Haydn to accept an offer to give a concert in London, England, where his music was very popular. Haydn left Vienna for London in December. For the concerts there, he composed an opera, symphonies, and chamber music, all of which were extremely popular. Haydn revisited London twice in the following years, 1791 to 1795, earning—after expenses—as much as he had in twenty years of employment with the Esterházys. Nonetheless, a new Esterházy prince decided to reestablish the family's musical foothold, so Haydn returned to their service in 1796. In the last years of his life, he wrote two important oratorios (he had been much impressed by performances of Handel's oratorios while in London) as well as more chamber music.

5.5.1 Overview of Haydn's Music

Like his younger contemporaries Mozart and Beethoven, Joseph Haydn composed in all the genres of his day. From a historical perspective, his contributions to the string quartet and the symphony are particularly significant: in fact, he is often called the Father of the Symphony. His music is also known for its motivic construction, use of folk tunes, and musical wit. Central to Haydn's compositional process was his ability to take small numbers of short musical motives and vary them in enough ways so as to provide interesting music for movements that were several minutes long. Folk-like as well as popular tunes of the day can be heard in many of his compositions for piano, string quartet, and orchestra. Contemporary audiences and critics seemed to appreciate this mixing of musical complexity and the familiar. Ernst Ludwig Gerber (1790-92), an important eighteenth-century musical connoisseur, wrote that Haydn "possessed the great art of ***appearing*** familiar in his themes" (***Historisch-biographisches Lexikon der Tonkünstler*** of 1790-1792). Additionally, many of his contemporaries remarked on Haydn's musical wit, or humor. Several of his music compositions play on the listeners' expectations, especially through the use of surprise rests, held out notes, and sudden dynamic changes.

Focus Composition:

Haydn, String Quartet in D Major, Op. 20, no. 4 (1772)

The string quartet was one of the important performing forces and genres of the Classical period, and Haydn was one of its most important composers. Over the course of his life, Haydn wrote sixty-eight quartets, many of which were played both by Haydn's aristocratic patrons and published and available for the amateur musician to purchase and play. In fact, many late eighteenth century writers (including the famous German poet Goethe) referred to the string quartet as "a conversation between four intelligent people," in this case, the four people being the first and second violinist, violist, and cellist.

The string quartet by Haydn which we will study is one of six quartets that he wrote in 1772 and published as opus twenty quartets in 1774 (roughly speaking, the "twenty" meant that this was Haydn's twentieth publication to date). In many ways, this follows the norms of other string quartets of the day. It is in four movements, with a fast first movement in sonata form, a slow second movement that uses a theme and variations form, a moderate-tempo third movement that is like a minuet, and a fourth fast movement, here in sonata form. As we will see, the third movement is subtitled "alla Zingarese," or "in the style of the Hungarians" (a good example of Haydn being "folky"). The entire quartet comprises a little over twenty minutes of music.

First, we will listen to the first movement, which is marked "allegro di molto," or very fast, and is in D major, as expected given the string quartet's title. It uses sonata form, and as stated earlier, in the exposition, the home key and musical themes of the movement are introduced, or "exposed." In the development, those themes are broken apart and combined in new and different ways, or "developed." In the recapitulation, the home key and original musical themes return; in other words, they are "recapitulated" or "recapped."

The exposition, development, and recapitulation are further broken into subsections to correspond to modulations in keys and the presentation of new and different themes. For the time being, simply listen for the main sections of sonata form in the first movement of Haydn's string quartet. You might also listen for Haydn's motivic style. In the first musical theme, you'll hear three motives. The first motive, for example, repeats the same pitch three times. The second motive consists of an arched musical phrase that ascends and descends and outlines the pitches of an important chord of the movement. The final motive that Haydn packs into his opening musical theme is a musical turn, or a decorative series of notes that move by step, revolving around a primary note. Each of these motives is heard repeatedly through the rest of the movement.

LISTENING GUIDE
For audio, go to: https://www.youtube.com/watch?v=d_Ly7d-wjco Performed by the New Oxford String Quartet, violinists Jonathan Crow and Andrew Wan, violist Eric Nowlin and cellist Brian Manker
Composer: Haydn
Composition: String Quartet in D major, Op. 20, no. 4 (I: Allegro di molto)

Date: 1772		
Genre: string quartet		
Form: I: Allegro di molto is in sonata form		
Performing Forces: string quartet, i.e., two violins, one viola, one cello		
What we want you to remember about this composition: • It uses sonata form: exposition, development, and recapitulation • It is in D major • Haydn's style here is very motivic		
Other things to listen for: • The interplay of the two violins, viola, and cello, in ways that might remind you of a "conversation between four intelligent people." • The subsections of the sonata form		
Timing	**Performing Forces, Melody, and Texture**	**Text and Form**
0:00	First theme in D major consists of three motives, including a first repeated note motive; first heard in the first violin and then passed to the other instruments, too.	EXPOSITION: First theme
0:38	Uses fast triplets (three notes per beat) in sequences to modulate to the key of A major	transition
1:12	New combinations of motives in themes in A major: starts with three-note motive, then a rapidly rising scale in the first violin, then more triplets, a more lyrical leaping motive, and ending with more triplets.	Second theme and closing theme
2:22	See above	EXPOSITION repeats; see above
4:44	Sequences the repeated note motive	DEVELOPMENT
5:12	Sounds like the first theme in the home key, but then shifts to another key. Repeated note and fast triplet motives follow in sequences, modulating to different keys (major and minor).	

5:44	A pause and the first motive, but not in the home key of D major; triplets, the more lyrical leaping motive and then a pause and the first motive, but still not in the home key.	
7:04	After a pause, the first theme in D major	RECAPITULATION: First theme
7:25	Uses fast triplets like the exposition's transition section, followed by more lyrical motives, but it does not modulate away from D major.	Transition-like section
7:48	Return of the three-note motive followed by a rapidly rising scale in the first violin, then more triplets, a more lyrical leaping motive, and ending with more triplets but still in D major (was in A major in the exposition).	Second theme and closing theme

The third movement of Haydn's String Quartet in D major, Op. 20, no. 4 uses a moderate tempo (it is marked "allegretto," in this case, a slow allegro) and the form of a minuet. Keeping with the popular culture of the day, a great number of Haydn's compositions included minuet movements.

Here, however, we see Haydn playing on our expectations for the minuet and writing a movement that is *alla zingarese*. The minuet was not a Hungarian dance, so the listener's experience and expectations are altered when the third movement sounds more like a lively Hungarian folk dance than the stately western-European minuet. (For comparison's sake, you can listen to the second movement of Haydn's String Quartet in E flat, Op. 20, no. 1, which is a much more traditional-sounding minuet.) Haydn retains the form of the stylized minuet, which consisted of a minuet and a trio. The trio consists of musical phrases that contrast with what was heard in the minuet: the trio got its name from an earlier practice of assigning this music to a group of three wind players. Here the entire string quartet plays throughout. After the trio, the group returns to the minuet, resulting in a minuet (A)—trio (B)—minuet (A). As was the custom, Haydn did not write out the minuet music at its return—remember paper was much more expensive 200 years ago than it is today. Instead, Haydn wrote two Italian words: "da capo" . As these words were used by all composers of the day, the players knew immediately to flip to the beginning of the movement and repeat the minuet, generally without repeats.

LISTENING GUIDE

For audio, go to:
https://www.youtube.com/watch?v=d_Ly7d-wjc0
Performed by the New Oxford String Quartet, violinists Jonathan Crow and Andrew Wan, violist Eric Nowlin and cellist Brian Manker

Composer: Haydn

Composition: String Quartet in D major, op. 20, no. 4 (III. Allegretto alla zingarese)

Date: 1772

Genre: string quartet

Form: III. Allegretto alla zingarese uses the form of a minuet and trio, that is, Minuet (A) Trio (B) Minuet (A).

Performing Forces: string quartet comprised of 2 violins, 1 viola, and 1 cello

What we want you to remember about this composition:

- It is in triple time and a moderate tempo, like most minuets
- The music for the repeat of the minuet is not written out; instead, Haydn writes "da capo" at the end of the Trio
- Instead of sounding like a stately minuet, it sounds more like a lively Hungarian dance

Other things to listen for:

- It hardly sounds like triple meter, because Haydn writes accents on beats two and three instead of mainly on beat one

Timing	Performing Forces, Melody, and Texture	Text and Form
0:00	Lots of unexpected accents on beats two and three of the triple time meter; homophonic texture: the first violin gets the solo and the other voices accompany; in D major	MINUET: A
0:09	"	a repeats
0:17	Similar to a, but the melody is even more disjunct, with more leaps.	B
0:27	"	b repeats
0:41	Accents back on the first beat of each measure (that is, of each measure of the triple meter); homophonic texture: the cello gets the solo and the other voices accompany; still in D major	TRIO: Cc

0:57	Similar to c; note the drone pitches in the 2nd violin and viola accompaniment at the beginning of the phrase	dd
1:14	See above	MINUET: A
1:20	See above	B

Focus composition:

Haydn, Symphony No. 94 in G Major, "Surprise"

Haydn is also often called the Father of the Symphony because he wrote over 100 symphonies, which, like his string quartets, span most of his compositional career. As already noted, the Classical orchestra featured primarily strings, with flutes and oboes (and, with Haydn's last symphonies, clarinets) for woodwinds, trumpets and horns for brass, and timpani (and occasionally another drums or the cymbals or triangle) for percussion. The symphony gradually took on the four-movement form that was a norm for over a century, although as we will see, composers sometimes relished departing from the norm.

Haydn wrote some of his most successful symphonies for his times in London. His Symphony No. 94 in G Major, which premiered in London in 1792, is a good example of Haydn's thwarting musical expectations for witty ends. Like most symphonies of its day, the first movement is in sonata form. (Haydn does open the symphony with a brief, slow introduction before launching into the first movement proper.)

Haydn's sense of humor is most evident in the moderately slow andante second movement which starts like a typical theme and variations movement consisting of a musical theme that the composer then varies several times. Each variation retains enough of the original theme to be recognizable but adds other elements to provide interest. The themes used for theme and variations movements tended to be simple, tuneful melody lines. In this case, the theme consists of an eight-measure musical phrase that is repeated. This movement, like many movements of Classical symphonies and string quartets, ends with a coda.

Why did Haydn write such a loud chord at the end of the second statement of the *a* phrase of the theme? Commentators have long speculated that Haydn may have noticed that audience members tended to drift off to sleep in slow and often quietly lyrical middle movements of symphonies and decided to give them an abrupt wakeup. Haydn himself said nothing of the sort, although his letters, as well as his music, do suggest that he was attentive to his audience's opinions and attempted at every juncture to give them music that was new and interesting: for Haydn, that clearly meant playing upon his listener's expectations in ways that might even be considered humorous.

LISTENING GUIDE
For audio, go to: https://www.youtube.com/watch?v=PhxZhDV9KHM Performed by The Orchestra of the 18th Century, conducted by Frans Brüggen.
Composer: Haydn
Composition: Symphony No. 94 in G major, "Surprise" (II. Andante)
Date: 1791
Genre: symphony
Form: II. Andante is in theme and variations form
Performing Forces: Classical orchestra here with 1st violin section, 2nd violin section, viola section, cellos/bass section, 2 flutes, 2 oboes, 2 trumpets, 2 horns, 2 bassoons, and timpani
What we want you to remember about this composition: • It is in theme and variations form • The very loud chord that ends the first phrase of the theme provides the "surprise"
Other things to listen for: • The different ways that Haydn varies the theme: texture, register, instrumentation, key

Timing	**Performing Forces, Melody, and Texture**	**Text and Form**
8:46	Theme: aa	Eight-measure theme with a question and answer structure. The "question" ascends and descends and then the "answer" ascends and descends, and ends with a very loud chord (the answer). In C major and mostly consonant. In homophonic texture, with melody in the violins and accompaniment by the other strings; soft dynamics and then very soft staccato notes until ending with a very loud chord played by the full orchestra, the "surprise."

9:21	b	Contrasting more legato eight-measure phrase ends like the staccato motives of the a phrase without the loud chord;
9:39	b	Repetition of b
9:57	Variation 1: aa	Theme in the second violins and violas under a higher-pitched 1st violin countermelody. Still in C major and mostly consonant Ascending part of the theme is forte and the descending part of the phrase is piano; the first-violin countermelody is an interesting line but the overall texture is still homophonic
10:30	bb	Similar in texture and harmonies; *piano* dynamic throughout
11:05	Variation 2: aa	The first four measures are in unison monophonic texture and very loud and the second four measures (the answer) are in homophonic texture and very soft; In C minor
11:41	Develops motives from a and b phrases	In C minor with more dissonance; very loud in dynamics; The motives are passed from instrument to instrument in polyphonic imitation.
12:20	Variation 3: aa	Back in C major. The oboes and flutes get the *a* phrase with fast repeated notes in a higher register; the second time, the violins play the a phrase at original pitch; uses homophonic texture throughout.
12:56	bb	The flutes and oboes play countermelodies while the strings play the theme.

13:27	Variation 4: ab	The winds get the first a phrase and then it returns to the first violin; very loud for the first statement of a and very soft for the second statement of a; homophonic texture throughout.
14:01	bb + extension	Shifting dynamics
14:50	Coda	

The third movement of Haydn's "Surprise" Symphony is a rather traditional minuet and trio movement. The fourth movement is equally traditional; it uses a light-hearted form called the rondo. As state above, in a rondo, a musical refrain, labeled as "A," alternates with other sections, alternately called B, C, D, etc. See if you can hear the recurrence of the refrain as you listen to this joyful conclusion to the symphony.

LISTENING GUIDE
For audio, go to: https://www.youtube.com/watch?v=PhxZhDV9KHM Performed by The Orchestra of the 18th Century, conducted by Frans Brüggen.
Composer: Haydn
Composition: Symphony No. 94 in G major, "Surprise" (IV. Finale: Allegro Molto)
Date: 1791
Genre: symphony
Form: IV. Finale: Allegro molto is in a (sonata) rondo form
Performing Forces: Classical orchestra here with 1st violin section, 2nd violin section, viola section, cellos/bass section, 2 flutes, 2 oboes, 2 trumpets, 2 horns, 2 bassoons, and timpani
What we want you to remember about this composition: • This movement uses a rondo form • It is at a very fast tempo • It uses a full orchestra
Other things to listen for: • The alternation of the different sections of the rondo form • The changes in key and texture

Timing	Performing Forces, Melody, and Texture	Text and Form
19:17	Fast and tuneful theme in duple time in homophonic texture; in G major, with more dissonances as the music modulates to...	A
20:19	D major for a different tuneful theme that opens descending motion;	B
20:42	Returns to G major and the first theme; texture becomes more polyphonic as it...	A'
20:49	modulates through several keys.	C
21:17	Return to the first theme in G major	A
21:26	Opening motive of the first theme in minor and then sequences on other motives that modulate through minor keys.	D
21:47	Back in G major with the first theme and other music of A that is extended into a coda that brings back b momentarily and juxtaposes *forte* and *piano* dynamics before its rousing close.	A and coda

Haydn's symphonies greatly influenced the musical style of both Mozart and Beethoven; indeed, these two composers learned how to develop motives from Haydn's earlier symphonies. Works such as the Surprise Symphony were especially shaping for the young Beethoven, who, as we will later discuss, was taking music composition lessons from Haydn about the same time that Haydn was composing the Symphony No. 94 before his trip to London.

5.6 MUSIC OF WOLFGANG AMADEUS MOZART (1756-1791)

Wolfgang Amadeus Mozart (b. 1756-91) was born in Salzburg, Austria. His father, Leopold Mozart, was an accomplished violinist of the Archbishop of Salzburg's court. Additionally, Leopold had written a respected book on the playing of the violin. At a very young age, Wolfgang began his career as a composer and performer. A prodigy, his talent far exceeded any in music, past his contemporaries. He began writing music prior to the age of five. At the age of six, Wolfgang performed in the court of Empress Maria Theresa.

Mozart's father was quite proud of his children, both being child prodigies. At age seven, Wolfgang, his father, and his sister Maria Anna (nicknamed "Nannerl") embarked on a tour featuring Wolfgang in London, Munich, and Paris. As was customary at the time, Wolfgang, the son, was promoted and pushed ahead with his musical career by his father. While his sister, the female, grew up traditionally, married, and eventually took care of her father Leopold in his later years. However, while the two siblings were still performing, these tours occurred from when Wolfgang was between the ages of six and seventeen. The tours, though, were quite demeaning for the young musical genius in that he was often looked upon as just a superficial genre of entertainment rather than being respected as a musical prodigy. He would often be asked to identify the tonality of a piece while listening to it or asked to sight read and perform with a cloth over his hands while at the piano. Still, the tours allowed young Mozart to accumulate knowledge about musical styles across Europe. As a composer prior to his teens, the young Mozart had already composed religious works, symphonies, solo sonatas, an opera buffa, and *Bastien and Bastienne*, an operetta; in short, he had quickly mastered all the forms of music.

Figure 5.5 | Wolfgang Amadeus Mozart
Author | Barbara Krafft
Source | Wikimedia Commons
License | Public Domain

Back in Salzburg, Mozart was very unhappy due to being musically restrained by the restrictions of his patron the Archbishop of Salzburg, Hieronymus von Colloredo. At approximately the age of twenty-five, he moved to Vienna and became a free artist (agent) and pursued other opportunities. Another likely reason for Wolfgang's ultimate departure to Vienna was to become independent of his father. Though Leopold was well-meaning and had sacrificed a great deal to ensure the future and happiness of his son, he was an overbearing father. Thus at the age of twenty-five, Mozart married Constance Weber. Mozart's father did not view the marriage favorably and this marriage served as a wedge severing Wolfgang's close ties to his father.

Wolfgang's new life in Vienna however was not easy. For almost ten years, he struggled financially unable to find the secure financial environment in which he had grown up. The music patronage system was still the main way for musicians to prosper and thrive: several times, Mozart was considered for patron employment but was not hired. Having hired several other musicians ahead of Mozart, Emperor Joseph II hired Mozart to basically compose dances for the court's balls. As the tasks were far beneath his musical genius, Mozart was quite bitter about this assignment.

While in Vienna, Mozart relied on his teaching to sustain him and his family. He also relied on the entertainment genre of the concert. He would write piano concertos for annual concerts. Their programs would also include some arias, solo improvisation, and possibly an overture of piece by another composer.

The peak of Mozart's career success occurred in 1786 with the writing of *The Marriage of Figaro* (libretto by Lorenza da Ponte). The opera was a hit in Prague and Vienna. The city of Prague, so impressed with the opera, commissioned another piece by Mozart. Mozart, with da Ponte again as librettist, then composed *Don Giovanni.* The second opera left the audience somewhat confused. Mozart's luster and appeal seemed to have passed. As a composer, Mozart was trying to expand the spectrum, or horizons, of the musical world. Therefore, his music sometimes had to be viewed more than once by the audience in order for them to understand and appreciate it. Mozart was pushing the musical envelope beyond the standard entertainment expected by his aristocratic audience, and patrons in general did not appreciate it. In a letter to Mozart, Emperor Joseph II wrote of *Don Giovanni* that the opera was perhaps better than *The Marriage of Figaro* but that it did not set well on the pallet of the Viennese. Mozart quickly fired back, responding that the Viennese perhaps needed more time to understand it.

In the final year of his life, Mozart with librettist (actor/poet) Emanuel Schikaneder, wrote a very successful opera for the Viennese theatre, *The Magic Flute.* The newly acclaimed famous composer was quickly hired to write a piece (as well as attend) the coronation of the new Emperor, Leopold II, as King of Bohemia. The festive opera that Mozart composed for this event was called *The Clemency of Titus.* Its audience, overly indulged and exhausted from the coronation, was not impressed with Mozart's work. Mozart returned home depressed and broken, and began working on a Requiem, which, coincidentally, would be his last composition.

The *Requiem* was commissioned by a count who intended to pass the work off as his own. Mozart's health failed shortly after receiving this commission and the composer died, just before his thirty sixth birthday, before completing the piece. Mozart's favorite student, Franz Xaver Sűssmayr, completed the mass from Mozart's sketch scores, with some insertions of his own, while rumors spread that Mozart was possibly poisoned by another contemporary composer. In debt at the time of his death, Mozart was given a common burial. As one commentator wrote:

> Thus, "without a note of music, forsaken by all he held dear, the remains of this Prince of Harmony were committed to the earth, not even in a grave of their own, but in the common fosse affected to the indiscriminate sepulture of homeless mendicants and nameless waifs."[2]

5.6.1 Overview of Mozart's Music

From Mozart's youth, his musical intellect and capability were unmatched. His contemporaries often noted that Mozart seemed to have already heard, edited, lis-

2 Crowest, "An Estimate of Mozart," *The Eclectic Magazine: Foreign Literature* Vol. 55; Vol 118 P. 464

tened to, and visualized entire musical works in his mind before raising a pen to compose them on paper. When he took pen in hand, he would basically transcribe the work in his head onto the manuscript paper. Observers also said that Mozart could listen and carry on conversations with others while transcribing his music to paper.

Mozart was musically very prolific in his short life. He composed operas, church music, a Requiem, string quartets, string quintets, mixed quintets and quartets, concertos, piano sonatas, and many lighter chamber pieces (such as divertimentos), including his superb *A Little Night Music* (*Eine kleine Nachtmusik*). His violin and piano sonatas are among the best ever written both in form and emotional content. Six of his quartets were dedicated to Haydn, whose influence Mozart celebrated in their preface.

Mozart additionally wrote exceptional keyboard music, particularly since he was respected as one of the finest pianists of the Classical period. He loved the instrument dearly and wrote many solo works, as well as more than twenty piano concertos for piano and orchestra, thus contributing greatly to the concerto's popularity as an acceptable medium. Many of these concerti were premiered at Mozart's annual public fundraising concerts. Of his many piano solo pieces, the ***Fantasia in C minor*** K 475 and the ***Sonata*** (in C minor) K 457 are representative of his most famous.

And Mozart composed more than forty symphonies, the writing of which extended across his entire career. He was known for the full and rich instrumentation and voicing of his symphonies. His conveying of emotion and mood are especially portrayed in these works. His final six symphonies, written in the last decade of his life, are the most artistically self-motivated independent of art patronage and supervision that might stifle creativity. Mozart's late and great symphonies include the ***Haffner*** in D (1782), the ***Linz*** in C (1783), the ***Prague*** in D (1786), and his last three symphonies composed in 1788. Mozart's final symphony probably was not performed prior to his death. In addition to the symphonies and piano concertos, Mozart composed other major instrumental works for clarinet, violin and French horn in concertos.

Focus Composition:

Mozart, *Don Giovanni* [1787]

The plot for *Don Giovanni* may be found at:

http://www.geocities.jp/wakaru_opera/englishdongiovanni.html

LISTENING GUIDE

For audio, go to:

http://semprelibera.altervista.org/wolfgang-amadeus-mozart/don-giovanni/deh-vieni-alla-finestra/

Composer: Wolfgang Amadeus Mozart
Librettist: Lorenzo Da Ponte

Composition: Deh, vieni alla finestra, Testo (Aria) from *Don Giovanni*, in Italian
Date: 1787, First performed October 29, 1787
Genre: Aria for baritone voice
Form: binary
Nature of Text: Originally in Italian Translation from Italian to English available at: http://semprelibera.altervista.org/wolfgang-amadeus-mozart/don-giovanni/deh-vieni-alla-finestra/
Performing Forces: Baritone and Classical Orchestra
What we want you to remember about this composition: This is a really a beautiful love-song where the womanizer Don Giovanni tries to woo Elvira's maid. The piece in D major begins in a 6/8 meter. The musical scoring includes a mandolin in the orchestra with light plucked accompaniments from the violins which supplement the feel of the mandolin. The atmosphere created by the aria tends to convince the audience of a heartfelt personal love and attraction The piece is written in a way to present a very light secular style canzonetta in binary form, which tends to help capture the playfulness of the Don Giovanni character.
Other things to listen for: This piece could very easily be used in a contemporary opera or musical.

Focus Composition:

Mozart, Piano Concerto No. 20 in D Minor, K. 466 [1785]

Classical composers like Mozart took the Baroque concerto for soloist and orchestra and expanded it into a much larger form. Like Vivaldi's concertos, Mozart's concertos were generally in three movements, with fast, slow, and fast tempos, respectively. The first movements of Mozart's concertos also featured the alternation of ritornello sections and solo sections, like we heard in the concerto by Vivaldi in the previous chapter. Mozart, however, also applied the dynamics of sonata form to the first movements of his concertos, resulting in a form that we now call **double exposition form**. In double exposition form, the first statement of the exposition was assigned to the orchestra, and the second statement of the exposition was assigned to the soloist with orchestral accompaniment in the background. The alternation between orchestra and soloist sections continues in the development and recapitulation. Near the end of the recapitulation and during the final orchestra exposition, the orchestra holds a suspenseful chord, at which point the soloist enters and the orchestra drops out. For a minute or longer, the soloist plays a **cadenza.** A cadenza is a solo section that sounds improvised, though sometimes composers or performers wrote these ahead of time, as is the case with this concerto (the recording cited by the text features a cadenza that was written by Beethoven). A cadenza normally ends with the pianist sustaining a chord (often with a trill) signaling the orchestra's final entrance in the piece, playing the last phrase of the ritornello to bring the movement to a conclusion. You can see an example how ritornello form and sonata form were merged in a double exposition form:

Table 5.1: Double Exposition Form							
Ritornello Form	Ritornello	Solo Section	Ritornello	Solo Section	Ritornello	Solo Section	Ritornello (including cadenza)
Sonata Form	[Orchestral] EXPOSITION	[Solo] EXPOSITION	DEVELOPMENT		RECAPITULATION		

The first movement of Mozart's *Concerto No. 20* in D minor, K. 466 is a good example of double exposition form. As the program annotator for the Burgess Hill Symphony Orchestra puts it:

> The orchestral tutti opens with the D minor first subject. This suggests dark threatening skies, emphasised [sic] by syncopation and dynamic contrasts. For a brief while the louring mood is relieved by the second subject, which has modulated into F major. The solo piano makes its entry with a plaintive new theme back in D minor - a little theme that refuses to go away. As the development progresses Mozart reviews all his themes, and presses onwards to a rather stormy climax leading to the cadenza. Mozart left no written cadenzas for this work. When the score came into the hands of Beethoven, he immediately decided that such a dramatic movement as this sorely needed one. He promptly sat down and wrote the shadowed brilliance that will be played by today's soloist.[3]

You might also listen to and take notes on to the lecture recital about the first movement of the concerto at:

http://www.bbc.co.uk/programmes/p01yh30s.

LISTENING GUIDE

For audio, go to:

https://www.youtube.com/watch?v=UGldgW6mDnY&list=RDUGldgW-6mDnY#t=517

Martha Argerich, piano, with the Orchestra di Padova e del Veneto, conducted by Alexandre Rabinovitch

Composer: Wolfgang Amadeus Mozart

3 "Mozart: Piano Concerto no 20 in D Minor." *Burgess Hill Symphony Orchestra.* Burgess Hill Symphony Orchestra, n.d. Web. 18 December 2015

<table>
<tr><td colspan="3">Composition: Piano Concerto No. 20 in D minor, K466, First Movement 1. Allegro (Cadenzas by Beethoven)</td></tr>
<tr><td colspan="3">Date: 1785</td></tr>
<tr><td colspan="3">Genre: Piano Concerto</td></tr>
<tr><td colspan="3">Form: Double exposition form</td></tr>
<tr><td colspan="3">Performing Forces: piano soloist and Classical orchestra</td></tr>
<tr><td colspan="3">What we want you to remember about this composition:<ul><li>It is in double exposition form.</li><li>At the end of the recapitulation, in the final ritornello, the orchestra drops out and the soloist plays a cadenza that sounds improvised.</li><li>The movement (like the concerto as a whole) starts and ends in D minor and is one of only two Mozart concertos in a minor key</li></ul></td></tr>
<tr><td>Timing</td><td>Performing Forces, Melody, and Texture</td><td>Text and Form</td></tr>
<tr><td></td><td>Orchestra alone, in a minor key throughout.</td><td>Orchestral Exposition</td></tr>
<tr><td>2:18</td><td>Spotlight on the solo piano, with some accompaniment from the orchestra; the key modulates to F majors.</td><td>Solo Exposition</td></tr>
<tr><td>5:05</td><td>Focus switches back and forth from solo piano and the orchestra while the music develops the themes, motives, and harmonies from the exposition.</td><td>Development</td></tr>
<tr><td>7:23</td><td>Back in D minor with the first themes from the exposition. Frequent alternation between the soloist and orchestra as they share the themes.</td><td>Recapitulation: Ritornello & solo sections</td></tr>
<tr><td>10:17</td><td>Orchestra begins the final ritornello and then sustains a suspenseful chord.</td><td>Recapitulation: Final ritornello</td></tr>
</table>

10:35	The pianist plays in a improvisatory manner, shifting suddenly between different motives, tempos, and styles. Listen for many ornaments such as trills and rapid and virtuosic scales. After a final, extended series of trills (starting at 12:17), the orchestra returns for...	Recapitulation: Cadenza
12:30	the final phrase of the ritornello and movement (which ends in D minor).	Recapitulation: Ritornello concludes

Focus Composition:

Mozart, Symphony No. 41 in C Major, K. 551 (1788)

Like Haydn, Mozart also wrote symphonies. Mozart's final symphony, the Symphony No. 41 in major, K. 551 is one of his greatest compositions. It very quickly acquired the nickname "Jupiter," a reference to the Greek god, perhaps because of its grand scale and use of complex musical techniques. For example, Mozart introduced more modulations and key changes in this piece than was typical. The symphony opens with a first movement in sonata form with an exposition, development, and recapitulation. Listen to the first movement with the listening guide below.

You can also find an animated listening guide providing guidance to various sections and identifying the different musical elements as they are introduced at: https://www.youtube.com/watch?v=YgUf2eMdi28.

LISTENING GUIDE
For audio, go to: https://www.youtube.com/watch?v=zK5295yEQMQ (Video of live orchestral performance); The Chamber Orchestra of Europe, conducted by Nikolaus Harnoncourt
Composer: Wolfgang Amadeus Mozart
Composition: Symphony No. 41 in C Major, K. 551 — 1st Movement, Allegro Vivace
Date: 1788
Genre: Symphony
Form: Sonata form
Performing Forces: Classical orchestra

What we want you to remember about this composition:

- Listen to the different sections identified in sonata form.
- During the development section you will feel the instability of the piece induced by the key changes and ever changing instrument voicings.

Other things to listen for:

- Its melodic line is mostly conjunct.
- Its melody contains many melismas.
- It has a Latin text sung in a strophic form.

I: Allegro Vivace

Time index follows the performance linked below:
https://www.youtube.com/watch?v=YgUf2eMdi28

Timing	Performing Forces, Melody, and Texture	Text and Form
0:00	Full orchestra. Stated twice-First loud and then soft short responses.	EXPOSITION: Opening triplet motive
0:18	The *forte* dynamic continues, with emphasis on dotted rhythms. Winds perform opening melody followed by staccato string answer; Full bowed motion in strings.	First theme in C major
1:30	Motive of three notes continues; Soft lyrical theme with moving ornamentation in accompaniment.	Pause followed by second theme of the exposition
2:08	Sudden forte dynamic. Energy increases until sudden softening to third pause; Brass fanfares with compliment of the tympani.	Second Pause followed by transition to build tension
2:41	Theme played in the strings with grace notes used. Melody builds to a closing; A light singable melody derived from Mozart's aria "Un baccio di mano"	After the third pause, the third theme is introduced
3:12		The entire exposition repeats itself

6:21	Transition played by flute, oboe and bassoon followed by third theme in strings; Music.	DEVELOPMENT SECTION: Transition to third theme
6:40	Modulations in this section add to the instability of the section; Starts like the exposition but with repetition in different keys.	Modulation to the minor
7:21	Slight introduction of third theme motif; Quiet and subdued.	Implied recapitulation: "Transition"
8:05	Now started by the oboes and bassoons; Now in C minor, not E flat major, which provides a more ominous tone.	Recapitulation in original key: First theme
9:29		Pause followed by second theme
10:39	After a sudden *piano* articulation of the SSSL motive, suddenly ends in a loud and bombastic manner: Fate threatens; Re-emphasizes C minor.	Third theme
10:53		Closing material similar to exposition
11:09	Full orchestra at forte dynamic.	Closing cadence for the movement

It is impossible to know how many more operas and symphonies Mozart would have written had he lived into his forties, fifties, or even sixties. Haydn's music written after the death of Mozart shows the influence of his younger contemporary, and Beethoven's early music was also shaped by Mozart's. In fact, in 1792, a twenty-something Beethoven was sent to Vienna with the expressed purpose of receiving "the spirit of Mozart from the hands of Haydn."

5.7 MUSIC OF LUDWIG VAN BEETHOVEN (1770-1827)

Beethoven was born in Bonn in December of 1770. As you can see from the map at the beginning of this chapter, Bonn sat at the Western edge of the Germanic lands, on the Rhine River. Those in Bonn were well-acquainted with traditions of the Netherlands and of the French; they would be some of the first to hear of the revolutionary ideas coming out of France in the 1780s. The area was ruled by the Elector of Cologne. As the Kapellmeister for the Elector, Beethoven's grandfather held the most important musical position in Bonn; he died when Beethoven was three years old. Beethoven's father, Johann Beethoven, sang in the Electoral Chapel his entire life. While he may have provided his son with music lessons at an early stage of Ludwig's life, it appears that Johann had given into alcoholism and depression, especially after the death of Maria Magdalena Keverich (Johann's wife and Ludwig's mother) in 1787.

Although hundreds of miles east of Vienna, the Electorate of Cologne was under the jurisdiction of the Austrian Habsburg empire that was ruled from this Eastern European city. The close ties between these lands made it convenient for the Elector, with the support of the music-loving Count Ferdinand Ernst Gabriel von Waldstein (1762-1823), to send Beethoven to Vienna to further his music training. Ferdinand was the youngest of an aristocratic family in Bonn. He greatly supported the arts and became a patron of Beethoven. Beethoven's first stay in Vienna in 1787 was interrupted by the death of his mother. In 1792, he returned to Vienna for good.

Perhaps the most universally-known fact of Beethoven's life is that he went deaf. You can read entire books on the topic; for our present purposes, the timing of his hearing loss is most important. It was at the end of the 1790s that Beethoven first recognized that he was losing his hearing. By 1801, he was writing about it to his most trusted friends. It is clear that the loss of his hearing was an existential crisis for Beethoven. During the fall of 1802, he composed a letter to his brothers that included his last will and testament, a document that we've come to know as the "Heiligenstadt Testament" named after the small town of Heiligenstadt, north of the Viennese city center, where he was staying. (To view the Testament go to https://en.wikipedia.org/wiki/Heiligenstadt_Testament#/media/File:Beethoven_Heiligenstaedter_Testament.jpg) The "Heiligenstadt Testament" provides us insight to Beethoven's heart and mind. Most striking is his statement that his experiences of social alienation, connected to his hearing loss, "drove me almost to despair, a little more of that and I have ended my life—it was only *my art* that held me back." The idea that Beethoven found in art a reason to live suggests both his valuing of art and a certain self-awareness of what he had to offer music. Beethoven and his physicians tried various means to counter the hearing loss and improve his ability to function in society. By 1818, however, Beethoven was completely deaf.

Figure 5.6 | Ludwig van Beethoven
Author | Joseph Karl Stieler
Source | Wikimedia Commons
License | Public Domain

Beethoven had a complex personality. Although he read the most profound philosophers of his day and was compelled by lofty philosophical ideals, his own writing was broken and his personal accounts show errors in basic math. He craved close human relationships yet had difficulty sustaining them. By 1810, he had secured a lifetime annuity from local noblemen, meaning that Beethoven never lacked for money. Still, his letters—as well as the accounts of contemporaries—suggest a man suspicious of others and preoccupied with the compensation he was receiving.

5.7.1 Overview of Beethoven's Music

Upon arriving in Vienna in the early 1790s, Beethoven supported himself by playing piano at salons and by giving music lessons. Salons were gatherings of literary types, visual artists, musicians, and thinkers, often hosted by noblewomen for their friends. Here Beethoven both played music of his own composition and improvised upon musical themes given to him by those in attendance.

In April of 1800 Beethoven gave his first concert for his own benefit, held at the important Burgtheater.

As typical for the time, the concert included a variety of types of music, vocal, orchestral, and even, in this case, chamber music. Many of the selections were by Haydn and Mozart, for Beethoven's music from this period was profoundly influenced by these two composers.

Scholars have traditionally divided Beethoven's composing into three chronological periods: early, middle, and late. Like all efforts to categorize, this one proposes boundaries that are open to debate. Probably most controversial is the dating of the end of the middle period and the beginning of the late period. Beethoven did not compose much music between 1814 and 1818, meaning that any division of those years would fall more on Beethoven's life than on his music.

In general, the music of Beethoven's first period (roughly until 1803) reflects the influence of Haydn and Mozart. Beethoven's second period (1803-1814) is sometimes called his "heroic" period, based on his recovery from depression documented in the "Heiligenstadt Testament" mentioned earlier. This period includes such music compositions as his Third Symphony, which Beethoven subtitled "*Eroica*" (that is, heroic), the Fifth Symphony, and Beethoven's one opera, *Fidelio*, which took the French revolution as its inspiration. Other works composed during this time include Symphonies No. 3 through No. 8 and famous piano works, such as the sonatas "Waldstein," "Appassionata," and "Lebewohl" and Concertos No. 4 and No. 5. He continued to write instrumental chamber music, choral music, and songs into his heroic middle period. In these works of his middle period, Beethoven is often regard-

Figure 5.7 | Burgtheater
Author | Michael Frankenstein
Source | Wikimedia Commons
License | Public Domain

ed as having come into his own because they display a new and original musical style. In comparison to the works of Haydn and Mozart and Beethoven's earlier music, these longer compositions feature larger performing forces, thicker polyphonic textures, more complex motivic relationships, more dissonance and delayed resolution of dissonance, more syncopation and **hemiola** (hemiola is the momentary simultaneous sense of being in two meters at the same time), and more elaborate forms.

When Beethoven started composing again in 1818, his music was much more experimental. Some of his contemporaries believed that he had lost his ability to compose as he lost his hearing. The late piano sonatas, last five string quartets, monumental *Missa Solemnis*, and Symphony No. 9 in D minor (*The Choral Symphony*) are now perceived to be some of Beethoven's most revolutionary compositions, although they were not uniformly applauded during his lifetime. Beethoven's late style was one of contrasts: extremely slow music next to extremely fast music and extremely complex and dissonant music next to extremely simple and consonant music.

Although this chapter will not discuss the music of Beethoven's early period or late period in any depth, you might want to explore this music on your own. Beethoven's first published piano sonata, the Sonata in F minor, Op. 2, No. 1 (1795), shows the influence of its dedicatee, Joseph Haydn. One of Beethoven's last works, his famous Ninth Symphony, departs from the norms of the day by incorporating vocal soloists and a choir into a symphony, which was almost always written only for orchestral instruments. The Ninth Symphony is Beethoven's longest; its first three movements, although innovative in many ways, use the expected forms: a fast sonata form, a *scherzo* (which by the early nineteenth century—as we will see in our discussion of the Fifth Symphony—had replaced the minuet and trio), and a slow theme and variations form. The finale, in which the vocalists participate, is truly revolutionary in terms of its length, the sheer extremes of the musical styles it uses, and the combination of large orchestra and choir. The text or words that Beethoven chose for the vocalists speak of joy and the hope that all humankind might live together in brotherly love. The "Ode to Joy" melody to which Beethoven set these words was later used for the hymn "Joyful, Joyful, We Adore Thee."

Focus Composition:

Beethoven, Symphony No. 5 in C minor, Op. 67 (1808)

In this chapter, we will focus on possibly Beethoven's most famous composition, his Fifth Symphony (1808). The premier of the Fifth Symphony took place at perhaps the most infamous of all of Beethoven's concerts, an event that lasted for some four hours in an unheated theater on a bitterly cold Viennese evening. At this time, Beethoven was not on good terms with the performers, several who refused to rehearse with the composer in the room. In addition, the final number of the performance was finished too late to be sufficiently practiced, and in the concert, it had to be stopped and restarted. Belying its less than auspicious first performance, once published the Fifth Symphony quickly gained the critical acclaim it has held ever since.

The most famous part of the Fifth Symphony is its commanding opening. This opening features the entire orchestra playing in unison a musical motive that we will call the short-short-short-long (SSSL) motive, because of the rhythm of its four notes. We will also refer to it as the Fate motive, because at least since the 1830s, music critics have likened it to fate knocking on the door, as discussed at http://www.npr.org/templates/story/story.php?storyId=5473894. The short notes repeat the same pitch and then the long, held-out note leaps down a third. After the orchestra releases the held note, it plays the motive again, now sequenced a step lower, then again at the original pitches, then at higher pitches. This sequenced phrase, which has become the first theme of the movement, then repeats, and the fast sonata-form movement starts to pick up steam. This is the exposition of the movement.

Figure 5.8 | Opening of Symphony No. 5, Op. 67
Author | Stelios Samelis
Source | Mutopia Project
License | Public Domain

After a transition, the second theme is heard. It also starts with the SSSL motive, although the pitches heard are quite different. The horn presents the question phrase of the second theme; then, the strings respond with the answer phrase of the second theme. You should note that the key has changed—the music is now in E flat major, which has a much more peaceful feel than C minor—and the answer phrase of the second theme is much more legato than anything yet heard in the symphony. This tuneful legato music does not last for long and the closing section returns to the rapid sequencing of the SSSL motive. Then the orchestra returns to the beginning of the movement for a repeat of the exposition.

The development section of this first movement does everything we might expect of a development: the SSSL motive appears in sequence and is altered as the keys change rapidly. Also, we hear more polyphonic imitative in the development than elsewhere in the movement. Near the end of the development, the dynamics alternate between piano and forte and, before the listener knows it, the music has returned to the home key of C minor as well as the opening version of the SSSL motive: this starts the recapitulation. The music transitions to the second theme—now still in the home key of C minor—and the closing section. Then, just when the listener expects the recapitulation to end, Beethoven extends the movement in a coda. This coda is much longer than any coda we have yet listened to in the music of Haydn or Mozart, although it is not as long as the coda to the final movement of this symphony. These long codas are also another element that Beethoven is known for. He often restates the conclusive cadence many times and in many rhythmic durations.

The second movement is a lyrical theme and variations movement in a major key, which provides a few minutes of respite from the menacing C minor; if you listen carefully, though, you might hear some reference to the SSSL fate motive. The third movement returns to C minor and is a scherzo. Scherzos retain the form of the minuet, having a contrasting trio section that divides the two presentations of the scherzo. Like the minuet, scherzos also have a triple feel, although they tend to be somewhat faster in tempo than the minuet.

This scherzo third movement opens with a mysterious, even spooky, opening theme played by the lower strings. The second theme returns to the SSSL motive, although now with different pitches. The mood changes with a very imitative and very polyphonic trio in C major, but the spooky theme reappears, alongside the fate motive, with the repeat of the scherzo. Instead of making the scherzo a discrete movement, Beethoven chose to write a musical transition between the scherzo and the final movement, so that the music runs continuously from one movement to another. After suddenly getting very soft, the music gradually grows in dynamic as the motive sequences higher and higher until the fourth movement bursts onto the scene with a triumphant and loud C major theme. It seems that perhaps our hero, whether we think of the hero as the music of the symphony or perhaps as Beethoven himself, has finally triumphed over Fate.

The fourth movement is a rather typical fast sonata form finale with one exception. The second theme of the scherzo (b), which contains the SSSL fate motive, appears one final time at the end of the movement's development section, as if to try one more time to derail the hero's conquest. But, the movement ultimately ends with a lot of loud cadences in C major, providing ample support for an interpretation of the composition as the overcoming of Fate. This is the interpretation that most commentators for almost two hundred years have given the symphony. It is pretty amazing to think that a musical composition might express so aptly the human theme of struggle and triumph. Listen to the piece and see if you hear it the same way.

LISTENING GUIDE For audio of the first and second movements performed by the Orchestre Révolutionnaire et Romantique (on period instruments) conducted by John Eliot Gardiner, go to: https://www.youtube.com/watch?v=jUrd2WPmQfY For audio of the third and fourth movements performed by the NBC Orchestra in 1952, conducted by Arturo Toscanini, go to: https://www.youtube.com/watch?v=9Mt7NIPFgQk https://www.youtube.com/watch?v=-mZ4_aWfH7s
Composer: Beethoven
Composition: Symphony No. 5 in C minor, Op. 67
Date: 1808
Genre: symphony

Form: Four movements as follows:

I. Allegro con brio – fast, sonata form
II. Andante con moto – slow, theme and variations form
III. Scherzo. Allegro – Scherzo and Trio (ABA)
IV. Allegro – fast, sonata form

Performing Forces: piccolo (fourth movement only), two flutes, two oboes, two clarinets, two bassoons, contrabassoon (fourth movement only), two horns, two trumpets, three trombones (fourth movement only), timpani, and strings (first and second violins, viola, cellos, and double basses)

What we want you to remember about this composition:

- Its fast first movement in sonata form opens with the short-short-short-long motive (which pervades much of the symphony): Fate knocking at the door?
- The symphony starts in C minor but ends in C major: a triumphant over fate?

Allegro con moto

For a guided analysis by Gerard Schwarz of the first movement go to:

https://www.khanacademy.org/partner-content/all-star-orchestra/masterpieces-old-and-new/beethoven-fifth-symphony/v/ludwig-van-beethoven-part-1

What we want you to remember about this movement

- Its fast first movement in sonata form opens with the short-short-short-long motive (which pervades much of the symphony): Fate knocking at the door?
- Its C minor key modulates for a while to other keys but returns at the end of this movement
- The staccato first theme comprised of sequencing of the short-short-short-long motive (SSSL) greatly contrasts the more lyrical and legato second theme
- The coda at the end of the movement provides dramatic closure.

Timing	**Performing Forces, Melody, and Texture**	**Text and Form**
0:00	Full orchestra in a mostly homophonic texture and *forte* dynamic. Melody starts with the SSSL motive introduced and then suspended with a fermata (or hold). After this happens twice, the melody continues with the SSSL motive in rising sequences.	EXPOSITION: First theme

0:21	The *forte* dynamic continues, with emphasis from the timpani. Falling sequences using the SSSL rhythm.	Transition
0:40	After the horn call, the strings lead this quieter section. A horn call using the SSSL motive introduces a more lyrical theme—now in a major key.	Second theme
1:01	SSSL rhythms passes through the full orchestra that plays at a forte dynamic. The SSSL rhythm returns in down-ward sequences.	Closing
1:17		EXPOSITION: Repeats
2:32	Some polyphonic imitation; lots of dialogue between the low and high instruments and the strings and winds. Rapid sequences and changing of keys, fragmentation and alternation of the original motive.	DEVELOPMENT
3:23	Music moves from louds to softs	Retransition
3:40	but ends with a short oboe cadenza. Starts like the exposition.	RECAPITULATION: First theme
4:09	Similar to the transition in the ex-position but does not modulate.	"Transition"
4:28	Now started by the oboes and bas-soons. Now in C minor, not E flat major, which provides a more ominous tone.	Second theme
4:53	As above	Closing
5:08	After a sudden *piano* articulation of the SSSL motive, suddenly ends in a loud and bombastic manner: Fate threatens. Re-emphasizes C minor.	Coda

Timing	Performing Forces, Melody, and Texture	Text and Form
II Andante For a guided analysis by Gerard Schwarz of the first movement from an orchestra conductor's perspective, go to: https://www.khanacademy.org/partner-content/all-star-orchestra/masterpieces-old-and-new/beethoven-fifth-symphony/v/gerard-schwarz-gives-a-conducting-lesson-beethoven-5th-part-1Andante		
For a guided analysis by Gerard Schwarz of the second movement, go to: https://www.khanacademy.org/partner-content/all-star-orchestra/masterpieces-old-and-new/beethoven-fifth-symphony/v/ludwig-van-beethoven-symphony-no-5-analysis-by-gerard-schwarz-mov-2		
What we want you to remember about this movement: • It is a slow theme and variations movement • Its major key provides contrast from the minor key of the first movement		
Timing	**Performing Forces, Melody, and Texture**	**Text and Form**
0:00 [6:32]	Mostly homophonic. Consists of two themes, the first more lyrical; the second more march-like.	Theme: a and b
1:40 [8:12]	More legato and softer at the beginning, although growing loud for the final statement of b in the brass before decrescendoing to *piano* again. Violas subdivide the beat with fast running notes, while the other instruments play the theme.	Variation 1: a and b
3:15 [9:47]	Starts with a softer dynamic and more legato articulations for the "a" phrase and staccato and louder march-like texture when "b" enters, after which the music decrescendos into the next variation. Even more rapid subdivision of the beat in the lower strings at the beginning of "a." Then the "b" phrase returns at the very end of the section.	Variation 2: a and b
5:30 [12:02]	Lighter in texture and more staccato, starting *piano* and crescendoing to *forte* for the final variation. The "a" phrase assumes a jaunty rhythm and then falls apart .	Variation 3: a

6:05 [12:37]	The full orchestra plays *forte* and then sections of the orchestra trade motives at a quieter dynamic. The violins play the first phrase of the melody and then the winds respond with its answer.	Variation 4: A
6:46 [13:17]	Full orchestra plays, soft at first, and then crescendoing, decrescendoing, and crescendoing a final time to the end of the movement. Motives are passed through the orchestra and re-emphasized at the very end of the movement.	Coda
III Scherzo. Allegro For a guided analysis by Gerard Schwarz of the third and four movements, go to: https://www.khanacademy.org/partner-content/all-star-orchestra/masterpieces-old-and-new/beethoven-fifth-symphony/v/beethoven-fourth-movement		
What we really want you to remember about this movement: • It is a scherzo movement that has a scherzo (A) trio (B) scherzo (A) form • The short-short-short-long motive returns in the scherzo sections • The scherzo section is mostly homophonic, and the trio section is mostly imitative polyphony • It flows directly into the final movement without a break		
Timing	**Performing Forces, Melody, and Texture**	**Text and Form**
15:26	Lower strings and at a quiet dynamics. Rapidly ascending legato melody.	Scherzo (A): A
15:49	Presented by the brass in a forte dynamic. Fate motive.	B
16:05		a b a b
17:09	Polyphonic imitation lead by the lower strings. Fast melody.	Trio (B): c c d d
18:30	Now the repetitious SSSL theme is played by the bassoons, staccato. Fast melody.	Scherzo (A): A

18:49	Strings are playing pizzicato (plucking) and the whole ensemble playing at a piano dynamic. Fate motive but in the oboes and strings.	B
19:31	Very soft dynamic to begin with and then slowly crescendos to the forte opening of the fourth movement. Sequenced motive gradually ascends in register.	Transition to the fourth movement

IV Allegro

What we want you to remember about this movement:

- It is a fast sonata form movement in C major: the triumph over Fate?
- The SSSL motive via the scherzo "b" theme returns one final time at the end of the development
- The trombones for their first appearance in a symphony to date
- It has a very long coda

Timing	Performing Forces, Melody, and Texture	Text and Form
20:02 [0:31]	Forte and played by the full orchestra (including trombones, contrabassoon and piccolo). Triumph triadic theme in C major.	EXPOSITION: First theme
20:41	Full orchestra, led by the brass and then continued by the strings. The opening motive of the first theme sequenced as the music modulates to the away key.	Transition
21:05 [1:31]	Full orchestra and slightly softer. Triumphant, if more lyrical, using triplet rhythms in the melody and in G Major.	Second theme
21:34 [2:11]	Full orchestra, *forte* again. Repetition of a descending them.	Closing theme
22:03 [2:29]	Motives passed through all sections of the orchestra. Motives from second theme appear, then motives from the first theme.	DEVELOPMENT

23:36 [4:00]	*Piano* dynamic with the theme in the winds and the strings accompanying. Using the fate motive	Return of scherzo theme
24:11 [4:35]	Performing forces are as before. C major.	RECAPITULATION: First theme
24:43 [5:08]	Performing forces are as before. Does not modulate.	"transition"
25:14 [5:39]	As before.	Second theme
25:39 [6:04]	Starts softly with the woodwinds and then played *forte* by the whole orchestra. Does not modulate.	Closing theme
26:11 [6:40]	Notice the dramatic silences, the alternation of of *legato* and *staccato* articulations, and the sudden increase in tempo near the coda's conclusion: full orchestra. Lengthy coda starting with motive from second theme, then proceeding through with a lot of repeated cadences emphasizing C major and repetition of other motives until the final repeated cadences.	CODA
For Leon Botstein's "An Appreciation" of Beethoven and his Symphony, go to: https://www.khanacademy.org/partner-content/all-star-orchestra/masterpieces-old-and-new/beethoven-fifth-symphony/v/ludwig-van-beethoven-symphony-no-5-an-appreciation-by-leon-botstein		

5.8 CHAPTER SUMMARY

As we have seen, around the 75 years that span the musical compositions of Haydn, Mozart, and Beethoven were rife with innovations in musical genre, style, and form. In many ways, they shaped music for the next 200 years. Composers continued to write symphonies and string quartets, using forms such as the sonata, theme, and variations. A large portion of late eighteenth and early nineteenth-century society continued playing music in the home and going to theaters for opera and to concerts at which orchestral compositions such as concertos and symphonies were performed. Although that live performance culture may not be as prevalent at the beginning of the twenty-first century, we might ask why it was so important for Western music culture for so long. We also might ask if any of its elements inform our music of today.

5.9 GLOSSARY

Cadenza – section of a concerto in which the soloist plays alone without the orchestra in an improvisatory style

Chamber music – music—such as art songs, piano character pieces, and string quartets—primarily performed in small performing spaces, often for personal entertainment

Coda – optional final section of a movement that reasserts the home key of the movement and provides a sense of conclusion

Da capo – instruction—commonly found at the end of the B section or Trio of a Minuet and Trio, to return to the "head" or first section, generally resulting in an A - B - A form

Development – the middle section of a sonata-form movement in which the themes and key areas introduced in the exposition are developed;

Double-exposition form – form of the first movement of a Classical period concerto that combines the exposition, development, and recapitulation of sonata form with the ritornello form used for the first movements of Baroque concertos; also called first-movement concerto form

Exposition – first section of a sonata form movement, in which the themes and key areas of the movement are introduced; the section normally modulates from the home key to a different key

Hemiola – the momentary shifting from a duple to a triple feel or vice versa

Minuet and trio form – form based on the minuet dance that consists of a Minuet (A), then a contrasting Trio (B), followed by a return to the Minuet (A)

Opera Buffa – comic style of opera made famous by Mozart

Opera Seria – serious style of eighteenth-century opera made famous by Handel generally features mythology or high-born characters and plots

Pizzicato – the plucking of a bowed string instrument such as the violin, producing a percussive effect

Recapitulation – third and final second of a sonata-form movement, in which the themes of the exposition return, now in the home key of the movement

Rondo – instrumental form consisting of the alternation of a refrain "A" with contrasting sections ("B," "C," "D," etc.). Rondos are often the final movements of string quartets, classical symphonies, concerti, and sonata (instrumental solos).

Scherzo – form that prominently replaced the minuet in symphonies and strings quartets of the nineteenth century; like the minuet, scherzos are ternary forms and have a triple feel, although they tend to be somewhat faster in tempo than the minuet.

Sonata form – a form often found in the first and last movements of sonatas, symphonies, and string quartets, consisting of three parts—exposition, development, and recapitulation

String quartet – performing ensemble consisting of two violinists, one violinist, and one cellist that plays compositions called string quartets, compositions generally in four movements

Symphony – multi-movement composition for orchestra, often in four movements

Ternary form – describes a musical composition in three parts, most often featurings two similar sections, separated by a contrasting section and represented by the letters A – B – A.

Theme and Variation form – the presentation of a theme and then variations upon it. The theme may be illustrated as A, with any number of variations following it – A', A'', A''', A'''', etc.

6 Nineteenth-Century Music and Romanticism

Jeff Kluball and Elizabeth Kramer

6.1 OBJECTIVES

1. Demonstrate knowledge of historical and cultural contexts of nineteenth-century music, including musical Romanticism and nationalism
2. Aurally identify selected genres of nineteenth century music and their associated expressive aims, uses, and styles
3. Aurally identify the music of selected composers of nineteenth century music and their associated styles
4. Explain ways in which music and other cultural forms interact in nineteenth century music in genres such as the art song, program music, opera, and musical nationalism

6.2 KEY TERMS AND INDIVIDUALS

- 1848 revolutions
- Antonín Dvořák
- art song
- Augmented second
- Bedřich Smetana
- Beethoven
- Caspar David Friedrich
- chamber music
- chromaticism
- concerto
- conductor
- drone
- Eugène Delacroix
- Exoticism
- Fanny Mendelssohn Hensel
- Felix Mendelssohn-Bartholdy
- Francisco de Goya
- Franz Liszt
- Franz Schubert
- Fryderyk Chopin
- Giuseppe Verdi
- *idée fixe*
- Johann Wolfgang von Goethe
- John Philip Sousa
- leitmotiv
- lied

- Louis Moreau Gottschalk
- Mary Shelley
- mazurka
- nationalism
- opera
- program symphony
- Pyotr Tchaikovsky
- Richard Wagner
- Robert and Clara Schumann
- Romanticism
- rubato
- salon
- scena ad aria (recitative, cantabile, cabaletta)
- soirée
- sonata
- sonata form (exposition, development, recapitulation)
- song cycle
- string quartet
- strophic
- symphonic poem
- Symphony
- ternary form
- through-composed
- V.E.R.D.I.
- William Wordsworth

6.3 INTRODUCTION AND HISTORICAL CONTEXT

This chapter considers music of the nineteenth century, a period often called the "Romantic era" in music. Romanticism might be defined as a cultural movement stressing emotion, imagination, and individuality. It started in literature around 1800 and then spread to art and music. By around 1850, the dominant aesthetic (artistic philosophy) of literature and visual art began to shift to what is now often called a time of realism (cultural expressions of what is perceived as common and contemporary). Cultural Nationalism (pride in one's culture) and Exoticism (fascination with the other) also became more pronounced after 1850, as reflected in art, literature, and music. Realism, nationalism, and Exoticism were prominent in music as well, although we tend to treat them as sub-categories under a period of musical Romanticism that spanned the entire century.

In his Preface to the second edition of the *Lyrical Ballads* (1801), English poet William Wordsworth declared that "all good poetry is the spontaneous overflow of powerful feelings." The power and expression of emotion exalted by literary Romanticism was equally important for nineteenth-century music, which often explicitly attempted to represent every shade of human emotion, the most prominent of which are love and sorrow. Furthermore, the Romantics were very interested in the connections between music, literature, and the visual arts. Poets and philosophers rhapsodized about the power of music, and musicians composed both vocal and instrumental program music explicitly inspired by literature and visual art. In fact, for many nineteenth-century thinkers, music had risen to the top of the aesthetic hierarchy. Music was previously perceived as inferior to poetry and sculpture, as it had no words or form. In the nineteenth century, however, music was understood to express what words could not express, thus transcending the material for something more ideal and spiritual; some called this expression "absolute music."

As we listen to nineteenth-century music, we might hear some similarities with music of the classical era, but there are also differences. Aesthetically speaking, classicism tends to emphasize balance, control, proportion, symmetry, and restraint. Romanticism seeks out the new, the curious, and the adventurous, emphasizing qualities of remoteness, boundlessness, and strangeness. It is characterized by restless longing and impulsive reaction, as well as freedom of expression and pursuit of the unattainable. There are many parallels between what was going on historically in society and what was occurring in music. We cannot study one without studying the other because they are so inter-related, though music will be our guiding focus.

Geo-politically, the nineteenth century extends from the French Revolution to a decade or so before World War I. The French Revolution wound down around 1799, when the Napoleonic Wars then ensued. The Napoleonic Wars were waged by Napoléon Bonaparte, who had declared himself emperor of France. Another war was the Unites States Civil War from 1861-1865. The United States also saw expansion westward as the gold rush brought in daring settlers. Even though the United States was growing, England was the dominant world power at this time. Its whaling trade kept ships sailing and lamps burning. Coal fueled the Industrial Revolution and the ever-expanding rail system. Economic and social power shifted increasingly towards the common people due to revolts. These political changes affected nineteenth-century music as composers who began to aim their music at the more common people, rather than just the rich.

Political nationalism was on the rise in the nineteenth century. Early in the century, Bonaparte's conquests spurred on this nationalism, inspiring Italians, Austrians, Germans, Eastern Europeans, and Russians to assert their cultural identities, even while enduring the political domination of the French. After France's political power diminished with the Congress of Vienna in 1814-1815, politics throughout much of Europe were still punctuated by revolutions, first a minor revolution in 1848 in what is now Germany, and then the Franco-Prussian War of 1870-1871. Later in the century, Eastern Europeans, in what is now the Czech Republic and Slovakia, and the Russians developed schools of national music in the face of Austro-German cultural, and sometimes political, hegemony. Nationalism was fed by the continued rise of the middle class as well as the rise of republicanism and democracy, which defines human beings as individuals with responsibilities and rights derived as much from the social contract as from family, class, or creed.

6.3.1 Philosophy

The nineteenth century saw some of the most famous continental philosophers of all time: Johann Wolfgang von Goethe (1749-1832), Georg Wilhelm Friedrich Hegel (1770-1831), Arthur Schopenhauer (1788-1860), and Friedrich Wilhelm Nietzsche (1844-1900). All responded in some way or another to the ideas of their eighteenth-century predecessor Immanuel Kant (1724-1804), who revolutionized the way human beings saw themselves in relation to others and to God by positing that human beings can never see "the thing in itself" and thus must relate as subjects to the objects that are exterior to themselves. Based on the work of Kant, as well as on a revival of ancient philosophical idealism, Hegel proposed some resolution of this subject-object dichotomy by characterizing human existence as thesis meeting its opposite in antithesis and thus yielding synthesis. Schopenhauer, on the other hand, maintained that Kant had been right to point to the divide between subject and object. (For our purposes here, consider music to be the human phenomenon in which one might experience the thing, or object, in itself.) His ideas influenced the musical philosophy of Richard Wagner, and both of Schopenhauer's and Wagner's ideas shaped Friedrich Nietzsche's early philosophy. In the middle of the nineteenth century, the ideas of Kant and Hegel, and to a lesser extent Schopenhauer, influenced American Transcendentalism, often reflected in the writings of Ralph Waldo Emerson (1803-1882) and Henry David Thoreau (1817-1862).

6.3.2 Science

Science and technology made great strides in the nineteenth century. Some of its inventions increased mobility of the individuals in the Western world, such as with the proliferation of trains running across newly-laid tracks and steamships sailing down major rivers and eventually across oceans. Other advances, such as the commercial telegraph (from the 1830s), allowed news to travel more quickly than before. All this speed and mobility culminated in the first automobiles that emerged at the very end of the century. Plate and then chemical photography were invented in the first half of the 1800s, with film photography emerging at the end of the century: we have photographs of several of the composers studied in this chapter. Experiments with another sort of recording, sound recording, would get started in the mid 1800s and finally become commercially available in the twentieth century. The nineteenth century saw ongoing experiments with electricity and electrically powered lamps such as the light bulb that would also blossom as the century turned.

Figure 6.1 | John James Audubon, 1826
Author | John Syme
Source | Wikimedia Commons
License | Public Domain

Figure 6.2 | Charles Darwin, 1854
Author | Henry Maull and John Fox
Source | Wikimedia Commons
License | Public Domain

Romantics were fascinated by nature, and the middle class public followed naturalists, like Americans John James Audubon (1785-1851) and John Muir (1838-1914) and the Englishman Charles Darwin (1809-1882), as they observed and recorded life in the wild. Darwin's evolutionary theories based on his voyages to locales such as the Galapagos Islands were avidly debated among the people of his day.

6.3.3 Visual Art

Romantics were fascinated by the imaginary, the grotesque, and by that which was chronologically or geographically foreign. Emphasis on these topics began to appear in such late eighteenth-century works as Swiss painter Henry Fuseli's *Nightmare* from 1781. Romantics were also intrigued by the Gothic style: a young Goethe raved about it after visiting the Gothic Cathedral in Strasbourg, France. His writings in turn spurred the completion of the Cathedral in Cologne, Germany, which had been started in the Gothic style in 1248 and then completed in that same style between the years of 1842 and 1880.

Romantic interest in the individual, nature, and the supernatural is also very evident in nineteenth-century landscapes, including those of Caspar David Friedrich (1774-1840). One of his most famous paintings, ***Wanderer Above the Sea of Fog*** (1818), shows a lone man with his walking stick, surrounded by a vast horizon. The man has progressed to the top of a mountain, but there his

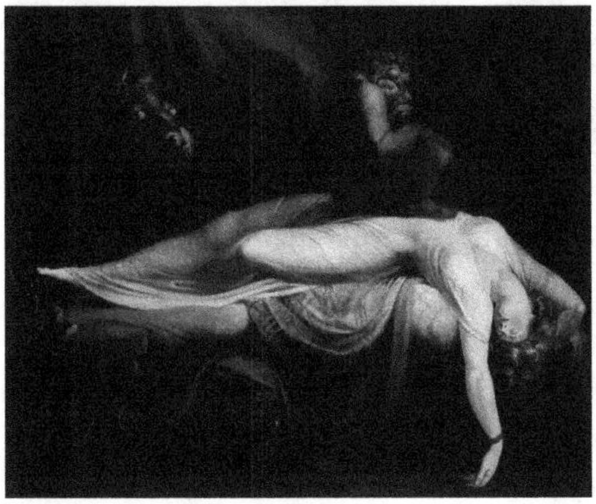

Figure 6.3 | *The Nightmare*
Author | Henry Fuseli
Source | Wikimedia Commons
License | Public Domain

Figure 6.4 | Cologne Cathedral
Author | Johann Franz Michiels
Source | Wikimedia Commons
License | Public Domain

Figure 6.5 | *The Wanderer Above the Sea of Fog*
Author | Caspar David Friedrich
Source | Wikimedia Commons
License | Public Domain

vision is limited due to the fog. We do not see his face, perhaps suggesting the solitary reality of a human subject both separate from and somehow spiritually attuned to the natural and supernatural.

In France, Eugène Delacroix (1798-1863) captured the revolutionary and nationalist fervor of the time in such paintings as *Liberty Leading the People* (1830). He was also a good friend with musicians Frydryk Chopin and Hector Berlioz, whom he immortalized in portraits.

Francisco de Goya (1746 -1828) was born in Fuendetodos, Spain. He painted for the Spanish Royal court, producing portraits of nobility. However, he also painted works criticizing the social and political problems of his era.

Figure 6.6 | *Liberty Leading the People*
Author | Eugène Delacroix
Source | Wikimedia Commons
License | Public Domain

Figure 6.7 | *Disasters of War, Plate 39*
Author | Francisco Goya
Source | Wikimedia Commons
License | Public Domain

Figure 6.8 | *The Third of May 1808*
Author | Francisco Goya
Source | Wikimedia Commons
License | Public Domain

One of Goya's personal projects, *Disasters of War*, however, was commissioned by no one. It was Goya's private project, which he never even published in his lifetime. *Disasters of War* unflinchingly depicts mutilation, torture, rape, and many other atrocities indiscriminately inflicted on Spanish citizens by French and Spanish alike. In *The Third Day of May*, Goya commemorated the Spanish resistance to Napoleon's Armies in 1808 in the Peninsular War. It portrays an execution by Napoleon's Troops.

As the nineteenth century progressed, European artists became increasingly interested in what they called "realist" topics, that is, in depicting the lives of the average human, as he or she went about living in the present moment. While the realism in such art is not devoid of idealizing forces, it does emphasize the validity of the everyday life as a topic for art alongside the value of craft and technique in bringing such "realist" scenes to life.

6.3.4 Literature

The novel, which had emerged forcefully in the eighteenth century, became the literary genre of choice in the nineteenth century. Many German novels focused on a character's development; most important of these novels are those by the German philosopher, poet, and playwright, Johann Wolfgang von Goethe who was fascinated with the supernatural and set the story of Faust. Faust is a man who sells his soul to the devil in exchange for knowledge, in an epic two-part drama. English author Mary Shelley (1797-1851) explored nature and the supernatural in the novel *Frankenstein, or the Modern Prometheus* (1818), which examines current scientific discoveries as participating in the ancient quest to control nature. Later in the century, British author Charles Dickens exposed the plight of the common man during a time of Industrialization. In France, Victor Hugo (1802-1885) wrote on a broad range of themes, from what his age saw as the grotesque in *The Hunchback of Notre-Dame* (1831) to the topic of French Revolution in *Les Misérables* (1862). Another Frenchman, Gustav Flaubert, captured the psychological and emotional life of a "real" woman in *Madame Bovary* (1856). And in the United States, Mark Twain created *Tom Sawyer* (1876).

Besides novels, poetry continued strong in the nineteenth century with such important English poets as George Gordon, Lord Byron, Wordsworth, Samuel Taylor Coleridge, and John Keats. In addition to Goethe, other German literary figures included Friedrich Schiller, Adrian Ludwig Richter, Heidrich Heine, Novalis, Ludwig Tieck, and E. T. A. Hoffmann; their works contributed librettos and settings for nineteenth-century music. Near the end of the century, French symbolism, a movement akin to Impressionism in art and music, emerged in the poetry of Paul Verlaine, Stéphane Mallarmé, and Arthur Rimbaud.

For a view of a comprehensive timeline that compares historical events of the Romantic time period to the musical events of the period go to:

http://www.wmea.com/index.php?module=cms&page=673

6.3.5 Nineteenth-Century Musical Contexts

We have already alluded to a new respect for vocal and instrumental music that emerged at the end of the eighteenth century. Music's influence only grew in the nineteenth century, becoming more prominent yet in the education of the still growing middle class; even the United States, which throughout most of the nineteenth century was deemed somewhat a cultural backwaters of the Western world, had music education in the public schools by the end of the century. An increasing number of music magazines was published, and amateur music making in the home and in local civic groups was at a height. Piano music was a major component of private music making. The salons and soirées of upper middle class and aristocratic women drew many of these private musical performances.

More concerts in public venues enjoyed increased attendance; some of these concerts were solo recitals and others featured large symphony orchestras, sometimes accompanied by choirs. Their performers were often trained in highly specialized music schools called conservatories, which took root in major European cities. By the end of the nineteenth century, traveling virtuoso performers and composers were some of the most famous personalities of their time. These musicians hailed from all over Europe. Some of them became quite wealthy from revenues of ticket sales and publications. Others fit the stereotype of the starving artist, paid in respect though not in the currency of their day.

Romantic aesthetics tended to conceptualize musicians as highly individualistic and often eccentric. Beethoven modeled these concepts and was the most influential figure of nineteenth-century music, even after his death in 1827. His perceived alienation from society, the respect he was given, and the belief in the transformative power of music that was often identified in his compositions, galvanized romantic perceptions. His music, popular in its own day, only became more popular after his death. Subsequent composers looked to his innovations in symphonic compositions, especially his use of recurring motives and themes, as we heard in the Fifth Symphony. For them, Beethoven was also something of a problem: how might one compose in the shadow of such a musical giant?

6.3.6 Musical Timeline

Events in History	Events in Music
1801: Wordsworth publishes his *Lyrical Ballades*	
1814-1815: Congress of Vienna, ending Napoleon's conquest of Europe and Russia	
	1815: Schubert publishes *The Erlking*
1818: Mary Shelley publishes *Frankenstein*	
1818: Caspar David Friedrich paints *Wanderer Above the Sea of Fog*	
	1827: Beethoven dies
	1829: Felix Mendelssohn leads a revival of Bach's *St. Matthew Passion,*which leads to a revival of Bach's music more generally
1830s: Eugène Delacroix captures revolutionary and nationalist fervor in his paintings	1830: Hector Berlioz premiers his most famous work, the *Symphonie fantastique*
	1830s: Clara Wieck and Franz Liszt tour (separately) as virtuoso pianists
	1831: Fryderyk Chopin immigrates to Paris, from the political turmoil in his native country of Poland
1832: Johann Wolgang von Goethe dies	
	1840: Clara and Robert Schumann marry
1850s: Realism becomes prominent in art and literature	1853: Verdi composes *La Traviata*
1861-1865: Civil War in the U.S.	
1870-71: Franco-Prussian War	
	1874: Bedřich Smetana composes *The Moldau*

	1876: Johannes Brahms completes his First Symphony 1876: Wagner premiers ***The Ring of the Nibelungen*** at his Festival Theatre in Bayreuth, Germany 1882: Tchaikovsky writes the ***1812*** Overture 1891-1892: John Philip Sousa tours the U.S. leading the U.S. Marine Band 1892-1895: Antonin Dvořák visits the U.S., helps establish the first American music conservatory, and composes the ***New World*** Symphony.

6.4 MUSIC IN THE NINETEENTH CENTURY

6.4.1 Music Comparison Overview

Classical Music	Nineteenth-Century Music
• Mostly homophony, but with variation • New genres such as the symphony and string quartet • Use of crescendos and decrescendos • Question and answer (aka antecedent consequent) phrases that are shorter than earlier phrases • New emphasis on musical form: for example, sonata form, theme and variations, minuet and trio, rondo, and first-movement concerto form • Greater use of contrasting dynamics, articulations, and tempos	• Lyrical melodies, often with wider leaps • Homophonic style still prevalent, but with variation • Larger performing forces using more diverse registers, dynamic ranges, and timbres • More rubato and tempo fluctuation within a composition • More chromatic and dissonant harmonies with increasingly delayed resolutions • Symphonies, string quartets, concertos, operas, and sonata-form movements continue to be written • Newly important miniature genres and forms such as the *Lied* and short piano composition • Program music increasingly prominent • Further development in performers' virtuosity • No more patronage system

6.4.2 General Trends in Nineteenth Century Music

Musical Style, Performing Forces, and Forms

The nineteenth century is marked by a great diversity in musical styles, from the conservative to the progressive. As identified by the style comparison chart above, nineteenth century melodies continue to be tuneful and are perhaps even more songlike than classical style melodies, although they may contain wider leaps. They still use sequences, which are often as a part of modulation from one key to another. Melodies use more chromatic (or "colorful") pitches from outside the home key and scale of a composition. Along with the continuing emphasis on tuneful melodies comes predominantly homophonic textures, although as compositions use more instruments, there are also increasing numbers of accompanying, but relatively interesting, musical lines.

Harmonies in nineteenth-century music are more dissonant than ever. More chords add a fourth note to the triad, making them more dissonant and chromatic. These dissonances may be sustained for some time before resolving to a chord that is consonant. One composition may modulate between several keys, and these keys often have very different pitch contents. Such modulations tend to disorient the listening and add to the chaos of the musical selection. Composers were in effect "pushing the harmonic envelope."

The lengths of nineteenth-century musical compositions ran from the minute to the monumental. Songs and short piano pieces might be only a couple of minutes long, although they were sometimes grouped together in cycles or collections. On the other hand, symphonies and operas grow in size. By the end of the century, a typical symphony might be an hour long, with the operas of Verdi, Wagner, and Puccini clocking in at several hours each. Performing forces reflected similar extremes. There is much nineteenth-century music for solo piano or solo voice with piano accompaniment. The piano achieved a modern form, with the full eighty-eight-note keyboard that is still used today and an iron frame that allowed for greater string tension and a wider range of dynamics. Crescendos and decrescendos became more common, alongside more tempo fluctuations, even within compositions. As we will see, Fryderyk Chopin was the first composer to make prevalent use of rubato as a performance instruction in his musical scores.

During the nineteenth century, the industrial revolution facilitated and enabled marked improvements to many musical instruments besides the piano with its improved and updated iron frame and tempered metal strings. Efficient valves were added to the trumpet and a general improvement in metal works tightened tolerances and metal fittings of all brass instruments. Along with the many improvements to instruments, new instruments were researched and created, including the piccolo, English horn, tuba, contrabassoon, and saxophone.

Orchestras also increased in size and became more diverse in makeup, thereby allowing composers to exploit even more divergent dynamics and timbres. With orchestral compositions requiring over fifty (and sometimes over 100) musicians, a conductor was important, and the first famous conductors date from this period. In fact, generally-speaking, the nineteenth-century orchestra looked not unlike what you might see today at most concerts by most professional orchestras (see Figure 6.9).

Nineteenth-century composers knew well the forms and genres used by their predecessors, most prominently the music of Beethoven, but also the music of composers such as Mozart, Handel, Haydn, and Bach. They continued to compose in these forms and genres, while sometimes transforming them into something quite different, especially among those composers who identified themselves as progressives, as opposed to conservatives. The wider nineteenth-century interest in emotion and in exploring connections between all of the arts led to musical scores with more poetic or prose instructions from the composer. It also led to more program music, which as you will recall, is instrumental music that represents something "extra musical," that is, something outside of music itself, such as nature, a literary text, or a painting. Nineteenth-century critics and philosophers sustained expansive debates about ways in which listeners might hear music as related to the extra musical. Extra musical influences, from the characteristic title to a narrative attached to a musical score, guided composers and listeners as they composed and heard musical forms.

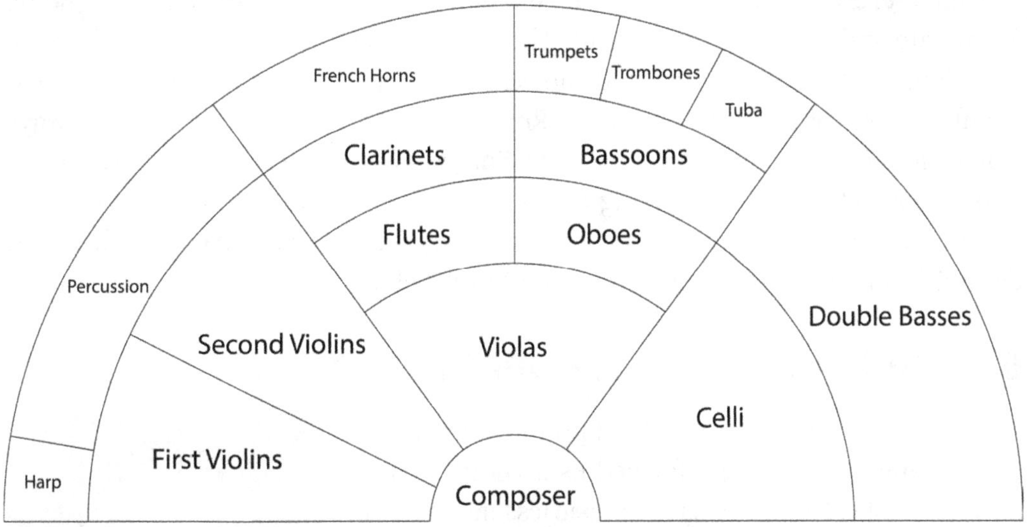

Figure 6.9 | Nineteenth-Century Orchestra Diagram
Author | Corey Parson
Source | Original Work
License | CC BY-SA 4.0

Genres of Instrumental Music

Some nineteenth-century compositions use titles similar to those found in classical style music, such as "Symphony No. 3," "Concerto, Op. 3," or "String Quartet in C Minor." These compositions are sometimes referred to as examples of absolute music (that is, music for the sake of music). Program music with titles came in several forms. Short piano compositions were described as "character pieces" and took on names reflecting their emotional mood, state, or reference. Orchestral program music included the program symphony and the symphonic poem (also known as the tone poem). The program symphony was a multi-movement composition for orchestra that represented something extra musical, a composition such as Hector Berlioz's *Symphonie fantastique* (discussed below). A symphonic or tone poem was a one-movement composition for orchestra, again with an extra musical referent, such as Bedřich Smetana's *Moldau.*

Genres of Vocal Music

Opera continued to be popular in the nineteenth century and was dominated by Italian styles and form, much like it had been since the seventeenth century. Italian opera composer Giacomo Rossini even rivaled Beethoven in popularity. By the 1820s, however, other national schools were becoming more influential. Carl Maria von Weber's German operas enhanced the role of the orchestra, whereas French grand opera by Meyerbeer and others was marked by the use of large choruses and elaborate sets. Later in the century, composers such as Giuseppe Verdi and Richard Wagner would synthesize and transform opera into an even more dramatic genre.

Other large-scale choral works in the tradition of the Baroque cantata and oratorio were written for civic choirs which would sometimes band together into larger choral ensembles in annual choral festivals. The song for voice and piano saw revived interest, and art songs were chief among the music performed in the home for private and group entertainment. The art song is a composition for solo voice and piano that merges poetic and musical concerns. It became one of the most popular genres of nineteenth-century Romanticism, a movement that was always looking for connections between the arts. Sometimes these art songs were grouped into larger collections called song cycles or, in German, *Liederkreis*. Among the important composers of early nineteenth-century German *Lieder* were Robert and Clara Schumann, Johannes Brahms, and Franz Schubert.

6.5 MUSIC OF FRANZ SCHUBERT (1797-1828)

Franz Schubert lived a short but prolific musical life. Like Joseph Haydn, he performed as a choirboy until his voice broke. He also received music lessons in violin, piano, organ, voice and musical harmony: many of his teachers remarked on the young boy's genius. Schubert followed in his father's footsteps for several years, teaching school through his late teens, until he shifted his attention to music composition fulltime in 1818. By that time he had already composed masterpieces for which he is still known, including the German *Lied, Der Erlkönig* (in English, *The Erlking*), which we will discuss.

Figure 6.10 | Franz Schubert
Author | Wilhelm August Rieder
Source | Wikimedia Commons
License | Public Domain

Schubert spent his entire life in Vienna in the shadow of the two most famous composers of his day: Ludwig van Beethoven, whose music we have already discussed, and Gioachino Rossini, whose Italian operas were particularly popular in Vienna in the first decade. Inspired by the music of Beethoven, Schubert wrote powerful symphonies and chamber music, which are still played today; his "Great" Symphony in C major is thought by many to be Schubert's finest contribution to the genre. He wrote the symphony in 1825 and 1826, but it remained unpublished and indeed perhaps unperformed until Robert Schumann discovered it in 1838. Schumann famously remarked on the "heavenly length" of this composition that can take almost an hour to perform. One reason for its length is its melodic lyricism, although the symphony also reflects the motivic developmental innovations of Beethoven.

Figure 6.11 | *Schubertiade 1868*
Author | Moritz von Schwind
Source | Wikimedia Commons
License | Public Domain

Schubert also wrote operas and church music. His greatest legacy, however, lies in his more than 600 *Lieder,* or art songs. His songs are notable for their beautiful melodies and clever use of piano accompaniment and bring together poetry and music in an exemplary fashion. Most are short, stand alone pieces of one and a half to five minutes in length, but he also wrote a couple of song cycles. These songs were published and performed in many private homes and, along with all of his compositions, provided so much entertainment in the private musical gatherings in Vienna that these events were renamed as Schubertiades (see the famous depiction of one Schubertiade by the composer's close friend Moritz Schwind (painted years after the fact from memory in 1868). Many of Schubert's songs are about romantic love, a perennial song topic. Others, such as *The Erlking*, put to music romantic responses to nature and to the supernatural. *The Erlking* is strikingly dramatic, a particular reminder that music and drama interacted in several nineteenth-century genres, even if their connections can be most fully developed in a lengthy composition, such as an opera.

Focus Composition:

Schubert, *The Erlking* (1815)

Schubert set the words of several poets of his day, and *The Erlking* (1815) is drawn from the poetry of the most famous: Johann Wolfgang von Goethe. *The Erlking* tells the story of a father who is rushing on horseback with his ailing son to the doctor. Delirious from fever, the son hears the voice of the Erlking, a grim reaper sort of king of the fairies, who appears to young children when they are about to die, luring them into the world beyond. The father tries to reassure his son that his fear is imagined, but when the father and son reach the courtyard of the doctor's house, the child is found to be dead.

As you listen to the song, follow along with its words. You may have to listen several times in order to hear the multiple connections between the music and the text. Are the ways in which you hear the music and text interacting beyond those pointed out in the listening guide?

LISTENING GUIDE

For audio, go to:
https://www.youtube.com/watch?v=5XP5RP6OEJI
Performed by baritone Dietrich Fischer Dieskau and pianist Gerald Moore.

Composer: Franz Schubert

Composition: *The Erlkönig* (in English, *The Erlking*)

Date: 1815

Genre: art song

Form: through-composed

Nature of Text:

Original Text

Wer reitet so spät dur ch Nacht und Wind?
Es ist der Vater mit seinem Kind.
Er hat den Knaben wohl in dem Arm,
Er faßt ihn sicher, er hält ihn warm.

Mein Sohn, was birgst du so bang dein Gesicht?
Siehst Vater, du den Erlkönig nicht!
Den Erlenkönig mit Kron' und Schweif?
Mein Sohn, es ist ein Nebelstreif.

Du liebes Kind, komm geh' mit mir!
Gar schöne Spiele, spiel ich mit dir,
Manch bunte Blumen sind an dem Strand,
Meine Mutter hat manch gülden Gewand.

Mein Vater, mein Vater, und hörest du nicht,
Was Erlenkönig mir leise verspricht?
Sei ruhig, bleibe ruhig, mein Kind,
In dürren Blättern säuselt der Wind.

Willst feiner Knabe du mit mir geh'n?
Meine Töchter sollen dich warten schön,
Meine Töchter führen den nächtlichen Reihn
Und wiegen und tanzen und singen dich ein.

Mein Vater, mein Vater, und siehst du nicht dort
Erlkönigs Töchter am düsteren Ort?
Mein Sohn, mein Sohn, ich seh'es genau:
Es scheinen die alten Weiden so grau.

Ich lieb dich, mich reizt deine schöne Gestalt,
Und bist du nicht willig, so brauch ich Gewalt!
Mein Vater, mein Vater, jetzt faßt er mich an,
Erlkönig hat mir ein Leids getan.

Dem Vater grauset's, er reitet geschwind,
Er hält in den Armen das ächzende Kind,
Erreicht den Hof mit Mühe und Not,
In seinen Armen das Kind war tot.

Translation

Who rides there so late through the night and wind?
The father it is, with his infant so dear;
He holds the boy tightly clasped in his arm,
He holds him safely, he keeps him warm.

"My son, why do you anxiously hide your face?"
"Look, father, is it not the Erlking!
The Erlking with crown and with train?"
"My son, it is the mist over the clouds."

"Oh, come, dear child! oh, come with me!
So many games I will play there with thee;
On my shoreline, lovely flowers their blossoms unfold,
My mother has many a gold garment."

"My father, my father, and do you not hear
The words that the Erlking softly promises me?"
"Be calm, stay calm, my child,
The wind sighs through the dry leaves."

"Will you come with me, my child?
My daughters shall wait on you;
My daughters dance each night,
And will cradle you and dance and sing to you."

"My father, my father, and do you not see,
The Erl-King's daughters in this dreary place?"
"My son, my son, I see it aright,
The old fields appear so gray."

"I love you, I'm charmed by your lovely form!
And if you're unwilling, then force I'll employ."
"My father, my father, he seizes me fast,
Full sorely the Erl-King has hurt me at last."

The father, horrified, rides quickly,
He holds in his arms the groaning child:
He reaches his courtyard with toil and trouble,—
In his arms, the child was dead.

Performing Forces: solo voice and piano

What we want you to remember about this composition:

- It is an art song that sets a poem for solo voice and piano
- The poem tells the story of three characters, who are depicted in the music through changes in melody, harmony, and range.
- The piano sets general mood and supports the singer by depicting images from the text.

Other things to listen for:

- Piano accompaniment at the beginning that outlines a minor scale (perhaps the wind)
- Repeated fast triplet pattern in the piano, suggesting urgency and the running horse
- Shifts of the melody line from high to low range, depending on the character "speaking"
- Change of key from minor to major when the Erlking sings
- The slowing note values at the end of the song and the very dissonant chords

Timing	**Performing Forces, Melody, and Texture**	**Text and Form**
0:00	Piano introduction Opens with a fast tempo melody that begins low in the register, ascends through the minor scale, and then falls. Accompanied by repeated triplet octaves. The ascending/descending melody may represent the wind. The minor key suggests a serious tone. The repeated octaves using fast triplets may suggest the running horse and the urgency of the situation.	
0:24	Voice and piano from here to the end; Performing forces are voice and piano in homophonic texture from here to the end. Melody falls in the middle of the singer's range and is accompanied by the repeated octave triplets.	Narrator: Who rides so late through night and wind?

0:56	Melody drops lower in the singer's range.	Father: My son, why are you frightened?
1:03	Melody shifts to a higher range	Son: Do you see the Erlking, father?
1:19	Melody lower in range.	Father: It is the fog.
1:28	The key switches to major, perhaps to suggest the friendly guise assumed by the Erlking. Note also the softer dynamics and lighter arpeggios in the piano accompaniment	The Erlking: Lovely child, come with me...
1:52	Back in minor the melody hovers around one note high in the singer's register; the minor mode reflects the son's fear, as does the melody, which repeats the same note, almost as if the son is unable to sing another	Son: My father, father, do you not hear it...
2:03	Melody lower in range	Father: Be calm, my child, the wind blows the dry leaves...
2:13	Back to a major key and *piano* dynamics for more from the Erlking	The Erlking: My darling boy, won't you come with me...
2:30	Back to a minor key and the higher-ranged melody that hovers around one pitch for the son's retort.	Son: My father, can you not see him there?
2:41	Melody lower in range and return of the louder repeated triplets	Father: My son, I see well the moonlight on the grey meadows....
2:58	Momentarily in major and then back to minor as the Erlking threatens the boy	The Erlking: I love you...if you do not freely come, I will use force...
3:09	Back to a minor key and the higher-ranged melody that hovers around one pitch.	Son: My father, he has seized me...
3:22	Back to a mid-range melody; the notes in the piano get faster and louder.	Narrator: The father, filled with horror, rides fast

3:37	Piano accompaniment slows down; dissonant and minor chords pervasive; song ends with a strong cadence in the minor key; Slowing down of the piano accompaniment may echo the slowing down of the horse. The truncated chords and strong final minor chords buttress the announcement that the child is dead.	Narrator: They arrive at the courtyard. In his father's arms, the child was dead.

The next generation of nineteenth-century composers—born in the first two decades of the century—included a number of talented pianists: Felix and Fanny Mendelssohn, Robert and Clara Schumann, Fryderyk Chopin, and Franz Liszt. They were joined by orchestra composer Hector Berlioz and a slightly younger composer who might be considered Berlioz's alter ego, Johannes Brahms.

6.6 MUSIC OF THE MENDELSSOHNS

In terms of musical craft, few nineteenth-century composers were more accomplished than Felix Mendelssohn-Bartholdy (1809-1847). Growing up in an artistically-rich, upper-middle class household in Berlin, Germany, Felix Mendelssohn received a fine private education in the arts and sciences and proved himself to be precociously talented from a very young age. He would go on to write chamber music for piano and strings, art songs, church music, four symphonies, and oratorios as well as conduct many of Beethoven's works as principal director of the Leipzig Gewandhaus Orchestra. All of his music emulates the motivic and organic styles of Beethoven's compositions, from his chamber music to his more monumental compositions. Felix was also well-versed in the musical styles of Mozart, Handel, and Bach.

Figure 6.12 | Felix Mendelssohn-Bartholdy
Author | James Warren Childe
Source | Wikimedia Commons
License | Public Domain

Felix descended from a family of prominent Jewish intellectuals; his grandfather Moses Mendelssohn was one of the leaders of the eighteenth-century German Enlightenment. His parents, however, seeking to break from this religious tradition, had their children baptized as Reformed Christians in 1816. Anti-Semitism was a fact of life in nineteenth-century Germany, and such a baptism opened some, if not all, doors for the family. Most agree that in 1832, the failure of Felix's application for the position as head of the Berlin *Singakadmie* was partly due to his Jewish ethnicity. This failure was a blow to the young musician, who had performed frequently with this civic choral society, most importantly in 1829, when he had led a revival of the *St. Matthew Passion* by Johann Sebastian Bach. Although today we think of Bach as a pivotal figure of the Baroque period, his music went through a period of neglect until this revival.

Initially, Felix's father was reluctant to see his son become a professional musician; like many upper-middle class businessmen, he would have preferred his son enjoy music as an amateur. Felix, however, was both determined and talented, and eventually secured employment as a choral and orchestral conductor, first in Düsseldorf, and then in Leipzig, Germany, where he lived from 1835 until his death. In Leipzig, Felix conducted the orchestra and founded the town's first music conservatory.

Felix's music was steeped in the styles of his predecessors. Although he remained on good terms with more experimental composers of his day, including Hector Berlioz and Franz Liszt, he was not fond of their music. It is not surprising, then, that he composed in genres passed down to him, including the symphony, string quartet, and oratorio.

Focus Composition:

Mendelssohn, Excerpts from *Elijah* (1846)

One of his last works, his oratorio *Elijah,* was commissioned by the Birmingham Festival in Birmingham, England. The Birmingham Festival was one of many nineteenth-century choral festivals that provided opportunities for amateur and professional musicians to gather once a year to make music together. Mendelssohn's music was very popular in England, and the Birmingham Festival had already performed another Mendelssohn oratorio in the 1830s, giving the premier of *Elijah* in English in 1846.

Elijah is interesting because it is an example of music composed for middle-class music-making. The chorus of singers was expected to be largely made up of musical amateurs, with professional singers brought in to sing the solos. The topic of the oratorio, the Hebrew prophet Elijah, is interesting as a figure significant to both the Jewish and Christian traditions, both of which Felix embraced to a certain extent. (In general, Felix was private about his religious convictions, and interpretations of *Elijah* as representing the composer's beliefs will always remain somewhat speculative.) This composition shows Felix's indebtedness to both Baroque composers Bach and Handel, while at the same time it uses more nineteenth-century harmonies and textures.

The following excerpt is from the first part of the oratorio and sets the dramatic story of Elijah's calling the followers of the pagan god Baal to light a sacrifice on fire. Baal fails his devotees; Elijah then summons the God of Abraham to a display of power with great success. The excerpt here involves a baritone soloist who sings the role of Elijah and the chorus that provides commentary. Elijah first sings a short accompanied recitative, not unlike what we heard in the music of Handel's *Messiah*. The first chorus is highly polyphonic in announcing the flames from heaven before shifting to a more homophonic and deliberate style that uses longer note values to proclaim the central tenet of Western religion: "The Lord is God, the Lord is God! O Israel hear! Our God is one Lord, and we will have no other gods before the Lord." After another recitative and another chorus, Elijah sings a very melismatic and virtuoso aria.

Elijah was very popular in its day, in both its English and German versions, both for music makers and musical audiences, and continues to be performed by choral societies today.

LISTENING GUIDE For audio, go to: https://youtu.be/pUOxpjiltGU?list=PL2DA5013E20B3E14A Performed by the Texas A&M Century Singers with orchestra and baritone soloist Weston Hurt.
Composer: Felix Mendelssohn-Bartholdy
Composition: Excerpts from *Elijah*
Date: 1846
Genre: Recitative, choruses, and aria from an oratorio
Form: Through-composed
Nature of Text: Elijah (recitative): O Thou, who makest Thine angels spirits; Thou, whose ministers are flaming fires: let them now descend! The People (chorus): The fire descends from heaven! The flames consume his offering! Before Him upon your faces fall! The Lord is God, the Lord is God! O Israel hear! Our God is one Lord, and we will have no other gods before the Lord. Elijah (recitative): Take all the prophets of Baal, and let not one of them escape you. Bring them down to Kishon's brook, and there let them be slain. The People (chorus): Take all the prophets of Baal and let not one of them escape us: bring all and slay them! Elijah (aria): Is not His word like a fire, and like a hammer that breaketh the rock into pieces! For God is angry with the wicked every day. And if the wicked turn not, the Lord will whet His sword; and He hath bent His bow, and made it ready.
Performing Forces: Baritone soloist (Elijah), four-part chorus, orchestra

What we want you to remember about this composition:

- It's an oratorio composed for amateurs and professionals to perform at a choral festival
- It uses traditional forms of accompanied recitative, chorus, and aria to tell a dramatic story

Other things to listen for:

- A much larger orchestra than heard in the oratorios of Handel
- A very melismatic and virtuoso aria in the style of Handel's arias
- More flexible use of recitatives, arias, and choruses than in earlier oratorios
- More dissonance and chromaticism than in earlier oratorios

Timing	Performing Forces, Melody, and Texture	Text and Form
0:00	Solo Baritone (Elijah); Orchestra. Minor key, orchestra punctuates the ends of each of singer's phrases.	Accompanied recitative: O Thou, who makest Thine angels spirits; Thou, whose ministers are flaming fires: let them now descend!
0:32	Chorus and Orchestra. Very forte and polyphonic until the end, when it becomes homophonic (with rests between phrases) and quieter in dynamics.	Chorus: The fire descends from heaven! The flames consume his offering! Before Him upon your faces fall!
1:29	Chorus and Orchestra. Very homophonic and legato with longer note values: a more deliberate style for central claim of Western faith.	Chorus: "The Lord is God..."
2:25	Soloist and Orchestra. Melody and texture as before.	Accompanied recitative: Take all the prophets of Baal, and let not one of them escape you. Bring them down to Kishon's brook, and there let them be slain.
2:40	Chorus and Orchestra. Homophonic, minor key.	Chorus: Take all the prophets of Baal and let not one of them escape us: bring all and slay them!

2:51	Soloist and Orchestra. Minor key and homophonic, with a frantic orchestral accompaniment; melody has a wide range with melismas.	Aria: Is not His word like a fire, and like a hammer that breaketh the rock into pieces! For God is angry with the wicked every day. And if the wicked turn not, the Lord will whet His sword; and He hath bent His bow, and made it ready.

Felix was not the only musically precocious Mendelssohn in his household. In fact, the talent of his older sister Fanny (1805-1847) initially exceeded that of her younger brother. Born into a household of intelligent, educated, and socially-sophisticated women, Fanny was given the same education as her younger brother (see figure of Fanny Mendelssohn, sketched by her future husband: https://en.wikipedia.org/wiki/Fanny_Mendelssohn#/media/File:Fannymendelssohn-improved.jpg). But for her, as for most nineteenth-century married women from middle-class families, a career as a professional musician was frowned upon. Her husband, Wilhelm Hensel supported her composing and presenting her music at private house concerts held at the Mendelssohn's family residence. Felix also supported Fanny's private activities, although he discouraged her from publishing her works under her own name. In 1846, Fanny went ahead and published six songs without seeking her husband's or brother's permission.

Musicians today perform many of the more than 450 compositions that Fanny wrote for piano, voice, and chamber ensemble. Among some of her best works are the four-movement Piano Trio in D minor, Op. 11, and several volumes of songs and piano compositions. This piano trio holds its own with the piano trios, piano quartets, piano quintets, and string quartets composed by other nineteenth-century composers, from Beethoven and Schubert to the Schumanns, Johannes Brahms, and Antonín Dvořák.

6.7 MUSIC OF THE SCHUMANNS

Husband and wife Robert and Clara Schumann were another prominent musical pair of the nineteenth century. The couple became acquainted after Robert (1810-1856) moved to Leipzig and started studying piano with Friedrich Wieck, the father of the young piano prodigy Clara (1819-1896). The nine-year-old Clara was just starting to embark on her musical career. Throughout her teens, she would travel giving concerts, dazzling aristocratic and public audiences with her virtuosity. She also started publishing her compositions, which she often incorporated into her concerts. Her father, perhaps realizing what marriage would mean for the career of his daughter, refused to consent to her marriage with Robert Schumann, a marriage she desired as she and Robert had fallen in love. They subsequently married in 1840, shortly before Clara's twenty-first birthday, after a protracted court battle with her father.

Figure 6.13 | Robert and Clara Schumann
Author | Eduard Kaiser
Source | Wikimedia Commons
License | Public Domain

Once the two were married, Robert's musical activities became the couple's first priority. Robert began his musical career with aims of becoming a professional pianist. When he suffered weakness of the fingers and hands, he shifted his focus to music journalism and music composition. He founded a music magazine dedicated to showcasing the newer and more experimental music then being composed. And he started writing piano compositions, songs, chamber music, and eventually orchestral music, the most important of which include four symphonies and a piano concerto, premiered by Clara in 1846. While Robert was gaining recognition as a composer and conductor, Clara's composition and performance activities were restricted by her giving birth to eight children. Then in early 1854, Robert started showing signs of psychosis and, after a suicide attempt, was taken to an asylum. Although one of the more progressive hospitals of its day, this asylum did not allow visits from close relatives, so Clara would not see her husband for over two years and then only in the two days before his death. After his death, Clara returned to a more active career as performer; indeed, she spent the rest of her life supporting her children and grandchildren through her public appearances and teaching. Her busy calendar may have been one of the reasons why she did not compose after Robert's death.

The compositional careers of Robert and Clara followed a similar trajectory. Both started their compositional work with short piano pieces that were either virtuoso showpieces or reflective character pieces that explored extra musical ideas in musical form. Theirs were just a portion of the many character pieces, especially those at a level of difficulty appropriate for the enthusiastic amateur pianist, published throughout Europe. After their marriage, they both merged poetic and musical concerns in *Lieder*—Robert published many song cycles, and he and Clara joined forces on a song cycle published in 1841. They also both turned to traditional genres, such as the sonata and larger four-movement chamber music compositions.

Focus Compositions:

Character Pieces by Robert and Clara Schumann

We'll listen to two character pieces from the 1830s. Robert Schumann's "Chiarina," was written between 1834 and 1835 and published in 1837 in a cycle of piano character pieces that he called *Carnaval,* after the festive celebrations that occurred each year before the beginning of the Christian season of Lent. Each short piece in the collection has a title, some of which refer to imaginary characters that Robert employed to give musical opinions in his music journalism. Others, such as "Chopin" and "Chiarina," refer to real people, the former referring to the popular French-Polish pianist Fryderyk Chopin, and the later referring to the young Clara. At the beginning of the "Chiarina," Robert inscribed the performance instruction *"passionata,"* meaning that the pianist should play the piece with passion. "Chiarina" is little over a minute long and consists of a two slightly contrasting musical phrases.

LISTENING GUIDE

For audio, go to:
https://www.youtube.com/watch?v=ihs68fFnT4Y
Played by Daniel Barenboim

Composer: Robert Schumann

Composition: "Chiarina" from *Carnaval*

Date: Published 1837

Genre: piano character piece

Form: aaba'ba'

Nature of Text: The title refers to Clara

Performing Forces: small ensemble of vocalists

What we want you to remember about this composition:

- This is a character piece for solo piano
- A dance-like mood is conveyed by its triple meter and moderately fast tempo

Other things to listen for:

- It has a leaping melody in the right hand and is accompanied by chords in the left hand.
- It uses two slightly different melodies

Timing	Performing Forces, Melody, and Texture	Text and Form
0:00	Forte rising, leaping melody, in homophonic texture throughout	a
0:09	Fortissimo (very loud) rising, leaping melody now doubled in octaves	a
0:19	Mezzo-forte melody has leaps but a smaller range and descends slightly	b
0:28	Played once and then crescendos as it is repeated in octaves	a

0:46	Melody has leaps but a smaller range and descends slightly	b
0:57	Played once and then repeated in octaves	a

The second character piece is one written by Clara Schumann between 1834 and 1836 and published as one piece in the collection *Soirées Musicales* in 1836 (a soirée was an event generally held in the home of a well-to-do lover of the arts where musicians and other artists were invited for entertainment and conversation). Clara called this composition Ballade in D minor. The meaning of the title seems to have been vague almost by design, but, most broadly considered, a ballade referred to a composition thought of as a narrative. As a character piece, it tells its narrative completely through music. Several contemporary composers wrote ballades of different moods and styles; Clara's "Ballade" shows some influence of Chopin.

Clara's Ballade like Robert's "Chiarina," has a homophonic texture and starts in a minor key. A longer piece than "Chiarina," the Ballade in D minor modulates to D major, before returning to D minor for a reprise of the A section. Its themes are not nearly as clearly delineated as the themes in "Chiarina." Instead phrases start multiple times, each time slightly varied. You many hear what we call musical embellishments. These are notes the composer adds to a melody to provide variations. You might think of them like jewelry on a dress or ornaments on a Christmas tree. One of the most famous sorts of ornaments is the trill, in which the performer rapidly and repeatedly alternates between two pitches. We also talk of turns, in which the performer traces a rapid stepwise ascent and descent (or descent and ascent) for effect. You should also note that as the pianist in this recording plays, he seems to hold back notes at some moments and rush ahead at others: this is called rubato, that is, the robbing of time from one note to give it to another. We will see the use of rubato even more prominently in the music of Chopin.

LISTENING GUIDE
For audio, go to: https://www.youtube.com/watch?v=wB34wOV3XYs Performed by Jozef de Beenhouwer (at 10:21)
Composer: Clara Wieck Schumann
Composition: Ballade in D minor, Op. 6, no. 4
Date: 1836
Genre: piano character piece
Form: ABA
Nature of Text: This is a ballade, that is, a composition with narrative premises

Performing Forces: piano

What we want you to remember about this composition:

- A lyrical melody over chordal accompaniment making this homophonic texture
- A moderate to slow tempo
- In duple time (in this case, four beats for each measure)

Other things to listen for:

- Musical themes that develop and repeat but are always varied
- Musical embellishments in the form of trills and turns

Timing	**Performing Forces, Melody, and Texture**	**Text and Form**
0:00 [10:21]	Theme starts three times before taking off; melody ascends and uses ornaments for variations; in D minor. *Piano* dynamics, slow tempo, duple time.	A
0:55	Transitional idea using trills (extended ornaments).	
1:26	New musical idea repeated a couple of times with variation. Ascending phrases crescendo and descending phrases decrescendo.	
2:09	Transitional idea returns. Slightly louder.	
2:24	Repeated note theme. More passionate and louder then subsiding in dynamics.	
2:50	First theme returns in D minor and then is varied. *Piano* with a crescendo to fortissimo and then a return to *piano*.	B
4:19	*Piano* dynamics quickly altered by crescendos and decrescendos.	A'
4:40	Return of rhythmic motive from opening. A section and then varied Dynamics move from soft to loud to soft.	Coda

6.8 MUSIC OF FRYDERYK CHOPIN

Figure 6.8 | Fryderyk Chopin
Author | Eugène Delacroix
Source | Wikimedia Commons
License | Public Domain

Fryderyk Chopin (1810-1849) grew up in and around Warsaw, Poland, son of a French father and Polish mother. His family was a member of the educated middle class; consequently, Chopin had contact with academics and wealthier members of the gentry and middle class. He learned as much as he could from the composition instructors in Warsaw—including the keyboard music of Bach, Mozart, and Beethoven—before deciding to head off on a European tour in 1830. The first leg of the tour was Vienna, where Chopin expected to give concerts and then head further west. About a week after his arrival, however, Poland saw political turmoil in the Warsaw uprising, which eventually led to Russian occupation of his home country. After great efforts, Chopin secured a passport and, in the summer of 1831, traveled to Paris, which would become his adopted home. Paris was full of Polish émigrés, who were well received within musical circles. After giving a few public concerts, Chopin was able to focus his attention on the salons, salons being smaller, semi-private events, similar to soirées, generally hosted by aristocratic women for artistic edification. There and as a teacher, he was in great demand and could charge heavy fees.

Much like Robert and Clara Schumann, Chopin's first compositions were designed to impress his audiences with his virtuoso playing. As he grew older and more established, his music became more subtle. Also, like the Schumanns, he composed pieces appropriate in difficulty for the musical amateur as well as work for virtuosos such as himself. Unlike many of the other composers we have discussed, Chopin wrote piano music almost exclusively. He was best known for character pieces, such as mazurkas, waltzes, nocturnes, etudes, ballades, polonaises, and preludes.

Focus composition:

Chopin Mazurka in F Minor, Op. 7, no. 1 (1832)

The composition on which we will focus is the Mazurka in F minor, Op. 7, no. 1, which was published in Leipzig in 1832 and then in Paris and London in 1833. The mazurka is a Polish dance, and mazurkas were rather popular in Western Europe as exotic stylized dances. Mazurkas are marked by their triple meter in which beat two rather than beat one gets the stress. They are typically composed in strains and are homophonic in texture. Chopin sometimes incorporated folk-like sounds in his mazurkas, sounds such as drones and augmented seconds. A drone is a sustained pitch or pitches. The augmented second is an interval that was commonly used in Eastern European folk music but very rarely in the tonal music of Western European composers.

All of these characteristics can be heard in the Mazurka in F minor, Op. 7, no. 1, together with the employment of rubato. Chopin was the first composer to widely request that pianists use rubato when playing his music.

LISTENING GUIDE

For audio, go to:
https://www.youtube.com/watch?v=nKgM1SkMiqY
Performed by Arthur Rubinstein on piano

Composer: Fryderyk Chopin

Composition: Mazurka in F minor, Op. 7, no. 1

Date: 1836

Genre: piano character piece

Form: aaba'ba'ca'ca'

Nature of Text: the title indicates a stylized dance based on the Polish mazurka

Performing Forces: solo piano

What we want you to remember about this composition:

- This mazurka is in triple time with emphasis on beat two
- The texture is homophonic
- Chopin asks the performer to use rubato

Other things to listen for:

- Its "c" strain uses a drone and augmented seconds
- Its form is aaba'ba'ca'ca'

Timing	Performing Forces, Melody, and Texture	Text and Form
8:23	Triple-meter theme ascends up the scale and then descends and then repeats; brief ornaments on beat two of the measure. In F minor, with homophonic boom-chuck texture.	aa
8:57	After a contrasting theme that oscillates, part of the first theme returns in a'.	ba'
9:24		ba'
9:53	Folk-like melody using augmented seconds. Listen for the drone as well as rubato (which Chopin asks for here).	c

9:36		a
9:53	C returns, then a.	ca

6.9 MUSIC OF FRANZ LISZT

Franz Liszt (b. 1811-1886) was born in Doborján, Hungary (now Raiding, Austria). His father, employed as a steward for a wealthy family, was an amateur musician who recognized his son's talent. A group of Hungarian noblemen sponsored him with a stipend that enabled Franz to pursue his musical interest in Paris. There, he became the friend of Mendelssohn, Hugo, Chopin, Delacroix, George Sand, and Berlioz; these friends influenced him to become part of the French Romanticism movement.

Also in Paris in 1831, Liszt attended a performance of virtuoso violinist Paganini, who was touring. Paganini's style and success helped make Liszt aware of the demand for a solo artist who performed with showmanship. The ever growing mass public audience desired gifted virtuoso soloists performers at the time. Liszt, one of the best pianists of his time, became a great showman who knew how to energize an audience. Up until Liszt, the standard practice of performing piano solos was with the solo artist's back to the audience. This limited—and actually blocked—the audience from viewing the artist's hands, facial expression, and musical nuance. Liszt changed the entire presentation by turning the piano sideways so the audience could view his facial expressions and the manner in which his fingers interacted with the keys, from playing loud and thunderously to gracefully light and legato. Liszt possessed great charisma and performance appeal; indeed, he had a following of young ladies that idolized his performances. During his career of music stardom, Liszt never married and was considered one of the most eligible bachelors of the time. But he did have several "relationships" with different women, one of whom was the novelist Countess Marie d'Agoult who wrote under the pen name of Daniel Stern. She and Liszt travelled to Switzerland for a few years and they had three children, including Cosima who ultimately married Wagner.

While at the height of his performance career, Liszt retreated from his piano soloist career to devote all his energy to composition. He moved to Weimer in 1948 and assumed the post of court musician for the Grand Duke, remaining in Weimer until 1861. There, he produced his greatest orchestral works. His position in Weimer included the responsibility as director to the Grand Duke's opera house. In this position, Liszt could influence the public's taste in music and construct musical expectations for future compositions. And he used his influential position to program what Wagner called "Music of the Future." Liszt and Wagner both advocated and promoted highly dramatic music in Weimer, with Liszt conducting the first performances of Wagner's ***Lohengrin,*** Belioz's ***Benevenuto Cellini,*** as well as many other contemporary compositions.

While in Weimer, Liszt began a relationship with a woman who had a tremendous influence on his life and music. A wife of a nobleman in the court of the Tsar, Princess Carolyne Sayn-Wittenstein met and fell in love with Liszt on his final performance tour of Russia. Later she left her husband and moved to Weimer to be with Liszt. She assisted Liszt in writing literary works, among which included a fabricated biography by Liszt on the *Life of Chopin* and a book on "Gypsy," a book also considered eccentric and inaccurate.

While Liszt had an eventful romantic life, he remained a Roman Catholic, and he eventually sought solitude in the Catholic Church. His association with the church led to the writing of his major religious works. He also joined the Oratory of the Madonna del Rosario and studied the preliminary stage for priesthood, taking his minor orders and becoming known as the Abbé Liszt. He dressed as a priest and composed Masses, oratorios, and religious music for the church.

Still active at the age of seventy-five, he earned respect from England as a composer and was awarded an honor in person by Queen Victoria. Returning from this celebration, he met Claude Debussy in Paris then journeyed to visit his widowed daughter Cosima in Bayreuth and attended a Wagnerian Festival. He died during that festival, and even on his death bed, dying of pneumonia, Liszt named one of the "Music of the Future" masterpieces: Wagner's ***Tristan.***

Liszt's primary goal in music composition was pure expression through the idiom of tone. His freedom of expression necessitated his creation of the **symphonic poem**, sometimes called a tone poem--a one movement program piece written for orchestra that portrays images of a place, story, novel, landscape or non-musical source or image. This form utilizes transformations of a few themes through the entire work for continuity. The themes are varied by adjusting the rhythm, harmony, dynamics, tempos, instrumental registers, instrumentation in the orchestra, timbre, and melodic outline, or shape. By making these slight-to-major adjustments, Liszt found it possible to convey the extremes of emotion—from love to hate, war to peace, triumph to defeat—within a thematic piece. His thirteen symphonic poems greatly influenced the nineteenth century, an influence that continues through today. Liszt's most famous piece for orchestra is the three portrait work ***Symphony after Goethe's Faust*** (the portraits include Faust, Gretchen, and Mephistopheles). A similar work, his ***Symphony of Dante's Divine Comedy,*** has three movements: ***Inferno***, ***Purgatory***, and ***Vision of Paradise.*** His most famous of the symphonic poems is ***Les Preludes*** (The Preludes) written in 1854.

His best known works include nineteen Hungarian Rhapsodies (Liszt's Hungarian Rhapsody No. 2 may be heard at the following link: http://www.52composers.com/liszt.html), Piano concertos (Piano concerto No. 1, Part 1 may be heard at the following link: http://www.52composers.com/liszt.html), Mephisto Waltzes, Faust Symphony (***Mephisto*** from ***Faust Symphony*** Part 1 may be heard at following link: http://www.52composers.com/liszt.html), and Lieberstaumes (may be heard at the following link: http://www.52composers.com/liszt.html).

LISTENING GUIDE

For audio, go to:

https://www.youtube.com/watch?v=LTBuNkUMW-I

Composer: Franz Liszt	
Composition: Hungarian Rhapsody No. 2	
Date: 1847	
Genre: The second of a set of 19 Hungarian Rhapsodies	
Performing Forces: Piano solo	
What we want you to remember about this composition: • Widely popular, this piece offers the pianist the opportunity to reveal exceptional skill as a virtuoso, while providing the listener with an immediate and irresistible musical appeal. • Listen to the dance rhythms and strong pulse even at the slower tempos	
Other things to listen for: • The piece begins with the "lasson", a brief dramatic introduction that is followed by the "friska", an energy building section that build to a tempest of sound and momentum. • This piece was used in many animated cartoons in contemporary culture, "Tom and Jerry", "Bugs Bunny", "Woody Woodpecker" and several others. • Interest in this piece is rooted in the period's interests in "Exoticism" (music from other cultures).	
Timing	**Performing Forces, Melody, and Texture**
00:00-04:26	The lasson opens at a slow tempo
04:26- to the end	The friska follows and builds feverishly. Dance rhythms with heavy pulse.

For more information and listening opportunities for Liszt selections, go to: http://www.classicfm.com/composers/liszt/guides/liszts-piano-music-where-start/#qhmCIMkIdTaD2088.97

We shift now from smaller compositions for small forces to larger-scale compositions written for entire orchestras.

6.10 MUSIC OF HECTOR BERLIOZ

Hector Berlioz (b. 1803-1869) was born in France in La Côte-Saint-André, Isère near Grenoble. His father was a wealthy doctor and planned on Hector's pursuing the profession of a physician. At the age of eighteen, Hector was sent to study medicine in Paris. Music at the Conservatory and at the Opera, however, became the focus of his attention. A year later, his family grew alarmed when they realized that the young student had decided to study music instead of medicine.

At this time, Paris was in a Romantic revolution. Berlioz found himself in in the company of novelist Victor Hugo and painter Delacroix. No longer receiving financial support from his parents, the young Berlioz sang in the theater choruses, performed musical chores, and gave music lessons. As a young student, Berlioz was amazed and intrigued by the works of Beethoven. Berlioz also developed interest in Shakespeare, whose popularity in Paris had recently increased with the performance of his plays by a visiting British troupe. Hector became impassioned for the Shakespearean characters of Ophelia and Juliet as they were portrayed by the alluring actress Harriet Smithson. Berlioz became obsessed with the young actress and also overwhelmed by sadness due to her lack of interest in him as a suitor. Berlioz became known for his violent mood swings, a condition known today as manic depression.

In 1830, Berlioz earned his first recognition for his musical gift when he won the much sought-after Prix de Rome. This highly-esteemed award provided him a stipend and the opportunity to work and live in Paris, thus providing Berlioz with the chance to complete his most famous work, the ***Symphonie Fastastique***, that year.

Upon his return to Rome, he began his intense courtship of Harriet Smithson. Both her family and his vehemently opposed their relationship. Several violent and arduous situations occurred, one of which involved Berlioz's unsuccessfully attempting suicide. After recovering from this attempt, Hector married Harriet. Once the previously unattainable matrimonial goal had been attained, Berlioz's passion somewhat cooled, and he discovered that it was Harriet's Shakespearean roles that she performed, rather than Harriet herself, that really intrigued him. The first year of their marriage was the most fruitful for him musically. By the time he was forty, he had composed most of his famous works. Bitter from giving up her acting career for marriage, Harriet became an alcoholic. The two separated in 1841 Berlioz then married his long time mistress Marie Recio, an attractive but average singer who demanded to perform in his concerts.

To supplement his income during his career, Berlioz turned to writing as a music critic, producing a steady stream of articles and reviews. He successfully utilized this vocation as a way to support his own works by persuading the audience to accept and appreciate them. His critical writing also helped to educate audiences so they could understand his complex and innovative pieces. As a prose writer, Berlioz wrote *The Treatise on Modern Instrumentation and Orchestration.* He also wrote *'Les Soirées de l'Orchestre'* (Evenings with the Orchestra), a compilation of his articles on musical life in nineteenth-century France, and an autobiography entitled *Mémoires.* Later in life, he conducted his music in all the capitals of Europe, with the exception of Paris. It was one location where the public would not accept his work; the Paris public would read his reviews and learn to welcome lesser composers, but they would not accept Berlioz's music. As over the years Berlioz saw his own works neglected by the public of Paris while they cheered and supported others, he became disgusted and bitter from the neglect. His last final work composed to gain acceptance by the Parisian audiences was the opera *Béatrice et Bénédict* with his own libretto based upon Shakespeare's *Much Ado about Nothing.* But the Parisian public did not appreciate it. After this final effort, the disillusioned and embittered Berlioz composed no more in his seven remaining years, dying rejected and tormented at the age of sixty-six. Only after his death would France appreciate his achievements.

His operas include *Benvenuto Cellini, Le Troyens* (to hear and view an excerpt, go to the link on http://www.52composers.com/berlioz.html)*, Béatrice et Bénédict, Les francs-juges (incomplete), Grande Messe des morts (Requiem)* (to view and hear the tuba mirum from the Requiem, go to the link found at http://www.52composers.com/berlioz.html)*, La damnation de Faust, Te Deum,* and *L'enfance du Christ*.

His major orchestral compositions include *Symphonie fantastique* (to hear the fifth movement, go to the link on http://www.52composers.com/berlioz.html)*, Harold en Italie, Romeo et Juliette* (to hear and view an excerpt, go to the link on http://www.52composers.com/berlioz.html)*, The Corsair, King Lear,* and *Grande symphonie funèbre et triomphale.* Berlioz is credited for changing the modern sound of orchestras.

Berlioz's *Symphonie fantastique* is important for several reasons: it is a program symphony, it incorporates an *idée fixe* (a recurring theme representing an ideology or person that provides continuity through a musical work), and it contains five movements rather than the four of most symphonies.

LISTENING GUIDE
For audio, go to: https://www.youtube.com/watch?v=l7chHNocFAc Performed by The BBC Philharmonic Orchestra, conducted by Yan Pascal Tortelier
Composer: Hector Berlioz
Composition: Symphonie Fantastique, Op.14: 1st movement Reveries – Passions
Date: 1830
Genre: Symphony, First movement
Form: Sonata form
Performing Forces: large Romantic symphony orchestra
What we want you to remember about this composition: • The largo (slow) opening is pensive and expressive, depicting the depression, the joy, and the fruitless passion Berlioz felt. It is followed by a long and very fast section with a great amount of expression, with the *idée fixe* (a short recurring musical theme/motive associated with a person, place or idea) indicating the appearance of his beloved. • The title for the movement is "Dreams, Passions." It represents his uneasy and uncertain state of mind. The mood quickly changes as his love appears to him. He reflects on the love inspired by her. He notes the power of his enraged jealousy for her and of his religious consolation at the end.

Other things to listen for:

- Berlioz is known for being one of the greatest orchestrators of all time. He even wrote the first comprehensive book on orchestration. He always thought in terms of the exact sound (tone or timbre) of the orchestra and the mixture of individual sounds to blend through orchestration. He gave very detailed instructions to the conductor and individual performers in regards to articulations and how he wanted them to play. Listen to the subtleties and nuance of the performance. Berlioz left little up to chance since he was so thorough in his compositions.

Timing	Music Measure (Bar) Numbers	Form, Melody, and Texture
00:12	3-6	The introductory four-bar phrase played by the violin one forms the basis for the following three phrases to bar sixteen, most of the music being played on muted strings. Here the composer portrays both depression and elation. 
1:45	17-71	The key changes from C major to Eb major to C minor and finally arriving to C major with a cadence in measure 62
5:30	72-111	Exposition-Allegro He sees his beloved and is overcome with many different emotions.  [Subject/*idée fixe*, bars 72-111] The major key of C is established by dominant pedal point.
6:33	133-149	Transition section that provides rising tension in the approach to the dominant.

6:47	150-166a	Second subject introduced and established in the key of G major at measure 160. See Music insert 3 for second subject notation.  [Second Subject found in bars 160-166]
8:36	167-228	Development Section—this section includes recapitulations and further developments. Two new motifs (musical segments) are featured in this section of the first movement. The first has become known as the "sigh motif." This motif musically represents the sighing figure of a long note followed by a shorter note. See music insert 4 for sighing motif notation.  [Sigh motif notations, measure 87.] The second motif has become known as the "heart beat motif." It is heard as a pair of detached pulses/quavers. These are brought out dynamically (volume emphasis) and represent heartbeats. See music insert 5 for heartbeat motif notation.  [Heartbeat motif notations, measure seventy-eight]
9:33	232-278	Recapitulation in the dominant key of G major
10:20	278- 311	Transitional Passage to upcoming second subject
10:51	311-329	Second subject resolving fortissimo in C major
11:50	358-409	Further development section continues and gradually increased tension setting up next unison section.
12:40	410-439	The full orchestra plays the first subject in C major
13:08	440-474	Further orchestral build up
13:43	475-526	Coda section: The final chords musically representing the consolation of religion ending with a plagal cadence (traditional Amen progression/ending).

6.11 MUSIC OF JOHANNES BRAHMS (1833-1897)

Whereas Berlioz's program symphony might be heard as a radical departure from earlier symphonies, the music of Johannes Brahms is often thought of as breathing new life into classical forms (see figure of Brahms: https://en.wikipedia.org/wiki/Johannes_Brahms#/media/File:JohannesBrahms.jpg). For centuries, musical performances were of compositions by composers who were still alive and working. In the nineteenth century that trend changed. By the time that Johannes Brahms was twenty, over half of all music performed in concerts was by composers who were no longer living; by the time that he was forty, that amount increased to over two-thirds. Brahms knew and loved the music of forebears such as Bach, Handel, Haydn, Mozart, Beethoven, Schubert, and Schumann. He wrote in the genres they had developed, including symphonies, concertos, string quartets, sonatas, and songs. To these traditional genres and forms, he brought sweeping nineteenth-century melodies, much more chromatic harmonies, and the forces of the modern symphony orchestra. He did not, however, compose symphonic poems or program music as did Hector Berlioz and Franz Liszt.

Brahms himself was keenly aware of walking in Beethoven's shadow. In the early 1870s, he wrote to conductor friend Hermann Levi, "I shall never compose a symphony." Continuing, he reflected, "You have no idea how someone like me feels when he hears such a giant marching behind him all of the time." Nevertheless, some six years later, after a twenty-year period of germination, he premiered his first symphony. Brahms's music engages Romantic lyricism, rich chromaticism, thick orchestration, and rhythmic dislocation in a way that clearly goes beyond what Beethoven had done. Still, his intensely motivic and organic style, and his use of a four movement symphonic model that features sonata, variations, and ABA forms is indebted to Beethoven.

The third movement of Brahms's First Symphony is a case in point. It follows the ABA form, as had most moderate-tempo, dance-like third movements since the minuets of the eighteenth-century symphonies and scherzos of the early nineteenth-century symphonies. This movement uses more instruments and grants more solos to the woodwind instruments than earlier symphonies did (listen especially for the clarinet solos). The musical texture is thicker as well, even though the melody always soars above the other instruments. Finally, this movement is more graceful and songlike than any minuet or scherzo that preceded it. In this regard, it is more like the lyrical character pieces of Chopin, Mendelssohn, and the Schumanns than like most movements of Beethoven's symphonies. But, it does not have an extra musical referent; in fact, Brahms' music is often called "absolute" music, that is, music for the sake of music. The music might call to a listener's mind any number of pictures or ideas, but they are of the listener's imagination, from the listener's interpretation of the melodies, harmonies, rhythms, and textures written by Brahms. In this way, such a movement is very different than a movement from a program symphony such as Berlioz's *Symphonie fantastique*. Public opinion has often split over program music and absolute music. What do you think? Do you prefer a composition in which the musical and extra musical are explicitly linked, or would you rather make up your own interpretation of the music, without guidance from a title or story?

LISTENING GUIDE

For audio, go to:
https://www.youtube.com/watch?v=dekswNoJqCs
Performed by the Berlin Philharmonic Herbert von Karajan conducting

Composer: Johannes Brahms

Composition: Symphony No. 1 in C minor, Op. 68, III. Un poco allegretto e grazioso [a little allegretto and graceful]

Date: 1876

Genre: Symphony

Form: ABA moderate-tempoed, dancelike movement from a symphony

Performing Forces: Romantic symphony orchestra, including two flutes, two oboes, two clarinets, two bassoons, one contrabassoon, four horns, two trumpets, three trombones, timpani, violins (first and second), violas, cellos, and double basses

What we want you to remember about this composition:

- Its lilting tuneful melodies transform the scherzo mood into something more romantic
- It is in ABA form
- It is in A-flat major (providing respite from the C minor pervading the rest of the symphony)

Other things to listen for:

- The winds as well as the strings get the melodic themes from the beginning

Timing	Performing Forces, Melody, and Texture	Text and Form
0:00	Clarinet solo with descending question phrases answer phrase in the flutes. (sparse string accompaniment)	A
0:26	Strings get the melodic theme with answer in the winds	
1:01	Second theme: starts with a clarinet solo and then with the whole woodwind section. Faster note values in the strings provide increased musical tension	

1:26	Return of opening theme (clarinet solo)	
1:41	New theme introduced and repeated by different groups in the orchestra. Gradually building dynamic and layers of the texture (more brass); phrase ends with hemiola. Climaxes to a forte dynamic	B
3:17	First theme returns answer theme in the strings (varied form). Sparser accompaniment again Softer dynamic	'A'
3:32	Second theme: This time it is extended using sequences	
4:00	Ascending sequential treatment of motives from the movement	Coda

As noted at the beginning of this chapter, political and cultural nationalism strongly influenced many creative works of the nineteenth century. We have already observed aspects of nationalism in the piano music of Chopin and Liszt. Later nineteenth-century composers invested even more heavily in nationalist themes.

6.12 MUSIC OF NATIONALISM

Nationalism, found in many genres, is marked by the use of folk songs or nationalist themes in operas or instrumental music. Nationalist composers of different countries include Russian composers such as Modest Mussorgsky, Alexander Borodin, and Nicolai Rimsky-Korsakov (members of the "Kuchka"); Bohemian composers such as Antonin Dvorak and Bedřich Smetana; Hungarian composers such as Liszt; Scandinavian composers such as Edvard Grieg and Jean Sibelius; Spanish composers such as Enrique Granados, Joaquin Turina, and Manuel de Falla; and British composers such as Ralph Vaughn Williams.

Composers looked to their native as well as **exotic** (from other countries) music to add to their pallet of ideas. Nationalism was expressed in several ways:

- songs and dances of native people
- mythology: dramatic works based on folklore of peasant life (Tchaikovsky's Russian fairy-tale operas and ballets)
- celebration of a national hero, historic event, or scenic beauty of country

6.13 MUSIC OF BEDŘICH SMETANA

Bedřich Smetana (b. 1824-1884) was born in Litomsyl, Bohemia while under Austrian rule (now the Czech Republic). Smetana was the son of a brewer and violinist and his father's third wife. Smetana was a talented pianist who gave public performances from the age of six. Bohemia under Austrian rule was politically very volatile. In 1848 Smetana aligned himself with those seeking independent statehood from Austria. After that revolution was crushed, Prague and the surrounding areas were brutally suppressed—especially those areas and people suspected of being sympathetic to Bohemian nationalism. In 1856, Smetana left for Sweden to accept a conductorship post. He hoped to follow in the footsteps of such music predecessors as Liszt. He thus expresses his admiration, "By the grace of God and with His help, I shall one day be a Liszt in technique and a Mozart in composition."[1]

As a composer, Smetana began incorporating nationalist themes, plots, and dances in his operas and symphonic poems. He founded the Czech national school after he left Sweden and was a pioneer at incorporating Czech folk tunes, rhythms, and dances into his major works. Smetana returned to Bohemia in 1861 and assumed his role as national composer. He worked to open and establish a theatre venue in Prague where performances would be performed in their native tongue. Of his eight original operas, seven are still performed in native tongue today. One of these operas, *The Bartered Bride*, was and is still acclaimed. To hear Smetana's *Bartered Bride Overture,* go to http://www.52composers.com/smetana.html and click on the link. He composed several folk dances, including polkas for orchestra. These polkas incorporated the style and levity of his Bohemian culture. To hear his *Louisa's Polka,* go to http://www.52composers.com/smetana.html and click on the link.

Smetana also is known for composing the cycle of six symphonic poems entitled *My Country*. These poems are program music, representing the beautiful Bohemian countryside, Bohemian folk dance and song rhythms, and the pageantry of Bohemian legends. The first of these symphonic poems is called *Má vlast (My Fatherland)* and is symbolic program music representing his birthplace. To hear Smetana's *My Fatherland*, go to http://www.52composers.com/smetana.html and click on the link.

The second of these, *Vltava, (The Moldau)* is recognized as Smetana's greatest orchestral work. Notes in the conductor's score state

> The Moldau" represents an exceptional expression of patriotic or nationalistic music. The musical poem reflects the pride, oppression, and hope of the Bohemian people. . . .
>
> Two springs pour forth in the shade of the Bohemian Forest, one warm and gushing, the other cold and peaceful. Their waves, gaily flowing over rocky beds, join and glisten in the rays of the morning sun. The forest brook, hastening on, becomes the river Vltava (Moldau.) Coursing through Bohe-

1 Taken from his *diary, 23 January, 1845 found at* www.quotesquotations.com/biography.

mia's valleys, it grows into a mighty stream. Through thick woods it flows, as the gay sounds of the hunt and the notes of the hunter's horn are heard ever nearer. It flows through grass-grown pastures and lowlands where a wedding feast is being celebrated with song and dance. At night wood and water nymphs revel in its sparkling waves. Reflected on its surface are fortresses and castles—witnesses of bygone days of knightly splendor and the vanished glory of fighting times. At the St. John Rapids the stream races ahead, winding through the cataracts, heaving on a path with its foaming waves through the rocky chasm into the broad river bed— finally. Flowing on in majestic peace toward Prague—finally. Flowing on in majestic peace toward Prague and welcomed by time-honored Vysehrad (castle.) Then it vanishes far beyond the poet's gaze."[2]

Figure 6.15 | A panoramic view looking north-west across the Vltava River to Prague Castle and the Charles Bridge
Author | User "Diliff"
Source | Wikimedia Commons
License | CC BY-SA 3.0

LISTENING GUIDE For audio, go to: https://www.youtube.com/watch?v=hYoBJOcEiOM Featuring Vilem Tausky conducting the BBC Symphony
Composer: Bedřich Smetana (1824-1884)
Composition: The Moldau (*Vlatava*)
Date: 1874
Genre: Symphonic poem
Form: Symphonic Poem (Tone Poem)
Performing Forces: piccolo, two flutes, two oboes , two clarinets, two bassoons, four French horns, two trumpets, three trombones, tuba, timpani, bass drum, triangle, cymbals, harp, strings

2 Preface to the original score, Philharmonic Symphony Society of New York, *The Concert Companion* p. 672

What we want you to remember about this composition:

- *The Moldau* (*Vlatava*) is a programmatic symphonic poem portraying the story of the main river in Bohemia as it flows through Smetana's homeland countryside. Each section portrays a different scene, often contrasting, that the river encounters.
- This piece is a good representation of Czech nationalism and also of a romantic setting of nature.
- The composer wrote the work following a trip he took down the river as part of a larger cycle of six symphonic poems written between 1874 and 1879 entitled *Má Vlast* (*My Country*).
- Note that each section of the work has its own descriptive title in bold print.

Timing	Performing Forces, Melody, and Texture
0:00	Two Springs.(Source of the river) Flutes begin with a flowing/rippling melodic passage soon joined by the clarinets. The harp and strings (pizzicato) are heard periodically. 
1:06	Rippling notes moves to lower strings that lead to the main river theme.
1:16	The River Theme. Violins present the river theme in a minor key (e minor). Melody moves step-wise with running-note accompaniment in strings. Repeated. 
1:31	River theme repeated.
1:46	Melodic answer to the river theme.
2:11	The river theme is expanded (note the triangle with orchestral crescendos).
2:18	Return of the river theme.
2:35	Answer to river theme.

2:52	Expansion/elaboration of river theme.
3:01	Return of the river theme.
3:20	Forest Hunting Scene. French horns and trumpets, hunting calls. 
4:10	Rippling continues (in strings); dies down to gently rocking motion. Transition to next section (strings). Repeated notes in strings lead to rustic folk tune, staccato in strings and woodwinds
4:38	Peasant Wedding. Strings present a dance-like tune (polka). Closes with repeated single note in strings 
6:15	Moonlight: Dance of Water Nymphs**.** Woodwinds, sustained tones. 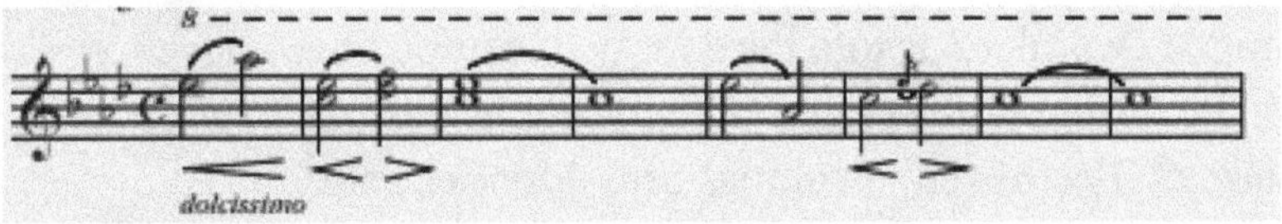
6:35	Flute passage (similar to opening of work). Rippling figures in flutes; muted string theme with harp, punctuated by French horn; brass crescendo, fanfare
7:02	Muted violins in high register with a legato melody.
9:06	Intensification.
9:29	Violins present the river theme. Played in the minor mode
10:17	River theme reappears in the major mode
10:29	St. John's Rapids. Full orchestra, ff. Brasses, timpani roll, piccolo, cymbal crashes.
12:09	River theme, Full orchestra, Loudest dynamic/volume. *The River at its Widest Point.* Full orchestra, river theme in major key. Faster tempo.
12:45	**The Ancient Castle.** The brasses and woodwinds portray Vyšehrad, the ancient castle in a hymn-like melody.  Slow then Accelerates

14:05	River Dies Away, Strings slow down, lose momentum
Final Cadence	Two forceful closing chords.

6.14 MUSIC OF ANTONÍN DVOŘÁK

Figure 6.16 | Antonín Dvořák
Author | Unknown
Source | Wikimedia Commons
License | Public Domain

Antonín Dvořák (b. 1841-1904) was born in a Bohemian village of Nelahozeves near Prague. Following in Smetana's footsteps, Dvořák became a leading composer in the Czech nationalism music campaign. Indeed, Dvořák and Smetana are considered the founders of the Czech national school. Dvořák, at the age of sixteen, moved to Prague. As a young aspiring violinist, Dvořák earned a seat in the Czech national Theater. Dvořák learned to play viola and became a professional violist; for a time in his career, he performed under Smetana. Dvořák became recognized by Brahms who encouraged Dvořák to devote his energy to composing. Early in his career he was musically under the German influence of Beethoven, Brahms, and Mendelssohn. Later, however, Dvořák explored his own culture, rooting his music in the dances and songs of Bohemia. Indeed, he never lost touch with his humble upbringing by his innkeeper and butcher father.

Dvořák's compositions received favorable recognition abroad and reluctant recognition at home. From 1892 to 1895, Dvořák served as director of the National Conservatory in the United States. During this time his compositions added American influences to the Bohemian. He fused "old world" harmonic theory with "new world" style. Very interested in American folk music, Dvořák took as one of his pupils an African-American baritone singer named Henry T. Burleigh who was an arranger and singer of spirituals. To hear Harry T. Burleigh sing the spiritual "Go Down Moses," go to https://www.youtube.com/watch?v=a7kpcps-7JxO. Dvořák's admiration and enthusiasm for the African-American spiritual is conveyed as he stated,

> I am convinced that the future music of this country must be founded on what are called Negro melodies. These can be the foundation of a serious and original school of composition, to be developed in the United States. These beautiful and varied themes are the product of the soil. They are the folk songs of America and your composers must turn to them.[3]

3 Gutmann, Peter. "Dvorak's "New World" Symphony". *Classical Classics. Classical Notes.* Retrieved 2012-09-09.

The spirituals, along with Native American and cowboys songs, interested Dvořák and influenced his compositions for years to come. His love for this American folk music was contagious and soon spread to other American composers. Up until this point, American composers were under the heavy influence of their European counterparts. Dvořák's influence and legacy as an educator and composer can be traced in the music of Aaron Copland and George Gershwin. Although he gained much from his time in America, Dvořák yearned for his homeland to which he returned after three years away, resisting invitations from Brahms to relocate in Vienna. Dvořák desired the more simple life of his homeland where he died in 1904, shortly after his last opera, *Armida*, was first performed.

6.14.1 Music for Orchestra

During his lifetime, Dvořák wrote in various music forms, including the symphony. He composed nine symphonies in all, with his most famous being the ninth, *From the New World* (1893). This symphony was commissioned by the New York Philharmonic who premiered it in New York on December 16, 1893, the same year as its completion. The symphony was partially inspired from a Czech translation of Henry Wadsworth Longfellow's poem *Hiawatha*.

Dvořák also composed a cello concerto for solo instrument and orchestra, a violin concerto, and a lesser known piano concerto. Dvořák received recognition for *Romance* for solo violin and orchestra and *Silent Woods* for cello and orchestra. These two pieces make significant contributions to the solo repertoire for both string instruments.

Dvořák composed several piano duets that he later orchestrated for symphony orchestra. They include his ten *Legends,* two sets of *Slavonic Dances,* and three *Slavic Rhapsodies*. His overtures include *In nature's realm, My Home, Carnival, Hussite,* and *Othello*. He also composed a polonaise *Scherzo capriccioso* and the much admired *Serenade for Strings*. His symphonic poems poems include *The World Dove, The Golden Spinning-Wheel, and The Noonday Witch.*

6.14.2 Music for Chamber Ensembles

Dvořák also composed chamber music, including fourteen string quartets. No 12, the "American" Quartet, was written in 1893, the same year as the *New World Symphony*. Also from the American period, Dvořák composed the G major Sonatinas for violin and piano whose second movement is known as "Indian Lament." Of the four remaining found Dvořák piano trios, the *Dumky* trio is famous for using the Bohemian national dance form. His quintets for piano and strings or strings alone for listening enjoyment are much appreciated, as are his string sextet and the trio of two violins and viola, *Terzetto*.

Humoresque in G-flat major is the best known of the eight Dvorak's piano pieces placed in a set. He also composed two sets of piano duets entitled *Slavonic Dances*.

6.14.3 Operas

From 1870 to 1903, Dvořák wrote ten operas. The famous aria 'O Silver Moon', 1900) from *Rusalka* is one of his most famous pieces. Dvořák wrote many of his operas with village theatres and comic village plots in mind—much the same as Smetana's *The Bartered Bride.* Other opera were based upon Czech legend.

6.14.4 Choral and Vocal Works

Several of Dvořák's choral works were composed for many of the amateur choral societies such as those found in Birmingham, Leeds, and London in England. The oratorio *St. Ludmilla* was composed for such societies, as were settings of the Mass, Requiem Mass, and the *Te Deum* which was first performed in 1892 in New York. Earlier choral works and settings, such as *Stabat Mater* and Psalm CXLIX, were performed in Prague 1879-1880.

Dvořák composed several songs, including the appreciated set of *Moravian Duets* for soprano and contralto. The most famous of his vocal pieces is the "Songs My Mother Taught Me" which is the fourth in the *Seven Gypsy Songs,* opus 55, set.

LISTENING GUIDE For audio, go to: https://www.youtube.com/watch?v=EvVonSkfhoo	
Composer: Antonin Dvorak	
Composition: From the New World, Symphony 9, movement 2 Largo	
Date: 1893	
Genre: Symphony Orchestra	
Performing Forces: Chicago Symphony Orchestra, Sir George Solti, conductor	
What we want you to remember about this composition: • The theme. The "coming home theme" is said to possibly be from a negro spiritual or Czech folk tune. It is introduced in what some call the most famous English horn solo.	
Other things to listen for: • The weaving of these very beautiful but simple melodies. Listen to how "western American" the piece sounds at times. The influence of American (western, spirituals, and folk) had a profound influence on Dvorak' compositions.	
Timing	**Performing Forces, Melody, and Texture**
0:00	Brass choral with string chord transition
0.45	English horn solo (theme 1) then woodwind transition to brass chords.
1:41	Theme is passed around then returns to English horn

5:34	Flute and oboe perform theme 2 over string tremolo, then clarinet duet above pizzicato strings. String then perform theme 2 to a transition
8:10	Theme/melody 3 played by violins-very smooth and connected
9:21	Oboe, clarinet , then the flute perform yet another theme, violins, cellos and basses-Light folk dance style in nature
9:47	Trombones enter with the first theme from the first movement-then trumpets and strings overlap with other earlier themes from the work. These style and compositional techniques create a very "western" sounding work.
10:28	English horn solo reintroduced followed by imitations in the strings (two silences) then scored reduction to a trio
11:40	Violin, viola, and cello trio. Transition in winds and strings
12:59	Opening chords without trumpets it is much darker sounding
13:29	Winds and strings pass the melodies around with ascension
13:51	Final three part chord in the double basses

You are encouraged to listen the entire symphony. For more information and a narrative guided tour of the Symphony no. 9 *"From the New World"*, go to:

- Antonín Dvořák: Symphony no. 9 *"From the New World"* analysis by Gerard Schwarz Part 1 First movement: https://www.khanacademy.org/partner-content/all-star-orchestra/masterpieces-old-and-new/dvorak-symphony-9/v/dvorak-one
- Antonín Dvořák: Symphony no. 9 *"From the New World"* analysis by Gerard Schwarz Part 2 Second Movement: https://www.khanacademy.org/partner-content/all-star-orchestra/masterpieces-old-and-new/dvorak-symphony-9/v/dvorak-two
- Antonín Dvořák: Symphony no. 9 *"From the New World"* analysis by Gerard Schwarz Part 3 Third Movement: https://www.khanacademy.org/partner-content/all-star-orchestra/masterpieces-old-and-new/dvorak-symphony-9/v/dvorak-three
- Antonín Dvořák: Symphony no. 9 *"From the New World"* analysis by Gerard Schwarz Part 4: https://www.khanacademy.org/partner-content/all-star-orchestra/masterpieces-old-and-new/dvorak-symphony-9/v/dvorak-four
- Another interpretation of the *"From the New World*", a commentary (from literature) by Joseph Horowitz: https://www.khanacademy.org/partner-content/all-star-orchestra/masterpieces-old-and-new/dvorak-symphony-9/v/joseph-horowitz-on-dvorak-minilecture

6.15 MUSIC OF PYOTR TCHAIKOVSKY

Figure 6.17 | Pyotr Tchaikovsky
Author | Nikolai Dmitriyevich Kuznetsov
Source | Wikimedia Commons
License | Public Domain

Pyotr (Peter) Ilyich Tchaikovsky (1840-1893) was born in Votinsk, a small mining town in Russia. He was a son of a government official, and started taking piano at the age of five, though his family intended him to have a career as a government official. His mother died of cholera when he was fourteen, a tragedy that had a profound and lasting effect on him. He attended the aristocratic school in St. Petersburg called the School of Jurisprudence and, upon completion, obtained a minor government post in the Ministry of Justice. Nevertheless, Pyotr always had a strong interest in music and yearned to study it.

At the age of twenty-three, he resigned his government post and entered the newly created Conservatory of St. Petersburg to study music. From the age of twenty-three to twenty-six, he studied intently and completed his study in three years. His primary teachers at the conservatory were Anton Rubinstein and Konstantin Zarembe, but he himself taught lessons while he studied. Upon completion, Tchaikovsky was recommended by Rubinstein, director of the school as well as teacher, to a teaching post at the new conservatory of Moscow. The young professor of harmony had full teaching responsibilities with long hours and a large class. Despite his heavy workload, his twelve years at the conservatory saw the composing of some of his most famous works, including his first symphony. At the age of twenty-nine, he completed his first opera *Voyevoda* and composed the *Romeo and Juliet* overture. At the age of thirty-three, he started supplementing his income by writing as a music critic, and also composed his second symphony, first piano concerto, and his first ballet, *Swan Lake*.

The reception of his music sometimes included criticism, and Tchaikovsky took criticism very personally, being prone as he was to (attacks of) depression. These bouts with depression were exacerbated by an impaired personal social life. In an effort to calm and smooth that personal life, Tchaikovsky entered into a relationship and marriage with a conservatory student named Antonina Ivanovna Miliukova in 1877. She was star struck and had fallen immediately and rather despairingly in love with him. His pity for her soon turned into unmanageable dislike to the point that he avoided her at all cost. Once in a fit of depression and aversion, he even strolled into the icy waters of the Moscow River to avoid her. Many contemporaries believe the effort was a suicide attempt. A few days later, nearly approaching a complete mental breakdown, he sought refuge and solace fleeing to his brothers in St. Petersburg. The marriage lasted less than a month.

At this darkest hour for Tchaikovsky, a kind, wealthy benefactress who admired his music became his sponsor. Her financial support helped restore Tchaikovsky to health, freed him from his burdensome teaching responsibilities, and permitted him to focus on his compositions. His benefactor was a widowed industrialist, Nadezhda von Meck, who was dominating and emotional and who loved his music. From her secluded estate, she raised her eleven children and managed her estate and railroads. Due to the social norms of the era, she had to be very careful to make sure that her intentions in supporting the composer went towards his music and not towards the composer as a man; consequently, they never met one another other than possibly through the undirected mutual glances at a crowded concert hall or theater. They communicated through a series of letters to one another, and this distance letter-friendship soon became one of fervent attachment.

In his letters to Meck, Tchaikovsky would explain how he envisioned and wrote his music, describing it as a holistic compositional process, with his envisioning the thematic development to the instrumentation being all one thought. The secured environment she afforded Tchaikovsky enabled him to compose unrestrainedly and very creatively. In appreciation and respect for his patron, Tchaikovsky dedicated his fourth symphony to Meck. He composed that work in his mid-thirties, a decade when he premiered his opera *Eugene Onegin* and composed the *1812 Overture* (excerpt may be viewed at the link on http://www.52composers.com/tchaikovsky.html) and *Serenade for Strings*.

Tchaikovsky's music ultimately earned him international acclaim, leading to his receiving a lifelong subsidy from the Tsar in 1885. He overcame his shyness and started conducting appearances in concert halls throughout Europe, making his music the first of any Russian composer to be accepted and appreciated by Western music consumers. At the age of fifty, he premiered *Sleeping Beauty* and *The Queen of Spades* in St. Petersburg. A year later, in 1891, he was invited to the United States to participate in the opening ceremonies for Carnegie Hall. He also toured the United States, where he was afforded impressive hospitality. He grew to admire the American spirit, feeling awed by New York's skyline and Broadway. He wrote that he felt he was more appreciated in America than in Europe.

While his composition career sometimes left him feeling dry of musical ideas, Tchaikovsky's musical output was astonishing and included at this later stage of his life two of his greatest symphonies: *The Nutcracker* and *Iolanta*, both of which premiered in St. Petersburg. He conducted the premier of his sixth symphony, *Pathétique*, in St. Petersburg as well, but received only a lukewarm reception, partially due to his shy, lack-luster personality. The persona carried over into his conducting technique that was rather reserved and subdued, leading to a less than emotion-packed performance by his orchestra.

A few days after the premier, while he was still in the St. Petersburg, Tchaikovsky ignored warnings against drinking unboiled water, warnings due to the current prevalence of cholera there. He contracted the disease and died within a week at the age of fifty-three years old. Immediately upon his tragic death, the *Symphonie Pathétique* earned great acclaim that it has held ever since.

In the nineteenth century and still today, Tchaikovsky is among the most highly esteemed of composers. Russians have the highest regard for Tchaikovsky as a national artist. Igor Stravinsky stated, "He was the most Russian of us all!" (Taken from http://www.tchaikovsky-research.net/en/forum/forum0291.html.) Tchaikovsky incorporated the national emotional feelings and culture—from its simple countryside to its busy cities—into his music. Along with his nationalism influences, such as Russian folk song, Tchaivovsky enjoyed studying and incorporating German symphony, Italian opera, and French Ballet. He was comfortable with all of these disparate sources and gave all his music lavish melodies flooding with emotion.

Tchaikovsky composed a tremendously wide spectrum of music, with ten operas including *Eugene Onegin, The Maid of Orleans, Queen of Spades,* and *Iolanthe;* internationally-acclaimed ballets, including *Swan Lake, The Sleeping Beauty, The Nutcracker* (excerpt may be viewed at the link on http://www.52composers.com/tchaikovsky.html)*, Snow Maiden,* and *Hamlet;* six symphonies, three piano concertos, various overtures, chamber music, piano solos, songs, and choral works.

LISTENING GUIDE For audio, go to: https://www.youtube.com/watch?v=-BbToE99oIQ
Composer: Pyotr (Peter) Ilyich Tchaikovsky (b. 1840-1893)
Composition: *1812* Overture
Date: 1882
Genre: Symphonic Overture
Form: Two-part overture—Choral and Finale
Performing Forces: Large orchestra, including a percussion section with large bells and a battery of cannons
What we want you to remember about this composition: • The piece depicts preparation for war, the actual conflict, and victory after the war is ended. It is quite descriptive in nature. • Tchaikovsky's *1812 Overture* is one of the most famous and forceful pieces of classical music. The *1812 Overture* is particularly famous for its epic finale. • It was made famous and mainstream to the public in the United States through public concerts on July 4th by city orchestras such as the Boston Pops. • Though the piece was written to celebrate the anniversary of Russia's victory over France in 1812, the piece's finale is very often used for the 4th of July during fireworks displays.

Timing	Performing Forces, Melody, and Texture
0:00–2:14	The Russian hymn "Spasi, Gospodi, Iyudi Tvoya" ("O Lord, Save Thy People") is performed in the strings
2:14– 3:46	The music morphs into a more suspenseful style creating tension of possible upcoming conflict.
3:46– 4:45	Snare drums set a military tone as the overtures theme is introduced. Listen how the rhythms line up clear and precise.
4:45– 6:39	An energetic disjunctive style portray an attack from the French. Brief motives of La Marseillaise, the French national anthem are heard. The energy continues to build. The tension diminishes.
6:39–8:10	A reference to a lyrical section is heard contrasting the previous war scene.
8:10–8:55	A traditional folkdance -tune "U vorot" ("At the gate") from Russia is introduced into the work.
8:5–10:26	The energetic conflicting melodies are reintroduced depicting conflict.
10:26-11:11	The lyrical peaceful tune is reintroduced..
11:11–11:31	The folk dance is reintroduced..
11:31–12:05	The French Marseillaise motive appears again in the horns.The tension and energy again build.
12:05–12:56	Percussion and even real cannons are used to depict the climax of the war conflict. This followed by a musical loss of tension through descending and broadening lines in the strings.
12:56–13:59	The Russian Hymn is heard again in victory with the accompaniment of all the church bells in celebration commemorating victory throughout Russia.
13:59–14:11	The music excels portraying a hasty French retreat
14:11–15:09	The Russian anthem with cannons/percussion overpowers the French theme, The church bells join in again symbolic of the Russian victory.

6.16 MUSIC OF JOHN PHILIP SOUSA

John Philip Sousa, (b. Nov. 6, 1854-1939) was born in Washington, D.C. to a father, John Antonio Sousa, who played trombone in the U.S. Marine band and a mother, Maria Elisabeth Trinkaus, of Bavarian descent. The young Sousa was raised in a very musical environment and began studying voice, violin, piano, flute, baritone, trombone, and alto horn when his peers were just beginning first grade.

Sousa was an adventurous young man. At the young age of thirteen, he unsuccessfully tried to run away to join a circus band. Immediately after this episode, his father enlisted him in the Marines as a band apprentice in the Marine Band. There he remained until he reached the age of twenty, complementing his Marine Band training in music by studying composition and music theory with the locally highly acclaimed orchestra leader, George Felix Benkert. During these early years with the Marine Band and under the music mentorship of Benkert, Sousa composed his first piece, *Moonlight on the Potomac Waltzes.*

Figure 6.18 | John Philip Sousa
Author | Elmer Chickering
Source | Wikimedia Commons
License | Public Domain

Upon his honorable discharge from the Marines in 1875, the twenty-one year old Sousa began performing on violin and touring. While playing violin, Sousa performed under the baton of Jacques Offenbach at the Centenary Exhibition in Philadelphia and Sousa's music later showed Offenbach's influence. While playing the violin in various theater orchestras, Sousa learned to conduct, a skill he would use for the remainder of his career. This period of Sousa's career eventually led to his conducting Gilbert and Sullivan's *H. M. S. Pinafore* on Broadway in New York. In 1879, while conducting in Broadway, Sousa met Jane van Middlesworth whom he married in December of that year. About a year later, Sousa assumed the leadership post of the Marine Band with the couple moving to Washington, D.C. Sousa conducted the Marine Band for the following twelve years, under the presidential administrations of Rutherford Hayes, James Garfield, Grover Cleveland, Chester Arthur, and Benjamin Harrison. Sousa composed and performed repertoire at the request of these presidents and their respective first families.

In 1895, Sousa successfully debuted his first opera. In 1886, *The Gladiator,* using his most recognizable music form of the march, received national recognition from military bandleaders. Two years later, he dedicated his newly composed march *Semper Fidelis* to the officers and men of the Marne Corps; that piece now is traditionally known as the "official" march of the Marine Corps.

The Marine Band made its first recordings under Sousa's leadership. The phonograph had just recently been invented, and the Columbia Phonograph Company, seeking a military band to record, selected the Marine Band. They first released sixty recording cylinders and, within the decade, recorded and released for sale more than 400 different titles. These recordings made Sousa's marches and their performance by the Marine Band among the most popular to be recorded.

Having achieved stardom, the Marine Band went on two limited but successful tours in 1891-92. After completing these tours, promoter David Blakely convinced Sousa to resign his post to organize a civilian concert band. Sousa did so, forming the New Marine Band which was a concert rather than a marching band. After receiving criticism from Washington for using the word "Marine" in the title of his civilian band, Sousa eventually dropped it from its name. The new band's first performance was on September 26, 1892 in Stillman Music Hall in Plainfield, New Jersey. Two days prior to the concert, acclaimed bandmaster, Patrick Gilmore, died in St. Louis. Eventually nineteen former musicians from Gilmore's band joined Sousa's band. The names of many of these nineteen musicians are still recognized today, including Herbert L. Clark on cornet and E. A. Lefebre on saxophone.

While conducting this new band, Sousa also continued to compose music. When vacationing in Europe with his wife in 1896, he received news that David Blakely had died. The couple immediately departed for home. During this time travelling back to the United States, Sousa wrote his most famous composition, *The Stars and Stripes Forever*.

From 1900 to 1910, the Sousa band toured extensively. Tours included performances in the United States, Great Britain, Europe, South Africa, Australia, Canada, New Zealand, Hawaii, and the South Pacific in the Canary Islands. These performances and tours contributed to Sousa's band's reputation as the most admired American band of its time.

After WWI, Sousa continued to tour with his band and became a champion and advocate for music education for all children; he also testified for composer's rights before Congress in 1927 and 1928. His success won him many titles and honorary degrees. Other successes included his serving as guest speaker and conductor for the Marine Band in Washington, D.C. in 1932, performing *The Stars and Stripes Forever*. Later that same year, following a rehearsal of the Ringgold Band in Reading, Pennsylvania, the seventy-seven year old Sousa passed away.

Sousa had composed 136 marches, many on the fly in preparation for a performance in the next town. Sousa's best known marches include *The Stars and Stripes Forever* (may be heard at http://www.marineband.marines.mil/Portals/175/Docs/Audio/Ceremonial/the_stars_and_stripes_forever.mp3), *Semper Fidelis* (may be heard at http://www.marineband.marines.mil/Portals/175/Docs/Audio/Ceremonial/the_thunderer.mp3), *The Washington Post, The Liberty Bell, Daughters of Texas, The Thunderer* (may be heard at http://www.marineband.marines.mil/Portals/175/Docs/Audio/Ceremonial/the_thunderer.mp3), *King Cotton* (may be heard at http://www.marineband.marines.mil/Portals/175/Docs/Audio/Ceremonial/king_cotton.mp3), and *Manhattan Beach.*

Sousa also wrote ten operas, including *El Capitan, The Queen of Hearts, The Smugglers*, and *Desiree,* as well as a series of music suites and seventy songs. Besides writing music, he authored several articles and letters to the editors on various subjects and wrote three novels, *The Fifth String, Pipedown Sandy,* and *The Transit of Venus. Marching Along* was his comprehensive autobiography.

A sign of his continuing fame, dedications and recognitions to the Sousa name include: a memory dedication of the newly-built 1939 Pennsylvania Avenue Bridge across the Anacostia River in Washington D.C., renaming of the of the Marine Barracks band hall in his honor in 1974, and many others. In 1987, *The Stars and Stripes Forever* march was designated as the national march of the United States. Sousa became known as the "March King."

For more information on Sousa, Read his obituary at:
http://www.nytimes.com/learning/general/onthisday/bday/1106.html

Focus Composition:

The Stars and Stripes Forever by John Philip Sousa (1896)

LISTENING GUIDE		
For audio, go to: http://www.marineband.marines.mil/Portals/175/Docs/Audio/Ceremonial/the_stars_and_stripes_forever.mp3 As performed by "The President's Own" United States Marine Corps Band, Washington, D.C.		
Composer: John Philip Sousa		
Composition: *The Star and Stripes Forever*		
Date: 1896		
Genre: March		
Performing Forces: large military band		
What we want you to remember about this composition: • It is the official National March of the United States		
Other things to listen for: • After the march introduction, the sections of the march are called strains and then a trio section. The trio sections often have a contrasting section traditionally called a dogfight strain. These often are representative of a traditional silent movie battle scene. The "fight scene" is staged between the different sections of the band (upper and lower voices, brass against the woodwind, brass, woodwind and percussion). The complete form unfolds as follows: (Intro) aabbcdcdc		
A score of the Stars and Stripes may be viewed at: file:///U:/My%20Documents/2014-2015/E%20Core/Chapter%20Six%20Romantic/StarsAndStripesForever-Conductor-scan.pdf		
Timing	**Performing Forces, Melody, and Texture**	**Text and Form**
00:00	Brief lecture introduction by the conductor	March Introduction

00:59	Starts in Eb major with the entire band and plays ff (fortissimo, or very loud) 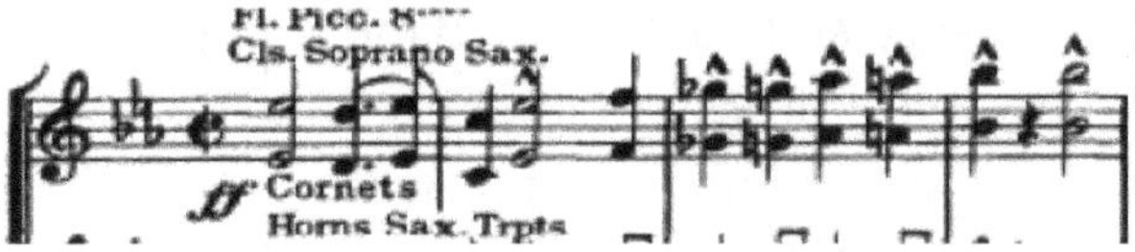	First Strain
01:03	The first strain remains loud. Notes are quick and detached/separated, and include cymbal crashes. Notice the sudden softness and crescendos (gradually gets louder).	
01:19	The first strain then repeats itself.	Second Strain
01:33	Starts piano (soft volume) the first time, melody has longer notes. Woodwind melody is heard. Euphonium compliments piccolo and woodwinds on the melody.	
01:50	The second strain repeats itself. Volume brought up to f (loud) on the repeat. Brass and percussion are prominent.	Trio
02:05	With key change/pitch center to Ab. P (Piano) soft volume with flowing and connected (legato style) melody in the clarinets and saxophones being heard. The bells compliment woodwind on the melody.	
02:37	The Dog Fight Strain depicts two opposing forcing battling one another musically. In this case, separated articulated accents descending between upper and lower voices in battle with one another. The fight goes back and forth between upper and lower voice. Percussion adds gun/cannon fire sounds to contribute to the battle scene. Then entire band descends to the potential final strain.	
03:00	Final Strain of the Trio Begins softy (p) with the famous and easily recognized piccolo solo above the previously introduced woodwind trio melody. This section features the woodwind section. But instead of ending, the woodwinds set up a repeat back to the dogfight strain.	
03:33	Repeated Dog Fight Strain	Final Strain of the trio and march

03:58	Final Strain of the trio and march-with the full compliment of the brass. The brass compliment and the piccolo solo to the end. Band plays fff (very very loud-fortississimo). Trumpets on the melody with trombones and euphoniums on the counter melody (polyphonic).	Stinger
04:29	Stinger—The march ends with the traditional musical exclamation point called the march stinger.	

We conclude this chapter with a consideration of two nationalist composers who made enduring contributions to the opera form. Some critics consider the opera form quintessential to the nineteenth century music world.

6.17 MUSIC OF GIUSEPPE VERDI

Giuseppe Verdi (1813-1901) succeeded Giacomo Rossini as the most important Italian opera composer of his day. Living during a time of national revolution, Verdi's music and name become associated with those fighting for an Italy that would be united under King Emmanuel. A chorus from one of his early operas about the ancient enslaved Hebrews would become a political song for Italian independent fighters. His last name, V.E.R.D.I. would become an acronymn for a political call to rally around King Emmanuel. Although Verdi shied away from the political limelight, he was persuaded to accept a post in the Italian parliament in 1861.

Figure 6.19 | Giuseppe Verdi
Author | Ferdinand Mulnier
Source | Wikimedia Commons
License | Public Domain

As was the case with many sons of nineteenth-century middle-class families, Verdi was given many and early opportunities to further his education. He began music instruction with local priests before his fourth birthday. Before he turned ten, he had become organist of the local church, and he continued music lessons alongside lessons in languages and the humanities through his adolescence. He assumed posts as music director and then in 1839 composed his first opera. Like his predecessor, Rossini, Verdi would prove to be a prolific composer, writing 26 operas in addition to other large-scale choral works. Like Rossini's music, Verdi's music used recitatives and arias, now arranged in the elaborate scena ad aria format, with an aria that contained both slower cantabile and faster cabaletta. Verdi, however, was more flexible in his use of recitatives and arias and employed a much larger orchestras than previous Italian opera composers, resulting in operas that were as dramatic as they were musical. His operas span a variety of subjects, from always popular mythology and ancient history to works set in his present that participated in a wider artistic movement called *verismo,* or realism.

Focus Composition:

Verdi, Excerpt from *La Traviata* (1853)

A good example of his operatic realism can be found in *La Traviata,* or *The Fallen Woman* (1853). This opera was based on a play by Alexandre Dumas. Verdi wanted it to be set in the present, but the censors at La Fenice, the opera house in Venice that would premiere the opera, insisted on setting it in the 1700s instead. Of issue was the heroine, Violetta—a companion-prostitute for the elite aristocrats of Parisian society—with whom Alfredo, a young noble, falls in love. After wavering over giving up her independence, Violetta commits herself to Alfredo, and they live a blissful few months together before Alfredo's father arrives and convinces Violetta that she is destroying their family and the marriage prospects of Alfredo's younger sister. In response, Violetta leaves Alfredo without telling him why and goes back to her old life. Alfredo is angry and hurt and the two live unhappily apart. A consumptive, that is, one suffering from tuberculosis, Violetta declines and her health disintegrates. Alfredo's father has a crisis of conscience and confesses to his son what he has done. Alfredo rushes to Paris to reunite with Violetta. The two sing a love duet, but it is soon clear that Violetta is very ill, and in fact, she dies in Alfredo's arms, before they can go to the church to be married. In ending tragically, this opera ends like many other nineteenth-century tales.

Figure 6.20 | *La Traviata*: Scene 1
Author | Carl Henning Lutzow d'Unker
Source | Wikimedia Commons
License | Public Domain

Verdi wrote this opera mid century with full knowledge of the Italian opera before him. Like his contemporary, Richard Wagner, Verdi wanted opera to be a strong bond of music and drama. He carefully observed how German opera composers such as Carl Maria von Weber and French Grand Opera composers such as Giacomo Meyerbeer had used much larger orchestras than had previous opera composers, and Verdi himself also employed a comparably large ensemble for *La Traviata.* Verdi also believe in flexibly using the operatic forms he had inherited, and so although *La Traviata* does have arias and recitatives, the recitatives are more varied and lyrical than before and the alternation between the recitatives, arias, and other ensembles, are guided by the drama, instead of the drama having to fit within the structure of recitative-aria pairs. A good example is "La follie...Sempre libera" from the end of Act I in which Violetta debates whether she is ready to give up her independence for Alfredo. Although at the end of the aria it seems that she has decided to remain free, Act II begins with the two lovers living happily together, and we know that the vocal injections sung by Alfredo as part of Violetta's recitative and aria of Act I have prevailed. This piece is also a good example of how virtuoso opera had gotten by the end of the nineteenth century. Earlier Italian opera had been virtuoso in its use of ornamentation. Verdi, however, required a much wider range of his singers, and this wider range is showcased in the scene we'll watch. Violetta has a huge vocal range and performers must have great agility to sing the melismas in her part. As an audience, we are awed by her vocal prowess, a fitting response, given her character in the opera.

LISTENING GUIDE
For audio, go to: https://youtu.be/RJzeD4HHnxs Featuring Edita Bruberova as Violetta, Neil Shicoff as Alfredo, and the Orchestra and Chorus of the Teatro La Fenice in Venice, Italy, conducted by Carlo Rizzi
Composer: Verdi
Composition: "Follie" and "Sempre libera" from *La Traviata*
Date: 1853
Genre: recitatives and aria from an opera
Form: alternates between singing styles of accompanied recitative, with some repetition of sections
Nature of Text: libretto by Francesco Maria Piave; Translation available at the following link: http://www.murashev.com/opera/La_traviata_libretto_English_Italian
Performing Forces: soprano (Violetta), tenor (Alfredo), and orchestra
What we want you to remember about this composition: • The virtuoso nature of Violetta's singing • The subtle shifts between recitative and aria, now less pronounced than in earlier opera • A large orchestra that stays in the background
Other things to listen for: • Alfredo's more lyrical melody in distinction to Violetta's virtuosity

Timing	Performing Forces, Melody, and Texture	Text and Form
0:00	Violetta sings a very melismatic and wide-ranged melody with flexible rhythm; the orchestra provides sparse accompaniment	Accompanied recitative: Follie! follie! Delirio vano è questo! Povera donna, sola, abbandonata in questo popoloso deserto che appellano Parigi. Che spero or più? Che far degg'io? Gioire, di voluttà ne' vortici perir.
0:26	Violetta sings wide leaps, long melismas, and high pitches to emphasize these words	Accompanied recitative: Gioir! (Pleasure!)
1:07	Stronger orchestral accompaniment as Violetta sings a more tuneful melody in a lilting meter with a triple feel	Aria: Sempre libera degg'io folleggiare di gioia in gioia, vo' che scorra il viver mio pei sentieri del piacer. Nasca il giorno, o il giorno muoia, sempre lieta ne' ritrovi, a diletti sempre nuovi dee volare il mio pensier.
2:06	Alfredo sings a more legato and lyrical melody in a high tenor range (this melody comes from earlier in the opera)	Alfredo's melody: Amore, amor è palpito . . . dell'universo intero – Misterioso, misterioso, altero, croce, croce e delizia, croce e delizia, delizia al cor.
2:41	Violetta sings her virtuoso recitative and then transitions into her aria style	Accompanied recitative and then aria: Follie . . . Sempre libera
3:56	Alfredo sings his lyrical melody and Violetta responds after each phrase with a fast and virtuosic melisma	Alfredo and Violetta sing: Repetition of text above

6.18 MUSIC OF RICHARD WAGNER

Figure 6.21 | Richard Wagner
Author | Cäsar Willich
Source | Wikimedia Commons
License | Public Domain

If Verdi continued the long tradition of Italian opera, Richard Wagner provided a new path for German opera. Wagner (1813-1883) may well have been the most influential European composer of the second half of the nineteenth century. Never shy about self-promotion, Wagner himself clearly thought so. Wagner's influence was both musical and literary. His dissonant and chromatic harmonic experiments even influenced the French, whose music belies their many verbal denouncements of Wagner and his music. His essays about music and autobiographical accounts of his musical experiences were widely followed by nineteenth-century individuals, from the average bourgeois music enthusiast to philosophers such as Friedrich Nietzsche. Most disturbingly, Wagner was rabidly anti-Semitic, and generations later his writing and music provided propaganda for the Nazi Third Reich.

Born in Leipzig, Germany, Wagner initially wanted to be a playwright like Goethe, until as a teenager he heard the music of Beethoven and decided to become a composer instead. He was particularly taken by Beethoven's Ninth Symphony and the addition of voices as performing forces into the symphony, a type of composition traditionally written for orchestra. Seeing in this work an acknowledgement of the powers of vocal music, Wagner set about writing vocal music. Coming to age during a time of rising nationalism, Wagner criticized Italian opera as consisting of cheap melodies and insipid orchestration unconnected to its dramatic purposes, and he set about providing a German alternative. He called his operas music dramas in order to emphasize a unity of text, music, and action; and declared that they would be *Gesamtkunstwerk*, or "total works of art." As part of his program, he wrote his own librettos and aimed for what he called unending melody: the idea was for a constant lyricism, carried as much by the orchestra as by the singers.

Perhaps most importantly, Wagner developed a system of what scholars have come to call Leitmotivs. Leitmotivs, or "guiding motives," are musical motives that are associated with a specific character, theme, or locale in a drama. Wagner integrated these musical motives in the vocal lines and orchestration of his music dramas at many points. Wagner believed in the flexibility of such motives to reinforce an overall sense of unity within his compositions, even if primarily at a subconscious level. Thus, while a character might be singing a melody line using one leitmotiv, the orchestration might incorporate a different leitmotiv, suggesting a connection between the referenced entities.

Wagner also designed and built a theatre for the performance of his own music dramas. The Festival Theatre in Bayreuth, Germany was the first to use a sunken orchestra pit, and its huge backstage area allowed for some of the most elaborate sets of Wagner's day. It was here that his famous cycle of music dramas, *The Ring of the Nibelungen*, was performed, starting in 1876. *The Ring of the Nibelungen* consists of four music dramas with over fifteen hours of music. Wagner took the story from a Nordic mythological legend that stems back to the Middle Ages. In it, a piece of gold is stolen from the Rhine River and fashioned into a ring, which gives its bearer ultimate power. The cursed ring changes hands, causing destruction around whoever possesses it. Eventually the ring is returned to the Rhine River, thereby closing the cycle. Into that story, which some may recognize from the much later fiction of J. R. R. Tolkien's *Lord of the Rings*, Wagner interwove stories of the Norse gods and men. Wagner's four music dramas trace the saga of the king of the gods, Wotan, as he builds Valhalla, the home of the gods, and attempts to order the lives of his children, including that of his daughter, the valkyrie warrior Brünnhilde.

Focus Composition:

Conclusion to *The Valkyrie* (1876)

In the excerpt we'll watch from the end of *The Valkyrie*, the second of the four music dramas, Brünnhilde has gone against her father, and, because Wotan cannot bring himself to kill her, he puts her to sleep before encircling her with flames, a fiery ring that both imprisons and protects his daughter. This excerpt provides several examples of the *Leitmotivs* for which Wagner is so famous. Their presence, often subtle, is designed to guide the audience through the drama. They include melodies, harmonies, and textures that represent Wotan's spear, the god Loge—a shape shifting life force that here takes the form of fire—sleep, the magic sword, and fate. The sounds of these motives is discussed briefly below and accompanied by excerpts from the musical score for those of you who can read musical notation.

The first motive heard in the video you will watch is **Wotan's Spear**. The spear represents Wotan's power. In this scene, Wotan is pointing it toward his daughter Brünnhilde, ready to conjure the ring of fire that will both imprison and protect here. Representing a symbol of power, the spear motive is played at a *forte* dynamic by the lower brass. Here it descends in a minor scale that reinforces the seriousness of Wotan's actions.

Figure 6.22 | Wotan's Spear
License | Public Domain

Wotan commands Loge to appear and suddenly the music breaks out in a completely different style. **Loge's music**—sometimes also referred to as the magic fire music—is in a major key and appears in upper woodwinds such as the flutes. Its notes move quickly with staccato articulations suggesting Loge's free spirit and shifting shapes.

Figure 6.23 | Loge's Music (aka The Magic Fire Music)
License | Public Domain

Depicting Brünnhilde's descent into sleep, Wagner wrote a chromatic musical line that starts high and slowly moves downward. We call this phrase the Sleep motive:

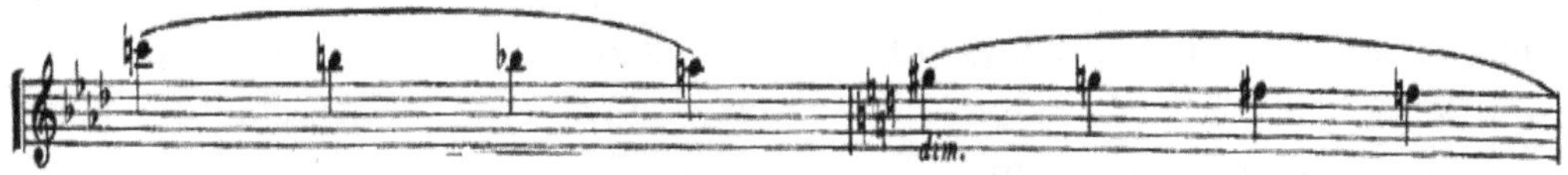

Figure 6.24 | Sleep
License | Public Domain

After casting his spell, Wotan warns anyone who is listening that whoever would dare to trespass the ring of fire will have to face his spear. As the drama unfolds in the next opera of the tetralogy, one character will do just that: Siegfried, Wotan's own grandson. He will release Brünnhilde using a magic sword. The melody to which Wotan sings his warning with its wide leaps and overall disjunct motion sounds a little bit like the motive representing Siegfried's sword.

Figure 6.25 | Siegfried's Sword
License | Public Domain

One final motive is prominent at the end of *The Vakyrie*, a motive which is referred to as Fate. It appears in the horns and features three notes: a sustained pitch that slips down just one step and then rises the small interval of a minor third to another sustained pitch.

Figure 6.26 | Wotan's Warning (subtly alluding to Siegfried's sword)
License | Public Domain

Figure 6.27 | Fate (the motive starts in the second measure of the excerpt)
License | Public Domain

Now that you've been introduced to all of the leitmotivs in the excerpt, follow along with the listening guide. As you listen, notice how prominent the huge orchestra is throughout the scene, how it provides the melodies, and how the strong and large voice of the bass-baritone singing Wotan soars over the top of the orchestra (Wagner's music required larger voices than earlier opera as well as new singing techniques). See if you can hear the *Leitmotivs*, there to absorb you in the drama. Remember that this is just one short scene from the midpoint of the approximately fifteen-hour-long tetralogy.

LISTENING GUIDE

For audio, go to:
https://www.youtube.com/watch?v=4tDP-K1dQ-M
Performed by Donald McIntyre (Wotan) and Gwyneth Jones (Brünnhilde), accompanied by the Bayreuth Festival Orchestra, conducted by Pierre Boulez (19746), starting at 13:53

Composer: Richard Wagner
Composition: *The Valkyries*, Final scene: Wotan's Farewell
Date: 1870
Genre: music drama (or nineteenth-century German opera)
Form: through-composed, using *Leitmotivs*

Nature of Text:

(He looks upon her and closes her helmet: his eyes then rest on the form of the sleeper, which he now completely covers with the great steel shield of the Valkyrie. He turns slowly away, then again turns around with a sorrowful look.)

(He strides with solemn decision to the middle of the stage and directs the point of his spear toward a large rock.)
Loge, hear! List to my word!
As I found thee of old, a glimmering flame,
as from me thou didst vanish,
in wandering fire;
as once I stayed thee, stir I thee now!
Appear! come, waving fire,
and wind thee in flames round the fell!

(During the following he strikes the rock thrice with his spear.)
Loge! Loge! appear!
(A flash of flame issues from the rock, which swells to an ever-brightening fiery glow.)
(Flickering flames break forth.)

(Bright shooting flames surround Wotan. With his
spear he directs the sea of fire to encircle the rocks; it
presently spreads toward the background, where it
encloses the mountain in flames.)

He who my spearpoint's sharpness feareth
shall cross not the flaming fire!

(He stretches out the spear as a spell. He gazes sorrowfully back on Brünnhilde. Slowly he turns to depart. He turns his head again and looks back. He diasappears through the fire.)

(The curtain falls.)

Wagner, Richard. *Die Walküre.* [English Transl. By Frederick Jameson; Version Française Par Alfred Eernst]. Leipzig: Eulenburg, 1900. Print. Eulenburgs kleine Partitur-Ausgabe.

Performing Forces: Bass-baritone Wotan, large orchestra		
What we want you to remember about this composition: • It uses *Leitmotivs* • The orchestra provides an "unending melody" over which the characters sing		
Other things to listen for: • Listen for the specific *Leitmotives*		
Timing	**Performing Forces, Melody, and Texture**	***Leitmotiv* and Form**
13:53	Descending melodic line played in octaves by the lower brass	Wotan's spear: Just the orchestra
14:06	Wotan sings a motivic phrase that ascends; the orchestra ascends, too, supporting his melodic line	Löge, hör! Lausche hieher! Wie zuerst ich dich fand, als feurige Glut, wie dann einst du mir schwandest, als schweifende Lohe; wie ich dich band
14:29	Appears as Wotan transitions to new words still in the lower brass	Spear again: Bann ich dich heut'!
14:29	Trills in the strings and a rising chromatic scale introduce Wotan's striking of his spear and producing fire introducing the . . .	Fire music: Herauf, wabernde Loge, umlo-dre mir feurig den Fels! Loge! Loge! Hieher!
15:03	fire music played by the upper woodwinds (flutes, oboes, and clar-inets).	Fire music: Just the orchestra
15:36	Slower, descending chromatic scale in the winds represents Brünnhil-de's descent into sleep	Sleep: Just the orchestra
16:04	As Wotan sings again, his melodic line seems to allude to the sword motive, doubled by the horns and supported by a full orchestra.	Sword motive: Wer meines Speeres Spitze fürchtet, durchschreite das Feuer nie!
16:31	Lower brass prominently play the sword motive while the strings and upper woodwinds play motives from the fire music; a gradual decrescendo	Sword motive; fire music con-tinues: Just the orchestra
17:42	The horns and trombones play the narrow-raged fate melody as the curtain closes	Fate motive: Just the orchestra

6.19 CHAPTER SUMMARY

As we have seen, nineteenth-century music was diverse and pervasive. Music was a part of everyday life, as middle class children received music education and as concerts became important social events across social strata. Aesthetic movements of Romanticism, Realism, Exoticism, and cultural nationalism shaped musical styles. Composers such as Franz Schubert, Felix and Fanny Mendelssohn, Robert and Clara Schumann, Fryderyk Chopin, Franz Liszt, Hector Berlioz, Johannes Brahms, Bedřich Smetana, Antonín Dvořák, John Philip Sousa, Pyotr Tchaikovsky, Giuseppe Verdi, and Richard Wagner wrote eclectic music across German, French, Italian, Czech, Polish, American, and Russian lands. Many of them continued with genres developed in the Baroque and classical periods, such as the concerto, symphony, opera, and oratorio, while others forged new paths, especially as music and poetry, drama, and visual art interacted in such new genres as the art song, piano character piece, program symphony, symphonic poem, and music drama, or opera. Despite the larger performing forces that were available, composers continued to privilege singable melodies, even if they were much more chromatic than before. These transformations of musical form and harmony continued into the early twentieth century as musicians sought to be more modern than ever before and, in so doing, questioned the very foundations basic to music of the previous two centuries.

6.20 GLOSSARY

Art song – a composition setting a poem to music, generally for one solo voice and piano accompaniment; in German, a Lied

Chamber music – music--such as art songs, piano character pieces, and string quartets--primarily performed in small performing spaces, often for personal entertainment

Chromaticism – use of "colorful," dissonant pitches, that included in the key of the composition

Concerto – a composition for a soloist or a group of soloists and an orchestra, generally in three movements with fast, slow, and fast tempos, respectively

Conductor – individual who leads an orchestra

drone – a sustained pitch or pitches often found in music of the middle ages or earlier and in folk music

Idée fixe – a famous melody that appears in all five movements of Berlioz's Symphonie fantastique to represent the beloved from the program

Leitmotiv – "guiding motive" associated with a specific character, theme, or locale in a music drama, and first associated with the music of Richard Wagner

mazurka – a Polish dance in triple time, with emphasis on beat 2

Nationalism – pride in one's nation or cultural identity, often expressed in art, literature, and music

Opera – a drama almost entirely sung to orchestral accompaniment, with accompanying costumes and staging

Plagal cadence – ending of a composition that consists of a IV chord moving to a I chord and most often associated with church music

Program music – instrumental music intended to represent a something extra musical such as a poem, narrative, drama, or picture, or the ideas, images, or sounds therein

Program symphony – program music in the form of a multi-movement composition for orchestra

Rubato – the momentary speeding up or slowing down of the tempo within a melody line, literally "robbing" time from one note to give to another

Scena ad aria – nineteenth-century operatic combination of a recitative ("scena") plus aria; here the aria generally has two parts, a slower cantabile and a faster cabaletta

Sonata – composition for a solo instrument or an instrument with piano accompaniment, generally in three movements with fast, slow, and fast tempos, respectively

Sonata form – a form often found in the first and last movements of sonatas, symphonies, and string quartets, consisting of three parts – exposition, development, and recapitulation

Song cycle – a collection of art songs, unified by poet, narrative, musical style, or composer

String quartet – performing ensemble consisting of two violinists, one violinist, and one cellist that plays compositions called string quartets, compositions generally in four movements

Strophic – a composition that uses the repetition of the same music ("strophes") for successive texts

Symphonic poem – program music in the form of a single-movement composition for orchestra; sometimes called a tone poem

Symphony – multi-movement composition for orchestra, often in four movements

Ternary form – describes a musical composition in three parts, most often featurings two similar sections, separated by a contrasting section and represented by the letters A – B – A.

Through-composed – a movement or composition consisting of new music throughout, without repetition of internal sections

7 The Twentieth Century and Beyond

N. Alan Clark and Thomas Heflin

7.1 OBJECTIVES

1. Demonstrate knowledge of historical and cultural contexts of the twentieth century through today
2. Recognize musical movements that occurred during the twentieth century
3. Aurally identify selected music of the twentieth century, making critical judgments about its style and uses

7.2 KEY TERMS

- Aaron Copland
- Alban Berg
- Anton Webern
- Arnold Schoenberg
- atom bomb
- Atonal
- Claude Debussy
- *Elektronische Musik*
- Expressionism
- George Gershwin
- Igor Stravinsky
- Impressionism
- John Williams
- Karlheinz Stockhausen
- Koji Kondo
- Laptop orchestra
- machine gun
- Maurice Ravel
- *Musique Concrète*
- Pierre Schaeffer
- Polytonality
- Primitivism, Neoclassicism
- Serialism
- Steve Reich
- Synthesizer
- telegraph
- telephone
- Thomas Edison
- through-composed
- twelve-tone techniques

7.3 INTRODUCTION AND HISTORICAL CONTEXT: 1900 TO TODAY

Music, like the other arts, does not occur in a vacuum. Changes brought on by advances in science, and inventions resulting from these advances, affected composers, artists, dancers, poets, writers, and many others at the turn of the twentieth century. Inventions from the late Romantic era had a great impact on economic and social life in the twentieth century. These inventions included the light bulb, the telephone, the automobile, and the phonograph. Thomas Edison invented the phonograph in 1877 and patented it in 1878. While researching means to improve the telegraph and telephone, Edison developed a way to record sound on tinfoil-coated cylinders. He would speak into a mouthpiece and the recording needle would indent a groove into the cylinder. The playing needle would then follow the groove, and the audio could be heard through a horn speaker (in the shape of a large cone). Edison improved his invention and formed the Edison Speaking Phonograph Company to market the invention. Edison's phonograph had an especially great influence on the spread of music to larger audiences; he also advertised the device's usefulness for dictation and letter writing, recording books for the blind, recording and archiving family members' voices, music boxes, toys, and clocks that verbally announce the time with prerecorded voices. In 1917, such audio phonograph devices were purchased by the U.S. Army for $60 each and used to make troops feel closer to home during World War I. Listen to this rare audio clip of Edison expressing his thanks to the troops for their service and sacrifice: http://www.americaslibrary.gov/assets/aa/edison/aa_edison_phonograph_3.wav

What defines twentieth-century music? Clearly, the twentieth century was a time of great upheaval in general, including in music. The sense of rapid change and innovation in music and art of this period is a reflection of the dramatic changes taking place in the world at large. On a political level, the twentieth century was one of the bloodiest and most turbulent periods in history. While wars are a constant throughout all of human history, the global nature of twentieth-century politics resulted in conflicts on a scale never before seen; World War II alone is widely regarded as the deadliest conflict in human history in terms of total deaths, partly due to advancements in technology such as machine guns, tanks, and eventually the atom bomb.

It's no surprise that music of this period mirrored the urgency and turmoil in the world at large. For many composers, the raw emotion and sentimentality reflected in the music of the nineteenth century had grown tiresome, and so they began an attempt to push the musical language into new areas. Sometimes, this meant bending long-established musical rules to their very limits, and, in some cases, breaking them altogether. One of the by-products of this urgency was fragmentation. As composers rushed to find new ways of expressing themselves, different musical camps emerged, each with their own unique musical philosophies. We now categorize these musical approaches with fancy terms ending in "-ism," such as "primitivism," "minimalism," "impressionism," etc. We will discuss many of these individual movements and techniques as well as address what makes them unique, but before we do this, let's first talk about those things that most (but not all) music of the twentieth century has in common.

7.3.1 Melody

One of the ways in which composers deviated from the music of the nineteenth century was the way in which they constructed melodies. Gone were the singable, sweeping tunes of the Romantic era. In their place rose melodies with angular shapes, wide leaps, and unusual phrase structures. In some cases, melody lost its status as the most prominent feature of music altogether, with pieces that featured texture or rhythm above all else.

7.3.2 Harmony

The most obvious difference between twentieth-century music and what preceded it is the level of harmonic dissonance. This is not a new phenomenon. The entire history of Western music can be viewed in terms of a slowly increasing acceptance of dissonance, from the hollow intervals of the Middle Ages all the way to the lush chords of the nineteenth century. However, in the twentieth century the use of dissonance took off like a rocket ship. Some composers continued to push the tolerance level for dissonance in the context of standard tonal harmony. One example is through the use of **polytonality**, a technique in which two tonal centers are played at the same time. Some composers sought to wash their hands of the rules of the past and invented new systems of musical organization. Often, this resulted in music that lacked a tonal center, music that we now refer to as **atonal**. Some composers such as Igor Stravinsky even tried their hand at more than one style.

7.3.3 Rhythm

In preceding centuries, music was typically relegated to logical, symmetrical phrases that fell squarely into strict meters. That all changed at the dawn of the twentieth century. Igor Stravinsky's *Rite of Spring* famously undermined the audience's expectation of the role of rhythm by abandoning strict meter for rapidly changing time signatures. Instead of the steady familiar time signatures containing three or four beats, Stravinsky peppered in measures containing an odd number of beats such as five or seven. This created a sense of unease in the audience by removing something from the music that they had previously taken for granted: a steady and unwavering sense of meter. In America, the rhythmic innovations of ragtime and jazz influenced both Western art music and popular music from that time on. Especially important was the use of syncopation, which was addressed in the first chapter.

7.3.4 Texture and Timbre

As memorable melodies and traditional harmonies began to break down, some composers looked to new tonal colors through the use of new instruments such as **synthesizers**, instruments that electronically generate a wide variety of sounds. In other cases, traditional instruments were used in nontraditional ways. For example, John Cage famously composed piano pieces that called for objects such as coins and tacks to be placed on the strings to create unique effects.

7.3.5 The Role of Music

Music has had many roles throughout history. The music of Josquin helped enhance worship. The works of Haydn and Mozart reflected the leisurely life of the aristocracy. Opera served as a form of musical escapism in the daring and ambitious works of composers such as Wagner. In the twentieth century, music began to move away from entertainment into the realm of high art. Composers sought to challenge the listener to experience music in new ways and in some cases to reevaluate their fundamental notions of what music is. This sense of revolution was not limited to music; it was also taking place throughout the art world. As we discuss the many "-isms" in music, we will see direct parallels with the visual arts.

7.3.6 Compositional Styles: The "-isms"

Near the beginning of the twentieth century, numerous composers began to rebel against the excessive emotionalism of the later Romantic composers. Two different styles emerged: the Impressionist style led by Claude Debussy and Maurice Ravel, and the atonal Expressionist style led by Arnold Schoenburg. Both styles attempted to move away from the tonal harmonies, scales, and melodies of the previous period. The impressionists chose to use new chords, scales, and colors while the expressionists developed a math-based **twelve-tone** system that attempted to completely destroy tonality.

7.3.7 Impressionism

The two major composers associated with the Impressionist movement are Claude Debussy and Maurice Ravel. Both French-born composers were searching for ways to break free from the rules of tonality that had evolved over the previous centuries. **Impressionism** in music, as in art, focused on the creator's impression of an object, concept, or event. The painting labeled Figure 7.1, by the French impressionist painter Claude Monet, suggests a church or cathedral, but it is not a clear portrait. It comprises a series of paint daubs that suggest something that we may have seen but that is slightly out of focus.

In the painting labeled Figure 7.2, we see how Monet distilled a scene into its most basic elements. The attention to detail of previous centuries is abandoned in favor of broad brushstrokes that are meant to capture the momentary "impression" of the scene. To Monet, the objects in the scene, such as the trees and boats, are less important than the interplay between light and water. To further emphasize this interplay, Monet pares the color palate of the painting down to draw the focus to the sunlight and the water.

Figure 7.1 | *Rouen Cathedral: The Portal (Sunlight)*
Author | Claude Monet
Source | Met Museum
License | Public Domain

Figure 7.2 | *Impression, soleil levant* (Impression Sunrise)
Author | Claude Monet
Source | Wikimedia Commons
License | Public Domain

Similarly, Impressionist music does not attempt to follow a "program" like some Romantic compositions. It seeks, rather, to suggest an emotion or series of emotions or perceptions.

Listen to the example of Debussy's *La Mer* (The Sea) linked below. Pay particular attention to the way the music seems to rise and fall like the waves in the sea and appears to progress without ever repeating a section. Music that is written this way is said to be "**through-composed**." The majority of impressionist music is written in this manner. Even though such music refrains from following a specific program or story line, *La Mer* as music *suggests* a progression of events throughout the course of a day at sea. Note that Debussy retained the large orchestra first developed by Beethoven and used extensively by Romantic composers. This music, unlike the **Expressionism** we will visit next, is tonal and still uses more traditional scales and chords.

Debussy, *La Mer*

https://www.youtube.com/watch?v=hlR9rDJMEiQ

Impressionist composers also liked using sounds and rhythms that were unfamiliar to most Western European musicians. One of the most famous compositions by Maurice Ravel is entitled *Bolero*. A Bolero is a Spanish dance in three-quarter time, and it provided Ravel with a vehicle through which he could introduce different (and exotic, or different sounding) scales and rhythms into the European orchestral mainstream. This composition is also unique in that it was one of the first to use a relatively new family of instruments at the time: the saxophone family. Notice how the underlying rhythmic pattern repeats throughout the entire composition, and how the piece gradually builds in dynamic intensity to the end.

Maurice Ravel, *Bolero*

https://www.youtube.com/watch?v=A2BYkJS8GE0

Unlike composers such as Bach, Ravel was not born into a family of musicians. His father was an engineer, but one who encouraged Ravel's musical talents. After attending the Paris Conservatory as a young man, Ravel drove a munitions truck during World War I. Throughout all this time, he composed compositions of such lushness and creativity that he became one of the most admired composers in France, along with Claude Debussy. His best known works are the aforementioned Bolero, Concerto in D for Piano, La valse, and an orchestral work entitled Daphnes et Chloe.

Daphnis et Chloé was originally conceived as a ballet in one act and three scenes and was loosely based on a Greek drama by the poet Longus. The plot on which the piece is based concerns a love affair between the title characters Daphnis and Chloe. The first two scenes of the ballet depict the abduction and escape of Chloe from a group of pirates. However, it is the third scene that has become so immortalized in the minds of music lovers ever since. "Lever du jour," or "Daybreak," takes place in a sacred grove and depicts the slow build of daybreak from the quiet sounds of a brook to the birdcalls in the distance. As dawn turns to day, a beautiful melody builds to a soaring climax, depicting the awakening of Daphnis and his reunion with Chloe.

After the ballet's premier in June of 1912, the music was reorganized into two suites, the second of which features the music of "Daybreak." Listen to the recording below and try to imagine the pastel colors of daybreak slowly giving way to the bright light of day.

LISTENING GUIDE For audio, go to: https://www.youtube.com/watch?v=tPuzMJNz9c8
Composer: Maurice Ravel
Composition: *Daphnis and Chloe, Suite No. 2: "Lever du jour"*
Date: 1913
Genre: Orchestral Suite
Form: Through-composed
Performing Forces: orchestra/chorus

Timing	Performing Forces, Melody, and Texture
0:00	Murmuring figures depicting a brook. Woodwinds, strings and harps, with more instruments entering periodically. Languid and flowing. Tonal, with ambiguous key centers and lush harmony typical of much Impressionistic music.
0:52	Sweeping melody reaches first climax, and then dies down slowly. Strings over murmuring accompaniment.
1:09	Strings and clarinet enter with song-like melody. Melody over murmuring strings.
1:30	Flute enters with dance-like melody. Melody over murmuring strings
1:48	Clarinet states a contrasting melody. Melody over murmuring strings.
2:13	Chorus enters while strings continue melody. Melody over murmuring strings and "Ah" of chorus.
2:53	Melody rises to a climax and then slowly diminishes. Full Orchestra and Chorus.
3:13	Sweeping melody enters in strings to a new climactic moment. Full Orchestra.
3:19	Motif starts in low strings and then rises through the orchestra. Full Orchestra.
4:05	Chorus enters for a final climactic moment, then slowly dies away. Full Orchestra and Chorus.
4:34	Oboe enters with repeating melody.
4:58	Clarinet takes over repeating melody and the piece slows to a stop. As the piece comes to an end, the texture becomes more Spartan with fewer instruments.

7.4 EXPRESSIONISM AND SERIALISM

While the Impressionist composers attempted to move further away from romantic forms and romantic harmony, some Expressionist composers succeeded in completely eliminating harmony and tonal melody (melody based on a particular key) from their music. The resultant sounds were often not very melodically and harmonically pleasant to hear and, as a result, the Expressionist style of music did not (and still does not) appeal to the majority of audiences.

The name of this style period can be confusing for some. The Expressionist period was not a time when composers sought to express themselves emotionally in a romantic, beautiful, or programmatic way. Due to the nature of the sounds produced by the system of composition described below, **Expressionism** seems more appropriate for evoking more extreme, and sometimes even harsh, emotions. Using this experimental style of writing, composers such as Arnold Schoenberg (1874-1951) attempted to intentionally eliminate what we call tonality; music that is based on scales and the progression (movement) of chords from one to another.

In Edward Munch's famous painting, *The Scream* (Figure 7.3), we see an excellent example of the parallel movement of expressionism taking place in the visual arts. Expressionists looked inward, specifically to the anxiety they felt towards the outside world. This was in stark contrast to the impressionists, who looked to the beauty of nature for inspiration. Expressionist paintings relied instead on stark colors and harsh swirling brushstrokes to convey the artist's reaction to the ugliness of the modern world.

Figure 7.3 | *The Scream*
Author | Edvard Munch
Source | Wikimedia Commons
License | Public Domain

Abstract Expressionism took this concept to a greater extreme, by abandoning shape altogether for pure abstraction. This style is typified by the works of the American painter Jackson Pollock (see Figure 7.4).

Many of the early works of Austrian-born Arnold Schoenberg (1874-1951) exemplified an expressionistic musical style. He is most famous for his experiments with atonality, that is, music without a tonal center. His music was highly dissonant and sounded quite radical when compared to earlier music, which utilized dissonance only as a means to eventually return to the stasis of consonance. However, Schoenberg saw dissonance not as a means to an end, but as the end itself. His music invited the listener to revel in various levels of dissonance, and many listeners were never able to adjust.

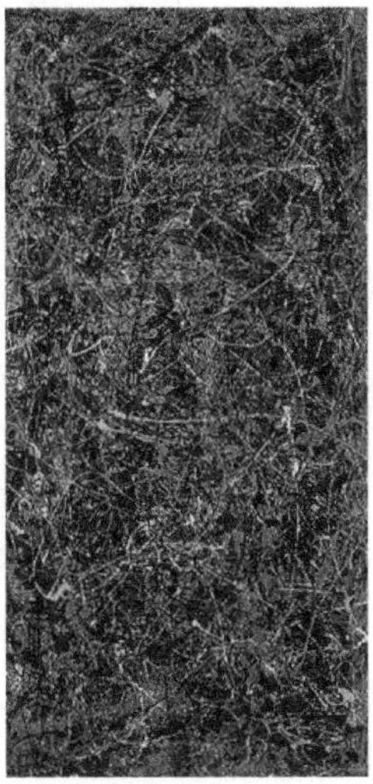

Figure 7.4 | *No. 5*
Author | Jackson Pollock
Source | Wikipedia
License | Fair Use

Born in Austria, and of Jewish descent, Schoenberg was already composing by the age of nine. While in his teens, he studied composition with the Austrian composer and conductor Alexander Zemlinsky. In 1901 he moved to Berlin where he was befriended and mentored by the German composer Richard Strauss. Three years later in 1903, Schoenberg returned to Austria and began a long association with the renowned composer Gustav Mahler who became one of his strongest supporters.

In 1909, Schoenberg composed the first complete work that completely did away with tonality. This piano composition was one of three that together are listed as his Opus 11 and was the first piece we now refer to as being completely atonal (without tonality). Schoenberg's most-important atonal compositions include: *Five Orchestral Pieces* (1909), *Pierrot Lunaire* (1912), *Die Jakobsleiter* (Jacob's Ladder - begun in 1917 but never finished), *Die glückliche Hand* (The Lucky Hand - 1924), and *Erwartung* (Expectation - 1924) for soprano and orchestra.

Schoenberg famously developed a system whereby the twelve notes of the chromatic scale were randomly organized into scale units that he called the **twelve-tone** row. These rows could then be further "serialized" (organized in random fashion) by a number of different techniques. This idea of assigning values to musical information is called **serialism.** In 1921 Schoenberg composed his Piano Suite opus 25, the first composition written using the 12-tone method. Each 12-tone composition is built from a series of 12 different pitches that may be arranged in a number of different ways. The original row may be played forward, backwards (retrograde), upside down (inverted), and backwards and inverted (retrograde inversion). All of the melodies and harmonies in a 12-tone piece must be derived in some way from the original row or from fragments of the original row.

In 1925 Schoenberg was hired by the Prussian Academy of Arts in Berlin to teach composition, and he would most likely have continued his career as teacher and composer in Europe were it not for the rise of the Nazi party and their subsequent persecution of European Jews. In 1933 he was released from the Academy and moved first to Paris and then to Boston. In 1934 he settled in California and held teaching positions first at the University of Southern California (1935-36) and then the University of Central Los Angeles (1936-44).

After immigrating to the United States, Schoenberg reconnected with the Jewish faith he had abandoned as a young man. The sadness he felt because of the personal accounts of the horrible treatment experienced by so many Jews during World War II led to his composition of A Survivor from Warsaw, which was composed for orchestra, male chorus, and narrator. The piece was completed in September 1947 and the entire piece is built on a twelve-tone row. This important work is Schoenberg's dramatization of a tragic story he heard from surviving Polish Jews who were victims of Nazi atrocities during World War II. Schoenberg created a story about a number of Jews who survived the war by living in the sewers of Warsaw. Interestingly, among Schoenberg's many and very specific performance instructions is the request that the narrator not attempt to sing his part throughout the performance.

LISTENING GUIDE
For audio, go to: https://www.youtube.com/watch?v=rGWaioSEpUQ
Composer: Arnold Schoenberg
Composition: *A Survivor from Warsaw*

Date: 1947	
Genre: 12-tone composition for small orchestra, male chorus, and narrator	
Form: through-composed	
Nature of Text: Narration of Germans' treatment of Jews in Warsaw during WWII	
Performing Forces: orchestra, male chorus, and narrator	
Timing	**Performing Forces, Melody, and Texture**
0:35	Trumpet introductory fanfare built from 12-tone row. Trumpets, snare drum, clarinets. Irregular rhythmic figures built from 12-tone row. 12-tone chordal structures built from 12-tone row.
0:46	Celli (cellos) enter with rhythmic motif. Brief medodic motifs move between celli, woodwinds, trumpets, and strings. Rhythms are derived from the 12-tone row and are irregular. 12-tone based chordal structures continue throughout piece.
1:06	Xylophone added.
1:16	Clarinet added. Clarinet completes instrumental introduction.
1:21	Narrator enters. Instrumentation and dynamics are altered to match rise and fall of phrases in narration.
1:57	French Horn enters.
2:19	Narration. Narration much more intense and trumpet fanfare underscores this change.
3:09	Narration. Bass drum begins a steady pulse with snare drum and xylophone irregular rhythms as drama in narration increases.
3:19	Narration switches to German. Narrator begins to shout in German.
3:38	Narration switches back to English. Strings play tremolo in background.
4:05	Narration becomes more introspective. Strings become more lyrical to underscore change in story.
4:20	Orchestra. Orchestra interlude decreases the intensity of the moment.
4:38	Narrator returns.

6:01	Narration. As narrator says "faster and faster" the music begins to accelerate as well.
6:19	Male chorus. Men begin to sing the Jewish prayer Shema Yisroel accompanied by strings. Brass and woodwinds are used as interjections throughout this section.
7:41	Brass join chorus. Intensity in Chorus and Orchestra build.
7:52	Brass continue as chorus ends. Brass and strings build to big climactic moment and conclude piece at 8:01.

Schoenberg's ideas were further developed by his two famous students, Alban Berg and Anton Webern. Together, the three came to be known as the Second Viennese School, in reference to the first Viennese School, which consisted of Hadyn, Mozart, and Beethoven. Born in Vienna, Alban Berg began studying with Schoenberg at the age of 19 and soon became known for his unique compositional style, which fused post-romantic concepts with Schoenberg's cutting edge twelve-tone techniques. Heavily influenced by Richard Wagner, Berg held on to techniques such as the leitmotif and sought to couch his harmonic ideas in tried-and-true forms such as the sonata and fugue. Although he composed many famous pieces, such as his Violin Concerto and his unfinished opera Lulu, he initially made his fame with Wozzeck, an opera based on the drama Woyzeck by German playright Georg Buchner. Berg served during World War I, and much of Wozzeck was composed in 1917, during a period of leave from the Austro-Hungarian Army. The opera consists of three acts, each with five scenes organized around the variations of a musical idea, such as the variations of a theme, a chord, or a rhythmic pattern. Berg himself adapted the libretto from Buchner's original play.

The story of the opera centers on the title character Wozzeck. Like the main character in many romantic operas, he is a tragic figure. However, whereas the operas of the nineteenth century often depicted gods and mythical figures, the story of Wozzeck is couched in a sense of realism and addresses the type of societal problems that Berg may himself have encountered during World War I, problems such as apathy and human cruelty. The character of Wozzeck is that of a pitiful and unremarkable soldier who is tormented by his captain and used for and subjected to medical experiments by a sadistic doctor. Wozzeck, who is often given to hallucinations, eventually goes mad and kills his love interest, Marie, who has been unfaithful. The opera ends after Wozzeck drowns trying to clean the murder weapon in a pond and wading out too far.

Listen to the recording below of act 3, scene 2, the scene in which Wozzeck kills Marie. The scene features a variation on a single note, namely B.

LISTENING GUIDE

For audio, go to:
https://www.youtube.com/watch?v=702knK1mopo

Composer: Alban Berg

Composition: *Wozzeck*

Date: 1924

Genre: Opera

Form: variation on a single note

Nature of Text: Wozzeck and Marie walk by a pond. Wozzeck stabs Marie in throat with a knife.

Performing Forces: orchestra, singers

Timing	**Performing Forces, Melody, and Texture**	**Text and Form**
0:00	Instrumental introduction evoking a low, and ominous feeling. Orchestra.	
0:24	Wozzeck and Marie enter. Marie wishes to leave. A syrupy melody in the strings reflects Wozzeck's pleas to Marie to sit down.	Marie: Dort links geht's in die Stadt. 's ist noch weit. Komm schneller! Wozzeck: Du Sollst dableiben, Marie. Kom, setz' Dich. Marie: Abe rich muss fort.
0:45	Marie leaps up, saying, "I must go!" and low ominous notes play underneath as Wozzeck lures her back.	Wozzeck: Komm. Bist weit gegangen, Marie. Sollst Dir die Fusse nicht mehr wund laufen. 's ist still hier! Und so dunkel. – Weisst noch, Marie, wi lang' es jetzt ist, dass wir uns kennen? Marie: Zu Pfingsten drei Jahre. Wozzeck: Und was meinst, wie lang' es noch dauern wird? Marie: Ich muss fort. Wozzeck: Furchst Dich, Marie? Und bist doch fromm! Und gut! Und true!

2:06	A sweet melody in the strings evokes the line by Wozzeck "What sweet lips you have, Marie."	Wozzeck: Was Du fur susse Lippen hast, Marie! Den Himmel gab' ich drum und die Seligkeit, wenn ich Dich noch of so kussen durft! Abe rich darf nicht! Was zitterst?
2:57	Wozzeck says, "Those who are cold shiver no more. You will not shiver in the morning dew," fortelling Marie's death. She asks what he means and the music ceases creating a tense silence.	Marie: Der Nachttau fallt. Wozzeck: Wer kalt ist, den friert nicht meher! Dich wird beim Morgentau nicht frieren. Marie: Was sagst Du da? Wozzeck: nix.
3:40	The music begins to build as Wozzeck prepares to kill Marie.	Marie: Wie der Mond rot aufgeht! Wozzeck: Wie ein blutig Eisen! Marie: Was zitterst? Was Willst?
4:07	The music echoes Wozzeck word by word as he says, "No one, Marie! If not me, then no one!" After the act is done, the orchestra dies down to a single note and Wozzeck exclaims, "Dead!"	Wozzeck: Ich nicht, Marie! Und kein Andrer auch nicht! Marie: Hilfe! Wozzeck: Tot!
5:00	Orchestra Orchestral interlude	

7.5 PRIMITIVISM IN MUSIC

The brilliant Igor Stravinsky (1882-1971) was truly a cosmopolitan figure, having lived and composed in Russia, France, Switzerland, and the United States. His music influenced numerous composers, including the famed French composition teacher Nadia Boulanger. Stravinsky caused quite a stir when the ballet entitled *The Rite of Spring* premiered in Paris in 1913. He composed the music for a ballet that was choreographed by Sergei Diaghilev, and it was so new and different that it nearly caused a riot in the audience. The orchestral version (without the dancing) has become one of the most admired compositions of the twentieth century.

Stravinsky's use of "primitive" sounding rhythms to depict several pagan ritual scenes makes the term "**primitivism**" seem appropriate. Use the listening guide below to follow Stravinsky's *The Rite of Spring*.

LISTENING GUIDE	
For audio, go to: https://www.youtube.com/watch?v=s7pV2cX0qxs	
Composer: Igor Stravinsky	
Composition: *Rite of Spring*, Sacrificial Dance	
Date: 1913	
Genre: Ballet music	
Form: Specific passages accompany changes in choreography	
Performing Forces: Full orchestra	
Timing	**Performing Forces, Melody, and Texture**
0:00	Flute repeated pattern based on scale tones. Wind and soft plucked stringed accompaniment. Steady slower pulse in accompaniment.
0:22	Muted trumpets state theme. Wind and plucked stringed accompaniment continues.
0:45	Violins enter softly. Wind and plucked stringed accompaniment continues.
0:56	Loud French horn entrance on fanfare-like part. French horn, bass drum, strings.
1:09	Oboe melody alternates with orchestra. Oboe, strings, brass, bassoons.
1:40	Restatement of loud French horn entrance. French horn, bass drum, cymbals, strings.
1:57	Low flute. English horn, flute, clarinet, bass clarinet, muted brass, drum.
2:45	Strings. String section with percussion. Short, hard notes, irregular rhythms.
3:16	Strings. Winds and soft plucked stringed accompaniment.
3:28	Trombones. Winds and soft plucked stringed accompaniment. Triplet trombone fanfare over plucked string parts. Muted trumpets and strings answer.

3:45	Strings. Plucked stringed accompaniment becomes immediately loud.
3:50	Trumpet fanfare. Plucked stringed accompaniment remains loud.
3:59	French horns join fanfare section. Plucked stringed accompaniment remains loud.
4:06	Plucked stringed accompaniment becomes the melody.
4:17	Winds and soft plucked stringed accompaniment.
4:31	Violins. Scale patterns become very fast and loud.
4:40	Silence.
4:41	Strings and percussion. Restatement of section at 2:50.
5:09	Brass and percussion. Brass and percussion. Percussion faster and louder.
5:43	Horn riffs up to high notes. Add high clarinet.
5:49	Silence.
5:50	Strings and percussion. Restatement of section at 2:50 and 4:41.
5:55	Full orchestra. Multiple loud fanfare-like parts in many sections. Piece builds.
6:19	Strings. Similar to 2:50, 4:41, 5:50 but more intense.
6:59	Brass. Full orchestra. Rhythmic figure carries intensity of the dance to end.

7.6 NEOCLASSICISM

In the decades between World War I and World War II, many composers in the Western world began to write in a style we now call **Neoclassicism**. When composing in a neoclassic manner, composers attempted to infuse many of the characteristics of the classic period into their music, incorporating concepts like balance (of form and phrase), economy of material, emotional restraint, and clarity in design. They also returned to popular classical forms like the Fugue, the Concerto Grosso, and the Symphony.

Numerous well-known composers incorporated neoclassic techniques and philosophy into their compositions. Stravinsky was among them, and his ballet entitled *Pulcinella* (1920) is an early example of neoclassical style. It was based on music that Stravinsky originally thought was written by the Baroque composer Giovanni Pergolesi. Music historians later deduced that the compositions were actually written by contemporaries of Pergolesi and not by Pergolesi himself. Stravinsky borrowed specific themes from these earlier works and combined them with more modern harmonies and rhythms. Listen to how in some sections the music closely approximates the style and sounds of Baroque composers, while in other sections it sounds much more aggressive, primitive, and modern.

Stravinsky, *Pulcinella*

https://www.youtube.com/watch?v=Fzoa_oyeQpQ

One composer who was able to combine elements of neo-Classicism with the traditions of his homeland was Béla Bartók (1881 – 1945). Bartok was born in Nagyszentmiklós, Hungary and was an important figure in the music of the early twentieth century. A noted composer, teacher, pianist, and ethnomusicologist, he was appointed to a position in the Royal Academy of Music in Budapest in 1907 and worked there until 1934. Along with his friend and colleague Zoltán Kodály, Bartók enthusiastically researched and sought out the music of Hungarian peasants, and both composers transcribed the music they found for piano, as well as using it as inspiration for their own original compositions.

In addition to Hungarian folk music, Bartók's style was also influenced by the Romantic music of Strauss and the Hungarian composer Franz Liszt. He was also influenced by Debussy's impressionism and the more modern music of Igor Stravinsky and Arnold Schoenberg. As a result of all of these influences, his music was often quite rhythmic, and it incorporated both tonal and chromatic (moving by half-steps) elements. Bartók composed numerous piano works, six string quartets, and an opera titled *Duke Bluebeard's Castle*, as well as a ballet entitled *The Wooden Prince* (1916), and a pantomime entitled *The Miraculous Mandarin* (1919). His string quartets and his *Concerto for Orchestra* have become part of the standard repertoire of professional performing groups around the world.

LISTENING GUIDE
For audio, go to: https://www.youtube.com/watch?v=bLtEnXinTbU
Composer: Béla Bartók
Composition: Concerto for Orchestra – Movement Five "Finale"
Date: 1944
Genre: Orchestral composition featuring all of the different sections of the orchestra
Form: Concerto in five movements – this is the fifth movement only

Performing Forces: Full Orchestra	
Timing	**Performing Forces, Melody, and Texture**
26:12	Chord tones. French horns. Tonal scales.
26:20	Violins. Strings and timpani. Fast scale patterns. Tonal scales.
26:38	Violins. Adds flute background figures. Fast scale patterns. Tonal scales.
26:40	Violins. Adds muted brass background figures. Fast scale patterns.
26:49	Violins. Adds full brass and woodwind fanfare like accompaniment. Violin scales and others playing chords.
26:55	Oboes. Brief interlude figure.
26:57	Celli. Scale patterns.
26:58	Violas. Scale patterns.
27:01	Violins. Very fast and high scale patterns.
27:14	Adds brass chords and figures from other strings. Strings and brass. Rhythm changes to include triplets.
27:25	Adds trombones and tuba on low note accents. Strings and brass.
27:33	Flutes and oboes. Begins section featuring different woodwinds.
27:36	Clarinet.
27:44	Oboe.
27:47	Woodwinds and violins. Section featuring alternation between fast string scale figures and fast woodwind scale figures.

28:01	Strings. Adds timpani.
28:05	Trombones.
28:15	Strings.
28:18	Bassoon. Section featuring bassoons, then clarinet, then oboe, then flute. Sections follow one another playing similar material.
28:30	Flute and adds bass clarinet. Lyrical section with flute melody and clarinet accompaniment.
28:42	Bassoon.
28:47	Violins. Oboes in background.
28:52	Violins. Clarinet in background.
28:56	Violins. Adds French Horn.
29:02	Oboe. Clarinet in background.
29:10	Violins. Tempo speeds up.
29:14	Trumpet. Fanfare begins. Rhythmic fanfare figures. Fanfare outlines minor sounding tonality.
29:25	Trumpet. Fanfare continues. Rhythmic fanfare figures. Fanfare outlines minor sounding tonality.
29:32	Trumpets. Adds French Horns to background. Fanfare continues.
29:43	Adds flute. Fanfare continues.
29:53	Rhythm changes.
30:02	Tympani and harp. Harp begins simple background beat pattern. Rhythm changes.
30:07	Violins.

30:14	Violas. Violas state a new melody - Woodwinds in background.
30:25	Violins take over the melody. Woodwinds in background.
30:40	Celli take over the melody. Violins and woodwinds in background.
30:56	String section. New section begins.
31:05	Oboes. Woodwinds and strings.
31:30	Oboe states new fragment of a theme.
31:35	Horn repeats fragment.
31:41	Woodwinds pass fragment around. Woodwinds and strings.
31:49	Strings. String section and woodwinds. New, faster and more intense rhythms.
32:06	Timpani enters.
32:09	Strings. Strings restate fast scale figures from earlier in movement. Fast scale figures.
32:25	Brass and strings alternate. Full orchestra with timpani. Fanfare rhythm.
32:34	Brass. Brass feature.
32:44	Strings. Strings begin to restate scale figures.
32:55	Strings. String parts get slower and softer. Rhythm slows.
33:04	Strings. Soft string interlude. Slower more relaxed.
33:31	Woodwinds. Woodwinds play quiet interlude section.
33:54	Bassoon followed by other woodwinds. Woodwinds build to final brass fanfare – strings in background.

34:12	Brass enters softly with fanfare figures and builds. Brass and strings. Complexity increases with dynamic increase.
34:29	Woodwinds join brass. Continues to build.
34:47	Brass. Big brass fanfare with fast string patterns in background. Slower but stronger brass, fast strings.
35:05	Strings and brass alternate. Strings alternate with loud brass fanfare figures to end. Faster, more aggressive rhythms.

7.7 MINIMALISM

Minimalism is a movement that began in New York during the 1960s, and it stands in stark contrast to much of the music of the early twentieth century. Minimalists composers sought to distill music down to its fundamental elements. Minimalist pieces were highly consonant (unlike the atonal music of earlier composers) and often relied on the familiar sounds of triads. Instead of featuring rhythmic complexity, minimalist composers established a steady meter. And, unlike twelve-tone music, which avoided repetition at all costs, minimalist composers made repetition the very focus of their music. Change was introduced very slowly through small variations of repeated patterns, and, in many cases, these changes were almost imperceptible to the listener. Arguably the most famous two composers of the minimalistic style were Stephen Reich (b.1936) and Philip Glass (b.1937). Glass composed pieces for small ensembles comprised of wind instruments, voices, or organ, while Reich's music often featured various percussion instruments.

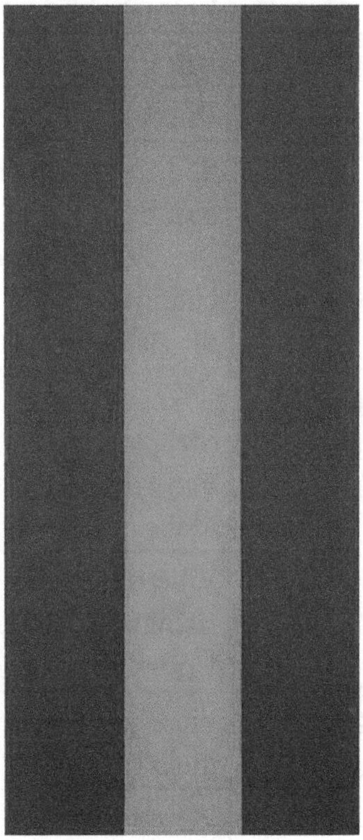

Figure 7.5 | *Voice of Fire*
Author | Barnett Newman
Source | Wikimedia Commons
License | Public Domain

But minimalism wasn't confined to the realm of music. In Barnett Newman's (1905-1970) painting (Image 7.5) *Voice of Fire* (1967), we see that many of these same concepts of simplification applied to the visual arts. Minimalist painters such as Newman created starkly simple artwork consisting of basic shapes, straight lines, and primary colors. This was a departure from the abstract expressionists such as Jackson Pollack in the same way that Steve Reich's compositions were a departure from the complexity of Arnold Schoenberg's music.

Steve Reich's *Music for 18 Musicians* is a composition featuring eleven related sections performed by an unorthodox ensemble consisting of mallet instruments, women's voices, woodwinds, and percussion. Section VII below is constructed of a steady six-beat rhythmic pattern that is established at the beginning of the piece. Over this unfaltering rhythmic pattern, various instruments enter with their own repeated melodic motifs. The only real changes in the piece take place in very slow variations of rhythmic density, overall texture, and instrumental range. All of the melodic patterns in the piece fit neatly into a simple three-chord pattern, which is also repeated throughout the piece. Most minimalistic pieces follow this template of slow variations over a simple pattern. This repetition results in music with a hypnotic quality, but also with just enough change to hold the listener's interest.

LISTENING GUIDE	
For audio, go to: https://www.youtube.com/watch?v=3hML1TuDcRI	
Composer: Steve Reich	
Composition: Music for 18 Musicians	
Date: 1976	
Genre: Minimalist Composition comprising eleven sections	
Performing Forces: orchestra	
Timing	**Performing Forces, Melody, and Texture**
0:00	Six-beat motif repeated by marimbas, mallet percussion, pianos and shaker. Steady meter is established throughout the piece. Only the texture changes. Single tonic minor chord.
0:20	Strings, woodwinds and voices enter with repeated motif, creating a more dense texture. Mallet percussion, pianos, shaker, strings, women's voices and clarinets.
0:40	Vibraphone enters, voice, woodwind and string parts begin to change, rising and becoming more dense. Underlying three-chord motif is established and repeated.
3:05	Piece has reached its apex. From here the string, voice, and woodwind melody slowly descends and becomes less rhythmically dense.
3:40	Piece returns to original texture of mallet instruments. mallet percussion, pianos, and shaker with simple closing melody played by vibraphone. Returns to single minor chord.

7.8 THE AMERICAN STYLE

As we will see in a later chapter, jazz is a uniquely American style. American orchestral composers were becoming aware of jazz in the early twentieth century, and George Gershwin (1898-1937) was no exception. Gershwin was a brilliant talent who dropped out of school at the age of fifteen to begin a professional career playing piano in New York's "Tin Pan Alley." After several years of success as a performer and composer, he was asked by the famous band leader Paul Whiteman to compose a work that would help raise people's perceptions of jazz as an art form. The resulting work, *Rhapsody in Blue,* combines the American blues style with the European symphonic tradition into a brilliant composition for piano and orchestra. Listen to how beautifully Gershwin combines these elements via the link below.

Gershwin, *Rhapsody in Blue* (1924)

https://www.youtube.com/watch?v=BxowOVIdnRo

In addition to *Rhapsody in Blue*, George Gershwin is also known for his opera, "Porgy and Bess." Although not a true opera in the strict sense of the term (Gershwin dubbed it a "folk opera"), the piece is considered one of the great American operatic works of the century. The story is set in a tenement in Charleston, South Carolina. Based on DuBose Heyward's novel *Porgy,* the opera incorporated classically trained black singers to depict the tragic love story between the two main title characters. Gershwin based the music for the opera on elements of folk music, referring to southern black musical style such as the blues and spirituals. Drawing on the nineteenth century opera tradition, Gershwin made use of leitmotifs to represent people or places. Near the beginning of the opera, we hear the famous aria "Summertime," which depicts the hot, hazy atmosphere in which the story is set.

George Gershwin – "Summertime"

https://www.youtube.com/watch?v=O7-Qa92Rzbk

Like Gershwin, American born Aaron Copland (1900-1990) was instrumental in helping to define a distinct American sound by combining his European musical training with jazz and folk elements. As an early twentieth-century composer, Copland was active during the Great Depression, writing music for the new genre of radio, the phonograph, and motion pictures. *El Salon Mexico (1935), Fanfare for the Common Man (1942),* and *Appalachian Spring* (1944) are three of Copland's most famous works. He won a Pulitzer Prize for his music for the ballet *Appalachian Spring* and was also an Oscar-winning film composer. *Appalachian Spring* is a ballet depicting a pioneer wedding celebration in a newly-built farmhouse in Pennsylvania. It includes the now well-known Shaker song *Simple Gifts.*

Copland, *Appalachian Spring* (1944)

https://www.youtube.com/watch?v=ZNHWcHEMy-Q

Copland's unique style evokes images of the landscape of the west, as we can hear in his score for the ballet *Rodeo* (1942) linked below.

Aaron Copland, *Rodeo* (1942)

https://www.youtube.com/watch?v=SXikDnYZYpM

One of the ways in which Copland was able to capture the sense of vastness of the American landscape was through his use of certain harmonic intervals, that is, two notes played together, which sound "hollow" or "open." These intervals, which are called "perfect 4ths" and "perfect 5ths," have been used since medieval times, and were named so due to their simple harmonic ratios. The result is music that sounds vast and expansive. Perhaps the best example of this technique is found in Copland's famous *Fanfare for the Common Man.*

While fanfares are typically associated with heralding the arrival of royalty, Copland wanted to create a fanfare that celebrated the lives of everyday people during a trying time in American history. The piece was premiered by the Cincinnati Symphony Orchestra on March 12, 1943 at the height of World War II. To this day, no other piece stirs up patriotic emotions like *Fanfare for the Common Man.* It has been used in countless movies, television shows, and even military recruitment ads. The piece came to define Copland's uniquely American compositional style and remains one of the most popular patriotic pieces in the American repertoire.

LISTENING GUIDE	
For audio, go to: https://www.youtube.com/watch?v=FLMVB0B1_Ts	
Composer: Aaron Copland	
Composition: *Fanfare for the Common Man*	
Date: 1942	
Genre: Fanfare	
Performing Forces: brass and percussion sections of symphony orchestra	
Timing	**Performing Forces, Melody, and Texture**
0:00	Opening crash heralds introduction by bass drum and timpani that slowly dies down. Slow and deliberate.
0:31	Slow fanfare theme enters. The melody itself is comprised of many perfect 4ths and perfect 5th intervals which convey a sense of openness. Unison trumpets. Slow tempo. No harmonic accompaniment creates a sense of starkness.

1:05	After brief notes from the percussion section, French horns enter, moving a perfect 5th below the trumpets. Trumpets and French horns, with periodic hits from the percussion Built primarily on perfect 4ths and 5ths.
1:46	Repeat of material from the introduction. Percussion.
1:48	Clarinet states a contrasting melody. Melody over murmuring strings.
1:59	Low brass enters with the main theme and is imitated by the horns and trumpets. Full brass and percussion.
3:01	Melody is restated at ½ speed (augmentation) and ends on climactic chord. Full brass and percussion.

7.9 THE LATE TWENTIETH CENTURY

Modern electronic inventions continue to change and shape our lives. Music has not been immune to these changes. Computers, synthesizers, and massive sound systems have become common throughout the western world. In this unit, we will touch on some of the important trends that started in the 1940s and 1950s and continue to the present. We will also look at an important genre, movie music!

7.9.1 Musique Concrète

Musique concrète (a French term meaning "concrete music") is a type of electro-acoustic music that uses both electronically produced sounds (like synthesizers) and recorded natural sounds (like instruments, voices, and sounds from nature). Pierre Schaeffer (in the 1940s) was a leader in developing this technique. Unlike traditional composers, composers of *musique concrète* are not restricted to using rhythm, melody, harmony, instrumentation, form, and other musical elements. The video linked below offers an excellent narrative on *musique concrète.*

Musique concrète

https://www.youtube.com/watch?v=c4ea0sBrw6M

Below is a link to one of Pierre Schaeffer's *musique concrète* compositions.

Pierre Schaeffer, *Études de bruits* (1948)

https://www.youtube.com/watch?v=CTf0yE15zzI

7.9.2 Elektronische Musik

Elektronische Musik (German term meaning "electronic music") is composed by manipulating only electronically-produced sounds (not recorded sounds.) Like Expressionism, both *musique concrète* and *elektronische Musik* did not last long as popular techniques. Karlheinz Stockhausen was a leader in the creation of *elektronische Musik.*

The link below is to an example of *elektronische Musik.*

Stockhausen: *Kontakte* (electronic version complete)

https://www.youtube.com/watch?v=-vjofqA2SNY

7.9.3 Laptop Orchestras

With the development of laptop computers, a new wave of interest has sprung up world-wide in electronic music of all types. Musicians can now easily link laptops together to form ensembles; they can also link laptops in other locations, even around the globe. Software is being developed that allows for all types of *musique concrète* and *elektronische musik* compositions and combinations. The Princeton Laptop Orchestra is a leader in this area of experimental composition and performance.

Princeton Laptop Orchestra

https://www.youtube.com/watch?v=gOsaANAfZcw

7.9.4 Film Music

Although modern audiences may no longer visit the local symphony or opera house on a regular basis, they do visit the local movie theater. In this way, symphonic music lives on in our everyday lives in the form of music for film, as well as for television shows, commercials, and video games.

More than any other form of media in the twentieth century, film has made an indelible mark on our culture. The first known public exhibition of film with accompanying sound took place in Paris in 1900, but not until the 1920s did talking pictures, or "talkies," become commercially viable. Inevitably, part of the magic of film is due to its marriage with music. After opera, film music was the next step in the evolution of music for drama. In fact, film music follows many of the same rules established by the nineteenth-century opera and before, such as the use of overtures, leitmotifs, and incidental music. Many of the most famous themes in the history of film are known throughout the world in the same way that an aria from a famous opera would have been known to the mass audiences of the previous century. For example, who of us cannot sing the theme from *Star Wars*?

Unlike the music of forward-thinking twentieth-century composers such as Schoenberg and Webern, music for film is not designed to push musical boundaries; instead, it draws on compositional devices from across the vast history of Western music. Music for a film depicting a love story might rely on sweeping melodies reminiscent of Wagner or Tchaikovsky. A science fiction movie might draw on dense note clusters and unconventional synthesized sounds to evoke the strangeness of encountering beings from another world. A documentary might feature music that is emotionally detached, such as the twentieth-century minimalistic style of Phillip Glass. It all depends on what style best complements the visuals.

The following example is one of the most famous melodies in cinema history, the main theme from *Star Wars*, composed by John Williams. Because *Star Wars* tells a story in a galaxy far, far away, its music should logically sound futuristic, but director George Lucas opted for an entirely different approach. He asked the film's John Williams to compose something romantic in nature so as to ground the characters of this strange universe in something emotionally familiar. Williams achieved this goal by creating a musical landscape deeply rooted in the style of Wagner, especially in his use of heroic themes and leitmotifs. Listen to the example below and pay special note to the sense of adventure it evokes.

LISTENING GUIDE	
For audio, go to: https://www.youtube.com/watch?v=_DoZQPqeJkk	
Composer: John Williams	
Composition: Star Wars Main Title	
Date: 1977	
Genre: Motion Picture Soundtrack	
Performing Forces: orchestra	
Timing	**Performing Forces, Melody, and Texture**
0:00	Opening Fanfare: Use of perfect fourths to evoke heroism. Orchestral: trumpets and brass. Triplet figures create a sense of excitement. Opens on a loud tonic chord to convey strength.
0:08	Main Theme. High brass alternating with strings. Heroic march. Strong tonal center.
1:11	Transition to space battle music as Imperial Star Destroyer looms over a smaller ship. Ascending strings followed by lone flute solo and stabbing brass notes Floating time followed by jarring triplet figures. Moves towards dissonance to create sense of impending danger.

2:03	Battle Music: Melody spells out a diminished chord, evoking conflict. Low brass takes over melody. Faster march creates a sense of urgency. Minor key depicts danger.
2:14	Main theme returns. Melody switches to the French horns. Heroic march. Returns to major key.
3:19	Leia's Theme. Sweeping romantic melody in strings. Slow moving tempo. Lush romantic chords.
4:06	Main Theme returns.
4:39	Battle Theme returns.
5:17	Closing Section (Coronation Theme). Full Orchestra. Slow and majestic. Ends on a strong tonic chord.

We talked about leitmotifs in our chapter on nineteenth-century music. The music of *Star Wars* relies heavily on this technique, and most of its characters have their own unique themes, which appear in different forms throughout the movies. Perhaps the most famous of these leitmotifs is the "Force Theme." The link below is a compilation of the various uses of this theme throughout the trilogy.

https://www.youtube.com/watch?v=QrbAg3zkpg4

7.9.5 Music for New Media

Although the movies continue to flourish in the twenty-first century, new technologies bring new media, and, with it, new music. One of the fastest growing examples of new media comes in the form of video games. The music of the first commercially-available video games of the 1970s was rudimentary at best. Fast-forward to the twenty-first century, and video games feature complex and original musical backdrops which complement incredibly realistic graphics and game play. These games require a cinematic style of music that can adapt to the actions of the player.

Listen to the example below from the original for the Nintendo Entertainment System. Early video game music is not unlike the music of the Renaissance in that it was limited to polyphony between a small number of voices. The original NES system put significant restraints on composers, as it was only possible to sound three to four notes simultaneously, and a great deal of effort was put into getting as rich a sound as possible within these constraints. Listen below to the two versions of the main Zelda theme (called the "Overworld Theme"). Conceived by acclaimed video game composer Koji Kondo, it is one of the most famous video game themes of all time. This theme has been featured in almost all of the Legend of Zelda games. Notice how the composer uses imitative polyphony to create the illusion of a full texture. Notice also the piece's similarity to Ravel's *Bolero,* which we heard earlier in this chapter. Kondo originally planned to use his own arrangement of Ravel's *Bolero* as the main theme for the game. However, in the end he chose to write instead an original piece with similar characteristics. Notice that both are built on a steady repeated percussive pattern.

LISTENING GUIDE	
For audio, go to: https://www.youtube.com/watch?v=lpEzYEoV9qY	
Composer: Koji Kondo	
Composition: *The Legend of Zelda (Overworld Theme)*	
Date: 1986	
Genre: Video Game Music	
Performing Forces: orchestra	
Timing	**Performing Forces, Melody, and Texture**
0:00	Introduction. Synthesized sounds. Heroic march implied by rudimentary percussion sounds. Basic chord structure implied through limited polyphony.
0:07	Main Theme. Synthesized sounds. Heroic march. Imitative polyphony creates a sense of full texture.

The second version of the theme is a testament to the advances made in the technological capabilities of video game music. An updated arrangement of the theme from Nintendo's 2011 release, *The Legend of Zelda: Skyward Sword,* it features the "Overworld Theme" in the game's credits sequence. If you didn't know this music belonged to a video game, you could imagine it as a soundtrack to a blockbuster adventure movie.

LISTENING GUIDE
For audio, go to: https://www.youtube.com/watch?v=5h2x18CtgZQ
Composer: Koji Kondo

Composition: *The Legend of Zelda (Overworld Theme)*	
Date: 1986 (2011 arrangement)	
Genre: Video Game Music	
Performing Forces: orchestra	
Timing	**Performing Forces, Melody, and Texture**
0:00	Introduction. Orchestral: Strings with brass hits. Heroic march. Rising chords create sense of anticipation.
0:14	Main Theme. Trumpets take melody followed by strings. Heroic march.

7.10 CHAPTER SUMMARY

In this chapter we examined the Impressionist style of music and its two main composers, Ravel and Debussy. We also looked at a new approach to harmony and composition developed by Schoenberg, Berg, and others that became known as Expressionism. We then briefly touched on the style called primitivism and the music of Igor Stravinsky and examined the Neoclassicism of Stravinsky and others. We saw how the minimalist composers sought to create music from its most fundamental rhythmic and melodic elements, returning to the consonant sounds of triads and the strict application of steady meter. We then discovered the uniquely American, yet contrasting styles of Aaron Copland and George Gershwin—Copland creating an American symphonic style and Gershwin creating a style which incorporated jazz music. We learned that *musique concrète* was a combination of recorded and electronic sounds and that the German composer Karlheinz Stockhausen was the leader in *elektronische Musik*. We saw that the Princeton University Laptop Orchestra is an important leader in laptop computer ensembles. Finally, we looked at music for motion pictures and at one of the most recent developments in electronic and digital entertainment: music for video games.

7.11 GLOSSARY

Atonal – Music that seeks to avoid both the traditional rules of harmony and the use of chords or scales that provide a tonal center

Chromaticism – a style of composition which uses notes that are not a part of the predominant scale of a composition or one of its sections.

Elektronische Musik - (German term meaning "electronic music") Music composed by manipulating only electronically-produced sounds (not recorded sounds.)

Expressionism – Style of composition where composers intentionally use atonality. Arnold Schoenberg devised a system of composing using twelve tones. His students Alban Berg and Anton Webern composed extensively in this twelve-tone style.

Impressionism – music composed based on the composer's impression of an object, concept, or event. This style included the use of chromaticism, whole-tone scales and chords, exotic scales, new chord progressions, and more complex rhythms

Laptop orchestra – an ensemble formed by linking laptop computers and speakers together to generate live and/or recorded performances using both synthesized and pre-recorded sounds

Musique Concrète – a type of electro-acoustic music that uses both electronically produced sounds (like synthesizers) and recorded natural sounds (like instruments, voices, and sounds from nature)

Neoclassicism – A musical movement that arose in the twentieth century as a reaction against romanticism and which sought to recapture classical ideals like symmetry, order, and restraint. Stravinsky's music for the ballet Pulcinella (1920) is a major early neoclassical composition.

Polytonality – a compositional technique where two or more instruments or voices in different keys (tonal centers) perform together at the same time

Primitivism – A musical movement that arose as a reaction against musical impressionism and which focused on the use of strong rhythmic pulse, distinct musical ideas, and a tonality based on one central tone as a unifying factor instead of a central key or chord progression.

Serialism – composing music using a series of values assigned to musical elements such as pitch, duration, dynamics, and instrumentation. Arnold Schoenberg's 12-tone technique is one of the most important examples of serialism.

Synthesizers - instruments that electronically generate a wide variety of sounds. They can also modify electronic or naturally produced recorded sounds

Through-Composed – Music that progresses without ever repeating a section

Twelve-tone Technique - Compositional technique developed by Arnold Schoenberg that derives musical elements such as pitch, duration, dynamics, and instrumentation from a randomly produced series of the twelve tones of the chromatic scale (the 12-tone row)

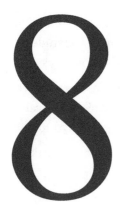

8 Popular Music in the United States

N. Alan Clark and Thomas Heflin

8.1 OBJECTIVES

- Basic knowledge of the history and origins of popular styles
- Basic knowledge of representative artists in various popular styles
- Ability to recognize representative music from various popular styles
- Ability to identify the development of Ragtime, the Blues, Early Jazz, Bebop, Fusion, Rock, and other popular styles as a synthesis of both African and Western European musical practices
- Ability to recognize important style traits of Early Jazz, the Blues, Big Band Jazz, Bebop, Cool Jazz, Fusion, Rock, and Country
- Ability to identify important historical facts about Early Jazz, the Blues, Big Band Jazz, Bebop, Cool Jazz, Fusion, and Rock music
- Ability to recognize important composers of Early Jazz, the Blues, Big Band Jazz, Bebop, Cool Jazz, Fusion, and Rock music

8.2 KEY TERMS

- 45's
- A Tribe Called Quest
- Alan Freed
- Arthur Pryor
- Ballads
- BB King
- Bebop
- Big Band
- Bluegrass
- Blues
- Bob Dylan
- Broadway Musical
- Charles "Buddy" Bolden
- Chestnut Valley
- Children's Song
- Chuck Berry
- Contemporary Country
- Contemporary R&B
- Count Basie
- Country

- Creole
- Curtis Blow
- Dance Music
- Dixieland
- Duane Eddy
- Duke Ellington
- Earth, Wind & Fire
- Elvis Presley
- Folk Music
- Frank Sinatra
- Fusion
- George Gershwin
- Hillbilly Music
- Honky Tonk Music
- Improvisation
- Jelly Roll Morton
- Joan Baez
- Leonard Bernstein
- Louis Armstrong
- LPs
- Michael Bublé
- Minstrel Show
- Musical Theatre
- Operetta
- Original Dixieland Jazz Band
- Oscar Hammerstein
- Protest Song
- Ragtime
- Rap
- Ray Charles
- Rhythm and Blues
- Richard Rodgers
- Ricky Skaggs
- Robert Johnson
- Rock and Roll
- Sampling
- Scott Joplin
- Scratching
- Stan Kenton
- Stan Kenton
- Stephen Foster
- Storyville
- Swing
- Syncopated
- The Beatles
- Victor Herbert
- Weather Report
- Western Swing
- William Billings
- WJW Radio
- Work Songs

8.3 INTRODUCTION

Popular music is by definition music that is disseminated widely. As such, it has been particularly significant with the twentieth-century proliferation of recording technologies and mass media. Sometimes we may forget that it was not until the 1920s that recording and playback technology allowed for the spread of music through records. To become popular before that time, a tune had to be spread by word of mouth, by traveling performers, and by music notation, which might appear in a music magazine or newspaper or in sheet music that could be bought at general stores, catalogs, and music stores.

Today the success of a popular music artist is most often measured by how many songs they sell. In the past, that meant record and CD sales, but today it essentially means numbers of downloads. Recording industry executives determine which artists to record and distribute based almost entirely on their perceived ability to sell units. Most popular music today is sold by downloading it to an electronic device, though CDs are still manufactured and distributed.

Popular music is also often thought of as ephemeral, that is, as remaining in the consciousness of a group of people for a limited time. For this chapter, we have chosen popular music that has either transcended that boundary or that was so important in or exemplary of its time and place that its discussion helps us understand music, history, and culture more broadly. It is, however, but a sampling of a huge body of popular music that exists in the United States since roughly the Colonial period. As you listen to these examples, perhaps you can think of similar examples of popular music that you know.

8.4 EARLY AMERICAN POPULAR MUSIC – OR NOT!

As music with the power to connect with large groups of people, popular music has sometimes been censored. In Colonial times, popular (pop) music was discouraged and, often, even illegal. Later, after church leaders began to lose some of their political power, with the separation of church and state, composers began to write popular music intended for singing at home by amateurs with some instrumental accompaniment. One popular political song of the 1700s was "Chester" by William Billings.

William Billings – "Chester"

http://www.youtube.com/watch?v=E_St8bsx31A

The birth and early development of Ragtime, New Orleans Jazz (Dixieland), and the Blues are all critical to the creation and growth of the popular music we enjoy today. The rhythm, melody, harmony, and instrumentation of all three styles were foundational to the big band, jazz, bebop, and rock and roll styles that followed.

The syncopated rhythms and the importance of a steady dance-like beat in ragtime, and the styles that followed originated in the African cultures accompanying the slaves brought to the American South. The use of scales, chords, and the rules of Western harmony—as well as the use of orchestral instruments like clarinets, saxophones, trumpets, trombones, tubas, pianos, and snare and bass drums—were all borrowed from the Western European tradition. The combination of these different musical cultures occurred almost exclusively in New Orleans, a city that included French, Spanish, English, Creole (Native American), and African populations in an environment that was unusually cooperative and open-minded for the late 1800s and early 1900s.

We must remember that most musical styles do not disappear when new styles evolve; they just fade in popularity. Ragtime, New Orleans jazz, and the Blues are still performed today—not only in New Orleans and St. Louis, but also across the United States, in Europe, and even parts of Asia.

8.4.1 Ragtime

One important point to realize is that most popular music from the 1890s on is heavily influenced by the dominance of syncopation. **Syncopation** is the act of disrupting the normal pattern of accents in a piece of music by emphasizing what would normally be weak beats. For instance, in a march in quadruple meter, the musicians would typically emphasize beats one and three. However, in Ragtime, the emphasis would be placed on beats two and four (or the "upbeats"). We attribute this practice largely to the music and culture of the Africans who were sold into slavery in the American South. Syncopation and the emphasis on beats two and four permeate ragtime, Dixieland jazz, the blues, and most of the rock music that follows these styles.

Figure 8.1 | Second edition cover of *Maple Leaf Rag*
Author | Scott Joplin
Source | Wikimedia Commons
License | Public Domain

The style of piano playing known as **"ragtime"** greatly influenced the development of American popular music. Indeed, all of our popular music styles grew out of ragtime and its New Orleans based cousin, jazz. Before the establishment of the recording industry, musicians supplied all live musical entertainment and background music. Music for these musicians to play was published in its written form for piano and other non-electric instruments.

Ragtime was first published as written piano sheet music in the 1890s; by the early 1900s, it had almost taken over the music publishing industry. In fact, ragtime was so popular that it even increased the sale of pianos and energized the early music recording industry.

After the Civil War much of the Midwest, particularly Missouri, sported numerous saloons, dance halls, and brothels. These establishments offered work to piano players because of the need for live music—remember there was no recorded music industry at that time. Many African American businessmen at this time came to enjoy financial success in a section of St. Louis called Chestnut Valley, one such man being John L. Turpin from Savannah who moved to St. Louis and opened the Silver Dollar saloon. Ten years later, in 1897, Turpin's son, a self-taught pianist, published "Harlem Rag," a defining piece of piano Ragtime and a model for future composers. That same year, W. H. Krell published "Mississippi Rag."

One of the most important ragtime composers, **Scott Joplin** was born sometime late 1867 and early 1868, probably in the northern part of Texas. Although most of the details of his early life are uncertain, his name appears in the 1880 census, listing him as twelve years of age. His father was a former slave and his mother worked in the home of a well to do white family in Texarkana. Scholars believe that Joplin probably had access to a piano in the home of his mother's employer and began at that time to learn the rudiments of music. While in Texarkana, Joplin's ability gained notice, and he began to study with Julius Weiss, a German-born music teacher. Scott later attended high school in Sedalia, Missouri then alternated between Texarkana, where in 1891 he was performing with a minstrel show, and Sedalia, where for several years he continued to perfect his compositional technique. In 1899, he convinced Civil War veteran, music lover, and music store owner John Stark to publish "Maple Leaf Rag"— a piece destined to become the most popular ragtime composition. By 1914, it had sold over 1 million copies.

Click on the links below to listen to Cory Hall perform two of Scott Joplin's better known compositions, "Maple Leaf Rag" and "The Entertainer." Pay attention to the steady beat of the music and then notice that many of the accented notes are not on the beat. Those are the syncopated notes, and they are what make the time sound "ragged." In the late 1800s and early 1900s, musicians often called music that was written with different beat patterns by the name of the purpose for which it was composed. For example, music written for dancing that was grouped in three beats per measure was called "waltz-time," and music written in two beats per measure for marching was called "march-time." So it seems reasonable that music written with many notes off the beat, or syncopated, would be called "ragged-time" or "ragtime."

Figure 8.2 | Scott Joplin
Author | Unknown
Source | Wikimedia Commons
License | Public Domain

***Maple Leaf Rag* – Scott Joplin**

https://www.youtube.com/watch?v=fagH03fxY7c

***The Entertainer* – Scott Joplin**

http://www.youtube.com/watch?v=t9gzZJ344Co

Arthur Pryor was the most famous trombone soloist of his era and a member of the world renowned band of John Philip Sousa. Prior was born in Missouri and wrote numerous successful ragtime compositions. When the Sousa Band toured Europe in 1900, Arthur Pryor's ragtime compositions did much to spread the fame of ragtime to Europe.

By the early 1900s, ragtime enjoyed tremendous popularity and could be found in many different forms, including the early example of mass-produced recorded music, the phonograph record. Listen to the following phonograph recording of the Sousa Band from 1906.

Sousa Band, "Arkansaw Huskin' Bee"

http://www.youtube.com/watch?v=JCDhpPGzCC4

The syncopated feel of ragtime encourages a feeling of movement—perhaps a desire to tap your foot, or bob your head, or dance. Many older people perceived this feeling as a threat that would lead young people down the road to sin and degradation; they associated the music with saloons, dance halls, and bordellos. Needless to say, they didn't approve! We will later see many similar warnings about the rock music of the 1960s.

You may have also noticed that "Maple Leaf Rag" and "The Entertainer" comprise sections that repeat. These three or four repeated sections make up the "form" of the vast majority of ragtime compositions. Music of all styles can either be built of sections that repeat (a repeating form), or be written in a way that does not repeat (through-composed). We will talk more about form later.

8.4.2 The Blues

The term "the blues" may have originated in two possible ways. The first possibility is that as early as the 1790s the term "blue devils" was used to refer to feelings of suffering and sadness. The term first appeared in print in Hart Wand's piece, "Dallas Blues" (1912), the first copyrighted blues composition. The second possibility suggests it derives from the mysticism associated with many West African cultures that used the Blue Indigo plant to dye the garments of those who were in mourning after the death of a loved one. The indigo plant was grown on many Southern plantations, and its use could have strengthened the slaves' connecting "blue" indigo with suffering.

Figure 8.3 | Robert Johnson
Author | User "Anetode"
Source | Wikipedia
License | Fair Use

Whatever the source, the term "the blues" became universally associated with a style of music that at the turn of the twentieth century began to form out of African American work songs, field hollers, and spirituals. Today, the word "blues" is used loosely and can mean several different things, like feeling sad or down. It can also describe any song played in a bluesy style.

In musical circles, the term "blues" most commonly describes a song that follows a blues form, which is a twelve-bar strophic song form. This musical structure of the blues has influenced the development of jazz, rock, techno, and other popular styles of music and is based on a few basic and recurring compositional and performance techniques. The form of the blues is repeating. It is usually eight, twelve, or sixteen bars in length, although some pieces vary this somewhat, and those sections are repeated several times. The blues uses a limited number of chords, usually three or four. Specific notes within these chords are often lowered (the third, fifth, and seventh notes above the root of the chord), and the scales associated with these "blue note" alterations are called "blues scales." Musicians often "bend" the pitch of these notes to give them their bluesy quality.

Over the years, the blues has found its way into many different styles of popular music. First, listen to two examples of traditional blues selections: **Robert Johnson** performs "Cross Road Blues," and **B. B. King** performs "How Blue Can You Get"

Robert Johnson – "Cross Road Blues"

https://www.youtube.com/watch?v=GsB_cGdgPTo

BB King - "How Blue Can You Get"

https://www.youtube.com/watch?v=6jCNXASjzMY

Next listen to Stevie Ray Vaughn perform a number of blues selections that use rock as the rhythmic basis, including a composition by Jimi Hendrix.
https://www.youtube.com/watch?v=grBmQwLSlDw

More than any other musical style, the blues is the foundation of all American music. It appears in virtually every other native musical style, including jazz, rock, rhythm and blues, and hip hop.

8.4.3 Jazz

Figure 8.4 | Louis Armstrong
Author | World-Telegram Staff
Source | Wikimedia Commons
License | Public Domain

New Orleans has, for centuries, been a city of many different cultural and ethnic groups. French, Spanish, Italian, German, and Irish immigrants all settled there before and during the 1800s, and it is in this city where their musical styles mixed with the different musical influences infused by the descendants of African slaves.

New Orleans jazz has its roots in Storyville, an area of New Orleans (NOLA) known for its bars, dance halls, and brothels—like Missouri's Chestnut Valley. In the early part of the 1900s, African American musical styles such as ragtime, blues, spirituals, and marches merged together to create a unique art form. Although jazz borrows much of its harmony and instrumentation from Europe, it differs fundamentally from European styles in its rhythmic makeup. Jazz emphasized syncopation and swing. **Swing** is a term used to describe the rhythmic bounce that characterizes the jazz style.

One of the most important aspects of the jazz style is that it often depends on performers being able to improvise. Improvisation is the act of creating melodies and harmonies on the spot without reading the music off a page. The blending of written and improvised performance has become an integral part of jazz performance and has continued in the later evolution of rock and other popular styles. Early jazz musicians learned to improvise entire new melodies over the chord structures of existing tunes.

Unlike with ragtime, which is largely a piano performance style, jazz musicians often provided music for dancing. By the early 1900s, dance music group instrumentation had changed from mostly string orchestras to jazz bands using instruments borrowed from marching bands; the band instruments were louder and more suited to noisy dance halls. Different combinations of trumpets, clarinets, saxophones, trombones, and tubas joined with drums, piano, guitar, and banjo to form the common jazz band instrumentation. However, piano players often traveled from city to city looking for work and it is easy to see how the music of these popular ragtime pianists influenced early jazz development in NOLA.

Figure 8.5 | Original Dixieland Jazz Band
Author | Unknown
Source | Wikimedia Commons
License | Public Domain

In 1917, Storyville was closed down due to the efforts of religious leaders in NOLA, so jazz musicians were forced to move to Chicago, New York, Los Angeles, Memphis, St. Louis, and other big cities to find work. Around this same time, the recording industry began to flourish, particularly in Chicago and New York. Soon groups like the **Original Dixieland Jazz Band** began recording New Orleans style jazz. Jazz eventually became part of a performing and recording revolution that swept the country (and Western world) and changed popular music and culture forever.

Charles "Buddy" Bolden is widely recognized as the first major figure in the early development of jazz in NOLA. Bolden, like most of the other top jazz performers at that time, was of African descent, a fact which points to the central importance of African Americans to the development of New Orleans jazz and later American popular music from this point forward. Unfortunately, no known recordings of Bolden exist. The Original Dixieland Jazz Band, an ensemble comprised of white musicians, is widely considered to have made the first recording of jazz. This recording sold over one million copies in the first six months of its release and did much to associate New Orleans with "jazz" in the new recording industry. Phonograph records soon replaced sheet music as a favorite way to experience new music because records allowed the listener to hear the subtle jazz performance practices that could not be accurately put down on paper.

Listen to the Original Dixieland Jazz Band's recording of "Livery Stable Blues" which was recorded in New York in 1917, linked below.

http://en.wikipedia.org/wiki/Original_Dixieland_Jass_Band#/media/File:ODJBcard.JPG

Original Dixieland Jazz Band – "Livery Stable Blues"

http://www.youtube.com/watch?v=5WojNaU4-kI

This early style of jazz, now known as **New Orleans Jazz**, or "**Dixieland**," is based almost entirely on the tradition of improvisation. The mature Dixieland style was in full swing by the 1920s and included syncopated rhythms, improvised solos and harmonies, as well as a common instrumentation that included trumpet, clarinet, saxophone, trombone, tuba, banjo, piano, guitar, and drums. The form of most Dixieland tunes, like almost all popular music, was based on repeated sections.

The late 1920s saw the rise of a New Orleans native who transformed jazz from a somewhat loose style with many parts being improvised at the same time, into a style that featured soloists taking turns playing improvised solos. **Louis Armstrong**, whose nickname was "Satchmo," became an international jazz superstar and movie and television personality in a career that stretched from the 1920s to the 1960s.

Armstrong was born in 1901 in a section of New Orleans with a violent reputation, so much so that it was called "The Battlefield." At the age of 11, Armstrong was arrested for firing a gun in the air to celebrate the New Year and was subsequently sent to the Colored Waif's Home for Boys. It was here that Armstrong learned to play the cornet (an early version of the trumpet). He quickly realized his aptitude for music and, upon being released two years later, soon began to build a reputation as one of the best trumpet players in New Orleans, performing everywhere from the seedy bars of Storyville to the riverboats that traveled up and down the Mississippi River.

Armstrong eventually moved to Chicago to join the band of his old mentor, Joe "King" Oliver. From 1925 to 1928, Armstrong made a series of recordings as a leader known as the "Hot Fives" and "Hot Sevens" that would cement his status as one of the most important jazz artists of the twentieth century. His innovations include the following: he established jazz as a solo art form firmly rooted in the blues and which celebrated individual expression; he introduced a jazz singing style, which included a loose phrasing style; he defined the new rhythmic feel of jazz known as swing; and he expanded the possibilities of the trumpet through bends and other techniques that allowed him to mimic the human voice.

Listen to "West End Blues" recorded by Louis Armstrong, America's first popular music superstar, in Chicago in 1928 (linked below.) In addition to common Dixieland instrumentation and improvised solos, this selection also contains a vocal solo by Louis Armstrong using a technique called "scat singing." Scat singing occurs when a vocalist improvises a melody using seemingly nonsense syllables, often in an attempt to imitate the style of a wind instrument.

LISTENING GUIDE

For audio, go to:
https://www.youtube.com/watch?v=W232OsTAMo8

Composer: Joe "King" Oliver

Composition: Louis Armstrong: "West End Blues"

Date: 1928

Genre: Early jazz or "Dixieland"

Form: 12-bar blues

Performing Forces: Early New Orleans Jazz Instrumentation:
Louis Armstrong – trumpet and vocal; Fred Robinson – trombone; Jimmy Strong – clarinet; Earl Hines – piano; Mancy Cara – banjo; Zutty Singleton – drums

What we want you to remember about this composition:

- Much of the piece is improvised over a repeating 12-bar blues form
- It features Armstrong's virtuosity on trumpet as well as his unique interpretation of the melody on trumpet and on vocals

Other things to listen for:

- Each time the twelve bar form is repeated, it is called a "chorus"
- Each chorus is an opportunity for a new soloist or a new ensemble passage
- Armstrong's vocals are "scat singing," and incorporate syllables instead of text
- The piano, banjo, and drums are collectively called the "rhythm section"

Timing	Performing Forces, Melody, and Texture	Text and Form
0:00	Trumpet. Improvised lines incorporate dramatic leaps, chromaticism, triplet figures, and elements of the blues.	
0:13	Full band. Trumpet plays the melody while clarinet and trombone improvise supporting parts.	
0:50	Trombone with rhythm section. Trombone plays the melody.	
1:25	Clarinet and voice with rhythm section. Call-and-response melody between clarinet and voice.	
2:00	Rhythm section featuring piano. Improvised piano solo.	

2:34	Full band. Improvised trumpet solo supported by full band.
2:57	Full band. Piano followed by trumpet.

No unit on New Orleans jazz would be complete without mentioning the Marsalis family. Father Ellis (piano) and sons Branford (saxophone), Wynton (trumpet), Delfeayo (trombone), and Jason (drums) are all artists of the first rate and world-renowned as individual jazz musicians. Listen to the Marsalis family continue the New Orleans jazz tradition as they perform "Struttin' with Some Barbeque."

***Struttin' With Some Barbeque* – The Marsalis Family**

https://www.youtube.com/watch?v=gUnWt21HxMQ

Later Jazz Styles

Big Bands

By the 1930s, jazz was the most popular music in the country. Most jazz ensembles at this time featured a large group of fifteen to twenty musicians. This increase in size was needed mainly because the larger venues used for dancing made it difficult to hear small combos over the noises in the room. Before long, the standard instrumentation of the performing dance band had become five saxophones, five trombones, five trumpets, a rhythm section (piano, bass, and drum set), and oftentimes one or more singers. The larger number of instruments made the normal improvised Dixieland parts impractical; fifteen musicians improvising at the same time just sounded like noise. Therefore, band leaders began to either arrange parts for the different sections (as Duke Ellington did) or hire arrangers to do it for them (as did Glenn Miller, Stan Kenton, and others). The standard big band instrumentation that resulted survives to this day.

Figure 8.6 | Duke Ellington
Author | Unknown
Source | Wikimedia Commons
License | Public Domain

Throughout the later 1930s, the 1940s, and to some extent the 1950s, big bands enjoyed enormous popularity performing both for dances and as concert performing groups. Today the terms dance band and big band are used interchangeably. During the heyday of big band popularity, a number of superstars rose with the tide. Many times the leaders of these bands became famous; Duke Ellington, Count Basie, Stan Kenton, Tommy Dorsey, and Glenn Miller were just a few that became household names. Listen to the traditional big band sound of Glenn Miller and his orchestra as they perform their number one hit "In the Mood."

Glenn Miller – "In the Mood"

https://www.youtube.com/watch?v=_CI-0E_jses

One of the most important figures in the big band era was **Duke Ellington**, a bandleader and composer who created some of most unique and innovative sounding music of the era. Ellington sought out musicians with their own personal sounds to incorporate into his orchestra. Some famous musicians from the Ellington band include trumpeter Cootie Williams, who created interesting vocal effects with a plunger mute; Cat Anderson, who could hit high notes that most trumpeters thought impossible, and alto saxophonist Johnny Hodges, a master at bending notes to create beautiful expressive melodies. Ellington was able write music that wove these unique playing styles together into a musical tapestry that was complex and dissonant, yet beautiful and accessible. Ellington wrote many big band hits of the 1930s and 1940s, such as the example below, "It Don't Mean A Thing If It Ain't Got That Swing."

LISTENING GUIDE For audio, go to: https://www.youtube.com/watch?v=YbwDRdRXP3k
Composer: Duke Ellington
Composition: *It Don't Mean A Thing If It Ain't Got That Swing*
Date: 1931 (recorded 1932)
Genre: Big Band Jazz
Form: AABA
Nature of Text: an upbeat song celebrating swing music
Performing Forces: Early Big Band Instrumentation: Arthur Whetsel, Freddie Jenkins, Cootie Williams – trumpet; Joe Nanton, Juan Tizol – trombone; Barney Bigard, Johnny Hodges, Harry Carney – woodwinds; Duke Ellington – piano, Fred Guy – banjo; Wellman Braud – bass; Sonny Greer – drums; Ivie Anderson – vocals
What we want you to remember about this composition: • The original song follows a standard AABA form, which is repeated over and over. Much like the blues, each time through the form is called a "chorus." • Take a look at the words to the song below to follow along with the form. **A** It don't mean a thing, if it ain't got that swing (doo-ah, doo-ah, doo-ah, doo-ah, doo-ah, doo-ah, doo-ah, doo-ah) **A** It don't mean a thing, all you got to do is sing (doo-ah, doo-ah, doo-ah, doo-ah, doo-ah, doo-ah, doo-ah, doo-ah) **B** It makes no difference if it's sweet or hot Just give that rhythm everything you've got **A** It don't mean a thing, if it ain't got that swing (doo-ah, doo-ah, doo-ah, doo-ah, doo-ah, doo-ah, doo-ah, doo-ah)

Other things to listen for: • In the A sections of the form, the brass players use standard toilet plungers on the bells of their horns to create a "wa, wa" sound		
Timing	**Performing Forces, Melody, and Texture**	**Text and Form**
0:00	Upright bass and vocals. Bluesy "scat singing" riff in vocals.	Introduction
0:13	Trombone with rhythm section. Improvised solos alternating with original melody.	First "chorus" of AABA form
0:47	Full Band. Main melody which includes a call and response between vocalist and horns.	Second chorus of AABA form
1:23	Alto sax solo over horn backgrounds. Improvised solo.	Interlude
1:58	Alto sax solo. Improvised solo.	First two A sections of third chorus
2:07	Sax section. New melodic material written in a soloistic manner.	B section of third chorus
2:16	Alto sax solo over horn backgrounds. Improvised solo.	Last A section of third chorus
2:25	Full Band (Shout Chorus). New melodic material written in a soloistic manner.	First two A sections of fourth chorus
2:42	Vocalist with rhythm section. Improvised "scat" solo.	B section of fourth chorus
2:52	Full Band. Main melody which includes a call and response between vocalist and horns.	Last A section of fourth chorus

Stan Kenton was an innovative big band leader who liked to incorporate music from other cultures into his repertoire. Listen to the Latin influence in his recording of "Malaga."

Stan Kenton – "Malaga"

https://www.youtube.com/watch?v=HEt13RILoko

This recording of the **Count Basie** band is a great example of the traditional swing style of jazz in a contemporary arrangement of "Sweet Georgia Brown."

Count Basie – "Sweet Georgia Brown"

https://www.youtube.com/watch?v=EbbBeU1vHew

Numerous vocalists also became stars in the Big Band movement. One of the most famous also became a movie star: **Frank Sinatra**.

Frank Sinatra – "New York, New York"

https://www.youtube.com/watch?v=odNmQiSC6dY

Ella Fitzgerald became world famous as a jazz vocalist and recording artist, and enjoyed a long and illustrious career as one of the leading jazz recording artists of all time.

Ella Fitzgerald – "The Lady is a Tramp"

https://www.youtube.com/watch?v=k9mssKqk6YE

The big band tradition continues to this day with vocal artists such as **Michael Bublé** recording and performing live concerts. Here Michael Bublé performs his hit "Moon Dance."

Michael Bublé - "Moon Dance"

https://www.youtube.com/watch?v=PBCJWJXeFzk

Bebop

In the early 1940s, World War II had put a serious damper on saloons and dance halls due to rationing, lower incomes, and the drafting of a large number of musicians. It was difficult for bandleaders to hire enough good players because many musicians had gone to war. Consequently, many musicians began to form smaller jazz ensembles consisting of a few wind instruments and a rhythm section. These ensembles are often called jazz "combos."

Figure 8.7 | Charlie Parker, Tommy Potter, Miles Davis, Dizzy Gillespie and Max Roach, Three Deuces, New York, N.Y.
Author | William P. Gottlieb
Source | Wikimedia Commons
License | Public Domain

At this same time, several important musicians, including Dizzy Gillespie, Bud Powell, and Thelonious Monk, began meeting at such clubs in uptown New York City as Minton's Playhouse. During late night jam sessions, they began exploring new ways to improvise in a small group setting. The bebop style developed when **Charlie Parker** arrived in New York from Kansas City. His nickname was "Bird," and he soon became perhaps the most influential bebop player. Bebop was a dramatic departure from the jazz that came before it in several ways. The music featured more complex, faster moving harmonies, angular melodies, and highly complex rhythms that were not conducive to dancing. Most importantly, bebop marked the beginning of the modern jazz era. From this point on, jazz was no longer perceived as a popular music. Dance halls gave way to basement clubs where jazz enthusiasts would come to sit and listen. While jazz never regained its initial popularity, musicians such as John Coltrane, Miles Davis, and others carried on the jazz tradition into the 1950s and beyond, creating some of the most groundbreaking recordings in American music.

Listen for the complex melodies and complex chords in the following selection.

Charlie Parker – "Donna Lee"

https://www.youtube.com/watch?v=o2apSoxB7B4

In the late 1960s and 1970s, some acoustic jazz musicians became interested in incorporating electronic instruments and rock beats into the jazz idiom. This style is often called **fusion** as it "fuses" jazz with other styles. A truly outstanding group from this era is **Weather Report**. The composition entitled "Birdland" from Weather Report's 1977 *Heavy Weather* studio album, *Heavy Weather* received numerous awards, as well as ranking #1 on the Billboard jazz charts. Although the title of the song pays tribute to an acoustic jazz club in New York City named after Charlie Parker, the music itself features a rock instrumentation, a straight beat, and electronic instruments. The group's bass player Jaco Pastorius is considered by many to be the best electric bassist of all time.

Weather Report – "Birdland"

https://www.youtube.com/watch?v=cH-WXR-Y2xs

8.5 THE R'S: ROCK, RHYTHM AND BLUES, AND RAP

The popular styles of music that we hear today, like most other Western musical styles, grew out of combinations of elements borrowed from the styles that preceded them. Rhythm and blues (R&B), rock and roll, and rap all resulted from combinations and changes of music practices that were borrowed from jazz, gospel, country, and the blues.

Elements of Contemporary Popular Music (the popular music we hear today) are the following: it is easy to listen to; its melody and lyrics, that is, words, are most important; it has a simple structure and strong melody; it is easy to sing and repetitive, with the form comprising repeating sections; it has a strong beat (with Rap, it IS the beat) and clear/regular phases; and it uses few chords.

8.5.1 Rhythm and Blues

Figure 8.8 | Ray Charles
Author | Heinrich Klaffs
Source | Wikimedia Commons
License | CC BY-SA 2.0

The term **"rhythm and blues (R&B)"** was first used by *Billboard* magazine in 1948 to refer to music recorded by black musicians and intended for use by the African American community. It has changed definitions several times over the years and is now very much in the mainstream. At one point, the term encapsulated several different musical styles, including soul and funk. Early rhythm and blues ensembles often featured a twelve-bar blues form with a strong backbeat (emphasis on beats two and four.) These early groups typically consisted of a rhythm section augmented by a saxophone or background vocalists. Georgia native **Ray Charles** was one of the early innovators of R&B.

Ray Charles – "Hit the Road Jack"

https://www.youtube.com/watch?v=Q8Tiz6INF7I&list=PL4417733726B17DBF

"Contemporary R&B" generally refers to music with jazz, gospel, and funk roots that uses electronic instruments, drums, horns, and vocals. This **Earth, Wind & Fire** example of contemporary R&B includes a rock rhythm section, brass, and synthesizer—plus a great groove. Many other excellent examples exist from groups like Kool and the Gang and The Ohio Players.

Earth, Wind & Fire – "In the Stone"

https://www.youtube.com/watch?v=rNNaKohSkrA

8.5.2 Rock and Roll

Early rock and roll grew directly out of the tradition of rhythm and blues. The term "rock and roll" is widely credited to the disk jockey Alan Freed, who used it to describe the R&B records he played on Cleveland's **WJW radio station**. Rock and Roll was marketed and consumed primarily by a teenage audience. Eventually, the term "rock and roll" was shortened to "rock" and evolved into an all-encompassing international music with a wide variety of subgenres such as glam rock, heavy metal, new wave and grunge. The cultural impact of rock and roll has been massive, influencing almost every facet of popular culture, from fashion to language.

Although early rock and roll bands often featured a variety of wind instruments such as the saxophone, by the 1950's, the typical rock and roll band was defined by the electric guitar. Invented in 1931, the instrument used an electronic device called a pickup to convert the vibration of the strings into electronic signals run to a speaker. The earliest electric guitars were merely used as a means of amplification, but rock and roll guitarists began to experiment with various effects, such as distortion that would alter the sound of the instrument.

Figure 8.9 | Elvis Presley
Author | Metro-Goldwyn-Mayer, Inc.
Source | Wikimedia Commons
License | Public Domain

A typical rock and roll band often included two guitarists. One guitarist typically played "rhythm guitar," which mean supporting the band by strumming the chords of the song. The second guitarist played "lead guitar, which meant playing solos in between the vocal lines or in open solo sections. These two guitarists were backed by a drum set and a bass. Often, one of the guitarists doubled as the lead vocalist, while other members might sing background harmonies.

Like R&B, rock and roll music places a strong emphasis on the backbeat. These accents are very noticeable in Chuck Berry's "rock and roll music," which features snare drum accents on beats two and four.

Figure 8.10 | Electric guitar, solidbody, Kramer XKG-20 circa 1980
Author | User "BellwetherToday"
Source | Wikimedia Commons
License | CC BY-SA 4.0

Chuck Berry – "Rock and Roll Music"

https://www.youtube.com/watch?v=oXSaKQlBZuE

Elvis Presley was one of the most important figures in the history of rock and roll, and one of the most celebrated recording artists of the twentieth century. He was born in Tupelo, Mississippi but grew up in Memphis, Tennessee. His recording career began in Memphis in 1954 when he worked with Sam Phillips, the owner of Sun Records. Elvis combined the sounds of country music and rhythm and blues into a style that was initially called **rockabilly**. Elvis soon moved to the RCA label, and his first single record "Heartbreak Hotel," released in 1956, became the number one hit in the United States. By embracing music from both sides of the civil rights movement, Elvis became both very popular and very controversial at the same time. In many ways, he helped bring the popular music of African Americans into the mainstream of white society and paved the way for groups like the Beatles and the Rolling Stones, who were heavily influenced by black artists. Elvis later branched out and recorded many successful ballads and rock tunes. He died of a drug overdose in 1977.

Listen to the blues influence in Elvis's singing and the guitar and piano solos in "Heartbreak Hotel."

LISTENING GUIDE For audio, go to: https://www.youtube.com/watch?v=e9BLw4W5KU8	
Composer: Tommy Durden and Mae Boren Axton	
Composition: Heartbreak Hotel	
Date: 1956 recording by Elvis Presley	
Genre: Rock and Roll	
Form: Strophic	
Nature of Lyrics: About a hotel that embodies the feelings of being heartbroken	
Performing Forces: Elvis Presley – lead vocals, Scotty Moore – electric guitar, Chet Atkins – acoustic guitar, Bill Black – double bass, D.J. Fontana – drums, Floyd Cramer – piano	
What we want you to remember about this composition: • Each verse repeats the same form, always ending with "Heartbreak is so lonely..." • Each verse follows an 8-bar chord progression • Notice how Presley's singing style is a mix of blues, country, and gospel influences	
Timing	**Text and Form**
0:00	Verse 1: Well, since my baby left me, I found a new place to dwell Its down at the end of lonely street At heartbreak hotel. Heartbreak is so lonely baby, Heartbreak so lonely, Heartbreak is so lonely I could die
0:21	Verse 2: And although it's always crowded, You still can find some room For broken hearted lovers To cry away their gloom. Heartbreak is so lonely baby, Heartbreak so lonely, Heartbreak is so lonely they could die

0:42	Verse 3: Well, the bell hops tears keep flowin', And the desk clerks dressed in black. Well they been so long on lonely street They ain't ever gonna look back. Heartbreak is so lonely baby, Heartbreak so lonely, Heartbreak is so lonely they could die
1:02	Verse 4: Hey now, if your baby leaves you, And you got a tale to tell. Just take a walk down lonely street To heartbreak hotel. Where you will be lonely baby, Where you will be lonely, You'll be so lonely you could die
1:22	Verse 5: Guitar solo followed by piano solo
1:43	Verse 6: And although it's always crowded, You still can find some room For broken-hearted lovers To cry away their gloom. Heartbreak is so lonely baby, Heartbreak so lonely, Heartbreak is so lonely they could die

One of the most famous rock and roll groups of all time was **The Beatles**. This British group toured the United States in 1964 and changed the face of popular music and the recording industry from that time forward. The Beatles popularized the use of electric guitars as the basis of the modern rock band and went on to add strings, brass, organ, and other instruments to the list of instruments used in rock performances and recordings. Their use of straight eighth notes on the cymbals and accents on beats two and four on the snare drum are classic rock and roll rhythm elements. Most Americans are unaware of the influence that Chuck Berry and other American artists had on the style and content of the Beatles' music.

The Beatles – "I Want To Hold Your Hand"

https://www.youtube.com/watch?v=01_zdt_FNmM

8.5.3 Rap

Rap is a form of spoken word delivered over a beat. It can be improvised or written out in advance. The history of rap music is intertwined with the history of hip hop and even disco music. An excellent history of hip hop and rap can be found on the site linked below.

https://www.britannica.com/topic/hip-hop

While the origins of rap can be traced back to Africa, rap as we know it came into being in the Bronx, NY in the 1970s. However, not until the art form was recorded did it enter the cultural mainstream. One of the first important rap recordings was the 1979 hit, "Rapper's Delight" by the Sugarhill Gang. **Kurtis Blow** (Kurt Walker, born August 9, 1959) is the first rapper to sign with a major record label. "The Breaks," a single from his 1980 debut album, is the first certified gold record rap song.

Kurtis Blow - "The Breaks" (1980)

https://www.youtube.com/watch?v=MAk2wlv1N1I

By the 1990s, rap had evolved into a more sophisticated musical style featuring complex rhythms and clever wordplay. The instrumentation of rap music varies greatly depending on the artist and, often, the individual song. Early rap concerts featured DJs creating beats on **turntables**, which allowed the DJ to create music on the spot by playing and manipulating records. One well-known technique on the turntables is **scratching**, or improvising a rhythmic solo on one turntable over a beat.

Figure 8.11 | A Tribe Called Quest
Author | James Chutter
Source | Wikimedia Commons
License | CC BY 2.0

A Tribe Called Quest is widely considered one of the greatest groups of the so-called golden age of hip hop during the late 1980s and early 1990s. Listen to the track below, "Can I Kick It" by **A Tribe Called Quest**. Like many rap songs, this track utilizes a technique called "**sampling**," in which a clip of a preexisting song is isolated and looped underneath the rapper (in this case, the bass line for Lou Reed's *Walk On The Wild Side)*. The song also features the use of scratching mentioned above.

LISTENING GUIDE

For audio, go to:
https://www.youtube.com/watch?v=71ubKHzujy8

Composer: A Tribe Called Quest (Q-Tip, Ali Shaheed Muhammad, Phife Dawg, Jarobi White)		
Composition: "Can I Kick It"		
Date: 1990		
Genre: Rap		
Form: Verse-chorus		
Nature of Text: recited to a steady beat		
Performing Forces: Rap vocals over looped music backdrop incorporating a variety of musical samples from previous recordings Rappers: Q-tip and Phife Dawg		
What we want you to remember about this composition: • Listen for the verse-chorus form • The first verse features clever wordplay, with the last word of each phrase rhyming. Notice how the last syllable of each line slowly evolves from words like "cuz" and "fuzz" to "rug" and "hug" and finally to "love" and "shove." • In the second verse, most of the phrases rhyme on the sound "ayer" as in "layer"or "player"		
Timing	**Performing Forces**	**Text and Form**
0:00	Q-tip	Chorus or "Hook": Hey y'all, we is havin' a ball And you know they ask me to get on the MIC And they ask me Can I kick it? Word yes you can Can I kick it? Yes you can Can I kick it? Yes you can Can I kick it? Yes you can Can I kick it? Yes you can Can I kick it? Yes you can Can I kick it? Yes you can Can I kick it? Yes you can Can I kick it? Yes you can Well I'm gone, gone

	Q-tip	Verse 1: Can I kick it? To all the people who can Quest like A Tribe does Before this, did you really know what live was? Comprehend to the track, for it's why cuz Gettin measures on the tip of the vibers Rock and roll to the beat of the funk fuzz Wipe your feet really good on the rhythm rug If you feel the urge to freak, do the jitterbug Come and spread your arms if you really need a hug Afrocentric living is a big shrug A life filled with fun that's what I love A lower plateau is what we're above If you diss us, we won't even think of Will Nipper the doggy give a big shove? This rhythm really fits like a snug glove Like a box of positives it's a plus, love As the Tribe flies high like a dove
0:13	Phife Dawg	Verse 1: Can I kick it? To all the people who can Quest like A Tribe does Before this, did you really know what live was? Comprehend to the track, for it's why cuz Gettin measures on the tip of the vibers Rock and roll to the beat of the funk fuzz Wipe your feet really good on the rhythm rug If you feel the urge to freak, do the jitterbug Come and spread your arms if you really need a hug Afrocentric living is a big shrug A life filled with fun that's what I love A lower plateau is what we're above If you diss us, we won't even think of Will Nipper the doggy give a big shove? This rhythm really fits like a snug glove Like a box of positives it's a plus, love As the Tribe flies high like a dove

0:50	Phife Dawg	Hook: Can I kick it? Can I kick it? Can I kick it? Yes you can Can I kick it? Yes you can Can I kick it? Yes you can Can I kick it? Yes you can Can I kick it? Yes you can Can I kick it? Yes you can Can I kick it? Yes you can Well I'm gone, gone

8.6 FOLK MUSIC

Folk music is a broad term used to describe a wide variety of musical forms that developed within different cultures, often for different reasons. American folk music varies widely depending on the region, but most American folk music was influenced by the European and African cultures from which many Americans descended. We will explore some of the more popular forms of folk music and folk-inspired music. Folk music in America largely developed from a combination of music from the British Isles and other European regions and music brought here by African slaves. Folk music often uses the form known as the ballad. **Ballads** most often tell a story that usually contains a moral or lesson.

Figure 8.12 | Woody Guthrie
Author | Al Aumuller
Source | Wikimedia Commons
License | Public Domain

Listen to this recording of the Scottish/English ballad "Barbara Allen."

Joan Baez performing "Barbara Allen"

https://www.youtube.com/watch?v=NqHJ4V893eo

Work songs often helped groups of people (including slaves) perform physical work. The music usually uses the tempo of the work itself and was sung by lumberjacks, railroad workers, and prison chain gangs, among others.

Listen to this recording of a Texas prison chain gang singing "Let the Hammer Reign" as they chop down trees. This piece is very similar to how slaves would sing while working on Southern plantations. Its compositional and style traits include the following: it uses a "Call and Response" technique, where a lead singer sings a line and then the group follows him with their response; it uses a simple melody; its instrumentation is only vocal; it possesses thicker texture (several singers);

its tempo is constant and matched to the speed of the axes; and its dynamics are fairly constant.

Prison chain gang – "Let the Hammer Reign"

https://www.youtube.com/watch?v=wFSlw8LlIwo

Children's songs also have a purpose, usually to teach a simple lesson. They are, therefore, simple to sing and easy to remember. In the case of "ABC Song," its lesson helped children remember the twenty-six letters of the alphabet.

The "ABC Song"

https://www.youtube.com/watch?v=75p-N9YKqNo

Protest songs are written to directly, or by suggestion, voice complaints about some injustice. Listen to Bob Dylan perform his composition "Blowin' in the Wind," a protest song written in the 1970s to indirectly protest social injustice and the Vietnam War. Its compositional and stylistic elements include the following: it uses the same music for each verse, its melody is simple, its instrumentation is voice and guitar, its texture is thin, and its tempo and dynamics are constant.

Bob Dylan – "Blowin' in the Wind"

https://www.youtube.com/watch?v=3l4nVByCL44

Dance music is folk music written for dancing. It's that simple! The instrumentation of various types of folk dance music varies with the style. Acoustic instruments were used before the 1950s simply because electric and electronic instruments didn't yet exist. Its compositional and stylistic components include the following: the form is almost always a repeating form; sometimes dance music comprises song with words while at other times, it is just instrumental; its form is almost always a repeating form; the dynamics are usually loud in order to be heard in a dance hall or other large space.

Below are links to three examples of different dance forms: a two-step, a waltz, and a square dance.

Gil Tanner & the Skillet Lickers, "Soldiers Joy"

https://www.youtube.com/watch?v=vd54F6bVvwo

Country Waltz
Ernest Tubb, "Waltz Across Texas"

https://www.youtube.com/watch?v=hK_qrg4Jz20

Square Dance
The Chuckwagen Team, "Golden Reel"

https://www.youtube.com/watch?v=i0zVE1ICidc

8.7 COUNTRY MUSIC

Figure 8.13 | Hank Williams
Author | WSM radio
Source | Wikimedia Commons
License | Public Domain

Like many musical terms discussed in this chapter, **Country Music** has come to define a broad variety of musical styles encompassing Bluegrass, Hillbilly Music, and Contemporary Country among others. Generally speaking, most types of music that fall under this category originated in the American South (although it also encompasses Western Swing and cowboy songs) and features a singing style with a distinctly rural southern accent, as well as an instrumentation that favors string instruments such as the banjo, guitar, or fiddle.

Bluegrass music is a variation of country music that developed largely in the Appalachian region; it features fiddle, guitar, mandolin, bass guitar, and the five-string banjo. Often associated with Appalachia, bluegrass combines many of the song forms that are common in the region's Scottish/English musical heritage. For example, bluegrass blends the Scottish/English ballad with blues inflections. Some bluegrass songs are fast instrumental pieces featuring amazing technique by the performers. Listen to **Ricky Skaggs** and the Bluegrass Thunder perform via the link below.

Ricky Skaggs, "Bluegrass Breakdown"

https://www.youtube.com/watch?v=oZIHSXpmilw

Hillbilly music was an alternative to the jazz and dance music of the 1920s. It was portrayed as wholesome and as the music of the "good old days." Nashville's *Grand Ole Opry* radio show became a very successful weekly network radio broadcast heard nationwide. Noticing an opportunity, record companies soon opened offices in Nashville. Country music became a source of big money for producers, song writers, and artists.

The Hillbillies – "Cluck Old Hen" 1927

http://www.youtube.com/watch?v=qizwcdHAWNU

Honky-tonk music developed as Hillbilly music went west to entertain in saloons called "honky tonks." Many of the songs dealt with subjects associated with honky tonks, such as infidelity and drinking. Although the first use of the term "honky tonk" referred to a ragtime-like piano style, it later came to refer to a country combo style that became quite popular in the 1940s and 1950s. D**uane Eddy's** combo example of the honky-tonk style shows a more modern variation of honky-tonk:

Hank Williams – "Honky Tonkin'" 1948

https://www.youtube.com/watch?v=88XvpkHS4UE

Western Music refers to music composed about the Great American West, such as the cowboy songs heard in movies of the 1930s and 1940s by singers such as Gene Autry and Roy Rogers.

One variation of this genre, **Western swing,** developed in Austin, Texas and other western cities and borrowed instruments from the dance band (saxophones, trombones, trumpets, piano, bass, and drums).

Mitch Ballard & The Western Swing Machine, "Ace in the Hole"

https://www.youtube.com/watch?v=TQawiRq-QDk

Contemporary country music has become a mixture of rock rhythm sections and a singer singing with a country accent about many of the same topics that traditional country singers have used over the decades. Contemporary country artists often use electric guitars, electric steel guitar, electric bass, keyboards (often synthesizers), and drum set. Country music is still big business, selling millions of units per year. Watch and listen to the Carrie Underwood and Miranda Lambert performance linked below:

Carrie Underwood and Miranda Lambert, "Something Bad"

https://www.youtube.com/watch?v=9RfT2KqPCoI

8.8 MUSIC FOR THE STAGE

Although music has been part of dramatic performances at least as far back as ancient Greece, American musical theatre has its own unique style, which developed from several earlier forms. The term **musical theatre** refers to a type of dramatic performance that tells a story through dialogue, with singing and dancing added to support and move the plot along. This differs from opera, which is presented purely through song, without any spoken word.

One precursor to modern musical theatre is the **minstrel show**. The first distinctly American form of theatre, minstrelsy was developed in the nineteenth century and featured white performers in blackface performing in a variety show of sorts. These three-act shows featured stock characters singing songs, performing in skits, and telling jokes. They often depicted black characters as happy participants in romanticized versions of the

Figure 8.14 | *West Side Story*
Author | Fred Fehl
Source | Wikimedia Commons
License | Public Domain

American slave south. One of the most well-known songwriters of minstrel music was **Stephen Foster**. Listen to his song Camptown Races, which depicts a group of men in a "camp town" (a community of transients) who bet on horses to try to make money.

Stephen Foster – "Camptown Races" (sung by Al Jolson)

https://www.youtube.com/watch?v=_tuu5YtkPIo

Foster was one of the first Americans to make a living as a professional songwriter, a feat which would become common in the twentieth century. Minstrelsy continued into the twentieth century and eventually evolved into other forms such as vaudeville, which featured variety shows with music, comedy, and talent acts. Although minstrelsy is now regarded by many as a remnant of the racism of the past, it was responsible for many songs that are still part of our repertory.

8.8.1 Early Broadway: Operettas

Operetta evolved in Europe in the middle of the nineteenth century and grew out of the French *opéra comique* tradition. An **operetta** can be characterized as "light opera" in which the focus is the music, but with less complex music than opera. Although not as technically demanding as opera, operettas typically required the use of classically trained singers. The operetta was popularized in America most famously by **Victor Herbert**, who wrote works at the beginning of the twentieth century. Operetta is important as a direct precursor to modern musical theatre. Listen to Victor Herbert's "Ah Sweet Mystery of Life" from *Naughty Marietta.*

Victor Herbert – "Ah Sweet Mystery of Life" from Naughty Marietta.

https://www.youtube.com/watch?v=1xpKeabZlEs

8.8.2 Broadway Musical

During the twentieth century, the operetta slowly gave way to a more cut-and-dry, vernacular American musical theatre style, which continues today. Modern musical theatre (also known as the **Broadway musical**) integrated a cohesive plot with songs and dances that advanced that plot. This more direct musical style reflected the American audiences of the twentieth century, who were less interested in the formal, Victorian style of the operetta.

Musicals are stage shows with music, acting, costumes, sets, and dance. They are closely related to opera and are an American art form, though they are also popular in parts of Europe. Some successful musicals were later turned into movies. Musicals usually use a full Romantic orchestra and often add synthesizer sounds as well. Listen to and watch the following segment from one of the most successful musical productions in Broadway history.

Phantom of the Opera - "All I Ask of You"

https://www.youtube.com/watch?v=uxs7qevmy50

The first half of the twentieth century marked the heyday of the Broadway musical, with shows like *Oklahoma!*, *South Pacific*, and *The Sound of Music* among many others. Broadway refers to the main thoroughfare in midtown Manhattan that serves as the theater district for New York City. To this day, it is considered the highest level of musical theatre in the United States and is home to the most popular shows in the country. Composers such as Cole Porter, **Richard Rodgers, Oscar Hammerstein**, and Irving Berlin composed hundreds of tunes for Broadway shows that are now considered American classics. Listen to the examples below from Rogers and Hammerstein's *Oklahoma!* from 1943.

Rogers and Hammerstein – *Oklahoma!*

https://www.youtube.com/watch?v=_C6J9gij5SQ

Listen to the example below of *West Side Story* from 1957, written by **Leonard Bernstein**. Bernstein, who was conductor of the New York Philharmonic, composed *West Side Story* as a depiction of Romeo and Juliet set in New York City. The musical dramatized the tensions between white and Puerto Rican street gangs, and updated the famous Shakespeare story for twentieth-century audiences. The music was also groundbreaking for its sophistication, use of modern harmonies, and incorporation of Latin music and jazz.

LISTENING GUIDE For audio, go to: https://www.youtube.com/watch?v=Qy6wo2wpT2k
Composer: Leonard Bernstein
Composition: *America* from *West Side Story*
Date: 1957
Genre: Broadway Musical
Form: Verse-chorus
Nature of Text: The Puerto-Rican characters lament on the dream of living as an immigrant in America versus the reality.
Performing Forces: Orchestra with solo vocals and chorus
What we want you to remember about this composition: • The piece is written in mixed meter, alternating between 6/8 time and 3/4 time • It features Latin American rhythms and percussion

Timing	Performing Forces	Text and Form
2:00	Percussion enters behind dialogue	Introduction Puerto Rico My heart's devotion Let it sink back in the ocean Always the hurricanes blowing Always the population growing And the money owing And the sunlight streaming And the natives steaming I like the island Manhattan Smoke on your pipe And put that in
2:20	Anita	Chorus: Chorus: I like to be in America Okay by me in America Everything free in America Bernardo: For a small fee in America
3:06	Chorus and Bernardo	Verse Anita: Buying on credit is so nice Bernardo: One look at us and they charge twice Rosalia: I'll have my own washing machine Indio: What will you have though to keep clean?
0:50	Exchange of lines between various characters	Chorus Anita: Skyscrapers bloom in America Rosalia: Cadillacs zoom in America Teresita: Industry boom in America Boys: Twelve in a room in America
3:31	Exchange of lines between various characters	Verse Anita: Lots of new housing with more space Bernardo: Lots of doors slamming in our face Anita: I'll get a terrace apartment Bernardo: Better get rid of your accent
3:45	Exchange of lines between various characters	Chorus Anita: Life can be bright in America Boys: If you can fight in America Girls: Life is all right in America Boys: If you're all white in America Girls: Here you are free and you have pride Boys: Long as you stay on your own side Girls: Free to be anything you choose Boys: Free to wait tables and shine shoes

3:57	Exchange of lines between choruses of boys and girls	Dance Break Boys: La, la, la, la, la, America America La, la, la, la, la, America America
4:08	Orchestra	Verse Girls: Here you are free and you have pride Boys: Long as you stay on your own side Girls: Free to be anything you choose Boys: Free to wait tables and shine shoes
4:50	Exchange of lines between choruses of boys and girls	
5:02	Bernardo and Anita	Chorus Bernardo: Everywhere grime in America Organized crime in America Terrible time in America Anita: You forget I'm in America
5:16	Orchestra	Dance Break N/A
5:54	Bernardo and Anita	Verse Bernardo: I think I'll go back to San Juan Anita: I know what boat you can get on Bernardo: Everyone there will give big cheers Anita: Everyone there will have moved here

8.8.3 American Opera

Although not a true opera in the strict sense, **George Gershwin's** "folk opera" *Porgy and Bess* is considered one of the great American operatic works of the century. The story is set in a tenement in Charleston, South Carolina. Based on DuBose Heyward's novel *Porgy*, the opera incorporated classically trained black singers to depict the tragic love story between the two main title characters. Gershwin based the music for the opera on elements of folk music, drawing on southern black musical style such as the blues and spirituals. Drawing on the nineteenth century opera tradition, Gershwin made use of leitmotifs to represent people or places. Near the beginning of the opera, we hear the famous aria "Summertime," which depicts the hot, hazy atmosphere in which the story is set.

George Gershwin – "Summertime"

https://www.youtube.com/watch?v=O7-Qa92Rzbk

8.9 CHAPTER SUMMARY

The musical styles that have developed in the United States are as varied as the people who live here. In this chapter, we learned that ragtime, New Orleans jazz, and the blues are all critical to the creation and growth of the popular music we enjoy today. We learned about the emphasis on rhythm inherited from African roots, and that syncopation refers to accented notes that are not on the beat. We also learned that from the country's colonial beginnings to the present day, the musical, societal, and cultural establishment has not always approved of popular music—particularly ragtime, blues, and jazz.

Scott Joplin and others developed the distinct style that was called "ragtime," which contributed, along with other African American music styles to the formation of jazz in and around New Orleans. We saw Louis Armstrong rise to international fame as a jazz performer, recording artist, and movie star. This was followed by the "big bands" of the 1930s and 1940s, and later the small groups, or combos that performed the highly sophisticated music known as bebop. We discussed the evolution of rhythm and blues (R&B) into modern R&B and learned to identify rap music as a style based on two central elements; a strong rhythmic beat and lyrics. We explored the wide variety of folk songs in America. We also learned that folk music in America largely developed from music of the British Isles and Europe, as well as the music brought here by African slaves. We also investigated how rock music incorporated the blues and an emphasis on beats two and four borrowed from jazz to create an exciting new music that appealed to the youth culture.

In the realm of country music, we learned about bluegrass music, which developed largely in the Appalachian region, as well as honky-tonk and hillbilly music, both of which were variations of country music. We examined Western swing as a subset of country music that often uses dance band instruments, and recognized contemporary country music as a mixture of rock and country styles.

America was also home to a wide variety of styles of musical theatre. From the minstrel songs of Stephen Foster, which glorified the plantation South, to the operettas of Victor Herbert, which dominated musical theatre at the turn of the nineteenth century, America has a rich history of song and dance. Today, American musical theatre takes the form of the Broadway musical, which features a strong plot conveyed through dialogue and supported by song and dance. We also discussed American opera in the form of Gershwin's folk opera, *Porgy and Bess*.

The importance of American popular music of the twentieth century cannot be overstated. Genres such as rock and roll and rap have now been exported around the globe. At their root, all forms of American popular music have been influenced by the blues, and thus owe their existence to the cultural contributions of African Americans. Although America was not yet discovered during much of the early development of Western art music, we have contributed much to the culture of the world in a relatively short span of time.

8.10 GLOSSARY

Ballads – a song form used often in folk music, which is used to tell a story that usually contains a moral or lesson.

Bebop - a style of small group jazz developed in the late 1940s, which featured fast moving harmonies, angular melodies, and highly complex rhythms

Big Band – large jazz ensembles (15-20 members) popular in the 1930's and 1940's. The term "Big Band" also refers to the era in which these bands were popular.

Bluegrass – a variation of country music featuring fiddle, guitar, mandolin, bass guitar, and the five-string banjo that developed largely in the Appalachian region

Blues – a style of music that, at the turn of the twentieth century, began to form out of African American work songs, field hollers, and spirituals. Today, the word "blues" is used loosely and can refer to feeling sad or down, to any song played in a bluesy style, or more specifically, to a song that follows a blues form, which is a twelve-bar strophic song form.

Broadway Musical – a style of Musical Theatre, which integrated a cohesive plot with songs and dances that advanced that plot. Broadway specifically refers to the street of the same name in New York City that became known for this style.

Children's Song – a type of folk song designed to teach a simple lesson. They are often simple to sing and easy to remember.

Contemporary Country – a mixture of rock rhythm sections and a singer singing with a country accent about many of the same topics that traditional country singers have used over the decades.

Contemporary R&B – generally refers to music with jazz, gospel, and funk roots that uses electronic instruments, drums, horns, and vocals.

Country Music – a term describing a broad variety of musical styles including Bluegrass, Hillbilly Music, and Contemporary Country. Generally speaking, most types of music that fall under this category originated in the American South (although it also encompasses Western Swing and cowboy songs) and features a singing style with a distinctly rural southern accent, as well as an instrumentation that favors string instruments such as the banjo, guitar, or fiddle.

Dance Music – music written for dancing. The instrumentation of various types of folk dance music varies with the style.

Dixieland – an early form of jazz developed in New Orleans during the turn of the twentieth century featuring syncopated rhythms, improvised solos and harmonies, as well as a common instrumentation that included trumpet, clarinet, saxophone, trombone, tuba, banjo, piano, guitar, and drums.

Folk Music – a term used to describe a wide variety of musical forms that developed within different cultures, often for different reasons. Folk music is often passed down not through written music, but orally from one generation to another.

Hillbilly Music – an early form of country music, Hillbilly Music was an alternative to the jazz and dance music of the 1920s and was portrayed as wholesome music of the "good old days."

Honky Tonk Music – a country combo style that became quite popular in the 1940s and 1950s. Originally performed in saloons known as "honky tonks,' many of the songs dealt with subjects associated with honky tonks such as infidelity and drinking.

Improvisation – the act of creating melodies and harmonies on the spot without reading the music off a page.

Minstrel Show – an American form of theatre developed in the nineteenth century and featuring white performers in blackface performing in a variety show, which depicted black characters as happy participants in romanticized versions of the American slave south.

Musical Theatre – a type of dramatic performance that tells a story through dialogue, with singing and dancing added to support and move the plot along.

New Orleans Jazz – (see Dixieland)

Operetta – a "light opera" developed in the nineteenth century that required classically trained singers, but featured less complex music than a typical opera.

Protest Song – a type of folk song written to directly, or by suggestion, voice complaints about some injustice.

Ragtime – a musical genre developed near the turn of the twentieth century that featured syncopated rhythms. The style became nationally popular after being widely published as sheet music.

Rap – a form of spoken word delivered over a beat. It can be improvised or written out in advance.

Rhythm and Blues (R&B) – a term originally referring to music recorded by black musicians and intended for use by the African American community. The term has evolved throughout the years and encompasses several different musical styles, including soul, funk and now contemporary R&B.

Rock and Roll – a style of music that grew out of Rhythm and Blues and came into prominence during the 1950s. The style features a strong backbeat and often features electric guitar, bass and drums. The style is now known as "rock" has spawned many subgenres.

Sampling – a technique in which a clip of a preexisting song is isolated and looped, often as a background for a rapper

Scratching – the technique of improvising a rhythmic solo on one turntable over a beat

Swing – a term used to describe the rhythmic bounce that characterizes the jazz style. The term can also refer to the big band music of the 1930s and 1940s.

Syncopation – the act of disrupting the normal pattern of accents in a piece of music by emphasizing what would normally be weak beats.

Western Swing – a style of country music that developed in western cities and borrowed instruments from the dance band such as saxophones, trombones, trumpets, piano, bass, and drums.

Work Songs – a type of folk song devised to help groups of people perform physical work. The music usually uses the tempo of the work itself and was sung by lumberjacks, railroad workers, and prison chain gangs, among others.

APPENDIX

Music of the World

N. Alan Clark and Thomas Heflin

A.1 INTRODUCTION

As we have seen, music in Western culture is part of a rich tradition beginning with the Greeks, developing through the music of the church, and eventually resulting in the music we hear today. But have you ever considered what music is like in non-Western cultures? As with Western music, the various cultures across the globe have their own traditions, musical styles, practices, and rules that are often vastly different from the music many Americans are used to.

The following is a sample of many different music styles from all over the world. This review will be a very cursory introduction to only a handful of the thousands of musical styles that exist across the globe with which you may not be familiar. Bear in mind that many of these musical traditions date back hundreds, and sometimes thousands, of years and deserve further exploration outside of the context of this textbook. Beyond these examples, much more music is available to you through YouTube. In this review, we will primarily focus on the musical elements of melody, rhythm, instrumentation, and harmony, and describe the processes that different societies use to combine these elements.

A.2 IMPORTANT TERMS

- cajun
- celts
- bodhran
- raga
- tala
- sitar
- tabla
- pentatonic scale
- koto
- shakuhachi
- mbira
- djembe
- tamtam

A.3 NORTH AMERICA

A.3.1 Native American Music

Throughout history, certain cultures have had more opportunity to develop music than others. Often, the effort required to hunt, gather, or raise food has been all encompassing and has left little time for leisure or artistic pursuits. Therefore, music was only performed when the people thought it was necessary or important. Like many other cultures, traditional Native American music was normally performed as a part of important rituals meant to ask specific deities for various benefits, such as increased health, successful hunting, success in war, or rain; or to contact the spirit world for other reasons.

Figure A.1 | Chasi, Bonito's Son, an Apache musician playing the "Apache fiddle"
Author | A. Frank Randall
Source | Wikimedia Commons
License | Public Domain

Most traditional Native American music was vocal music. It was used to tell a story, express a wish, or to describe an emotional state, and it was almost always accompanied with percussion. The percussion instruments used were normally drums made of stretched animal skins, rattles, and, later, metallic bells. Vertical flutes and panpipes were sometimes used to accompany love songs. These songs had a small range with a few different pitches and were quite often based on the **pentatonic scale**, a five-note scale used in many different cultures. Most Native American music was not harmonized and did not have any form of harmonic accompaniment.

Listen to the Native American music linked below. Listen for the drums and the limited range of the voices and their use of the pentatonic scale.

Native American Line Dance Music

https://www.youtube.com/watch?v=txFWJbHgcMM

A.3.2 Tejano (TexMex)

Tejano or TexMex music is a blend of Central American and European influences. TexMex specifically refers to the music that grew out of both Mexico and Texas. It is dance oriented and uses European scales and chords. Instruments often include upright bass, drums, guitar, accordion, and solo vocal.

TexMex Music – *Ay te Dejo en San Antonio* – (Flaco Jimenez)

https://www.youtube.com/watch?v=Z--fJolAWQg

The following example is based on the Western European dance called the waltz. It is in three-quarter time, with the emphasis on beat one. Listen for the ukulele, trumpet, drums, guitar, vocal harmony, and the trombone.

TexMex Music – *Arboles de la Barranca* – (El Coyote)

https://www.youtube.com/watch?v=XNjXv4rajHE

A.3.3 Southwest Louisiana

Cajun Zydeco is another form of American folk music that grew from European roots. This style was developed by Cajuns, the descendants of Acadian immigrants (French speakers from Acadia), who settled in the swamps of Southwest Louisiana, later to be called Acadiana. Almost all Zydeco music is vocal and is almost always designed for dancing. Instruments were traditionally acoustic since electricity is not easy to come by in Acadiana! Instruments include upright bass (later the electric bass), drums, accordion, fiddle, guitar, and solo vocal. The words are almost always in French, the language of the Cajun settlers.

Figure A.2 | Clifton Chenier on accordion, brother Cleveland on washboard and John Hart on tenor saxophone
Author | User "Bozotexino"
Source | Wikimedia Commons
License | CC BY 3.0

Zydeco Music - *Tu le Ton Son Ton* - Clifton Chenier

https://www.youtube.com/watch?v=NiexKQt8FyQ

A.4 EUROPEAN FOLK MUSIC

A.4.1 France

Much of European folk music is largely built around song forms that are tied together by the lyrics of the songs. In the following example of folk music from France you may notice that the scales and instruments sound a little like those of our modern American folk music (except for the language). The development and use of major and minor scales is what gives our Western European music its distinctive sound.

French Folk Song - M'en Suis Allé Aux Noces 1980s

https://www.youtube.com/watch?v=SrBm7RYRdoE

A.4.2 Celtic (Ancient Scotland, Ireland, and a small portion of France)

The **Celts** refers to a diverse group of people who lived during the Iron Ages in what is now Great Britain and Western Europe. In addition to speaking Celtic languages, these people shared a common musical heritage, one that is still used by their descendants. Celtic music is often recognized by its instrumentation, which combines bagpipes, various stringed instruments, and drums. Celtic music also has a distinctive melodic style, with wide leaps that outline the harmonies of the song, creating a feeling of jubilance. This Celtic example is a modern version of a traditional dance song. However, once you get past 0:50 on the counter, it becomes much more traditional with flute and **bodhrans** (stretched skin drums.)

Figure A.3 | Rapalje
Author | Sander van der Wel
Source | Wikimedia Commons
License | CC BY-SA 2.0

Celtic folk music - Cry of the Celts

https://www.youtube.com/watch?v=DlHmGy4Aq_g

Many modern performance groups focus on music from the Celtic tradition, as can be heard in the example below.

Modern Celtic Ensemble (Celtic Woman) - Téir Abhaile Riú

https://www.youtube.com/watch?v=EjyljC5fSeU

A.4.3 Norway

Norway has a centuries-long history of vocal and instrumental music. Indeed, many of their folk ballads and songs date back to the Middle Ages; often, they describe the dramatic tales of historical figures from that period. The Norwegian folk music linked below is one such Norwegian ballad of the Middle Ages era. It uses European sounding scales as well as several wind instruments.

Norwegian folk music - Kalenda Maya - Heming og Gygri

https://www.youtube.com/watch?v=UwWojrmqo5c

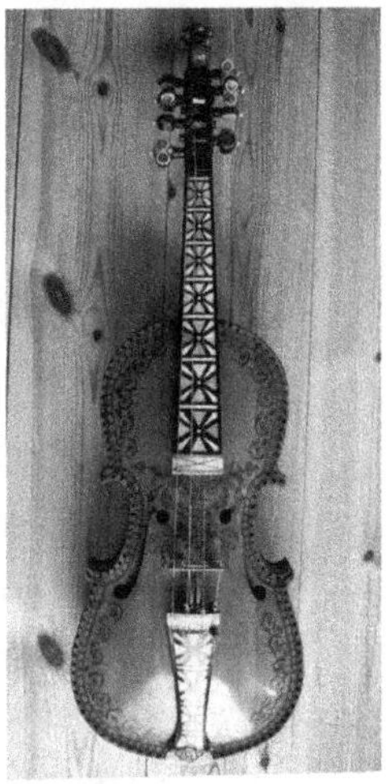

Figure A.3 | A Hardanger fiddle made by Knut Gunnarsson Helland
Author | Frode Inge Helland
Source | Wikimedia Commons
License | CC BY-SA 3.0

A.4.4 Russia

Russian folk music uses what we would call the modern minor scale. Listen to how distinctive this Russian folk music sounds as its slow introduction gradually gives way to faster and faster verses, until it reaches a very fast and exciting dance-like conclusion.

Russian folk music - Hej sokoly - Krzysztof

https://www.youtube.com/watch?v=fCXcfDli3yo

Figure A.5 | Russian Boy with Balalaika
Author | Wilhelm Amandus Beer
Source | Wikimedia Commons
License | Public Domain

A.4.5 Balkan Peninsula (Southeastern Europe)

The region of Southeastern Europe that includes Hungary, Romania, Macedonia, Turkey, and several other countries, is called the Balkans. This region has a rich musical heritage with many fast, exciting, dance-like songs using accordion and clarinet. Balkan music is unique in that it incorporates complex rhythms that we do not often hear in Western music.

Balkan Traditional Music - Mirjan Hasi, Clarinet

https://www.youtube.com/watch?v=Eczarul7300

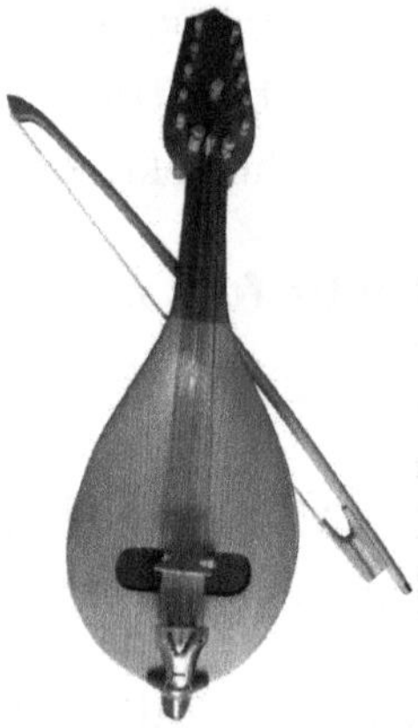

Figure A.6 | Gadulka Bulkarian knee-violin with bow
Author | User "Arent"
Source | Wikimedia Commons
License | CC BY-SA 3.0

A.5 ASIAN MUSIC

A.5.1 India

Indian classical music is almost always performed in small groups. Indian musicians do not use scales and harmony like we do in our Western music. Their music includes improvisation and is based on rhythmic melodic patterns. The example here is a traditional improvised Indian piece that employs the stringed **sitar** and the **tabla** drum.

Indian Music - Ravi Shankar - *Raga Ramkali*

https://www.youtube.com/watch?v=mCJkjhNmsoI

SIDEBAR:

The melodic patterns Indian music uses are called **raga**, which are more of a shape than a scale. The rhythmic patterns are called **tala**, which are established patterns that repeat over and over. Often the raga and tala don't line up exactly, so there never seem to be any repeated sections. Indian musicians use a large stringed instrument called a sitar, and stretched skin drums called tabla.

Figure A.7 | A Lady Playing the Tanpura
Author | User "Arent"
Source | Wikimedia Commons
License | Public Domain

A.5.2 Japan

Like Indian music, Japanese music is also performed in small groups and uses pentatonic scales, but that is where the similarities end. Japanese folk music is not improvised. Rather, it is composed and is almost always built around lyrics that are either borrowed from poetry or composed for the specific song. The music is made up of regular rhythms, but there is no intentional harmony as in Western music. Japanese musicians pride themselves on memorizing each composition and then performing it exactly the same way every time. They use a large thirteen string instrument called a **koto**, and an end blown flute called a **shakuhachi**.

Figure A.8 | Japanese folkwoman playing shamishen
Author | Christopher Wagner
Source | Wikimedia Commons
License | Public Domain

Listen for the koto and the shakuhachi in the traditional Japanese selection below.

Japanese Music – *Tsuki no shizuku* (Played on Koto and Shakuhachi)

https://www.youtube.com/watch?v=IITn9XHXT8k

A.5.3 China

At first glance, Chinese Opera is not that different than Italian Opera in that it is a musical drama incorporating costumes, song, and dance. However, a closer examination reveals that the music of Chinese Opera differs greatly from Western opera. Chinese Opera singing style often involves singing melodies derived from the pentatonic scale. Also, Chinese singers can be heard sliding between notes of the melody, giving the music a "slippery" quality that is unique to Eastern Music. Give this piece a listen, and you will hear this quality!

Figure A.9 | Sichuan Opera in Chengdu
Author | User "Zoharby"
Source | Wikimedia Commons
License | CC BY-SA 3.0

Chinese Opera

https://www.youtube.com/watch?v=sPYKQhsx_HQ

A.5.4 Indonesia

When we think of a gong, we often envision a large brass thing that looks like a giant cymbal. True, gongs come in many different sizes and can actually be used to play melodies but this often envisioned image is one variant of a gong named **tamtam**. In Indonesia, gongs have been used in traditional music for centuries. The following video shows musicians using many different sized gongs while performing Indonesian music.

Figure A.10 | Gamelan ceremonial Munggang, Kraton Surakarta
Author | Giovanni Sciarrino
Source | Wikimedia Commons
License | CC BY-SA 3.0

Indonesian Gong Music

https://www.youtube.com/watch?v=sZZT-fu4jWcI

A.6 SOUTH AND CENTRAL AMERICAN FOLK MUSIC

Folk music in many parts of South America is similar to folk music of Native Americans as well as folk music from parts of Africa. Stretched skin drums, wooden flutes, rattles, pentatonic sounding scales, and vocal music are all popular in this region. The first example is a modern performance of traditional Aztec music and the second is a modern adaptation a traditional Inca song Compare and contrast the similarities and differences of the pieces.

Aztec Music of Mexico

https://www.youtube.com/watch?v=tiFljznibKo

Inca Music - ***Ecos del tiempo***

https://www.youtube.com/watch?v=49WVkZrWTDg

A.7 CARRIBEAN POP MUSIC

Numerous cultures currently thrive in the Caribbean. One of the more popular styles of music in the Caribbean is called **Reggae** and is from the island of Jamaica. The following example by Bob Marley combines American electronic instruments with the distinctive reggae beat, which involves the guitar playing staccato chords of the off beats of each measure.

Reggae Music - ***Get Up, Stand Up*** **- Bob Marley**

https://www.youtube.com/watch?v=JuMlHdxiIZ8

Figure A.11 | Bob Marley
Author | Eddie Mallin
Source | Wikimedia Commons
License | CC BY 2.0

A.8 AFRICAN FOLK MUSIC

A.8.1 Zimbabwe

The **mbira** is an integral part of the folk music of Zimbabwe. It is a common small keyboard type instrument that is played by the performers' thumbs. Its metal reeds are tuned to different pitches, and it is usually used to accompany vocalists.

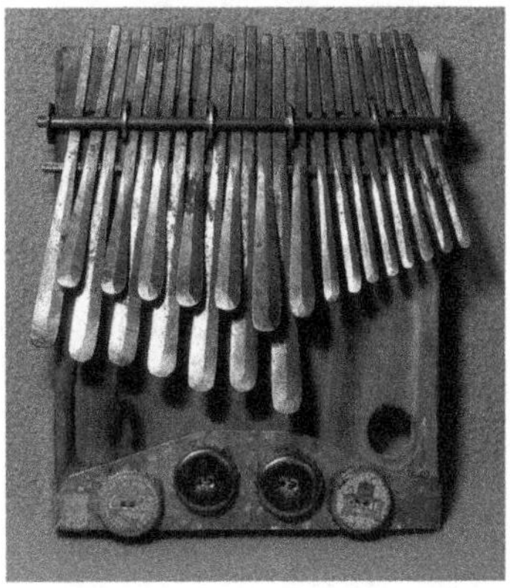

Figure A.12 | Mbira Dzavadzimu
Author | Alex Weeks
Source | Wikimedia Commons
License | CC BY-SA 3.0

Zimbabwe - Mbira music at Copacabana Harare Zimbabwe

https://www.youtube.com/watch?v=-2cIOdnG-Fw

A.8.2 Senegal

Senegal is a country located on the far coast of West Africa. In Senegal, the traditional stretched skin drum is called the **djembe**. By way of contrast, modern **Senegalese** music shows an American influence; synthesizer sounds, drum set, and electric bass and guitar are often used.

Figure A.13 | Djembe
Author | Djembe Art
Source | Wikimedia Commons
License | CC BY-SA 3.0

Senegal - Traditional djembe drummers

https://www.youtube.com/watch?v=RfXnuG6X7cw

Senegal Music - Modern – (Bakane featuring Viviane Yayu Diere)

https://www.youtube.com/watch?v=OJCh9eMnlX-M&list=PLfoK9L3f5inQOQPFEW_S8ZXd7Mf89YK-CL&index=2

A.9 GLOSSARY

Bodhran - a traditional Celtic open-ended frame drum with a low, resonant sound

Cajun Zydeco – American folk music developed by Cajuns, the descendants of Acadian immigrants (French speakers from Acadia), who settled in the swamps of Southwest Louisiana.

Celts – a term referring to a diverse group of people who lived during the Iron Ages in what is now Great Britain and Western Europe.

Raga - a pattern of notes that used as the basis for improvisation in Indian classical music

Tala – a repeating rhythmic pattern that that forms the rhythmic foundation for Indian classical music

Sitar – a plucked string instrument used in Indian classical music.

Tabla - a pair of hand drums used in Indian classical music

Pentatonic scale – a five-note scale used in traditional music throughout the world

Koto – a traditional Japanese string instrument with thirteen strings over movable bridges

Shakuhachi – a bamboo flute used in traditional Japanese music

Mbira – and African thumb piano

Djembe – a hand drum used in the music of West Africa

Tamtam – a large metal gong

GLOSSARY

A cappella – vocal music without instrumental accompaniment

Accidentals – notes that are not normally found in a given key

Acoustical Engineer – a person who works in the area of acoustic technology

Acoustician – a person who studies the theory and science of acoustics

Acoustics – the study of how sound behaves in physical spaces

Amplitude – refers to how high the wave form appears to vibrate above zero when seen on an oscilloscope; louder sounds create higher oscilloscope amplitude readings

Anthem – a musical composition of celebration, usually used as a symbol for a distinct group, particularly the national anthems of countries. Originally, and in music theory and religious contexts, it also refers more particularly to short sacred choral work and still more particularly to a specific form of Anglican

Antiphonal – A genre of sacred music featuring multiple choirs, or a choir that has been divided into different groups that can perform call and responses.

Aria – Homophonic compositions featuring a solo singer over orchestral accompaniment. homophonic compositions featuring a solo singer over accompaniment. Arias are very melodic primarily utilized in operas, cantatas, and oratorios.

Art song – a composition setting a poem to music, generally for one solo voice and piano accompaniment; in German, a Lied

Atonal – Music that seeks to avoid both the traditional rules of harmony and the use of chords or scales that provide a tonal center

Ballads – a song form used often in folk music, which is used to tell a story that usually contains a moral or lesson.

Bar – see measure

Basso continuo – continuous realization of harmony throughout a musical piece, usually by a harpsichord and/or cello. The Basso continuo provides a framework/template for harmonic accompaniments.

Beat – the basic unit of time in music

Bebop - a style of small group jazz developed in the late 1940s, which featured fast moving harmonies, angular melodies, and highly complex rhythms

Big Band – large jazz ensembles (15-20 members) popular in the 1930's and 1940's. The term "Big Band" also refers to the era in which these bands were popular.

Bluegrass – a variation of country music featuring fiddle, guitar, mandolin, bass guitar, and the five-string banjo that developed largely in the Appalachian region

Blues – a style of music that, at the turn of the twentieth century, began to form out of African American work songs, field hollers, and spirituals. Today, the word "blues" is used loosely and can refer to feeling sad or down, to any song played in a bluesy style, or more specifically, to a song that follows a blues form, which is a twelve-bar strophic song form.

Bodhran - a traditional Celtic open-ended frame drum with a low, resonant sound

Brass – instruments traditionally made of brass or another metal (and thus often producing a "bright" or "brassy" tone) whose sound is generated by blowing into a mouthpiece that is attached to a coiled tube

Broadway Musical – a style of Musical Theatre, which integrated a cohesive plot with songs and dances that advanced that plot. Broadway specifically refers to the street of the same name in New York City that became known for this style.

Cadence – the ending of a musical phrase providing a sense of closure, often through the use of one chord that resolves to another

Cadenza – section of a concerto in which the soloist plays alone without the orchestra in an improvisatory style

Cajun Zydeco – American folk music developed by Cajuns, the descendants of Acadian immigrants (French speakers from Acadia), who settled in the swamps of Southwest Louisiana.

Cantata – A composite major church choir form from the Baroque period that involves soloist, choir, and orchestra. Cantatas have several movements and last for fifteen to thirty minutes. Cantatas are performed without staging but they utilize narration, arias, recitatives, choruses and smaller vocal ensembles.

Celts – a term referring to a diverse group of people who lived during the Iron Ages in what is now Great Britain and Western Europe.

Chamber music – music--such as art songs, piano character pieces, and string quartets--primarily performed in small performing spaces, often for personal entertainment

Chanson – is in general any lyric-driven French song, usually polyphonic and secular. A singer specializing in chansons is known as a "chanteur" (male) or "chanteuse" (female); a collection of chansons, especially from the late Middle Ages and Renaissance, is also known as a chansonnier.

Chant – text set to a melody written in monophonic texture with un-notated rhythms typically used in religious worship

Chapel Master – Director of music, secular and sacred, for the courts' official functions and entertainment.

Children's Song – a type of folk song designed to teach a simple lesson. They are often simple to sing and easy to remember.

Chorale – Originally the result from the German protestant church's reformation, the chorale is the hymn (tune) is a four part homophonic work that is sung by the church congregation. Chorales became the foundation for several cantatas and chorale preludes for organ.

Chord – the simultaneous sounding of three or more pitches; like intervals, chords can be consonant or dissonant

Chord Progression – a series of chords

Chromatic – musical pitches which move up or down by successive half-steps

Chromaticism – a style of composition which uses notes that are not a part of the predominant scale of a composition or one of its sections.

Church Music – Sacred music written for performance in church, or any musical setting of ecclesiastical liturgy, or music set to words expressing propositions of a sacred nature, such as a hymn. Church Music Director is a position responsible the musical aspects of the church's activities.

Coda – optional final section of a movement that reasserts the home key of the movement and provides a sense of conclusion

Composition – the process whereby a musician notates musical ideas using a system of symbols or using some other form of recording

Concerto – a composition for a soloist or a group of soloists and an orchestra, generally in three movements with fast, slow, and fast tempos, respectively

Concerto Grosso – a musical composition for a small group of soloists and orchestra.

Conductor – individual who leads an orchestra

Conjunct – a melody that moves mostly by step, in a smooth manner

Consonant – (adjective) term used to describe intervals and chords that tend to sound sweet and pleasing to our ears; consonance (noun), as opposed to dissonance, is stable and needs no resolution.

Consort – A renaissance consort is a group of renaissance instrumentalists playing together. A whole consort is an ensemble performing with instruments from the same family. A broken consort is an ensemble comprised of instruments from more than one family.

Contemporary Country – a mixture of rock rhythm sections and a singer singing with a country accent about many of the same topics that traditional country singers have used over the decades.

Contemporary R&B – generally refers to music with jazz, gospel, and funk roots that uses electronic instruments, drums, horns, and vocals.

Cori spezzati – A divided choir that is utilized to perform in a polychoral style—able to perform "call and response". Large churches were designed with multiple choir seating sections to perform such works.

Counter-Reformation – The preservation movement or "Counter-Reformation" against the protestant reform led to the development of the Jesuit order (1540) and the later assembling of the Council of Trent (1545-1563) which considered issues of the church's authority and organizational structure.

Country Music – a term describing a broad variety of musical styles including Bluegrass, Hillbilly Music, and Contemporary Country. Generally speaking, most types of music that fall under this category originated in the American South (although it also encompasses Western Swing and cowboy songs) and features a singing style with a distinctly rural southern accent, as well as an instrumentation that favors string instruments such as the banjo, guitar, or fiddle.

Courtly Love – love for a beloved, without any concern for whether or not the love will be returned, called "courtly" because it was praised by those participating in medieval courts

Cycles per Second (cps) – a definition of frequency of vibration; replaced by Hertz in 1960

Da capo – instruction—commonly found at the end of the B section or Trio of a Minuet and Trio, to return to the "head" or first section, generally resulting in an A - B - A form

Dance Music – music written for dancing. The instrumentation of various types of folk dance music varies with the style.

Dance Music [WM1] – is music composed specifically to facilitate or accompany dancing

Development – the middle section of a sonata-form movement in which the themes and key areas introduced in the exposition are developed;

Disjunct – a melody with wide leaps and rapid changes in direction

Dissonant – (adjective) intervals and chords that tend to sound harsh to our ears; dissonance (noun) is often used to create tension and instability, and the interplay between dissonance and consonance provides a sense of harmonic and melodic motion in music

Dixieland – an early form of jazz developed in New Orleans during the turn of the twentieth century featuring syncopated rhythms, improvised solos and harmonies, as well as a common instrumentation that included trumpet, clarinet, saxophone, trombone, tuba, banjo, piano, guitar, and drums.

Djembe – a hand drum used in the music of West Africa

Double-exposition form – form of the first movement of a Classical period concerto that combines the exposition, development, and recapitulation of sonata form with the ritornello form used for the first movements of Baroque concertos; also called first-movement concerto form

Drone – a sustained pitch or pitches often found in music of the middle ages or earlier and in folk music

Dynamic – the variation in the volume of musical sound (the amplitude of the sound waves)

Elektronische Musik - (German term meaning "electronic music") Music composed by manipulating only electronically-produced sounds (not recorded sounds.)

Equalization (EQ) – the process of raising or lowering different frequencies of sound, either in a recording, or within a tone (overtones)

Exposition – first section of a sonata form movement, in which the themes and key areas of the movement are introduced; the section normally modulates from the home key to a different key

Expressionism – Style of composition where composers intentionally use atonality. Arnold Schoenberg devised a system of composing using twelve tones. His students Alban Berg and Anton Webern composed extensively in this twelve-tone style.

Folk Music – a term used to describe a wide variety of musical forms that developed within different cultures, often for different reasons. Folk music is often passed down not through written music, but orally from one generation to another.

Form – the structure of the phrases and sections within a musical composition (Does it repeat?)

Frequency – how quickly or slowly a medium (solid, liquid, gas) vibrates and produces a sound

Frets – is a raised strip on the neck of a stringed instrument. Frets usually extend across the full width of the neck and divide the string into half steps for most western musical instruments. Most guitars have frets.

Fugue – perfected by J.S. Bach during the baroque period, fugues are a form written in an imitative contrapuntal style in multiple parts. Fugues are based upon their original tune that is called the subject. The subject is then imitated and overlapped by the other parts by the called the answer, countersubject, stretto, and episode

Fundamental Pitch – the lowest pitch in the harmonic series

Galliard – was a form of Renaissance dance and music popular all over Europe in the 16th century.

Guido of Arezzo – a medieval music theorist who developed a system of lines and spaces that enabled musicians to notate the specific notes in a melody

Harmony – any simultaneous combination of tones and the rules governing those combinations (the way a melody is accompanied is also another way to define harmony)

Hemiola – the momentary shifting from a duple to a triple feel or vice versa

Hertz (Hz) – the unit of frequency defined as one cycle per second and named after Heinrich Hertz (1957-1894) in 1960

Hillbilly Music – an early form of country music, Hillbilly Music was an alternative to the jazz and dance music of the 1920s and was portrayed as wholesome music of the "good old days."

Homophonic – musical texture comprised of one melodic line accompanied by chords

Homophony – Music where the melody is supported by a chordal accompaniment the move in the same rhythm. Homophony is generally the opposite of polyphony where the voices imitative and weave with each other.

Honky Tonk Music – a country combo style that became quite popular in the 1940s and 1950s. Originally performed in saloons known as "honky tonks,' many of the songs dealt with subjects associated with honky tonks such as infidelity and drinking.

Hymn – religious song most generally having multiple strophes of the same number and length of lines and using strophic form

Idée fixe – a famous melody that appears in all five movements of Berlioz's Symphonie fantastique to represent the beloved from the program

Impressionism – music composed based on the composer's impression of an object, concept, or event. This style included the use of chromaticism, whole-tone scales and chords, exotic scales, new chord progressions, and more complex rhythms

Improvisation – the process whereby musicians create music spontaneously using the elements of music as building blocks

Instrumentation – the instruments comprising a musical group (including the human voice)

Interval – the distance in pitch between any two notes

Jig – is the accompanying dance tune for an energetic fold dance usually in a compound meter.

Key – the set of pitches on which a composition is based

Keyboard – instruments that are characterized by keyboards, such as the piano, organ, vibraphone, and accordion

Koto – a traditional Japanese string instrument with thirteen strings over movable bridges

Laptop orchestra – an ensemble formed by linking laptop computers and speakers together to generate live and/or recorded performances using both synthesized and pre-recorded sounds

Leitmotiv – "guiding motive" associated with a specific character, theme, or locale in a music drama, and first associated with the music of Richard Wagner

Libretto – The text or actual words of an opera, musical, cantata or oratorio, written or compiled by a librettist

Madrigal – a musical piece for several solo voices set to a short poem. They originated in Italy around 1520. Most madrigals were about love.

Mass – Catholic celebration of the Eucharist consisting of liturgical texts set to music by composers starting in the middle ages

mazurka – a Polish dance in triple time, with emphasis on beat 2

Mbira – and African thumb piano

Measure – a unit of time that contains a specific number of beats defined by the meter/time signature

Melisma – More than one note sung during one syllable of the text. The melismatic style was used extensively in gregorian chant.

Melody – a succession of single tones in musical compositions

Meter – the way in which the beats are grouped together in a piece

Minstrel Show – an American form of theatre developed in the nineteenth century and featuring white performers in blackface performing in a variety show, which depicted black characters as happy participants in romanticized versions of the American slave south.

Minuet and trio form – form based on the minuet dance that consists of a Minuet (A), then a contrasting Trio (B), followed by a return to the Minuet (A)

Monophonic – musical texture comprised of one melodic line; a melodic line may be sung by one person or 100 people

Motet – is a highly varied sacred choral musical composition. The motet was one of the pre-eminent polyphonic forms of Renaissance music.

Motive – the smallest musical unit of a melody, generally a single rhythm of two or three pitches

Motor rhythm – The constant repeated subdivision of the beat. The motor rhythm provide unity and stability within the musical piece.

Movement – a subsection or independent section/piece of a larger work. (Ex. A symphony is divided into movements.)

Music – sound and silence organized in time

Musical Theatre – a type of dramatic performance that tells a story through dialogue, with singing and dancing added to support and move the plot along.

Musique Concrète – a type of electro-acoustic music that uses both electronically produced sounds (like synthesizers) and recorded natural sounds (like instruments, voices, and sounds from nature)

Nationalism – pride in one's nation or cultural identity, often expressed in art, literature, and music

Neoclassicism – A musical movement that arose in the twentieth century as a reaction against romanticism and which sought to recapture classical ideals like symmetry, order, and restraint. Stravinsky's music for the ballet Pulcinella (1920) is a major early neoclassical composition.

New Orleans Jazz – (see Dixieland)

Noise – a disorganized sound with no observable pitch

Octave – the distance between two musical pitches where the higher pitch vibrates exactly twice as many times per second as the lower

Opera – A staged musical drama for voices and orchestra. Operas are fully blocked and performed in costume with sets. Operas utilize arias and recitatives without no narration.

Opera Buffa – comic style of opera made famous by Mozart

Opera Seria – serious style of eighteenth-century opera made famous by Handel generally features mythology or high-born characters and plots

Operetta – a "light opera" developed in the nineteenth century that required classically trained singers, but featured less complex music than a typical opera.

Oratorio – a major work with religious or contemplative character for solo voices, chorus and orchestra. Oratorios do not utilize blocking, costumes, or scenery.

Oscilloscope - an electronic device that displays a visual representation of the different types of sound waves

Overtones (also known as harmonics) – a musical tone heard above a fundamental pitch

Partials – the sounds of different frequency that naturally occur above a fundamental (primary) tone

Pavanne – is a slow processional dance common in Europe during the 16th century Renaissance.

Pentatonic scale – a five-note scale used in traditional music throughout the world

Percussion – instruments that are typically hit or struck by the hand, with sticks, or with hammers or that are shaken or rubbed by hand

Performing Forces – see instrumentation

Phrase – smaller sub-sections of a melody

Pitch – a tone that is composed of an organized sound wave

Pizzicato – the plucking of a bowed string instrument such as the violin, producing a percussive effect

Plagal cadence – ending of a composition that consists of a IV chord moving to a I chord and most often associated with church music

Polychoral (style) – a compositional style where the chorus/choir is divided into two or more groups that can perform with or independently for each other (see antiphonal).

Polyphony – musical texture that simultaneously features two or more relatively independent and important melodic lines

Polyrhythm – two or more different rhythms played at the same time

Polytonality – a compositional technique where two or more instruments or voices in different keys (tonal centers) perform together at the same time

Primitivism – A musical movement that arose as a reaction against musical impressionism and which focused on the use of strong rhythmic pulse, distinct musical ideas, and a tonality based on one central tone as a unifying factor instead of a central key or chord progression.

Program music – instrumental music intended to represent a something extra musical such as a poem, narrative, drama, or picture, or the ideas, images, or sounds therein.

Program symphony – program music in the form of a multi-movement composition for orchestra

Protest Song – a type of folk song written to directly, or by suggestion, voice complaints about some injustice.

Raga - a pattern of notes that used as the basis for improvisation in Indian classical music

Ragtime – a musical genre developed near the turn of the twentieth century that featured syncopated rhythms. The style became nationally popular after being widely published as sheet music.

Range – the number of pitches, expressed as an intervallic distance

Rap – a form of spoken word delivered over a beat. It can be improvised or written out in advance.

Recapitulation – third and final second of a sonata-form movement, in which the themes of the exposition return, now in the home key of the movement

Recitative – An operatic number using speech-like melodies and rhythms, performing using a flexible tempo, to sparse accompaniment, most often provided by the basso continuo. Recitatives are often performed between arias and have texts that tend to be descriptive and narrating.

Reformation – was a succession and division from the practices of the Roman Catholic Church initiated by Martin Luther. Led to the development of Protestant churches.

Refrain – a repeating musical section, generally also with repeated text; sometimes called a "chorus"

Register – the low, medium, and high sections of an instrument or vocal range

Rhythm – the way the music is organized in respect to time

Rhythm According to the Text – rhythm that follows the rhythm of the text and is not notated

Rhythm and Blues (R&B) – a term originally referring to music recorded by black musicians and intended for use by the African American community. The term has evolved throughout the years and encompasses several different musical styles, including soul, funk and now contemporary R&B.

Ritornello Form – repeated unifying sections founds in between the solo sections of a concerto grosso

Rock and Roll – a style of music that grew out of Rhythm and Blues and came into prominence during the 1950s. The style features a strong backbeat and often features electric guitar, bass and drums. The style is now known as "rock" has spawned many subgenres.

Rondo – instrumental form consisting of the alternation of a refrain "A" with contrasting sections ("B," "C," "D," etc.). Rondos are often the final movements of string quartets, classical symphonies, concerti, and sonata (instrumental solos).

Rubato – the momentary speeding up or slowing down of the tempo within a melody line, literally "robbing" time from one note to give to another

Sampling – a technique in which a clip of a preexisting song is isolated and looped, often as a background for a rapper

Scale – a series of pitches, ordered by the interval between its notes

Scena ad aria – nineteenth-century operatic combination of a recitative ("scena") plus aria; here the aria generally has two parts, a slower cantabile and a faster cabaletta

Scherzo – form that prominently replaced the minuet in symphonies and strings quartets of the nineteenth century; like the minuet, scherzos are ternary forms and have a triple feel, although they tend to be somewhat faster in tempo than the minuet.

Scratching – the technique of improvising a rhythmic solo on one turntable over a beat

Sectional form – A piece where distinct sections can be identified due to changes in texture and other musical compositional techniques.

Sequence – a repetition of a motive or phrase at a different pitch level

Serialism – composing music using a series of values assigned to musical elements such as pitch, duration, dynamics, and instrumentation. Arnold Schoenberg's 12-tone technique is one of the most important examples of serialism.

Seventh Chord – a chord that has four pitches stacked in intervals of thirds

Shakuhachi – a bamboo flute used in traditional Japanese music

Sine Wave – the simplest sound wave that occurs in nature. A pure sine wave contains no partials and is perfectly smooth and rounded in appearance on an oscilloscope.

Sitar – a plucked string instrument used in Indian classical music.

Solo – A musical piece that features on musician either with or without accompaniment. In larger scored piece, the solo is the main part that should be brought out while performing.

Sonata – composition for a solo instrument or an instrument with piano accompaniment, generally in three movements with fast, slow, and fast tempos, respectively

Sonata form – a form often found in the first and last movements of sonatas, symphonies, and string quartets, consisting of three parts – exposition, development, and recapitulation

Song – a composition sung by voice(s)

Song cycle – a collection of art songs, unified by poet, narrative, musical style, or composer

Sound – the mechanical movement of an audible pressure wave through a solid, liquid, or gas

Sound Waves – longitudinal waves (compression and rarefaction waves) that travel through a solid, liquid, or gas

Step – the distance between adjacent notes in a musical scale

String quartet – performing ensemble consisting of two violinists, one violinist, and one cellist that plays compositions called string quartets, compositions generally in four movements

Strings – instruments whose sound is produced by setting strings in motion

Strophe – section of a poem or lyric text generally of a set number of lines and line length; a text may have multiple strophes

Strophic – a composition that uses the repetition of the same music ("strophes") for successive texts

Stylized dance – piece of music that sounds like a dance but that was not designed for dancing. In other words, a stylized dance uses the distinct characteristics of a dance and would be recognized as sounding like that dance but might be too long or too complicated to be danced to.

Subject – The main melody or tune of a fugue.

Suite – A multi-movement instrumental musical composition of baroque music—usually in dance form.

Swing – a term used to describe the rhythmic bounce that characterizes the jazz style. The term can also refer to the big band music of the 1930s and 1940s.

Syllabic – music in which each syllable of a text is set to one musical note

Symphonic poem – program music in the form of a single-movement composition for orchestra; sometimes called a tone poem

Symphony – multi-movement composition for orchestra, often in four movements

Syncopation – the act of disrupting the normal pattern of accents in a piece of music by emphasizing what would normally be weak beats.

Synthesizers - instruments that electronically generate a wide variety of sounds. They can also modify electronic or naturally produced recorded sounds

Tabla - a pair of hand drums used in Indian classical music

Tala – a repeating rhythmic pattern that that forms the rhythmic foundation for Indian classical music

Tamtam – a large metal gong

Tempo –the speed at which the beat is played

Ternary form – describes a musical composition in three parts, most often featurings two similar sections, separated by a contrasting section and represented by the letters A – B – A.

Terraced dynamics – Used during the Baroque period, this is where the different sections have a piece of music have a set volume unique for that particular section. The next section may be written to be performed at another volume.

Texture – the ways in which musical lines of a musical piece interact

Theme and Variation form – the presentation of a theme and then variations upon it. The theme may be illustrated as A, with any number of variations following it – A', A'', A''', A'''', etc.

Through-composed – a movement or composition consisting of new music throughout, without repetition of internal sections

Timbre – the tone color or tone quality of a sound

Time signature – the numeric notation at the beginning of a line of music where the top number indicates how many beats are in each measure and the bottom number indicates which type of note will represent that beat

Tonic – the most important pitch of a key; the note from which the other pitches are derived

Triad – a chord that has three pitches stacked in intervals of thirds

Tutti – Where the entire musical ensemble performs together as a whole as opposed to a soloist.

Twelve-Bar Blues – a twelve-bar musical form commonly found in American music

Twelve-tone Technique – Compositional technique developed by Arnold Schoenberg that derives musical elements such as pitch, duration, dynamics, and instrumentation from a randomly produced series of the twelve tones of the chromatic scale (the 12-tone row)

Verse and Refrain Form – a musical form (sometimes referred to as verse and chorus) in which one section of music is sung to all the verses and a different section of music is sung to the repeating refrain or chorus

Vocal – having to do with the human voice

Western Swing – a style of country music that developed in western cities and borrowed instruments from the dance band such as saxophones, trombones, trumpets, piano, bass, and drums.

Woodwinds – instruments traditionally made of wood whose sound is generated by forcing air through a tube, thus creating a vibrating air column

Word painting – was utilized by Renaissance composers to represent poetic images musically. For example, an ascending melodic line would portray the text "ascension to heaven." Or a series of rapid notes would represent running.

Work Songs – a type of folk song devised to help groups of people perform physical work. The music usually uses the tempo of the work itself and was sung by lumberjacks, railroad workers, and prison chain gangs, among others.

ABOUT THE AUTHORS

N. ALAN CLARK, PhD

N. Alan Clark, a native of Lakeland, Florida, has taught and conducted at all levels; middle school, high school, college and professional military bands. He holds Bachelor of Music Education and Master of Music degrees from the University of Florida and a PhD in Music Education from Louisiana State University. During his twenty year Air Force career Major Clark served as Deputy Commander of the Band of the United States Air Forces in Europe; Deputy Commander of the Air Force Band of Flight; Rehearsal Conductor of the Miami Valley Symphony Orchestra; and Commander and Conductor of The Band of the USAF Reserve. Dr. Clark has published numerous articles and books and is currently Director of Bands at Middle Georgia State University in Cochran, Georgia.

THOMAS HEFLIN, DMA

Thomas Heflin received his bachelor's degree in music (2000) from the University of Tennessee, his masters degree in music performance from William Paterson University (2002) and his Doctorate of Musical Arts from the University of Texas (2009). Upon completing his DMA, he lived in New York City for five years and served as a member of the faculty at the Manhattan School of Music Precollege Division. He now serves as Assistant Professor of Jazz at Abraham Baldwin Agricultural College in Tifton, GA. A jazz trumpeter, he has released three albums for Blue Canoe Records, and has performed all over the US and internationally, including Europe, Canada and Australia.

JEFFREY KLUBALL, EdD

Originally from Valdosta, GA, Jeffrey Kluball earned a bachelor's degree in music education (1980) from Valdosta State College, and a master's degree in music education (1983) from the VanderCook College of Music in Chicago where he studied conducting under Victor Zajec. He continued his study in music conducting and band repertoire with Dr. William D. Revelli and received his Education Specialist Degree from Troy State University (1990). Jeffrey completed his Doctorate of Education in Curriculum and Instruction at the University of Sarasota (2001). His extensive research revolved around the influence of music study on academic achievement and brain development. His research is cited in multiple studies and on many music advocacy websites. He has also done extensive research into the history of the Joliet (Illinois) HS Band. Dr. Kluball is currently a Professor of Music and serves as Chair of Fine Arts Department at Darton State College (Albany, GA).

ELIZABETH KRAMER, PhD

Dr. Elizabeth Kramer is an Associate Professor of Music History and Strings at the University of West Georgia. In addition to working with undergraduate and music students, she has led introductory music courses for non majors for many years. Her three favorite things about teaching music appreciation are helping students think more critically about all the music they encounter, introducing students to music styles new to them, and exploring with students ways in which music has interacted with other cultural phenomenon across time. She is currently serving as Associate Dean for the UWG College of Arts and Humanities.